Gender and International Security

D0217129

This book explores the relationship between gender and international security, analyzing and critiquing international security theory and practice from a gendered perspective.

Gender issues have an important place in the international security landscape, but have been neglected both in the theory and practice of international security. The passage and implementation of UN Security Council Resolution 1325 (on Security Council operations), the integration of gender concerns into peace-keeping, the management of refugees, post-conflict disarmament, and reinte-gration and protection for non-combatants in times of war show the increasing importance of gender sensitivity for actors on all fronts in global security.

This book aims to improve the quality and quantity of conversations between feminist Security Studies and Security Studies more generally, in order to demonstrate the importance of gender analysis to the study of inter-national security, and to expand the feminist research program in Security Studies. The chapters included in this book not only challenge the assumed irrelevance of gender, they argue that gender is not a subsection of Security Studies to be compartmentalized or briefly considered as a side issue. Rather, the contributors argue that gender is conceptually, empirically, and norma-tively essential to studying international security. They do so by critiquing and reconstructing key concepts of and theories in international security, by looking for the increasingly complex roles women play as security actors, and by looking at various contemporary security issues through gendered lenses. Together, these chapters make the case that accurate, rigorous, and ethical scholarship of international security cannot be produced without taking account of women's presence in or the gendering of world politics.

Gender and International Security will be of interest to all students of critical Security Studies, gender studies and International Relations in general.

Laura Sjoberg is Assistant Professor of Political Science at the University of Florida. She has a PhD in International Relations and Gender Studies from the University of Southern California, and a JD from Boston College Law School. She is the author of *Gender, Justice, and the Wars in Iraq* (2006) and, with Caron Gentry, *Mothers, Monsters, Whores: Women's Violence in Global Politics* (2007).

Routledge Critical Security Studies series

Gender and International Security

Feminist perspectives

**Edited by
Laura Sjoberg**

Routledge
Taylor & Francis Group

LONDON AND NEW YORK

First published 2010
by Routledge
2 Park Square, Milton Park, Abingdon, Oxon, OX14 4RN

Simultaneously published in the USA and Canada
by Routledge
711 Third Avenue, New York, NY 10017

Routledge is an imprint of the Taylor & Francis Group, an informa business

First issued in paperback 2012

Typeset in Times New Roman by
Taylor & Francis Books

British Library Cataloguing in Publication Data
A catalogue record for this book is available from the British Library

Library of Congress Cataloging in Publication Data
Gender and international security : feminist perspectives / edited by Laura
Sjoberg.
   p. cm.
  1. Security, International. 2. Feminist theory. 3. Women and war. 4.
Women and peace. I. Sjoberg, Laura, 1979-
   JZ5588.G47 2009
   355'.03300082–dc22

                                                        2009017537

ISBN13: 978-0-415-47546-4 (hbk)
ISBN13: 978-0-415-47579-2 (pbk)
ISBN13: 978-0-203-86693-1 (ebk)

In loving memory of Fred Sjoberg, who was one of my first sources of security

Contents

Contributors

Nicole A. Detraz is an Assistant Professor in the Department of Political Science at the University of Memphis. Her research explores the theoretical and practical application of environmental security concepts and seeks to introduce gender considerations into these discussions. She is the 2009 winner of the Best Paper prize for the Feminist Theory and Gender Studies Section of the International Studies Association.

Heidi Hudson is Professor of Political Science and Academic Program Director of the Centre for Africa Studies, University of the Free State, Bloemfontein, South Africa. She is also a former chairperson of the Department of Political Science at the same university. Her area of specialization is International Relations and she is particularly interested in questions relating to IR theory, globalization, security, and gender. Heidi has been the recipient of several scholarships such as Fulbright, Rotary and was guest researcher at the Nordic Africa Institute in Uppsala, Sweden, in 2006. She is a rated National Research Foundation (NRF) researcher and has published articles in, among others, *Security Dialogue*, *African Security Review* and *Agenda*. Heidi Hudson serves on the editorial board of the *Journal for Contemporary History* and is currently President of the South African Association of Political Studies (SAAPS). She is also convenor of the NRF rating panel for Philosophy, Political Science and Policy Studies.

Jennifer K. Lobasz is a PhD candidate at the University of Minnesota Department of Political Science. Her work focuses on the intersection of feminism, poststructural International Relations theory, and international security. Jennifer's work has been published in *Security Studies* and the *Journal of Women, Politics, and Policy*. She has presented her research at the Annual Meetings of the International Studies Association, the Methodology Workshop at the International Studies Association-Northeast, and the Minnesota International Relations Colloquium, and was an invited speaker at the workshop "Gender and Security Studies" in Chicago in February of 2007.

Jennifer Heeg Maruska is a PhD candidate in International Relations at Georgetown University, and Assistant Lecturer in Political Science at

Texas A& M University at Qatar. Her research interests include critical and feminist Security Studies, and IR theory more broadly. Her dissertation focuses on the securitization of migration in Qatar. Jennifer is the recipient of three conference paper awards, from the Annual Meetings of the Northeast Political Science Association (Women's Caucus), the International Studies Association (FTGS section), and ISA-Northeast (Hartmann Award).

Megan MacKenzie is a Lecturer in the Department of Political Science and International Relations at Victoria University of Wellington, NZ. She recently completed a year as a post-doctoral Fellow in residence at the Women and Public Policy Program and the Belfer Center for International Security at Harvard University. Her research areas include gender and development, International Relations, Security Studies, and post-conflict reconstruction. She has published in areas related to female soldiers, Sierra Leone's disarmament process, empowerment policies, and wartime sexual violence and female soldiers. Her unique research experience includes extensive work in Sierra Leone where she interviewed over 50 former female soldiers.

Sandra McEvoy is Associate Director of the Consortium on Gender, Security and Human Rights and former post-doctoral Fellow at the Five Colleges Women's Studies Research Center at Mt. Holyoke College. Her research centers on women perpetrators of political violence with a focus on women's participation as loyalist paramilitaries in Northern Ireland. She has presented her work at academic conferences both within the United States and internationally, and has been invited to speak on her research in Northern Ireland on several occasions. She is currently working on a book manuscript based on her PhD thesis.

Swati Parashar is currently a PhD candidate at Lancaster University, UK. She specializes in gender, feminist IR theories and "terrorism" and political violence in South Asia. Prior to entering the doctoral program, Swati was a Research Analyst with the International Centre for Political Violence and Terrorism Research at the S. Rajaratnam School of International Studies (RSIS), Singapore. Additionally, she has worked as an Associate Fellow at the Observer Research Foundation, New Delhi, where she coordinated the International Terrorism Watch Programme. Swati was a Fulbright Fellow on a National Security Programme at the Institute of Global Conflict and Cooperation, University of California, San Diego, USA (Jan.–Feb. 2006). She has published extensively on "terrorism," gender, and security in South Asia, and has presented papers at several international conferences including the annual conventions of the ISA. She has traveled to Sri Lanka, Kashmir, Nepal, and Israel as part of her field research.

Laura Sjoberg is Assistant Professor of Political Science at the University of Florida. She holds a PhD in International Relations and Gender Studies and a law degree specializing in International Law. She has taught at the University of Southern California, Brandeis University, Merrimack College, Duke University, and Virginia Tech. Her research focuses on gender in international security. She is the author of *Gender, Justice, and the Wars in Iraq* (2006) and (with Caron Gentry) *Mothers, Monsters, Whores: Women's Violence in Global Politics* (2007). Laura is the Chair of the Feminist Theory and Gender Studies Section of the International Studies Association, and President of the International Studies Association-West. Her work has recently appeared in *International Studies Quarterly, International Studies Review, International Studies Perspectives, International Relations, International Politics,* and *Politics and Gender.* Her research has been supported by the Women and Public Policy Program and the International Security Program at the Kennedy School of Government at Harvard University, the Center for the Study of Sexuality in the Military at the University of California Santa Barbara, the Law School at Boston College, the Kenan Institute for Ethics at Duke University, the Center for International Studies at the University of Southern California, and the Institute for Society, Culture, and the Environment at Virginia Tech.

Judith Hicks Stiehm is Professor of Political Science at Florida International University where she served as Provost and Academic Vice President for four years. Her specialties include political theory, social change, the status of women, and civil–military relations. She has taught at the University of Wisconsin, University of California at Los Angeles, and the University of Southern California. She has been a Visiting Professor at the U.S. Army Peacekeeping Institute and at the Strategic Studies Institute at Carlisle Barracks. Her books include *Nonviolent Power: Active and Passive Resistance* (Heath, 1972), *Bring Me Men and Women: Mandated Change at the U.S. Air Force Academy* (California, 1981), *Women's and Men's Wars* (Pergamon, 1983), *Arms and the Enlisted Woman* (Temple, 1989), *It's Our Military Too!: Women and the US Military* (Temple, 1996), and *U.S. Army War College: Military Education in a Democracy* (Temple, 2002). She has served on the Defense Advisory Committee on Women in the Military, the California Postsecondary Education Commission, the California Vocational Education Commission, as a consultant to the United Nations Commission for the Advancement of Women and to the Lessons Learned Unit of the Department of Peacekeeping Operations, and as an Expert Witness to the Senate Armed Services Committee.

Christine Sylvester is Professor of International Relations and Development in the Politics and International Relations Department at Lancaster University, UK. She was Vice President of the International Studies Association (ISA, 2004–5), Leverhulme Professor of International Relations at London University, School of Oriental and African Studies (2003–4), inaugural chair of the Feminist Theory and Gender Studies section of the International Studies Association (1990–92), and the 2009 recipient of the

Susan S. Northcutt Award from the Women's Caucus of the ISA. She has authored five books: *Art/Museums: International Relations Where We Least Expect It* (Paradigm Press, 2009), *Feminist International Relations: An Unfinished Journey* (Cambridge University Press, 2002), *Feminist Theory and International Relations in a Postmodern Era* (Cambridge University Press, 1994), *Producing Women and Progress in Zimbabwe: Narratives of Women and Work from the 1980's* (Heinemann Press, 2000), and *Zimbabwe: The Terrain of Contradictory Development* (Westview Press, 1991). Projects underway include a book, *War, Feminism, and International Relations,* and *Key Works in Feminist IR,* four volumes in an edited collection, both projects for Routledge.

Jonathan D. Wadley is a PhD candidate at the University of Florida. His research focuses on sexual politics and European identity. Jonathan has presented his work at the Annual Meetings of the American Political Science Association and International Studies Association, as well as at numerous regional conferences and workshops. He is currently finishing work on his dissertation, which examines the effect of the European Union's prostitution and trafficking policies upon its status as an international actor.

Lauren Wilcox is a PhD candidate at the University of Minnesota, where she works on issues of gender and technology in war. Lauren has presented her work at the Annual Meetings of the International Studies Association and the Northeast Political Science Association, as well as at the Institute for Qualitative Research Methods (IQRM), the "Gender and Security" Workshop, and the Methodology Workshop at the International Studies Association-Northeast. Lauren is working on a dissertation outlining the relationships between gender theory, the cyborg body, and technology in global politics.

Susan Wright is Research Scientist in History of Science and International Relations in the Institute for Research on Women and Gender at the University of Michigan. Over the past thirty years, her research and writing have focused on the history and politics of molecular biology and biotechnology and on the international and national politics of biological warfare and disarmament. Her books include *Molecular Politics: Developing American and British Regulatory Policy for Genetic Engineering, 1972–82* (University of Chicago Press, 1994), *Preventing a Biological Arms Race* (MIT Press, 1990), and *Biological Warfare and Disarmament: New Problems/New Perspectives* (Rowman & Littlefield, 2002). Her most recent publication is "Terrorism and Biological Weapons: Forging the Linkage in the Clinton Administration," *Politics and the Life Sciences* 25 (1–2) (2007): 57–115. From 1979 to 1998, she directed the Residential College Science and Society Program at the University of Michigan. From 1998 to 1999, she was a Senior Research Fellow at the UN Institute for Disarmament

Research in Geneva where she directed an international project, "Forming a North–South Alliance to Address Current Problems of Biological Warfare and Disarmament." From 2003 to 2005, she was a consultant for a research project, "The Bioterrorism Challenge", supported by Princeton University's Program on Science and Global Security. She is currently a Visiting Professorial Fellow at the School of Social Sciences, University of Wollongong, Australia, where she directs a research project, "Gender and Security: Bridging the Gulf between Theory and Practice."

Acknowledgments

This project exists because of the financial, institutional, and creative support of the Women and Public Policy Program at the Kennedy School of Government at Harvard University, and the personal efforts of the Executive Director, Victoria Budson; the Associate Director for Research, Theresa Lund; and the Program Manager, Kerry Conley. Funding and institutional support were also provided by the International Studies Association, the Department of Political Science at Virginia Polytechnic Institute and State University, the Institute for Research on Women and Gender at the University of Michigan, the Political Science Department at Duke University, the Law School at the University of North Carolina, and Rudman & Winchell in Bangor, Maine.

Portions of this book were published as a special issue of the journal *Security Studies* entitled "Security Studies: Feminist Contributions." Those essays in particular and the project in general owe a debt to the journal's editors over the course of the project, Susan Peterson, Michael Desch, and William Wohlforth, as well as two anonymous reviewers who read and commented on all seven essays twice. This book was first discussed as a collection at a workshop held at the 2007 Annual Meeting of the International Studies Association, where a number of contributors and other scholars shared ideas that evolved into this project.

My personal inspiration for this project, and my motivation to bring it to fruition at a tough time in my life, comes from Ann Tickner, whose intellectual inspiration, leadership, and tireless work is only matched by her kindness of spirit and personal toughness. I believe in this project because of Ann's work, and I believe in my ability to do it because of her friendship and mentorship. I am inspired to work even when I am exhausted because Ann's tireless dedication serves as a constant reminder of the importance of feminist work in International Relations.

A number of people have been careful readers and advisers over the course of this project. Those include (but certainly are not limited to) the contributors to this volume (Judith Hicks Stiehm, Christine Sylvester, Jonathan D. Wadley, Lauren Wilcox, Nicole A. Detraz, Sandra McEvoy, Megan MacKenzie, Swati Parashar, Susan Wright, Jennifer K. Lobasz, Jennifer Heeg Maruska, and Heidi Hudson). Several colleagues read versions of the

Introduction, including Amy Eckert, Caron Gentry, Ilja Luciak, Janice Bially Mattern, Spike Peterson, and Ann Tickner. Carol Cohn, Annick Wibben, Lene Hansen, and Jacqueline Berman have read and provided comments on substantial parts of this project. Participants in the workshop at ISA 2007 who did not end up writing for the book contributed to its conceptualization and shaping, including Annick Wibben, Gunhild Hoogenson, Runa Das, Laura Shepherd, Cristina Masters, Rebecca Grant, Theresa Lund, Chris Jones, and Brandon Valeriano. Dozens of panel discussants and commentators at meetings of ISA and APSA have also helped shape this project. As an editor, I also owe a debt to conversations with Brooke Ackerly, Francine D'Amico, Sandy Whitworth, and Anne Runyan.

Personally, this book could not have been constructed without the love and support of my family, including my parents, Marie and David Sjoberg, my grandmother Jean, my aunts, Jenny and Debby, and my brother, JD. I am closer to all of those people than I was at the start of this project, and better for it. I've learned a good bit about gender and war from my chihuahuas: Max, the youngest, and April, the oldest, have been engaged in a constant and apparently never-ending fight for dominance/relative power during the compilation of this book; Gizmo, the "middle child", has been an adorable combination of empathy and fear. Co-celebrants at my 30th birthday party in New York have been sources of strength, as friends and colleagues. Overall, I am energized by a network of friendships and support more amazing than I could imagine, and better than I deserve, without which this book would not exist.

Those of you who know me know that my acknowledgments usually conclude with a negative interaction with the discipline that inspired me to do the counter-hegemonic work that I have done. I am sure there will be plenty more of those in books in the future, given the youth of my career and the nature of my work. This time, though, I would like to deviate from that pattern and tell a story of a positive relationship of building mutual trust and understanding in cross-field interaction. As I mentioned above, many of the essays in this book were originally published as a part of a feminist special issue of the journal *Security Studies*. When I approached the journal, I expected the sort of closed-minded reaction to feminist approaches that I have chronicled in other acknowledgment-ending stories. The editor's reaction was exactly the opposite—a willingness to engage and excitement about including feminist work. In the editing process, we encountered a number of ontological, epistemological, and methodological misunderstandings and disagreements (what is constitutive reasoning?, how do you account for variation?, what is gender if not male/female?, what does race have to do with it?), but the journal editors were fair, open-minded, and attuned to bridging divides rather than alienating new ideas. This book exists as a follow-up to the special issue to demonstrate that Feminist Security Studies is both what the journal included, and what it excluded on format, methodological, or epistemological/ontological grounds. Still, my experience with *Security Studies* makes me optimistic (if cautiously) that the future of feminism in International Relations generally and Security Studies specifically is not doomed to marginality and mis-understanding, even when feminist scholars insist on not compromising the key ideas that make their scholarship not just gender-based, but explicitly feminist.

That said, the point of this as a book project is that gathering the best work by feminist scholars addressing the sub-field that International Relations (IR) labels "Security Studies" or "International Security" cannot be contained within the epistemological, methodological, or ontological boundaries that the "mainstream" in the discipline is flexible enough to accommodate. Something is lost when work that does not talk "to" or "in the language of" a subfield built by men around masculinized concepts and ideal-types is excluded. Much like intellectual communities centered around other IR paradigms, the feminist community in IR is not substantively or methodologically homogenous. In fact, many of the most important insights coming from feminist scholarship in IR come in the form of work considered "incommensurable" or "without a research program" by "the discipline" of IR. It is ironic, then, that the real strength of feminist contributions of Security Studies (and any other part of IR) comes in the intersections and totalities of those diverse approaches. Many of the chapter in this book were excluded (not in theory but in actuality) from the conversation of "*Security Studies*: Feminist Contributions" by (my and others') editorial decisions about commensurability and disciplinary fit. This book was put together to make/embody the argument that feminist theorizing about global politics/global security should not be bound by those concerns, and makes a stronger contribution to IR narrowly and knowledge writ large without those chains.

Permissions

The book project is indebted to the journals *Security Studies* and the *Cambridge Review of International Affairs* for permission to reprint modified forms of the following articles:

Laura Sjoberg, "Introduction to Security Studies: Feminist Contributions," *Security Studies*, 18(2) 2009, 183–213, Taylor & Francis Ltd, www.informaworld.com, reprinted by permission of the publisher.
Lauren Wilcox, "Gendering the 'Cult of the Offensive'," *Security Studies*, 18(2) 2009, 214–40, Taylor & Francis Ltd, www.informaworld.com, reprinted by permission of the publisher.
Nicole A. Detraz, "Environmental Security and Gender: Necessary Shifts in an Evolving Debate," *Security Studies*, 18(2) 2009, 345–69, Taylor & Francis Ltd, www.informaworld.com, reprinted by permission of the publisher.
Sandra McEvoy, "Loyalist Women Paramilitaries in Northern Ireland: Beginning a Feminist Conversation about Conflict Resolution," *Security Studies*, 18(2) 2009, 262–86, Taylor & Francis Ltd, www.informaworld.com, reprinted by permission of the publisher.

Megan MacKenzie, "Securitization and De-Securitization: Female Soldiers and the Reconstruction of Women in Post-Conflict Sierra Leone," *Security Studies*, 18(2) 2009, 241–61, Taylor & Francis Ltd, www.informaworld.com, reprinted by permission of the publisher.

Swati Parashar, "Feminist International Relations and Women Militants: Case Studies from Sri Lanka and Kashmir," edited from *Cambridge Review of International Affairs*, 22(2) 2009, 235–56, Taylor & Francis Ltd, www. informaworld.com, reprinted by permission of the publisher.

Jennifer K. Lobasz, "Beyond Border Security: Feminist Approaches to Human Trafficking," *Security Studies*, 18(2) 2009, 319–44, Taylor & Francis Ltd, www.informaworld.com, reprinted by permission of the publisher.

Heidi Hudson, "Peace Building through a Gender Lens and the Challenges of Implementation in Rwanda and Côte d'Ivoire," *Security Studies*, 18(2) 2009, 287–318, Taylor & Francis Ltd, www.informaworld.com, reprinted by permission of the publisher.

Introduction

Laura Sjoberg

In 1988, *Millennium* published a special issue on "Women and International Relations" now widely recognized as the start of a research program of feminist approaches to International Relations (IR). In a critique of Hans Morgenthau's political realism in that issue, Ann Tickner pointed out that "international relations is a man's world, a world of power and conflict in which warfare is a privileged activity."[1] Based on this realization, Robert Keohane characterized feminist International Relations as "likely to begin a productive debate involving international relations scholars, feminist thinkers, and others concerned about security in the most inclusive sense."[2] Feminist scholars aspired to "move the suspicion of officially ungendered IR texts to their subversion and to replace their theories,"[3] and several IR scholars predicted that their insights should "fundamentally change IR's greatest debates."[4]

In the intervening decades, feminist scholars have critiqued and reformulated many of the foundational theoretical assumptions of IR. Still, the productivity of conversations between feminists and other IR scholars has been more mixed than original predictions envisioned. In some areas of IR, scholarship that uses gender as an analytical category has successfully engaged in dialogue with more "mainstream" approaches. In other areas of study, however, feminists have experienced "awkward silences and miscommunications" brought about by a lack of understanding between IR audiences and feminist speakers.[5]

Security Studies is one area of IR where unsatisfactory encounters "illustrate a gendered estrangement that inhibits more sustained conversations" between feminists and IR scholars.[6] As Ann Tickner laments, "feminist theorists have rarely achieved the serious engagement with other IR scholars for which they have frequently called."[7] In many ways, the theory and practice of international security remain a man's world. Women in privileged positions in international security policy-making remain rare (and are often identified primarily by their gender when they do reach those positions), and entire scholarly texts can be found with no reference to women or gender at all.

This lack of communication between the field of Security Studies and feminist scholars exists despite the growing influence of feminist thought and practice in the policy world. The passage and implementation of United Nations

Security Council Resolutions 1325 and 1820 (which mainstream gender in Security Council operations and oblige member-states to include women in peace negotiations and post-conflict reconstruction), and similar initiatives throughout the United Nations, the World Bank, and the IMF, show that gender is a salient concern in global governance.[8] Furthermore, specific international phenomena all show not only women's significance in international security, but also the relevance of gender as a factor in understanding and addressing security matters—such as, the increase in female suicide bombers,[9] growing evidence of the use of sexual violence as a tool of war in conflicts from South Korea to the Democratic Republic of Congo,[10] women's participation as soldiers in armed conflicts around the globe,[11] and women's activism and protests against conflicts (including the war in Iraq).[12] Practitioners interested in peacekeeping,[13] the study and management of refugees,[14] and protecting noncombatants in times of war[15] reveal the increasing importance of gender sensitivity to many of the actors that we study in global politics. As Spike Peterson explains, "'real world' events are not adequately addressed by androcentric accounts that render women and gender relations invisible."[16]

This book was assembled with the goal of improving the quality and quantity of conversations between feminist Security Studies and Security Studies more generally, in order to demonstrate the importance of gender analysis to the study of international security, and to expand the feminist research program in Security Studies. The chapters included in this book not only challenge the assumed irrelevance of gender, they argue that gender is not a subsection of Security Studies to be compartmentalized or briefly considered as a side issue. Rather, feminists argue that gender is conceptually, empirically, and normatively essential to studying international security. As such, accurate, rigorous, and ethical scholarship cannot be produced without taking account of women's presence in or the gendering of world politics.

In this Introduction, I provide a brief discussion of what it means to approach IR from a feminist perspective, giving a brief summary of some of the accomplishments of and common themes in feminist Security Studies to this point. I then introduce chapters in this book as analyses of the concept of security, traditional security theories, women as actors in international security, and security problematiques through gendered lenses.

Feminist approaches to international security

It has been argued that all scholars approach their particular subject matter with lenses that "foreground some things, and background others."[17] In other words, scholars' investigations start with the variables that they find meaningful in global politics. For the studies in this book, that lens is gender.[18] As Jill Steans explains, "To look at the world through gendered lenses is to focus on gender as a particular kind of power relation, or to trace out the ways in which gender is central to understanding international processes."[19]

In order to understand feminist work in IR, it is important to note that gender is not the equivalent of membership in biological sex classes. Instead, gender is a system of symbolic meaning that creates social hierarchies based on perceived associations with masculine and feminine characteristics. As Lauren Wilcox explains, "Gender symbolism describes the way in which masculine/feminine are assigned to various dichotomies that organize Western thought" where "both men and women tend to place a higher value on the term which is associated with masculinity."[20] Gendered social hierarchy, then, is at once a social construction and a "structural feature of social and political life" that "profoundly shapes our place in, and view of, the world."[21]

This is not to say that all people, or even all women, experience gender in the same ways. While genders are lived by people throughout the world, each person lives gender in a different culture, body, language, and identity. Still, as a structural feature of social and political life, gender is "a set of discourses that represent, construct, change, and enforce social meaning."[22] Feminism, then, "is neither just about women, nor the addition of women to male-stream constructions; it is about transforming ways of being and knowing" as gendered discourses are understood and transformed.[23] Therefore, there is not one gendered experience of global politics, but many. By extension, there is not one gender-based perspective on IR or international security, but many. Feminists can approach global politics from a number of different perspectives, including realist, liberal, constructivist, critical, poststructural, postcolonial, and ecological. These perspectives yield different, and sometimes contradictory, insights about and predictions for global politics.

Feminist work from a realist perspective is interested in the role of gender in strategy and power politics between states.[24] Liberal feminist work calls attention to the subordinate position of women in global politics and argues that gender oppression can be remedied by including women in the existing structures of global politics.[25] Critical feminism explores the ideational and material manifestations of gendered identity and gendered power in world politics.[26] Feminist constructivism focuses on the ways that ideas about gender shape and are shaped by global politics.[27] Feminist poststructuralism focuses on how gendered linguistic manifestations of meaning, particularly strong/weak, rational/emotional, and public/private dichotomies, serve to empower the masculine, marginalize the feminine, and constitute global politics.[28] Postcolonial feminists, while sharing many of the epistemological assumptions of poststructural feminists, focus on the ways that colonial relations of domination and subordination established under imperialism are reflected in gender relations, and even relations between feminists, in global politics and academic work.[29] Ecological feminism, or "ecofeminism," identifies connections between the treatment of women and minorities, on one hand, and the nonhuman environment, on the other.[30] While each of the chapters in this book approach international security from a feminist perspective, each of their feminist perspectives differ.

Still, feminists looking at global politics share a normative and empirical concern that the international system is gender-hierarchical. In feminist scholarship, gender is not a variable that can be measured as a "yes" or "no" (or "male" or "female" question), but as a more complicated symbolic and cultural construction.[31] Fundamental to this understanding is that gender hierarchy is seen as a normative problem, which can be revealed and analyzed through scholarly evaluation. While gender hierarchy is a normative problem, the failure to recognize it presents an empirical problem for IR scholarship. Failing to recognize gender hierarchy makes IR scholarship less descriptively accurate and predictively powerful for its omission of this major force in global politics. Scholars looking through gender lenses "ask what assumptions about gender (and race, class, nationality, and sexuality) are necessary to make particular statements, policies, and actions meaningful."[32] As such, feminist scholars have argued that "gender matters in what we study, why we study, and how we study global politics,"[33] and it matters in a way that "transforms knowledge in ways that go beyond adding women" to critiquing, complicating, and improving Security Studies.[34]

Feminist theorists have contributed to the field of Security Studies through analyses and reformulations of the traditional contents of Security Studies, explorations of the roles that women and gender play in combat and combat resolution, and by bringing attention to new or neglected subjects revealed by taking gender seriously. In analyzing traditional concepts in Security Studies, feminists have demonstrated the gender bias in security's core concepts, such as the state, violence, war, peace, and even security itself, urging redefinition in light of that bias.[35] Feminist scholars have also gained empirical and theoretical insights from analyzing the various roles of women and gender in conflict and conflict resolution. Feminists have found gender-based language and assumptions at the foundation of debates about nuclear strategy,[36] the noncombatant immunity principle,[37] peacekeeping,[38] and various aspects of militarization and soldiering.[39] In addition to critiquing concepts traditionally employed in the study of security, gender-based perspectives have also uncovered new empirical knowledge about sexual violence in war and gendered participation in armed conflict.[40] For example, feminist scholars have pointed out that rape is more prevalent in times of war than in times of peace.[41] In addition to pointing out the serious threat to women's security posed by wartime rape,[42] feminists have demonstrated that rape is institutionalized in war, as recreational and as a weapon.[43] This book aims to consolidate and build on these gains, expanding on common tenets of feminist work in security to explore new empirical situations and develop new theoretical insights.

The first common tenet is a broad understanding of what counts as a security issue, and to whom the concept of security should be applied. Feminist approaches define security broadly in multidimensional or multilevel terms. In this view, security threats include not only war and international violence, but also domestic violence, rape, poverty, gender subordination, and ecological destruction.[44] Feminist scholars not only broaden what is meant by security but also who merits security. Fueled by the recognition that secure states often contain insecure women, feminists analyze the security of individuals and communities as well as of states and international organizations. Feminists have argued that "the personal is international [and] the international is personal."[45]

The second common theme in feminist Security Studies is an understanding of the gendered nature of the values prized in the realm of international security. If "masculinism is the ideology that justifies and naturalizes gender hierarchy by not questioning the elevation of ways of being and knowing associated with men and masculinity over those associated with women and femininity,"[46] then the values socially associated with femininity and masculinity are awarded unequal weight in a competitive social order, perpetuating inequality in perceived gender difference. Social processes select for values and behaviors that can be associated with an idealized, or hegemonic, masculinity.[47] This selection occurs because traits associated with hegemonic masculinities dominate social relations while other values are subordinated. This cycle is self-sustaining—so long as masculinity appears as a unitary concept, dichotomous thinking about gender continues to pervade social life.[48] This dichotomous thinking about gender influences how scholars and policy-makers frame and interpret issues of international security.

A third common theme for feminist Security Studies is the broad and diverse role that feminist scholars see gender playing in the theory and practice of international security. In each of these chapters, gender matters in the theory and practice of international security in three main ways: (1) it is necessary, conceptually, for understanding international security; (2) it is important in analyzing causes and predicting outcomes; and (3) it is essential to thinking about solutions and promoting positive change in the security realm. First, gender can be a constitutive category which defines (and is defined by) international actors' understandings of their security as well as those left out of security analyses. International security practice often relies on the invisibility of women (both as labor and as a *casus belli*) specifically and gender generally.[49] Second, gender can be a causal variable, which causes (or is caused by) states' security-seeking behavior. Feminist scholars have argued that states' foreign policy choices are guided by their identities, which are based on association with characteristics attached to masculinity, manliness, and heterosexism.[50] Finally, feminists' interest in remedying gender subordination could be epistemologically constitutive for the theory and practice of security. If we were to re-envision security as starting from the perspective of individual women's lives, it would change not only what security is, but how it is conceptualized, operationalized, and acted on. The chapters in this book argue that gender adds something to Security Studies, but that it is also a transformative force in the constitution of security generally and security scholarship specifically.

These observations lead to a final common theme for feminist Security Studies: that the omission of gender from work on international security does not make that work gender-neutral or unproblematic. Instead, feminist work on issues of international security has served to "question the supposed non-existence of and irrelevance of women in international security politics," to interrogate "the extent to which women are secured by state 'protection' in times of war and peace," to contest "discourses where women are linked unreflectively with peace," and to critique "the assumption that gendered security practices address only women."[51]

Gender and international security: feminist perspectives

In Part I, "Gendered lenses envision security," each chapter presents a different point of departure for, and direction in, the theorizing of security through gendered lenses. Chapter 1, Judith Hicks Stiehm's "Theses on the military, security, war, and women," is modeled after Martin Luther's "95 Theses" and Karl Marx's "Theses on Feuerbach." It is a creative project "offering for discussion" theses exploring people's ethical responsibility to know and engage with militaries and militarism from a feminist perspective. Switching easily between telling quips like "do you know where your special forces are tonight?" to bold statements like declaring terrorism "not unusual," Stiehm addresses many uncomfortable themes particularly related to contemporary American civilian–military relations. Stiehm demonstrates that feminist approaches emphasize empathy and responsibility and question the assumed naturalness of war as protection as gender dichotomy, as something done "over there."

Chapter 2, Christine Sylvester's "War, sense, and security," argues that we desperately need new ways of thinking and looking at the world and of overturning the fear and banality of security. In particular, Sylvester is interested in Security Studies' unwillingness to look at war as a sense experience. She asks, crucially, about the relationships between senses of war and experiences of war. Using recent texts by Anthony Burke, Lene Hansen, Laura Sjoberg, Caron Gentry, and Erin Manning, Sylvester explores what she calls the war sense/the security sense. Her feminist lenses recognize that people experience war both physically and emotionally, and both are crucial parts of the sensory experience of war, a dimension all the more important to explore at a time when globalization extends the reach of international conflicts. Writing about sense, Sylvester contends, can lead to "escape from wrong-footed security" and its current exclusionary domains.

In Chapter 3, "Gendering the state: performativity and protection in international security," Jonathan D. Wadley turns from sensing war to questions of anthropomorphism and the state. Wadley points out that anthropomorphic images of the state are consistently employed by IR theorists of most stripes in discussions of security issues. Still, he observes, the practice of humanizing the state remains understudied in IR, especially as it relates to the problematic presentation of the state's humanity as ungendered. Arguing that presenting the state-person as ungendered does not make it so, Wadley undertakes an exploration of the discipline's tendency to treat states as genderless persons by looking at the role of gender in security performances of states. Using Judith Butler's idea of performativity as a starting point, Wadley argues that "performances within the field of security" have to be understood within webs of symbolic meaning and "cannot be but gendered." Wadley contends that the masculine and feminine subjects in international security are created performatively through states' behaviors as masculinized protectors, and suggests that it is important to understand security performances with "an eye towards their constitutive effects" in order to understand the nature of the hierarchical relations that are endemic to global politics.

Part II, "Gendered security theories," features chapters which interpret particular theoretical approaches to international security through gendered lenses. The section opens with Lauren Wilcox's Chapter 4, "Gendering the cult of the offensive," which explores a topic that has long been of interest to traditional scholars in Security Studies, the offense–defense balance. Wilcox focuses on the claim in offense–defense theory that misperceived offensive dominance has been the cause of numerous international conflicts, including, but not limited to, the First World War. Her chapter starts with a question offense–defense theory has not definitively answered: why do states misperceive the dominance of the offense? Wilcox suggests that the roots of these misperceptions can be found in a combination of states' "gendered perceptions of technology, gendered nationalism, and definitions of citizenship and honor based on the gendered concept of protection." In other words, Wilcox explains that "gender may provide the missing link in explaining the cult of the offensive." Through the analysis of offense–defense theory, Wilcox demonstrates that gender is constitutive of perceptions of military strength. This chapter shows that a feminist analysis of offense–defense theory is one instance in which gender can add explanatory leverage to "mainstream" security theories and suggest a transformative agenda for the theory and practice of international politics.

Chapter 5, "Gendering power transition theory," which I wrote, takes a look at the power transition theory (PTT) research program through gendered lenses. Power transition theory is interested in when and why states with power parity at the top of the international hierarchy fight wars, with a particular interest in the question of whether the "transition" between the United States and China will be peaceful. After introducing the central tenets of PTT, this chapter uses feminist insights to "ask how PTT contains, reproduces, and reflects gender relations, gender stereotypes, and gender subordination," critiquing PTT's understandings of core concepts in international security, including power, agency, and the causes of conflict. The chapter presents alternatives to key PTT hypotheses consistent with reading great power politics through feminist lenses, and finish the chapter with a feminist (re)evaluation of the likelihood and nature of China "overtaking" the United States in the global hierarchy.

In Chapter 6, "The genders of environmental security," Nicole A. Detraz argues that gender analysis can shed helpful light on the question of the links between the environment and security. For years scholars in Security Studies have asked if the environment is a security issue, but as Detraz points out, "gender has not been incorporated into these debates in a meaningful way." Detraz contends that gender may be the missing link in theorizing the relationship between the environment and security. Combining theoretical analysis with two case studies, Detraz uses feminist lenses to demonstrate that not only is the environment a security issue, it is a gendered security issue. This chapter reformulates the environmental security approach from a feminist perspective, presenting a combination of feminist and environmental security that provides more theoretical leverage than either approach does separately.

In Part III, "Gendered security actors," the chapters deal with the theoretical implications of women as (particularly violent) actors in international security. In Chapter 7, "Loyalist women paramilitaries in Northern Ireland: beginning a feminist conversation about conflict resolution," Sandra McEvoy challenges traditional conceptions about conflict resolution by foregrounding the experiences and opinions of women combatants. McEvoy argues that the conflict in Northern Ireland remained intractable in part because the peace negotiators' perceptions of the conflict were flawed by their exclusion of the perspectives of Loyalist women combatants. She reveals the unique perceptions of Loyalist women paramilitaries on the four cross-border agreements between 1974 and 2007, arguing that the inclusion of combatant women in their negotiation and execution would have made these agreements more likely to succeed. McEvoy's analysis demonstrates to conventional accounts of conflict resolution that women should not be left out of the process and points out to feminists that they should not only be asking whether women are involved in peace processes, but also asking which women are invited to the table when women are included. Reading the conflict through the experiences of women paramilitaries, McEvoy argues for a theoretical and practical reformulation of both gender role expectations and conflict resolution processes, in Northern Ireland and beyond.

Chapter 8, "Securitization and de-securitization: female soldiers and the reconstruction of women in post-conflict Sierra Leone," by Megan MacKenzie, is based on 50 interviews with female former combatants in Sierra Leone. Her analysis focuses on the gendered construction of "soldier" and "victim" in the DDR process in Sierra Leone, based on her interviews and her observation that reintegration agencies are reluctant to acknowledge women who participated in the war as soldiers. Instead, in the language of the Copenhagen School, MacKenzie recognizes that men and masculinity are securitized post-conflict, while former female soldiers are desecuritized. The result is that the reintegration of men into society post-conflict is prioritized as essential for the transition to peace, while women's reintegration, when considered at all, is treated as a social issue. MacKenzie argues that the gendered perceptions of former combatants in Sierra Leone not only cause the DDR process to be less effective for women, but to be less effective more generally.

Using this information, MacKenzie critiques the concept of securitization through gendered lenses, arguing that gendered power dictated who was securitized and who was desecuritized (that is, ignored) in the post-conflict reconstruction process in Sierra Leone.

Swati Parashar's Chapter 9, "Women, militancy, and security: the South Asian conundrum," explores the theoretical and practical implications of women's militancy in the conflicts in Kashmir and Sri Lanka. Parashar argues that "terrorism" is gendered as a concept and in action, and that it is important for IR theory generally and feminist IR theory specifically to hear and understand the voices of marginalized, militant women not only to understand those women but also to fully understand the nature of, and the differences between, ethno-national and religio-political conflicts. Using substantial first-hand interview material from both conflicts, Parashar convincingly argues that women's participation in conflict should not be ignored, but should not be treated as a simple question of whether or not participation in militancy "liberates" or "subordinates" women, as elements of both are present in the conflicts that she studies. Instead, Parashar suggests that the study of women's participation in militancy suggests that international security be approached with an understanding that it is constituted by a number of factors that are not strict, essential values but instead porous categories, including but not limited to race, caste, class, culture, religion, and gender. Parashar suggests that understanding women's participation in militancy will improve scholarly understandings of gender and of conflict.

Part IV, "Gendered security problematiques," includes chapters which address issues of security that have been marginalized in Security Studies for one reason or another. Some of these issues have been marginalized because of the field's perceived irrelevance of gender issues specifically and human security issues generally, while others have been treated, though they are related to war, not as "war proper," which often excludes pre- and post-conflict security issues.

Susan Wright, in Chapter 10, "Feminist theory and arms control," explores two unexplored territories, since arms control theorists have neglected gender and feminist theorists have not addressed issues of arms control. Wright asks what kind of insights feminist analysis can bring to the nature of present forms of arms control. Analyzing the theoretical insights of two prominent theorists of arms control (Thomas Schelling and Hedley Bull), Wright argues that arms control theory and practice are informed by stereotypically masculine—or masculinist—values of reducing the human complexity of the state to impersonal units, distancing Self from Other, exerting power over, and seeking military advantage over human security. She applies these arguments to the negotiations within the UK government and between the UK and the US governments that shaped the British proposal for an international convention banning biological weapons in 1968 and to the influence of Hedley Bull on the substance of these negotiations. She argues that the well-known problems with the 1972 Biological Weapons Convention negotiated following the British proposal can be traced to the masculinist values that dominated these discussions. Wright suggests that a feminist reading of arms control policies such as the one in her chapter is a first step towards a reconstruction that replaces such values with an alternative, feminist-inspired approach that places human security at the center of the analysis.

In Chapter 11, "Beyond border security: feminist approaches to human trafficking," Jennifer K. Lobasz addresses an issue rarely considered by mainstream scholars in international security—human trafficking. Lobasz points out that, when traditional security approaches do deal with human trafficking, they "emphasize border security, migration controls, and international law enforcement cooperation." She argues that feminist perspectives reject both the marginalization of human trafficking in traditional security approaches and those approaches' policy priorities in dealing with trafficking. Instead, Lobasz uses feminist theory to argue that trafficking should be a high-priority security issue and that key issues concerning trafficking to be addressed include the security of trafficked persons, the security threats posed by both traffickers and states, and the sexist and racist stereotypes that constitute the category of trafficking victims in the policy world. Lobasz's chapter demonstrates both that trafficking deserves attention in Security Studies and that "mainstream" approaches to trafficking as a security issue can be improved and transformed by the addition of feminist analysis.

If Lobasz and Wright analyze issues that are frequently theorized but neglected in Security Studies, Jennifer Heeg Maruska's Chapter 12, "When are states hypermasculine?," suggests a relatively new area for theorization in IR and security—state hypermasculinity. Maruska argues that American hegemonic masculinity became hypermasculine following the September 11, 2001, attacks. She explains the popular support for the war in Iraq and the 2004 re-election of George W. Bush in terms of gendered tropes and expectations dominating US foreign policy-making. Maruska elaborates on the concepts of hegemonic masculinity in cultural and political institutions, and then defines hypermasculinity as gendered stereotypes and expectations taken to their extremes. She explains two previous periods where a hypermasculine hegemonic masculinity in US culture was manifested in foreign and domestic policy: in the 1890s with the closing of the "frontier," and in the late 1940s and early 1950s with the end of World War I and the onset of the Cold War. Maruska then explains both the early popular support for the invasion of Iraq and the 2004 reelection of George W. Bush in terms of a shift to hypermasculinity in the American hegemonic masculinity. Maruska shows that gender can be a key constitutive element of the making and manifestation of foreign policies in the security realm.

The book concludes with Chapter 13, by Heidi Hudson, entitled "Peace building through a gender lens and the challenges of implementation in Rwanda and Côte d'Ivoire," which looks at peace-building processes from a different perspective, through the lens of African feminisms with special attention to the cases of Côte d'Ivoire and Rwanda. Building on previous work proposing that "gender mainstreaming" be adopted in peace-building processes, Hudson contends that mainstreaming strategies, while important to peace building, need to take account not only of including women in peace processes, but also of the cultural context in which a conflict occurs. Using examples from several African conflicts, Hudson contends that the success of peace building generally depends on the inclusion of women, and that the success of the inclusion of women depends on the cultural sensitivity of the mainstreaming process, the strength and commitment of local women's movements, and the translation of international legal frameworks to local contexts. Hudson demonstrates that neither peace building nor gender emancipation are cookie-cutter processes, and that both gender and cultural sensitivity "could have substantial payoffs in terms of gender rights ... [and] could serve as the missing link to lend coherence to peace building processes." Hudson's feminist analysis also shows that post-conflict security requires the interaction of a number of actors, including states, social movements, and individuals (women) who "make various and important contributions to modeling and implementing African peace building process."

Independently, the chapters in this book show that gender matters in particular concepts, theories, and situations crucial to understanding international security. In conversation, they show that the ways gender matters are complex and diverse. As a whole, they demonstrate that gender is necessary, conceptually, to understanding security; crucial to explaining the causes and effects of events in the international security arena; and essential to constructing workable solutions to the world's most serious security problems.

Notes

1 J. Ann Tickner, "Hans Morgenthau's Principles of Political Realism: A Feminist Reformulation," *Millennium: Journal of International Studies* 17, no. 3 (December 1988): 429–40.
2 This is Robert Keohane's endorsement on the back cover of Ann Tickner's book, *Gender in International Relations: Feminist Approaches on Achieving Global Security* (New York: Columbia University Press, 1992).
3 Christine Sylvester, "Feminists and Realists on Autonomy and Obligation in International Relations," in *Gendered States: Feminist (Re)Visions on International Relations Theory*, ed., V. Spike Peterson (Boulder, CO: Lynne Rienner, 1992).
4 Robert Keohane, "International Relations Theory: Contributions of a Feminist Standpoint," *Millennium: Journal of International Studies* 18, no. 2 (1989): 245–53.
5 J. Ann Tickner, "You Just Don't Understand: Troubled Engagements Between Feminists and IR Theorists," *International Studies Quarterly* 41, no. 4 (December 1997): 611–32; and V. Spike Peterson, "Transgressing Boundaries: Theories of Knowledge, Gender, and International Relations," *Millennium: Journal of International Studies* 21, no. 2 (June 1992): 183–206.
6 Tickner, "You Just Don't Understand," p. 613.
7 Ibid., p. 628.
8 Jacqui True, "Gender Mainstreaming in Global Public Policy," *International Feminist Journal of Politics* 5, no. 3 (2003): 368–96; and Jacqui True and Michael Mintrom, "Transnational Networks and Policy Diffusion: The Case of Gender Mainstreaming," *International Studies Quarterly* 45, no. 1 (March 2001): 27–57.

9 Laura Sjoberg and Caron Gentry, *Mothers, Monsters, Whores: Women's Violence in Global Politics* (London: Zed Books, 2007).

10 Claudia Card, "Rape as a Weapon of War," *Hypatia* 11, no. 4 (Fall 1996): 5–18.

11 Cynthia Enloe, *Does Khaki Become You?: The Militarization of Women's Lives* (Boston: South End Press, 1983); see also Megan MacKenzie and Sandra McEvoy's chapters in this book.

12 Concerning Iraq, see Judy El-Bushra, "Feminism, Gender, and Women's Peace Activism," *Development and Change* 38, no. 1 (January 2007): 131–47; generally, see Alice Cook and Gwyn Kirk, *Greenham Women Everywhere: Dreams, Ideas, and Actions from the Women's Peace Movement* (London: Pluto Press, 1983).

13 See Dyan Mazurana, "International Peacekeeping Operations: To Neglect Gender Is to Risk Peacekeeping Failure," in *The Postwar Moment: Militaries, Masculinities and International Peacekeeping*, eds., Dubravka Zarkov and Cynthia Cockburn (London: Lawrence and Wishart, 2002); and Dyan Mazurana, Angela Raven-Roberts, and Jane Parpart, eds., *Gender, Conflict, and Peacekeeping* (Oxford: Rowman & Littlefield, 2005).

14 See Nira Yuval-Davis, and Pnina Werbner, eds., *Women, Citizenship, and Difference* (London: Zed Books, 2006); Doreen Indra, "Gender: A Key Dimension of the Refugee Experience," *Refugee* 6, no. 3 (1987).

15 See Jean Bethke Elshtain, *Just War Theory: Readings in Social and Political Theory* (New York: New York University Press, 1992); Judith Gardam and Hilary Charlesworth, "Protection of Women in Armed Conflict," *Human Rights Quarterly* 22, no. 1 (February 2000): 148–66; Laura Sjoberg, *Gender, Justice, and the Wars in Iraq* (New York: Lexington Books, 2006); and Laura Sjoberg, "The Gendered Realities of the Immunity Principle: Why Gender Analysis Needs Feminism," *International Studies Quarterly* 50, no. 4 (December 2006): 889–910.

16 Peterson, "Transgressing Boundaries," p. 197.

17 V. Spike Peterson and Anne Sisson Runyan, *Global Gender Issues* (Boulder, CO: Westview Press, 1999), p. 21.

18 Ibid., p. 2.

19 Jill Steans, *Gender and International Relations: An Introduction* (New Brunswick, NJ: Rutgers University Press, 1998), p. 5.

20 Lauren Wilcox, "Gendering Offense–Defense Theory." Paper presented at the 2007 Annual Meeting of the International Studies Association, Chicago, IL, February 26–March 1, 2007. See also Chapter 4 in this book.

21 Ibid.

22 R. W. Connell, *Masculinities* (Berkeley, CA: University of California Press, 1995); and J. K. Gibson-Graham, "'Stuffed if I Know!' Reflections on Post-Modern Feminist Social Research," *Gender, Place, and Culture: A Journal of Feminist Geography* 1, no. 2 (September 1994): 205–44.

23 Peterson, "Transgressing Boundaries," p. 205.

24 Most typologies leave out a feminist/realist approach from their list of types of feminist theories. Still, several feminists have suggested that the research programs have potentially fruitful commonalities, for example, Sandra Whitworth, "Gender and the Interparadigm Debate," *Millennium: Journal of International Studies* 18, no. 2 (June 1989): 265–72; Laura Sjoberg, "Feminism and Realism, Strategy in (Apparently) Gender-Emancipatory Policies," paper presented at the 2007 Annual Meeting of the International Studies Association, Chicago, Illinois, 28 February–3 March 2007; and Jacqui True, "Feminism and Realism," paper presented at the 2008 Annual Meeting of the International Studies Association, San Francisco, CA, 26–29 March 2008.

25 For example, liberal feminists have tested the relationship between woman-inclusive policies at the domestic level and a state's violence internationally, arguing that states will be less violent if and when women are integrated into their

structures. See Mary Caprioli and Mark Boyer, "Gender, Violence, and International Crisis," *Journal of Conflict Resolution* 45, no. 4 (August 2001): 503–18.

26 Critical feminism builds on the work of Robert Cox, studying the interacting forces of material conditions, ideas, and institutions, committed to understanding the world in order to change it. See Sandra Whitworth, *Feminism and International Relations* (London: Macmillan, 1994); and Christine Chin, *In Service and Servitude: Foreign Female Domestic Workers and the Malaysian Modernity Project* (New York: Columbia University Press, 1998).

27 See Elisabeth Prugl, *The Global Construction of Gender* (New York: Columbia University Press, 1999).

28 See Charlotte Hooper, *Manly States: Masculinities, International Relations, and Gender Politics* (New York: Columbia University Press, 2001).

29 See Chandra Mohanty, "Under Western Eyes," in *Third World Women and the Politics of Feminism*, eds., Chandra Mohanty, Anne Russo, and Lourdes Torres (Indianapolis: Indiana University Press, 1991), pp. 51–80; and Geeta Chowdhry and Sheila Nair, eds., *Power, Postcolonialism, and International Relations: Reading Race, Gender, and Class* (New York: Routledge, 2002).

30 See Maria Mies and Vandana Shiva, *Ecofeminism* (London: Zed Books, 1993); and Karen Warren, ed., *Ecofeminism: Women, Culture, Nature* (Indianapolis: Indiana University Press, 1997).

31 Lauren Wilcox makes this argument most articulately in a yet-unpublished manuscript, "What Difference Gender Makes: Ontologies of Gender and Dualism in IR."

32 Wilcox, "Gendering Offense–Defense Theory."

33 Brooke Ackerly, Maria Stern, and Jacqui True, eds., *Feminist Methodologies for International Relations* (Cambridge: Cambridge University Press, 2006), p. 5.

34 Tickner, "You Just Don't Understand," p. 621.

35 Tickner, *Gendering World Politics*; Peterson, *Gendered States*; and J. J. Pettman, *Worlding Women: A Feminist International Politics* (London: Routledge, 1996).

36 Carol Cohn, "Sex and Death in the World of Rational Defense Intellectuals," *Signs: Journal of Women in Culture and Society* 12, no. 4 (Summer 1987): 687–718.

37 Sjoberg, *Gender, Justice, and the Wars in Iraq*.

38 Sandra Whitworth, *Men, Militarism, and Peacekeeping* (Boulder, CO: Lynne Rienner Publishers, 2004).

39 For example, Cynthia Enloe, *Maneuvers: The International Politics of Militarizing Women's Lives* (Berkeley, CA: University of California Press, 2000).

40 See, for example, Card, "Rape as a Weapon of War," p. 5; Anne Barstow, ed., *War's Dirty Secret: Rape, Prostitution, and Other Crimes Against Women* (Cleveland, OH: Pilgrim Press, 2000); Caroline O. N. Moser and Fiona C. Clark, eds., *Victims, Perpetrators, or Actors? Gender, Armed Conflict, and Political Violence* (New York: Zed Books, 2001); and Cynthia Enloe, *The Morning After: Sexual Politics at the End of the Cold War* (Berkeley, CA: University of California Press, 1993).

41 Enloe, *The Morning After*; and Steans, *Gender and International Relations*.

42 Lene Hansen, "Gender, Nation, Rape: Bosnia and the Construction of Security," *International Feminist Journal of Politics* 3, no. 1 (April 2001): 55–75; and Gardam and Charlesworth, "Protection of Women in Armed Conflict."

43 Peterson and Runyan, *Global Gender Issues*, p. 127.

44 Tickner, *Gender in International Relations*.

45 Enloe, *Maneuvers*.

46 Charlotte Hooper, "Masculinist Practices and Gender Politics: The Operation of Multiple Masculinities in International Relations," in *The "Man" Question*, p. 31.

47 Hooper, *Manly States*; and Connell, *Masculinities*.

48 Hooper, *Manly States*, p. 48.
49 Enloe, *Maneuvers.*
50 See Peterson, "Sexing Political Identities"; and Hooper, *Manly States.*
51 Eric Blanchard, "Gender, International Relations, and the Development of Feminist Security Theory," *Signs: Journal of Women in Culture and Society* 28, no. 4 (Summer 2003): 1290.

Part I

Gendered lenses envision security

1 Theses on the military, security, war and women

Judith Hicks Stiehm

(With apologies to Martin Luther and Karl Marx)

Out of concern that issues related to war and security are narrowly construed, and believing that both moral and intellectual responsibility require an inclusive analysis, the following theses are offered for discussion.

I

In *Just and Unjust Wars* Michael Walzer asserts (Osama Bin Laden implicitly agrees) that, "In a democracy the citizen is responsible for the kind of military the state possesses and how it is used."[1] This means that if we can participate in choosing our government, we are accountable for the nature of our military and where and how it is deployed.

II

Holding no official position does not relieve one of responsibility. Being a non-combatant does not make one innocent, nor does ignorance, especially not deliberate ignorance. "Conscious avoidance" or "deliberate ignorance" is a legal term which diminishes or negates a claim of innocence. For instance, if an individual stops at a corner where her car door is opened and a package is placed on the car seat and she then proceeds to another corner where someone else opens the door and removes the package, her claim that she did not know the package contained drugs is considered "deliberate avoidance" and culpability can be inferred. Similarly, ignorance about one's military does not make a citizen innocent.

III

Governmental secrecy does not absolve a citizen. Citizens who accept the necessity for governmental secrecy are complicit. In time of war, operational secrets are permissible. However, citizens should insist that *every* member of Congress have access to *every* government file, and that *no* file be kept secret longer than ten years. Withholding information from citizens subverts democracy. Lying to them is criminal/treasonous.

IV

It is absurd that a foreign regime which a democracy is trying to destabilize or "change" may know more about the activities of a democratic government than do its own citizens. Do you know where your Special Forces are tonight?

V

Military personnel kill on behalf of citizens. If killing is truly necessary, citizens should stand ready to be conscripted. They should be ashamed of asking or requiring others to do that grim work for them. If it is not necessary, they should be ashamed that the military is killing in their name.

VI

In many developed countries military technology has created such impunity for its users that the moral question, "What is worth dying for?" has been replaced with "What is worth killing for?" Heroes risk their lives. Killing at a distance is not heroic. Camus has given us this test for honor in his pamphlet "Neither a Victim nor an Executioner Be."[2]

VII

Army leaders are cautious about committing to force because their troops are likely to have to kill people they can see, because they are the most exposed to danger, and because they will be the occupiers of any invaded territory. Navy personnel and especially Air Force personnel kill at a distance. The advice of Army leaders should be given more weight by civilian leaders than advice given by the other services.

VIII

Republics (the United States is one) have for centuries proclaimed the value of a citizen army in contrast to that of a mercenary army. A citizen army can be a conscripted army if it is inclusive. However, conscription is rarely inclusive. Women are seldom conscripted, the upper class finds ways to avoid service, and in the US the lower class is largely ineligible, mostly because of educational deficiencies. (The most "over-represented" group in the US military is the Army's African-American enlisted women. They are 40 percent of the Army's enlisted women.)

IX

A "volunteer" army could be a citizen army but is likely to be a mercenary army because it recruits lower middle-class men and women with promises of benefits otherwise unattainable. In 2008, enlistment bonuses were as much as $40,000.

X

A military that "outsources" is a military which makes war profitable. Contracts let without standard procedures because of an "emergency" are not only enriching but a likely source of corruption.

XI

Many, including Alfred Nobel of Peace Prize fame, have deplored the "standing army." While described as preventing war, the availability of a standing army leads to its use. For example, US forces developed to deter a hot war with the USSR were immediately put to use in the Gulf when the USSR collapsed. Similarly, once NATO determined the USSR was not a threat, it sent forces into Afghanistan. Again, a standing army gets used.

XII

In democracies, the military is sent to war by civilian officials who are charged with protecting the citizenry. The role of "protector" leads officials to authorize actions they might not take even in self-defense. The problem is that those charged with protection know that they cannot guarantee it. Therefore, they are prone to seek ever more weaponry v. the "enemy" and ever more control of the citizenry whether through curfews, wiretaps, stops and searches, and/or preventive detention.

XIII

Security means both safety and well-being. It attaches to people not necessarily to the state, or to corporations, or religious or other institutions. Importantly, even "opponents" need to be and feel secure.

XIV

A crucial tool in diplomacy *and* in warfare is to be able to think as the person one is dealing with thinks. It is always possible that an opponent is evil and or a threat. However, historians have concluded that too often calamities occur because of misjudgments about others' thinking. Therefore, security specialists must try to develop the capacity to think as a perceived opponent thinks. They must be slow to see others either as evil *or* as "just like us."

XV

Security specialists might consider the value of the "golden rule." If one does not want other countries meddling in one's elections by organizing demonstrations and funding candidates, one should not charge governmentally supported organizations to do so in other people's countries.

XVI

To think critically and to design a new security strategy citizens need to be familiar with documents like the US National Security Policy, the Department of Defense's (DOD's) Quadrennial Review, its Global Defense Posture Review, and the long-range strategy papers which support DOD budget requests.

XVII

The last US National Security Strategy document prepared by the Bush administration establishes a "no competitor" policy even though "competition" was the administration's mantra as applied to everything else.[3]

XVIII

That National Security Strategy also justifies "preemption." The most recent US preemption, Iraq, has been described as a "war of choice." "Fighting over there so we won't have to fight at home" is, in fact, a way of describing a war of aggression.

XIX

"Terrorism" has been used to justify preemption but terrorism is not special. It is experienced everywhere, including in democracies like England, India, Sri Lanka, the Philippines and Spain. In fact, if the number of casualties in Northern Ireland during "The Troubles" were extrapolated to the United States, there would have been 600,000 deaths in the US.

XX

"Terrorism" is not necessarily more heinous than the random killing of non-combatants as "collateral damage." Both involve the killing of non-participating civilians. In both cases the actor(s) know that will be the result.

XXI

Because terrorism is not unusual, breaking domestic or international law in reacting to it is not justified.

XXII

Instead of focusing on war's cost and its horror, attention should be given to whether or not the outcome of a conflict fulfills its stated purpose. World War I did destroy four empires (Russian, Ottoman, Austro-Hungarian, and Prussian), but instead of making the world "safe for democracy" one of the new democracies launched World War II less than twenty years later. The United States has invaded Haiti numerous times. Though it is small and nearby, the US has not succeeded in creating either democracy or prosperity there.

XXIII

The US should make Haiti a demonstration project for how to democratize a country. If it cannot accomplish that goal, it should reconsider more ambitious goals in larger, more distant countries with cultures quite different from our own.

XXIV

The stationing of any country's troops abroad should be prohibited unless they are part of a United Nations sanctioned force. This particularly applies to the US which even before 9/11 had more than 250,000 troops at sea and in more than 30 countries. This includes troops now stationed in some former Soviet Republics.

XXV

Arguments that x dollars spent on the military could provide x number of schools, x number of hospitals, or support for x number of scientists have little effect. Nor do estimates of the costs of war like the analysis of the Iraq War by Joseph Stiglitz and Linda Bilmes.[4] It is necessary to learn the content of the Department of Defense (DOD) budget and to then target specific offensive (in both senses of the word) military expenditures. Examples might include moneys now being spent for the development of new nuclear weapons, space weaponry, and a missile defense system. One might also want to consider the expense and efficacy of the 100,000 spies scattered through 16 agencies and budgeted at $44,000,000,000.[5]

XXVI

Taking a stand against nuclear proliferation requires consideration of the countries which already have such weapons. It may be that the world was spared the routine use of nuclear weapons after 1945 precisely because the USSR obtained those weapons. If India and Pakistan are less likely to go to war because each now has nuclear weapons, isn't a country like Iran, which has a valuable asset (oil), safer, more secure, if it has a nuclear weapon given that it is surrounded by China, Russia, Pakistan, India and Israel all of whom (and the US too) can reach Tehran with a nuclear weapon?

XXVII

Article VI of the 1968 Nuclear Non-proliferation Treaty calls for nuclear disarmament. Even, if the US were to destroy (not mothball, destroy) 9000 of its existing nuclear weapons, it would still have enough left to destroy civilization.[6] The goal of non-proliferation should be expanded to include the goal of eliminating all nuclear weapons just as the treaty says.

XXVIII

"Gender" is a confusing concept. Usually when we talk about gender we actually mean either sex or sex role (behavior expected because of one's biological sex). In practice, a policy of "gender mainstreaming" involves bringing females into an institution. It does not involve screening individuals for their gender, their deep-rooted sense of identity as feminine/woman or masculine/man.

XXIX

Scholars speculate that women's gender (their deep-rooted identity) could bring new direction to Security Studies, but it may be more important to examine men's gender because (mostly) men make and execute security policy. Is it men's gender that leads to their belief in (1) the importance of dominance; and (2) the efficacy of force? Or is it only a matter of males acting out a sex role, something which is more malleable than is "gender"?

XXX

The government is said to have a monopoly on the legitimate use of force. If men have a near monopoly on force, what can we learn from how women manage in a culture where they are, essentially, unilaterally disarmed?

XXXI

Official militaries may be largely male, but during war sex roles are suspended. They are not reinforced nor are they changed. Irregular forces also regularly suspend sex roles whether those forces be Buddhist, Christian or Islamic or without a religious base.

XXXII

Conflict is a social leveler. Immediately after a conflict, women, minorities and the lower classes may win rights like the vote and immigrants may win citizenship. Soon thereafter, however, efforts to reconstruct the social order begin. In particular, peace often brings "remasculinization" to the dismay of some women who believed change had occurred.

XXXIII

When women focus on issues like rape in war, a military tactic, their energy and thoughts are diverted from the larger issue, which is replacing strategies which select force as a legitimate means to achieving a goal. The goal should not be to make war more humane but to eliminate it.

XXXIV

Women in developed countries who are concerned about the use of force focus on weapons of mass destruction and on terrorism. This is because these are the only forms of violence they perceive as threatening them personally, the one because of the scale of destruction, the other because of the randomness of victims. This limited view is not responsible. Most victims in today's wars are killed by small arms, mines and improvised bombs.

XXXV

Enforcement of UN Security Council Resolution 1325 which requires women's presence at all peace negotiations would serve as a useful reminder that women are participants in every conflict and have a stake in every conflict's resolution.

XXXVI

The world can be interpreted in various ways; the point is to change it.

Notes

1 Michael Walzer, *Just and Unjust Wars* (New York: Basic Books, 1973), p. 184.
2 Albert Camus, "Neither a Victim Nor an Executioner Be," serial in *Combat*, Autumn 1946.
3 George W. Bush, "The National Security Strategy of the United States," *New York Times*, September 20, 2002.
4 Joseph Stiglitz and Linda Bilmes, "The Three Trillion Dollar War," *The Times*, February 23, 2008. Available at: www.timesonline.co.uk/tol/comment/columnists/guest_contributors/article3419840.ece, accessed April 7, 2009.
5 Mark Mazzetti, "Spymaster Tells Secret of Size of Spy Force," *New York Times*, 21 April 2006, p. A18.
6 The *Bulletin of the Atomic Scientists* reported that as of January 2009 the US had reduced its operationally deployed strategic warheads to 2200 as agreed to by the Strategic Offensive Reduction (Moscow) Treaty signed in 2002. However, it also reported the existence of 500 operational, nonstrategic warheads, 2500 warheads "in reserve" and 4200 warheads awaiting dismantlement. See www.thebulletin.org/files/o65002008.pdf, retrieved April 13, 2009.

2 War, sense, and security

Christine Sylvester

It is noteworthy that both mainstream International Relations (IR) and its critical Security Studies camp shy away from analyzing war and other forms of violence as sensory experiences. Conventionalists define, game, strategize, correlate, map causes, and trace historical trajectories of wars, weapons, alliance structures, civil–military relations and outcomes of violence. Critical Security Studies looks at political, economic, social, and environmental dimensions of human security as well as the technologies of securitization that bring more and more daily activities into national security frameworks. War as an experience of the body has not usually been on these agendas in IR

Recently, some feminists have been looking closely into the links between war, security, and what people see, feel, hear, smell and even taste when they are confronted with violence in International Relations. Anne Orford, for example, places the sense of touch high on her list of missing elements in humanitarian war analysis.[1] Judith Butler offers a powerful set of arguments about grief and mourning as potential backbones of an international politics with real anti-war clout.[2] Jean Bethke Elshtain earlier spoke of the good soldier being like the good mother in their mutual concerns about the body, its fluids, its discipline, its errors.[3] I have written about the ways that art looting during the second Iraq war touched people internationally, galvanizing a war for art within the war for Iraq that thrust art/museums into the international limelight.[4]

Sense is especially significant at a time when globalization enables international conflict to impact and involve so many. People can experience war physically through the pain of wounds and acts of wounding, through giving or receiving medical or emergency aid, through the sights of the rifle or the lens of the camera, through acts of revenge such as raping or being raped, through regarding dead comrades and family members and handling dead bodies, through capture and confinement, through the physical effort to escape a war zone, through sleeplessness, drugs, alcohol, and so on.

People who find themselves in war zones can also experience war through emotions. They might fear or excitedly wish to face an enemy, because of what they have heard or think about "him" and his society. They might be moved to action by religious beliefs, nationalist feelings, or ethnic loyalties.

They can also experience the painful loss of people, property, art and architectures around them and end up repulsed by what they see, paralyzed by grief or trauma, or saddened by popular opinion about a war. They might become disgusted with war while others take from the same experience a certain exhilaration. Meanwhile, a person who is not directly involved in war can be moved for or against a war—or war in general—by the justifications given for it, by how well or poorly it is going for one's group and oneself, by popular opinion, by one's political party affiliation, by reports in the media, by religion and identity politics, by representations of war in the arts and in novels, by what one learns about war in classrooms, by the effects of war on the economy or on one's family or future, by memories of war and war memorials.

Not everyone touches war in the same way but everyone can be touched by it in this time of globalization—as citizens, refugees, observers, participants, victims, recorders and researchers of war experiences.[5] Indeed, the many wars of the post-Cold War era in Europe, Africa, and the Middle East have put all of us in an insecure zone that overflows with bodily senses. The UN Human Development Report of 1994 made the sense and human security link explicit in its calls for freedom from fear and freedom from want, rather than, as has been common in statist logics, freedom from invasion.[6] But Anthony Burke argues that it is difficult to get security as "freedom from" right, because we have become addicted to suffering—"to a rational, functional suffering embedded in the very patterns of politics and order that regulate global life."[7] Our politics create and then pander to fear and dread, those twin-set emotions people are so accustomed to as part of the fabric of everyday life.

To Erin Manning, "sense does not pre-exist experience." Perhaps our experiences with violence have curdled our senses.[8] We help generously at times of tsunamis, earthquakes and hurricanes and then feel sour watching shocked parents close to our safe homes groping for words to express what it could possibly be like to learn that their 11-year-old son has been shot dead on his way home from soccer practice in Liverpool. A Long Beach, California high school student writes:

> If you look Asian or Latino, you're gonna get blasted on or at least jumped. The war has been declared, now it's a fight for power, money, and territory; we are killing each other over race, pride, and respect … They might think they're winning by jumping me now, but soon enough, they're all going down![9]

Freedom from fear, want, and dread goes missing in such prosaic contexts. We experience surveillance instead—oversecuring, annoyingly securitizing, or insecuring us with measures that supposedly keep us free from all manner of dangers—except the ones that affect us.

Statist security measures can get "silly" when they are not being deadly. Ministries in the UK and Homeland Security officials in the USA insist that the ever numerous body and mind intrusions we experience at airports, for example, are required to secure us. Why then do we dread them? Insecurely we shuffle along in the queue, suffering, hateful, or numbed by a bureaucratic politics that targets individuals where it once leveled its security logic on villainous states. The old security dilemma of the Cold War more or less confined insecurity in International Relations to states madly building arms and keeping us on board that mission by blowing nuclear dust in our eyes. Today, human security has been bribed into silence as it faces the dilemma of jostling, waiting, watching our bottle of water or lipstick seized, enduring repetitive questions about who packed the bags. Compared to people in war zones, air travelers get off easy. No one, however, gets to bow out of the security stakes.

We desperately need new ways of looking at the world and of overturning the fear in security. We might start where security hurts or annoys us as individuals. We might think, that is, about what security feels like and does not feel like. Ideas along these lines appear in inspiring new IR texts on security that carry a critical edge and are not afraid to go into sensory spaces. To ponder new ways to think about sense and security, consider four such texts: Anthony Burke's (2007) *Beyond Security, Ethics and Violence*, Lene Hansen's (2006) *Security as Practice*,[10] Laura Sjoberg and Caron Gentry's (2007) *Mothers, Monsters, Whores: Women's Violence in Global Politics*,[11] and Erin Manning's (2007) *Politics of Touch*. Not every section of each book is directly relevant to sense and security, but all zero in on sense forms that entail suffering for security when they could be leading us to experience security differently.

Getting beat up

Burke's book is poignantly framed by a sensory lesson he learned early in life. Aged 6 years old, he was at boarding school in Australia, itself a wretched thing to manage, and was set upon by a group of school bullies. They beat him up: "I flinch from their blows and wonder if I will die."[12] Apparently, this violence—"their sudden, inexplicable malice"[13]—was not unique in his surrounds. Imagine that the "world shrinks to blackness" and he looks up to see nothing but "contorted, horror-film faces."[14] Then, suddenly, it is over. He does not know what starts the violence and what ends it. He cries.

Now the adult is speaking:

> I learned much from those formative years: how it felt to be displaced, torn from what is familiar and comforting and placed in a strange and ambivalent environment, where one is watched and nurtured yet exposed to vulnerability and horror.[15]

Years later he sees people chased down by Indonesian troops, Palestinians arguing ferociously with Israeli police, Iraqis torn apart by suicide bombs, and asylum seekers held by his Australian government in the worst of conditions. He is touched, his old fears ignited, his antennae for danger on alert. Sense does not pre-exist experience and Burke is clearly aware of this. He was touched physically by violence then and is touched emotionally and intellectually now. He knows his childhood experiences, terrifying as they were, could never equate with the wickedly prosaic beatings in Baghdad and Kabul today. He simply tells of an innocent unprotected child beaten by a less innocent group of violence-empowered children in a schoolyard war called bullying. It is a particularly Anglo-Australian cowardice. Americans have their own:

> My heart was beating fast as the tears ran down my face because all of those painful memories that came back. I had constant flash-backs of all the guns put to my head, all of the bullets that barely missed me, and all the times I thought to myself, 'Just give up, they're gonna kill you anyway.' But I couldn't give up, I didn't give up, and I will never give up![16]

Taking a bit of distance from excruciating sense experiences, Burke suggests that "not only are global patterns of insecurity, violence and conflict getting ever more destructive and out of hand, but ... the dominant conceptual and policy frameworks we use to understand and respond to them are deeply inadequate and dangerous."[17] Security is set up in western political circles and in IR texts as the be all and end all of the state. It is the quality, value, or assurance that sews up the heart of a good community, maintains identity and rights, and keeps one free. But the logic is odd: watch for bullies and beat them up first or hunt out the suspects and retaliate fiercely everywhere. Such was the explicit *raison d'état* of George W. Bush's response to 9/11.

If we really felt the beating heart of security, most heads of state could be out of a job. The Promised Land would have been delivered. The power that comes from screaming SECURITY a thousand times would have lost its capacity to put us on edge by now. That power would be gone and so would the system of politics that has no real security end in mind. Burke:

> as a global community, we need no longer be beholden to such existential visions of exclusion, dominance and violence, where life exists at the whim and mercy of power. No more war against the Other; we can light our own paths out.[18]

Sovereign state narcissism, however, puts only itself in mind, which means, says Burke, that "our fears and desires may not be our own."[19] How to exorcise them?

And whose fears are they? Wary of anything that smacks of parental power to command our thoughts and force us into insecurity in the name of security—be it a school or one's own family situation—Burke recommends the sense-freeing enablement that Sylvia Plath puts into her poem, "Daddy." Anyone who knows the American poet Plath, who lived a distressed existence in England with her husband Ted Hughes, recalls her struggles over her father, who died when she was 9 years old. "Daddy" is a father exorcism that pulls no punches in expressing her sense of an evil controlling man, whose influence over her she finally "kills" with a poetic stake through his fat black heart. His telephone line to her head disconnects at that point and she joins the villagers dancing—stomping, as she puts it—on his grave.

Burke: "By beginning with Sylvia Plath's most (in)famous poem I want to present security as a malevolent, vampyric, indeed *parental* power, which ought to be as much a source of revulsion and struggle, as of comfort."[20] In other words, Burke thinks Plath's struggle against the father is our struggle against patriotism as an historic investment of identity in the (founding) father. Her words are harsh, the sentiments vengeful, and she is walking the line of cruelty; but it is tough freeing oneself of the parental ritual of instilling fear in the child in the name of securing his or her security. Perhaps Burke underwent a similar exorcism from a difficult childhood, determined that the beatings and displacements, the losses and the parental decisions that hurt, would not define him forever.

Plath does not leave things in a personal space relieved of bad vibes. Daddy is the master of ovens, Lucifer, Herr God, who harnesses all resources to a "remorseless suppression of difference" as a way of gaining über-freedom from want and fear.[21] Her leap in level of analysis, the epitome of poetic justice, moves "from the most private experience of subjectivity to the larger historical culture that contains and informs it."[22] It is a move, Burke claims, that parallels the logic of state security, promising to keep demons away so that the people can just be. "If there is any hope of being secure, this Satanic security must be escaped. Beware the blackmail of fear and pleasure."[23] To sidestep "Him," and focus instead on the possible connections between "subjectivity, responsibility and social transformation," one must get outside security.[24] Plath's "Daddy" achieves that, suggests Burke, because poetry's rules are not the rules of the state. One can get away with those words.

The beat-up Burke trails away in the slipstream of ethical abstractions and reconsidered *raisons d'état* and comes back only at the end to touch freedom. He says,

> Freedom, at its most naked and unborn, is a wish sent into a space of existence; a simplistic, childlike hunger growing in a space of complexity and life. It is this "space" that is most important. Who lives there? What do we all want, in our tension and complexity? How do we adjudicate, mediate, and meet our diverse and so often conflicting claims?[25]

He is worried about these and myriad questions of sense and security; but he is both less afraid now—less the Ron Mueck sculpture of an enormous boy crouched with his arms cradling his head, watchful for the inevitable big blow, than that same boy protecting himself from the inevitability of melancholia as he hears the voiceless say: "We're all dying."[26]

We see how the image has been put together: "modern man has combined ever more powerful and unpredictable forms of freedom with a discourse of historical inevitability that effaces all trace of its political authority, its unequal beneficiaries, and its terrible human and natural costs."[27] And so the poet removes her arms of self-protection, takes her hands from her ears, writes poems and dies of insecurity. For at the end of the day, we are struck by the knowledge that Plath's poetic exorcism of insecuring daddies did not make her happy. She ended up crouched with her head in an oven, her children nicely tucked up, secure, in their beds.

Sacrificing

Hansen is not one for poetics, but she does make sense of mermaids and worry about their security. In 2000, she wrote an intriguingly entitled piece, "The Little Mermaid's Silent Security Dilemma and the Absence of Gender in the Copenhagen School," which took the Copenhagen School of critical Security Studies on for neglecting the important problematic of gender.[28] Her sensory angle here highlighted the realms of sound and sight. It seemed to her that some of her colleagues' major writings were ignoring the sounds of insecurity that women choke back in difficult situations. They were also tending to subsume gender problematics within larger security concerns, where women could not be seen in order to be addressed properly. Hansen says, "Security as silence occurs when insecurity cannot be voiced, when raising something as a security problem is impossible or might even aggravate the threat being faced."[29] Subsuming security puts gender in some social location apart from salience. It is removed from security frameworks that locate issues of security and insecurity in issues of nationality, religion, or race. Groups falling under these categories can risk existential threats by states or communal actions designed to insecure through fear, and sometimes through enforced deprivation and want. As members of nations, religions, and races under threat, women are subsumed: they do not compose a group in and of themselves. So says the Copenhagen School.

Hansen maintains that in not recognizing women as a potentially threatened group, the "potential subject of security has no, or a limited, possibility of speaking its security problem."[30] Hansen's case in point is rape during wartime. Depending on the nation or other group identity women hold, the security strategies available to them at such scary moments of physical assault can be "silence, denial, or if the incident has become known, flight."[31] Women can find it nearly impossible to speak of the rape, because to do so would put them in harm's way, perhaps in the way of *zina* in Pakistan, the law against sexual intercourse outside bona fide marriage. When religious or national law is pitched against women, and their families are in a fury about humiliations suffered as a result of bodily transgressions on their woman, the victims go silent. It is the only way they can create some security.

Subsuming security dovetails with the silencing example. Without recognizing that raped women are silenced as members of a distinctive gender collectivity, there is little that critical Security Studies can do to ease women out of their security dilemma. They become like H.C. Anderson's little mermaid in Copenhagen harbor. She silently hopes that love will liberate her from her watery prison and give her the human perambulation required to be with her beloved prince. She takes the decision to leave the water world and become human, to have a soul, only to discover that her man cannot recognize her now as a proper subject, as the mermaid he loved. Trapped in an existential netherworld, she cannot be at home with him or return to familiar waters. She sits stuck to stone in Copenhagen harbor, at once sad and quietly commanding of the waters around her. Glass-topped tourist boats sail in to memorialize her pain, their passengers photographing her exquisite distress. Few hear her call, her wails.

In *Security as Practice*, Hansen leaves the mermaid to her own musings in that harbor and segues to the Balkan wars of the 1990s.[32] There, she shows us two basic and several correlative discourses that were used by the western countries to make sense of those troubles. One was a so-called Balkan discourse that put the war down to ethnicity and ancient animosities. The other was a genocide discourse emphasizing that Bosnian Muslims were being targeted for extermination by Serbs. Because the Balkan discourse cast the region into the historical story of a crazy or "sick man" in Europe, the West was not insecured by its logic. The genocide discourse was something else. Not only did it recall more recent historical genocides, it brought to the fore the (vaguely worded) 1948 Convention on the Prevention and Punishment of the Crime of Genocide, which commanded that something be done to prevent this crime. Having shamefully stood by while genocide was committed earlier in Rwanda, the EU and the UN tried an initial response of peacekeeping combined with efforts to broker a political solution in the region. The US, however, connected up the Balkan and genocide discourses, deciding, claims Hansen, that civilians were innocent in a conflict between leaders of warring parties. "Innocent civilians" could not be differentiated by ethnicity, religion, or, apparently, gender; they simply needed security from fear and want. Under the Clinton administration, the genocide discourse brought to the fore norms of fairness and responsibility, as well as a worry about slow diplomatic measures that could prolong suffering and end in appeasement. Operation Deliberate Force against Serbian positions was the result, itself a half-way measure.

Choices. We are beset with choices. None of them are very heartening, it seems. Either we swim in the sea with a fish tail or have love and soul with a human. Either we have silence post-rape or retribution by one's own relatives. Either we see ourselves as part of a larger group under threat or risk not being seen at all (or seen as a lone malcontent). Either we sacrifice or we are sacrificed. Thus is any physical and emotional sense of security—freedom from fear and from want—a chimera. I made that argument about security a bit differently in 1994 and hold to it still, more tightly, in fact, as insecuring events of our time have unfolded.[33] The Balkans: which experiences predate which senses? Are we secure there? Ask Burke.

Doing what?

Here is an insecuring moment: sitting across the table from Biljana Plavsic, circa 1993. Were women innocent victims in the genocidal discourse about the Balkans wars and the Balkan discourse of ethnic animosities?

The two discourses together "explained" why the Serbs went after Muslim Bosnians in their own province and did so through massacres, a host of war crimes, and quite possibly genocide under a policy of ethnic cleansing. The International Criminal Tribunal for the Former Yugoslavia has since brought around eighty cases to book. One of those indicted for war crimes is Biljana Plavsic, former acting president of the Republic of Serbia (which was established against the decision of Bosnians to declare independence from Yugoslavia) and Dean of Natural Sciences and Mathematics at the University of Sarajevo. She pleaded guilty to crimes against humanity.

Plavsic was an academic who took biopolitics to fascist levels of perversion. She argued that Bosnian Muslims were genetically deformed Serbs. She opposed mixed ethnic marriages on the basis that an exchange of genes would cause the degeneration of Serb nationhood. She hung out lovingly with some of the most notorious male war criminals in the Serbian population (like the nasty "Arkan"), allegedly coaching them on the fine points of being real men for the Republic. Often, the duty she urged on them was genocidal rape of Croat and Bosnian Muslim women. And, supposedly, she reveled in her bad-girl reputation, enjoying comparisons with Margaret Thatcher's toughness: she was the iron lady of Serbia. Some found her behavior symptomatic of mental health problems (ironically, the Miloševićs were supporters of this view), and to others she was a madam teaching her troops the dirty tricks of war, an errant whore of war. In any of these guises, Biljana Plavsic's touch could be terrible. She bargained her way out of the genocide charge leveled at her and into "only" eleven years of prison. Many believe she got off lightly—like someone who routinely kicks 6-year-olds to the ground and then walks away—as a consequence of her willingness to cooperate, her gender, her advancing age, whatever.

She is not the only cheerleading woman for the types of violence we associate with aberrant militarism and sadistic politics. Pauline Nyiramasuhuko, Gertrude Mukangango, Sister Maria Kisito, Rose Karushara, Odette Nyirabagenzi, Anhanasie Mukabatana, and Julienne Kizito number among those charged for genocidal acts of 1994 in Rwanda. Indeed, we know that more than 3,000 Rwandan women are being tried in Rwanda alone for their contributions to that killing spree against Tutsis and moderate Hutus. Pauline Nyiramasuhuko's involvement has been widely publicized, partly, it seems, because she is the first woman to be charged internationally with genocide and with using rape as a crime against humanity. In addition, people are intrigued that she could metamorphose from being a social worker, and then Minister for the Family and the Advancement of Women, to mass killer. Not only did she assist in planning the genocide, she helped carry it out in Butare, where she arrived and announced that food was available from the Red Cross at a nearby sports stadium, when what was available there was death at the hands of Hutus under her direction. She told supporters to rape women before killing them but to keep some of them alive for multiple rape sessions. She allegedly said: get all Tutsis, no matter their age. Plavsic denied most of these charges on the grounds that women and mothers are incapable of such acts, and that she herself had been a victim of sexism. Her trial continues.

Laura Sjoberg and Caron Gentry present Plavsic and Nyiramasuhuko as two among the many violent women they studied for their book, *Mothers, Monsters, Whores: Women's Violence in Global Politics.*[34] At issue for the authors is the usual transcultural equation of women with nonviolence. Sjoberg and Gentry show that women can and do engage in violent activities of International Relations, oftentimes with considerable élan, imagination, and ultimate agency. Their violence does not make these women heroines for the co-authors. What it does is to put violent women on the record instead of putting them in the category of impossible, silent, subsumed, deviant or mad people. It is a revealing move against the strength of common assumptions.

To get violent women recognized and then seen as people who make choices and have influence in their respective spheres of the international is no small matter. The bulk of feminist literature, popular understandings of "women" in the West, and academic studies of war depict women as victims, spies, or soldiers with support roles off the front lines. It can seem that they hold to these depictions because

> *Women* are not supposed to be violent ... A conservative interpretation of gender sees women as peaceful and apolitical, a liberal view understands women as a pacifying influence on politics, and feminists who study global politics often critique the masculine violence of interstate relations.[35]

And yet, for all the silencing, subsuming, and assuming, women clearly do engage in political violence. They did so in the Balkans, in Rwanda, in the national liberation struggles of the 1990s, in Chechnya recently, and in "terrorist" organizations in Kasmir, Sri Lanka, and throughout the Middle East. Women can engage in genocidal activities and they can be front and center in related acts, like prisoner humiliation at Abu Ghraib.

The authors argue that gender discourses are so evident in other areas of life today—in discussions of development, labor practices, marriage, human rights and educational achievement, to name a few—that it is time for the light of recognition to illuminate their instances of violence, as well. The problem is that it can be difficult to distinguish the myths, the accusations, and the easy condemnations from the truth about women and violence. The women indicted for genocide, for example, have been paraded in the press in gender particularistic ways. Their attire has been commented on. Their personalities and careers have been excavated for clues to their later behavior. In Nyiramasuhuko's case, her relationship with her own son has been scrutinized. These women have been analyzed in more depth than most of the male perpetrators of genocide.

When mothers go wrong, something in society is fearfully in disarray. Is that the belief that has so many people thinking that violence does not become a "her?" Or is it the related assumption that women are not supposed to feel the kinds of emotions that urge or force men into the violence we see in our communities and the larger world? Women's emotions are meant to be different, and that difference is this: no one is supposed to feel insecure around or insecured by the presence of women. And if we do feel insecurity around women, we are disinclined to see this as a case of security as chimera. It is, rather, security willfully and perversely or monstrously destroyed. Around such pillars of society knocked to the ground, there is fear and there is want.

Move your body

"Might we conceive of touch as the original sin?" asks Erin Manning.[36] Might touch be the thing that leads us into temptations, sacrifices, and displacements? From apple to flesh to gun to mass militaries to mass rape to mass flight? Or is touch the ultimate gift, the laying on of hands, healing? Is it the thing that can make the difference between a healthy and well-adjusted baby and one that grows into depression, drug dependency, anxiety disorders, obesity and the like? At this point in the chapter, we are probably feeling too jaded to say. We might want to console ourselves with the soft touch option or just nod cynically about touch and sin. We have seen beatings of youngsters, silencings and subsumings of women into others' security framework, and real live killer women egging on a politics of extermination. Touch is not feeling very good.

But what if we think of the senses as relational rather than as properties that people possess and show or hide? Manning says the senses are about the many ways bodies move and interact, with touch being "the act of reaching toward, of creating space-time through the worlding that occurs when bodies move."[37] This is not your everyday sense of touch. "I reach out to touch you in order to invent a relation that will, in turn, invent me."[38] We move the relation through touch. It is not straightforward, touching and inventing and relating; it combines several edgy elements. To Manning, the proverbial touching and eating of an apple can be thought of as the "violent entry into the political."[39] At that biblical moment, two people chose an imperfect and chaotic life on earth over a perfect heavenly paradise. Their decision can be thought of as political because it "engages us toward the world and therefore toward each other."[40] And that decision was also our fall, our condemnation to death, the slipping away of what we could know perfectly for the ominous hint of what would come next. The dual legacy of that originary touch is the bold reaching toward freedom and the equally audacious slap of sin. "The apple is about experience, even if this experience is that of the 'baseness' of humanity."[41] Sense does not pre-exist experience, and politics and authority are part of the mythical experience influencing our senses.

Burke thinks our experience is one of suffering through the wrong-mindedness of repetitive statist approaches to violence and security. Manning sees the wrong-mindedness in the idea that violence is the usual political means "through which the self is constituted and maintained."[42] What she would like us to see is that the violence occurs "in the decision to reach toward. The violence exists in the reaching out toward that which will remain unknowable," rather than, in the lexicon of the state, simply reaching something unknown and therefore conquerable.[43] The unknowable is the realm of God, not us. Following the Genesis story further, Manning reminds us that "the only one who is allowed to challenge the unknowable is the savior himself, the one who has been sent to heal us from the unknowable, the one who solves the mysteries of [fallen] humanity through his miracles."[44]

Yet if Michelangelo had connected the finger of God with the finger of Adam on his great Sistine Chapel fresco, perhaps unknowability would have been breached—by God, who would get a sense of what being human really feels like. That moving of the relation is not achieved. Hierarchy and unknowability thereby persist, as does a nonconnection that enables the continuing violence of original sin. At the same time, the reaching without connection maintains the human self and keeps it from being subsumed into God's sameness. That is to say, the violence of the original sin of touch is what keeps us embodied rather than operating as spirits who cannot be killed. Our bodies remain alive to touch, to spatializing, and to reciprocity with other bodies. Bodies can know the war touch as a reach that violently transforms the spaces between one another. We can also reach to evade the Manichean wars that state sovereignty—secular God—demands that we experience. It can go both ways.

Here is a good thought: "To live sensually is to discover the infinite in all things and to be persuaded by our beliefs. Nothing can be proven: there is no truth."[45] Living without proof and truth liberates some bodies from the touch of the state and of war, and unnerves other bodies, for whom stability of expectation is the preferred experience. The only solution is to reach, to put body in motion, to move the body as a condition of possibility that can take us, stretchingly, beyond what it is said we already know, embody, and experience as security. We can angle purposively into insecure spaces rather than allow security requirements and sacred texts to make us bodies to the Word. Something was lost when we went for the apple instead of the infinity of a fixed environment. Something was equally gained in that move. Whether we are making full use of the move or acquiescing to a variety of sovereign securitizations that promise freedom from fear and want—ah, perfection—is the question. Manning is hopeful: "A free body is not a secured body."[46]

Simultaneities of sense

The war sense/the security sense. According to these authors, there is much that we must wrestle. Parental figures promise the opposite of what they want to deliver and bullies lurk about waiting to kick the ribs of someone who dares walk free from fear. There are tricks of security in parts of critical Security Studies that sustain a certain violence towards women in not-hearing and not-giving proper space for their security needs. Sacrificed, they are, to communitarian security scripts. There are also violent communitarian women out there to wrestle, women who want to insecure and to war against their alter egos in society. And then there are those who move their bodies toward one another in the interest of touching, not knowing, perhaps, that touch is the freedom and the fall, the war that must be endured after peace is gone, the reaching out that bends the body to open spaces, to others, and away from the patronizing certitude of paradise.

We also wrestle with some ambivalence and some more questions: Why didn't exorcist poetry save Plath from her inner war? Why did it (did it?) save Burke? Is it liberating and securing for women to be violent or violent of them to presume themselves liberated and powerful through war? Does the context of the violence matter, as in not being ok if masterminded through the state and perhaps a bit more ok at the hands of women in militant liberation struggles? Can we really transform spaces by moving through them touchingly? Can we write ourselves poetically out of our security dilemmas and war touches?

Hard to say. War in all its forms is quite determined and so is our present climate of security. The determined ones regularly tell lies about what it is they are trying to achieve. Burke is right: vampires charm themselves into our spaces of subjectivity and history, and yet to touch them is to be undone by them. Sjoberg and Gentry are also right that women do violence and therefore the security problematic must be enlarged to encompass them. Hansen is right that we are beset with choices and often end up with sacrifices instead, because not everyone is interested in our stories or appreciate our emotional and physical struggles. And Manning is right when she says that the "politics of touch is about potential energy," albeit energy also runs in several directions, to and away from violence and war's enthusiasms.[47]

What we have here is a wave of fluid senses coming at us. It is gaining strength as more analysts get under its curl and look out from its crest to see all the screaming, laughing, crying, listening, snuggling, shooting and confessing. For my part, the thing is to keep thinking and writing about sense, whether the forms and outcomes are poetic or not. Some escape from wrong-footed security can be harbored in a well-sensed sentence and mise-en-scène. Here's one:

As she hung up the phone, she turned around to see me standing there confused and scared. I didn't know what was wrong. She quickly held me as tight as she could, hugged me, and said that she was sorry. She began to cry again, this time more so than when I walked in. Her tears hit my shirt like bullets.[48]

But they were not bullets, and that is the point.

Notes

1 Anne Orford, *Reading Humanitarian Intervention: Human Rights and the Use of Force in International Law* (Cambridge: Cambridge University Press, 2003).
2 Judith Butler, *Precarious Life: The Powers of Mourning and Violence* (London: Verso, 2004).
3 Jean Bethke Elshtain, *Women and War* (New York: Basic Books, 1987).
4 See Christine Sylvester, "The Art of War/The War Question in (Feminist) IR," *Millennium: Journal of International Studies*, 33, no. 3 (2008): 855–78 and *Art/Museums: International Relations Where We Least Expect It* (Boulder, CO: Paradigm Publishers, 2009).
5 This came across clearly in the special Touching War program of speakers, films, and workshops that I directed at Lancaster University during the 2009–10 academic year (with IAS, Film Society, and Politics/IR departmental support). See the Touching War website: www.lancs.ac.uk/fass/events/touchingwar/.
6 United Nations Development Programme, Human Development Report, UNDP/HDR/1994. Curiously, however, that document translates feelings of "freedom from" into mostly materialist outcomes, in a conflation of "development" with "security."
7 Anthony Burke, *Beyond Security: Ethics and Violence: War Against the Other* (London: Routledge, 2007), p. 1.
8 Erin Manning, *Politics of Touch: Sense, Movement, Sovereignty* (Minneapolis: University of Minnesota Press, 2007), p. 131.
9 Freedom Writers, *The Freedom Writers Diary, with Erin Gruwell* (New York: Broadway Books, 1999).
10 Lene Hansen, *Security as Practice: Discourse Analysis and the Bosnian War* (London: Routledge, 2006).
11 Laura Sjoberg and Caron Gentry, *Mothers, Monsters, Whores: Women's Violence in Global Politics* (London: Zed Books, 2007).
12 Burke, *Beyond Security*, p. 1.
13 Ibid.
14 Ibid.
15 Ibid., p. 2.
16 Freedom Writers, *The Freedom Writers Diary*, p. 178.
17 Burke, *Beyond Security*, p. 2.
18 Ibid., p. 13.
19 Ibid., p. 6.
20 Ibid., p. 55, emphasis in original.
21 Ibid., p. 64.
22 Ibid., p. 57.
23 Ibid., p. 61.
24 Ibid.
25 Ibid., p. 235.
26 Ibid., p. 237.

27 Ibid.
28 Lene Hansen, "The Little Mermaid's Silent Security Dilemma and the Absence of Gender in the Copenhagen School," *Millennium: Journal of International Studies*, 29, 2 (2000): 285–306.
29 Ibid., p. 287.
30 Ibid., p. 294.
31 Ibid., p. 295.
32 Hansen, *Security as Practice.*
33 Christine Sylvester, *Feminist Theory and International Relations in a Postmodern Era* (Cambridge: Cambridge University Press, 1994).
34 Sjoberg and Gentry, *Mothers, Monsters, Whores.*
35 Ibid., p. 2, emphasis in original.
36 Manning, *Politics of Touch*, p. 49.
37 Ibid., p. xiv.
38 Ibid., p. xv.
39 Ibid., p. 49.
40 Ibid.
41 Ibid., p. 50.
42 Ibid., p. 52.
43 Ibid., p. 53.
44 Ibid.
45 Ibid., p. 82.
46 Ibid., p. 159.
47 Ibid., p. 102.
48 Freedom Writers, *The Freedom Writers Diary*, p. 52.

3 Gendering the state

Performativity and protection in international security

Jonathan D. Wadley

For analytical purposes, scholars of International Relations (IR) tend to treat the state as if it were a person. It is assumed to have "interests" and "intentions," said to "act" (and often, to "act rationally"), even allowed to experience "death." In the most extreme cases of anthropomorphization, the state is explicitly given "a body" and "a life." For most scholars, it seems perfectly natural—common sense, even—to speak of the state in this way. Indeed, so commonplace is the attribution of personhood that it is hard to think of the state *without* appropriating the language used to describe the beliefs, emotions, motivations, and actions of individual human beings. Such naturalness is reflected in the fact that metaphors of personhood are not restricted to one or two subfields, but characterize the discipline as a whole, so much so that "in a field in which almost everything is contested, this seems to be one thing on which almost all of us agree."[1] And yet, despite the stubbornness of these metaphors and the consistency with which they are used, rarely are they reflected upon. Surprisingly few studies have considered explicitly the ontological status of the state and the degree to which it may be said to exist as if it were a person. Even fewer scholars have looked at this foundational assumption through a gender lens.[2] When one does, one thing becomes abundantly clear: The state, though understood as a person, remains a strangely ungendered being.

For anyone who wishes to bring a more thorough consideration of gender into the study of International Relations, this should set off alarm bells. Feminists have shown that it is problematic to study actors as if they are genderless things. Ignoring gender too often means elevating the masculine subject to universal status, leading to the production of theories that not only are partial, but that mask their partiality through claims to universality. In IR, ignoring gender means not recognizing the ways in which key actors are defined and differentiated by their relationship to norms of masculinity and femininity. Leaders, states, international organizations—all of these act in accordance with gender norms, albeit in different ways at different times. Additionally, by ignoring gender, the analyst remains blind to processes through which these gendered identities are produced—processes that are in many ways central to the operation of world politics. The arenas in which the actors engage each other are saturated with gendered meaning and it is this fact that enables, for example, a state to "act like a man" or "act like a woman." Thus, gender, which was defined earlier in this volume as "a system of symbolic meaning that creates social hierarchies based on perceived associations with masculine and feminine characteristics,"[3] is not simply an attribute possessed by certain actors, but a system through which those actors are constituted and positioned relative to each other. One great contribution of feminist IR has been to draw the attention of other IR scholars to these arguments, despite the reluctance of "conventional" theorists to incorporate gender into the processes they are attempting to explain. Given the work that has been done to demonstrate the dangers of theorizing without gender, it is highly questionable for the bulk of IR scholars to write about the state as if it is not gendered, especially when it is understood, conceptually, to exist and act *as if it were a person*. Failing to consider the role of gender does not make one's theory gender-neutral, and conceptualizing the state as a generic, non-gendered actor does not make it so.

Nowhere is the silence toward gender more deafening than in the field of International Security. The study of war, anarchy, alliances—all observably gendered processes—stands to benefit the most from the recognition that the key actors do not act without, or outside of, gender. Yet, the field has been slow to incorporate the study of gender, even though almost twenty years have passed since Ann Tickner criticized its dominant paradigm for projecting the "values associated with hegemonic masculinity" onto the international behavior of states. Within realism, she argued, the state has been conceptualized through an historical worldview that privileges the experiences of men. Other approaches can be, and have been, criticized on the same grounds, offering similarly partial theories owing to their common reliance upon "the Western political and philosophical tradition," which has produced "a foundation of political concepts" that assumes the political actor is a man. The proliferation of constructivist and post-structuralist scholarship over the past twenty years has, despite much promise, brought little help, largely side-stepping questions of gender. Nonetheless, the epistemological pluralism of Security Studies today means that the field is much more amenable to approaches that incorporate gender, and that incorporate it in new ways, than it was at the time when feminists within IR first raised these concerns. The argument that states are produced within, and not outside of, their environment is no longer esoteric. Security and insecurity are understood by many to be interpretations made within an intersubjective realm of interaction among states, rather than the absence or presence of objective threats.[4] And the role of representation, speech acts, and discursive structures in outlining the parameters of security practices and giving them meaning is better appreciated, as well.[5] As a result of these developments, the field of feminist Security Studies is well positioned to theorize the role of gender in innovative ways. Specifically, there is more room now to apply post-positivist insights into how gender works onto the field of Security Studies.

The analysis presented here challenges the discipline's tendency to treat states as genderless persons by exploring the role of gender in the security performances of states. In so doing, it draws upon the concept of performativity—the idea that, in the words of Judith Butler, "identity is performatively constituted by the very 'expressions' that are said to be its results."[6] It argues that performances within the field of security, much like performances within the daily lives of people, carry no intrinsic meaning, but must be made sense of through "a system of symbolic meaning" that cannot be but gendered. Through such performances, identities become salient, and masculine and feminine subjects are created. While this process is less palpable for states than it is for humans, it is nonetheless observable in broad patterns. States can be observed reifying themselves through performances of security, particularly through those which establish them as stable and masculine protectors. Recent work on the politics of protection, particularly that done by Didier Bigo, suggests the constitutive effects that protection has upon both providers and recipients. It stops short, however, of recognizing that these effects may be enabled by the gendered meaning that different forms of protection carry. When such meanings are considered, it becomes evident that by "being" masculine protectors, states can position themselves favorably in relation to other international actors and gain legitimacy from their domestic audiences.

This means that states are gendered, and are gendered in much the same way as people are: through repeated performances. When state identity is viewed in this light, the anthropomorphic assumption, as it is commonly used, appears woefully inadequate. To be clear, it is not being suggested that drawing parallels between human subjects and state subjects is bad in-and-of-itself. Indeed, useful parallels can be drawn, despite (or, perhaps, *because of*) the notion that "both states and persons are fuzzy sets."[7] The trouble lies in assuming that states, or people, are constituted outside processes of interaction, and that either can be made sense of without considering the relational identities they take on through the systems of symbolic meaning through which they operate. Anthropomorphic assumptions tend to treat the state as a genderless, unitary actor—often, one that is ontologically primitive to its interactions—while neglecting the ways that the "actor-ness" and "unity" of the state are an effect of iterated, gendered performances, particularly in the realm of security. By viewing security performances with an eye toward their constitutive effects, and by moving gender to the center of that analysis, one gains not only a richer understanding of how states reproduce themselves (i.e. where their person-like "identities" come from), but a clearer picture of the hierarchical relations that exist among states and between states and domestic populations.

This chapter begins with a consideration of how the state has been conceived of as a person throughout the discipline, arguing that such practices almost always import an inadequate understanding of how people are constituted. In both cases—conceptualizing states and conceptualizing humans—this is a result, largely, of substance-oriented, as opposed to process-oriented, approaches. It argues that by making processes, rather than substances, the core of research, scholars will be able to more fully explain how states reproduce themselves as actors in world politics, how they garner power for themselves (in relation to other international actors, particularly states), and how they gain legitimacy from their subjects. Following that, the chapter argues that a theory of performativity can fill this need, especially in the realm of Security Studies. Moreover, such a theory would facilitate the study of gender within these processes and shed light on the incentives states have to behave as masculine actors. The final section of the chapter offers, tentatively, a way forward for scholars within feminist Security Studies who wish to bring empirical research to bear on the theoretical sketches presented here. It submits that "the rational protector model" may be examined as a type of dominant masculinity for states, one which allows them to "do" security in ways that cast them as unitary, masculine actors.

The state as a (genderless) person

Most IR scholars have not understood states to be gendered—presumably because they have not focused on how states are made and how gender works. The state is typically believed to possess its core identity prior to interaction with others. Gender is, therefore, given no room within the theory to have a constitutive relationship with that identity. As a result, the state "body" and "life" are written about without reference to gender, or to any other systems of meaning that can code a state's performances. This happens largely because most scholars adhere, in Patrick Jackson's and Daniel Nexon's typology, to some form of substantialism. "Substantialism," they explain, "maintains that the ontological primitives of analysis are 'things' or entities—entities exist before interaction and all relations should be conceived as relations between entities."[8] Substantialism ranges from the belief that states possess internally generated interests or ideas and are, as a result, self-motivated (which Jackson and Nexon label "self-action substantialism") to the more common view that interaction changes the variable attributes of states, but not the states themselves (termed "inter-action substantialism").

The anthropomorphic assumption in IR goes hand in hand with the substantialist assumption. The antecedent of the anthropomorphic assumption may be traced back to antiquity, where one finds an association of the citizen-warrior with the public realm of the Greek city-state. This association continues today, so that "in times of war, the state itself becomes a citizen-warrior: military commanders refer to the enemy as a singular 'he.'"[9] More directly, the anthropomorphic assumption is a product of Medieval Christian theology and its lasting effects upon the political imaginary of dynastic subjects. But this leaves unanswered an important question: Why has this anthropomorphic form maintained its currency in our modern day, when, unlike in the dynastic era, no measure of the state's existence may be traced to the body of a single man? No doubt, the frequent recourse of IR theory to state of nature theorizing has played a role. Theorists of all stripes have extended descriptions of the conditions of society at the time of state formation to the international realm. Often treating the narratives of Hobbes and Rousseau as analogies, they have cast states into the role of men acting absent an overarching sovereign power.

According to Iver Neumann, it is not the humanness of the metaphors that are so appealing, but their organicism. Viewing the state as an organism, human or not, presents a conveniently dualistic ontology. A clear "inside" and "outside" are given, and the relevant "stuff" of International Relations may be said to belong either to the organism or to the realm external to it. The state becomes a container, of a sort, and as a result the world becomes much more categorizable. Also, such metaphors give the state a *telos* (survival and adaptation) and the state system a mode (evolution), which corresponds well with prominent social thought in other disciplines (e.g. with Durkheimian frameworks).[10] Neumann does not explain why states are so consistently thought of as *humans*, nor does he try to, but his observations raise an important point: There is no necessary connection between substantialist ontologies and the *person*hood of the state. One could theorize the state as a unitary actor possessing a pre-social identity without imagining it to be analogous to a person. Other metaphors, organic or not, could be used. Additionally, there is no necessary connection between anthropomorphization and substantialism because one could anthropomorphize the state without recourse to substantialist beliefs. This would be accomplished by adopting a performative or purely structural theory of human identity, in which the latter is an *effect*, and then transferring that theory onto the state. Recasting identity as, before all else, an effect, breaks the connection between substantialism and anthropomorphization, enabling one to view the state as a person, while viewing neither as a preformed entity.

Still, these beliefs appear to be mutually reinforcing. Viewing the state as a person transfers the habit of seeing people as unitary, already-formed actors onto one's understanding of states. And conversely, theorizing the state as an entity facilitates (even if it does not *necessitate*) the analogy of personhood by making it possible for a state to have a "body" and a "life." The conflation of substantialism and anthropomorphization is clearest in Alexander Wendt's *Social Theory of International Politics*. Wendt, more than anyone else in the discipline, has brought the ontological status of the state to center stage and has done much to draw attention to relational components of state identity. His theory, however, strongly reinforces the connection between substantialism and anthropomorphization, going so far as to build an argument for the former upon the "reality" of the latter. "States are people too," he claims, and the ramification of this claim is that they may be treated as ontologically primitive entities (as humans most often are).[11] Every state has, by definition, a "body" and a "life," and in much more than the metaphorical sense. Although Wendt places the terms "body" and "life" in quotations, he takes state personhood to be real. As he explains, "I argue that states are real actors to which we can legitimately attribute anthropomorphic qualities like desires, beliefs, and intentionality."[12]

Wendt's goal in positing the existence of a state "body" (anthropomorphization) is to advance the argument that states are ontologically prior to the state system (substantialism), which, in turn, allows him to perform the systemic-level analysis that is common to the discipline. To posit the state "body" as an "exogenously given, relatively stable platform,"[13] he attributes to it five properties, or parts of the "body:" "(1) an institutional-legal order, (2) an organization claiming a monopoly on the legitimate use of organized violence, (3) an organization with sovereignty, (4) a society, and (5) territory."[14] Together, these parts compose the state's *personal*, or *corporate*, identity. This is not the only identity that states have, but is the precursor to other, more social identities. Once these social identities are stripped away, it is what remains. Wendt elaborates:

> Two things are left if we strip away those properties of the self which presuppose interaction with others. The first is the material substrate of agency, including its intrinsic capabilities. For human beings, this is the body; for states, it is an organizational apparatus of governance. In effect, I am suggesting for rhetorical purposes that the raw material out of which members of the state system are constituted is created by domestic society before states enter the constitutive process of international society, although this process implies neither stable territoriality nor sovereignty, which are internationally negotiated terms of individuality. The second is a desire to preserve this material substrate, to survive.[15]

The "desire to preserve this material substrate" is the "life" of the state—the "intrinsic motivational dispositions" that are more commonly captured by the term "the national interest."[16]

The problem is not so much that Wendt is attempting to operationalize the analogy, but that he is attempting to do so in regards to the actors rather than the process. Contrast this with David Campbell's formulation, in which the same analogy is made, but arrived at from the similarity of the processes in which states engage:

> Whether we are talking of "the body" or "the state," or particular bodies and states, the identity of each is performatively constituted. Moreover, the constitution of identity is achieved through the inscription of boundaries which serve to demarcate an "inside" from an "outside," a "self" from an "other," a "domestic" from a "foreign."[17]

Ultimately, the inscriptions and demarcations are the result of ongoing political processes, ones that states have great interest in successfully reproducing. For those who study statecraft—"the practices and activities that engender the effect called the sovereign state"[18]—this is a familiar point. It is through statecraft that the state's body, taken to be pre-social in substantialist accounts, is carved out and reified. If the state is posited as a person (metaphorical or not) who exists in some meaningful sense prior to social interaction, then much of this is missed. One may still recognize the state to be a partially-socialized entity, as Wendt does, but many of those processes which construct the state as a subject will be left out of the analysis.

The state as a (gendered) process

Drawing on the scholarship within feminist Security Studies, one sees quickly how the story could be different. Viewing Wendt's theory through a gender lens reveals each of its components to be gendered in some way, and to become so through security performances undertaken by the state. Society, for instance, is often reconstituted in gendered terms through war, which has long been viewed as a means of masculinizing a people. Through war, power is valorized and identified with a heroic kind of masculinity.[19] Kristin Hoganson's work shows that Theodore Roosevelt saw the Spanish-American War as a way to re-masculinize America's young men, who were otherwise at risk of succumbing to the "sedentary life."[20] Jean Bethke Elshtain demonstrates that the will-to-sacrifice is constitutive of an individual's selfhood, and that this will is most fully recognized in war.[21] War—a means through which states and individuals are crafted together—can impart upon its performers a masculinity that cannot be accomplished through other means. This is what Ralph Pettman means when he claims, "Statemaking and warmaking are cognate activities and warmaking has long been a way of defining and demonstrating a range of stereotypically masculinist traits."[22] Finally, David Campbell, whose work contains little discussion on gender, observes nevertheless that societies have a history of being viewed in feminine terms in relation to the masculine leaders who control them: "The body of the body politic is taken to have a 'female' identity to which the head (the 'male' ruler) is married."[23]

War has the ability to masculinize leaders, as well. It helped George H.W. Bush overcome the "wimp factor." The Iranian hostage crisis even turned Jimmy Carter into a man (at least temporarily). Likewise, George W. Bush appears to have been rescued from a less-heroic corporate masculinity (suited to the managerial duties of, say, a global CEO) by the events of September 11th.[24] This phenomenon is relatively easy to understand: War is, to a significant degree, performed by the leaders who participate in it. War provides for a leader the opportunity to perform in ways that are in accordance with recurring masculine ideas. He may do so through a number of means, such as associating himself with the men who are fighting the war or simply by demonstrating traits characterized as masculine (such as decisiveness, an embrace of violence, or a willingness to protect his "vulnerable" subjects). Bruce Curtis describes these masculine traits being performed "through action, often violent, to protect women, children, and country, and by the use of willpower, strength, and firepower."[25]

Though it is beyond the bounds of this study to submit each possible component of the state's corporate identity to a gendered analysis, there is enough work within feminism, and within feminist Security Studies, to indicate that this could be done. Territory may be gendered, as is evident when one considers the shared symbolism of intervention and rape. As Cynthia Weber explains, intervention, like any violation of a state's territory, redraws the boundaries of sovereignty, which then "produces, represents or writes the state."[26] The institutional–legal order that Wendt considers to be a component of the state "body" may be gendered, as well. It has been observed regularly that this order constitutes a public realm that marginalizes women (by relegating them to the private realm of the family), establishes men as the political and civil subjects, and orients subjects "toward autonomy, autarky, and individual power"—all generally considered to be masculine qualities.[27] Sovereignty—a third component of the state "body"—has proven equally problematic when viewed through a gender lens. The idea that sovereignty is an ordered realm, set apart from the dangers of the state system, has been called into question by the particular vulnerabilities of women within states, and the connection between those vulnerabilities and the wider power relations that extend into the international realm.[28] Instead, some scholars have argued that the state project, operating within and beyond borders, makes possible the inside/outside, order/anarchy distinction, which then produces the "effect" of the state.[29] The final component of the state "body"—an organization claiming a monopoly on the legitimate use of organized violence—may be usefully examined as an effect, thereby denaturalizing its presumed status as a pre-social characteristic of states. By studying how performances of protection in International Relations reestablish the prerogative power, or claim to violence, of the state, this component of the state body can be embedded in processes that it has been posited to proceed.

All this points to the idea that the creation of the state as a unitary, person-like actor in International Relations is an ongoing process, rather than something that has been accomplished before International Relations begin. Such an observation need not devalue the work done within feminism on the domestic structures or the internal organization of the state.[30] Indeed, as much research shows, these are important sources of masculinism and patriarchy. But it does remove the assumptions that reify the state, abstract it from the processes of its own reproduction, and obscure the contestation over its meaning. It does this by foregrounding the processes through which those structures are given meaning as domestic structures—processes that simultaneously carve out the space for the state that is said to contain them. And it is consistent with a belief recurrent in much feminist work, that a more complete understanding of the forces perpetuating the hierarchical relations between masculine and feminine subjects must incorporate those processes that transcend (and produce) the context of the state.[31]

To replace essentialist ontologies, Jackson and Nexon propose a *processual relational* approach to International Relations. In contrast to substantialism, in which some aspects of the state's identity is held outside of process and relation, processual relationalism treats states (and all other entities) as entirely embedded. Social interaction, rather than the entities doing the interacting, becomes the starting point of analysis. Within that interaction, the state appears as a particular pattern of ties or processes—or, as Jackson and Nexon label it, a *project*. At that level, the state may be thought of as "an aggregation of processes," but is not yet the purposeful actor that exists in the minds of most people. It is through an additional process, termed *yoking*, that the state achieves such status. Through yoking, the myriad sites of difference (i.e. the boundaries) among projects within the patterns of processes are connected, then rationalized (in the Weberian sense of being made more formal and abstract), resulting in entity-formation. Jackson and Nexon draw two important implications from this process of state formation. First, the process of yoking, which is necessary for the state to appear as a substance, implies that the production and reproduction of boundaries are necessary for the creation of the state. Second, the coming into "being" of the state does not happen randomly—the connections formed through yoking must be intersubjectively meaningful; they must cohere in the eyes of the audience, thus giving meaning to the various activities that produce the state. The effect is the appearance of a distinct, unitary actor, possessing purpose and capable of exercising agency—in common usage, a state.

This view of how states are made has much in common with Judith Butler's theory of how human subjects are made. For her, neither subjects nor their bodies exist pre-socially in any meaningful sense. Instead, they are constituted and reconstituted performatively within broader matrices of relations, prominent among which is gender.[32] "It would be wrong," Butler explains, "to think that the discussion of 'identity' ought to proceed prior to a discussion of gender identity for the simple reason that 'persons' only become intelligible through becoming gendered in conformity with recognizable standards of gender intelligibility."[33] There is no subject, then, that is not already gendered. This runs counter to common conceptions of the relationship between the subject and gender, in which the former is assumed to exist (in the form of a sexed body) before the latter is acquired (through socialization). In Butler's theory, the subject cannot pre-exist gendering processes, nor can the gender that the subject is said to have be the cultural expression of "its biological sex," for neither the subject nor "its sex" can be conceptualized pre-culturally. On this point there is much convergence with the processual relational approach described above. Much as the "sexed body" loses its foundational status within Butler's theory, the "state body" (to use Wendt's term) loses its foundational status within a processual relational approach. The focus, then, turns to the processes through which the subject (human or state) is constituted.[34]

Butler terms this process performativity. It is much more than "a performance" of gender, which would imply, mistakenly, that the action is done by a preexisting actor. Butler's point is that the action *produces* the actor. Performativity is conceptualized, then, as repetitive imitations of a subject, a "reiterative and citational practice," through which the subject is produced discursively.[35] Butler, in modifying a quote from Nietzsche, sums up the ontological commitment this theory entails: "There is no gender identity behind expressions of gender ... identity is performatively constituted by the very 'expressions' that are said to be its results."[36] Yet, despite being a performatively-generated effect, the actor maintains the appearance of continuity and solidity. This is not due to any essential characteristics the actor possesses; rather, "continuity" and "solidarity" appear as iterated performances and are read through "socially instituted and maintained norms of intelligibility."[37] For instance, within the dominant heterosexual matrix and the norms of intelligibility it encompasses, acting "like a man" constitutes the subject as "a man." Additionally, acting "like a man" constitutes the subject as one who was "a man" before "he acted."

Again the similarities between a theory of performativity for humans and a processual relational approach for states are apparent. For a state to emerge out of a web of relations, it must follow a process that is intersubjectively meaningful to its audience.[38] For this reason, the boundaries that are drawn in the yoking process are necessarily drawn according to some "generic plan" that "lend[s] interpretive coherence to the various actions which make up the project."[39] There is, in other words, a "recipe" for making a state—"'instructions for stateness'" without which the process lacks unity and the state cannot gain the appearance of being an entity.[40] Thus, boundaries must be drawn in meaningful ways for the state to become intelligible as a subject. This is quite compatible with Butler's theory of performativity, which, too, suggests that a "recipe" for intelligible subjects exists. That recipe, however, includes gender (among other, related constructions like race) as it is regulated by a compulsory, naturalized, and normative heterosexuality. The cultural grid of heterosexuality structures the meanings that gender performances must assume to make sense. As a result, a subject must be performatively constituted as a heterosexual masculine subject or a heterosexual feminine subject to be intelligible within the heterosexual matrix. But whether the cultural grid serves heterosexuality, in Butler's theory, or something else (perhaps, in International Relations, sovereignty), the point is that the subject can only be constituted through its relations to those norms.

Given these similarities, the application of Butler's theory of performativity to the constitution of states in International Relations can be helpful. If states are intelligible as people, then her theory, which explains how people become intelligible, can be used to better understand states. It can shed light not only on the processes through which states are naturalized, but also on the unacknowledged relationships that exist among states by virtue of the norms through which they become intelligible. Gender must be counted among these norms. To apply Butler's theory of performativity, without attempting to abstract gender from it, is to argue that states are gendered, and that their gendering is no more metaphorical than is the gendering of humans. Because both Butler's work and the approach advocated by Jackson and Nexon are process-oriented, both forms of subjects—humans and states—can be studied as discursively-constituted effects, formed within a cultural grid that contains ideas about gender and that structures the meanings of the subjects' performances. Ontologically, both are productions, performatively established in relation to gender norms of intelligibility, though seldom recognized as such.

This assumes, of course, that there are norms of intelligibility shaping the conceptualization of the state. On the one hand, the pervasiveness of the anthropomorphic assumption within IR implies that there must be. If people cannot be conceptualized without gender, and states are conceived of as people, then that conception must contain gender within it, even if implicitly so. The details of such a conceptualization, and the norms of gender upon which it draws, will vary by local context. Specific, interrelated discourses of gender and statehood will determine the ways in which the state is gendered. Meanwhile, the pervasiveness of those discourses will determine who shares that conception. There is valuable work that has been done by examining how states become gendered within specific discourses. Cynthia Weber has gone farther down this road than anyone else, applying Butler's theory of performativity to US-Caribbean relations.[41] She argues that within discourses on the US role vis-à-vis Caribbean countries, US foreign policy has been geared toward the production of a straight, masculine, hegemonic identity where one no longer exists. Within some of the same discourses, Jutta Weldes considers briefly how, during the Cuban Missile Crisis, the fear of appearing effeminate meant that "the United States not only had to be strong, courageous, determined, and firm, it also had repeatedly to reenact these characteristics."[42] Iris Marion Young examines performances of the US security state within post-9/11 discourses of danger and finds that they masculinize the state while feminizing the population.[43] By approaching the idea of gendered states within the confines of specific discourses, these works reflect well upon the sentiment that "the relations between gender and the state cannot be studied in general terms ... instead, attention must be on the construction of gender within specific state discourses and practices."[44]

Masculinity and protection

But can it be said that states are gendered in recognizable ways, *in general*? If so, then through what kind of performances, and through what gendered norms of intelligibility? The rest of this chapter offers a preliminary answer to these questions by suggesting that certain security performances gender the state through the widely-held norm of masculine protection. While the precise forms that this protection takes, and the meaning that it "writes" upon the state, will vary, the norms through which the performances are read are culturally pervasive enough to be theorized as masculinizing or feminizing.[45] R. W. Connell's concept of hegemonic masculinity can help observers find a benchmark for the meaning of such performances. And while one must be careful not to homogenize state identities when viewing them in relation to system-wide norms, a project focused on the masculinizing effects of performances of protection can elucidate how states naturalize their status and improve their standing among other states.

In applying society-level theories, like those offered by Butler and Connell, to the global scale, one problem is immediately apparent: the "cultural grid" that structures gender norms is much thinner there than it is within local contexts. But this does not render those norms ineffectual. The qualities that compose them account for some of the basic, relational identities that recur in the international realm. Although a more complete understanding of those identities requires situating them within local discourses, they may be observed—relationally and in broad terms—to connect to more global discourses on gender. Connell, for instance, proposes that a model of "transnational business masculinity" has been developing in response to globalization.[46] As a global model, it does not supplant local and regional masculinities. Instead, it reveals some broad, gendered qualities that are in play. These qualities can then be studied with attention to how models of masculinity are articulated through each other across levels.

Often, the qualities of gender norms are structured as dichotomous pairs. As signifiers of identity, they establish hierarchy among the actors upon which they are "written." They include, among other things: rationality/irrationality, civilized/barbaric, autonomous/dependent, active/passive, and powerful/weak—all of which map onto the dominant signifier pair of masculine/feminine.[47] The examination of gender dichotomies such as these has been helpful in accounting for how unequal, relational identities have been maintained and how they have privileged some actors and marginalized others. However, there are limits to this kind of analysis. By viewing relational gender identities in dichotomous terms, one risks neglecting the variation that exists within those categories.[48] Simply put, there are different and unequal types of masculinity and femininity. Within the range of masculinities, there are dominant and subordinate types. A hegemonic masculinity is an idealized, relational, and historical model of masculinity—one to which other forms of masculinity are subordinate. Although the qualities associated with it characterize a small percentage of masculine actors, its idealization and cultural pervasiveness require other actors to position themselves in relation to it.[49] And while it is continually evolving, incorporating other forms of masculinity even as it subordinates them, it remains identifiable.[50]

By performing in accordance with a dominant model of masculinity, states can constitute (and thus, position) themselves relationally as powerful subjects. For Connell, this kind of positioning is at the heart of the concept of masculinity, to such a degree that the term "represents not a certain type of man but, rather, a way that men position themselves through discursive practices."[51] Cynthia Enloe argues similarly that patriarchy is perpetuated by "men who are recognized and claim a certain form of masculinity, for the

sake of being more valued, more 'serious,' and 'the protectors of/and controllers of those people who are less masculine.'"[52] A comparable process
occurs among states. As with men, the more that states are able to constitute
themselves in alliance with the norms of the hegemonic masculinity, the more
they will improve their position and boost their credibility.[53] Thus, states have
constant incentives to perform in ways that not only are masculine, but that
constitute them as a certain form of masculine actor, one who embodies the
elements of the hegemonic masculinity.

Performances that masculinize states by positioning them closer to the ideal
of the hegemonic masculinity are likely to be most effective in the realm of
security. This is because security performances are central to the production
of the state as a unitary subject and because, so often, security performances
are rendered intelligible by highly pronounced ideas about masculinity and
femininity. War, in particular, demonstrates this claim. Long ago, Kenneth
Waltz observed that in times of war the state is united (and, therefore, a single
entity) to a greater degree than at any other time.[54] Tickner makes a similar
observation but concludes that gender plays a big role in producing state
unity: the state becomes a citizen-warrior in times of war.[55] Jean Bethke
Elshtain and Susan Jeffords go one step further, arguing that collective identities are constructed through the types of men and women that war creates or
brings out. But absent war, security performances are still crucial for state
production and reproduction.[56] By taking dangers, threats, and other signs of
insecurity to be their objects, security performances reproduce the boundaries
between a secure self and a dangerous other. Boundary reproduction is central to processes of statecraft, and security performances occur where the
integrity of the state's boundaries are discursively challenged, often in an
explicit manner. Whether such threats are internal or external, the effect is the
same. Indeed, the distinction often collapses.

One effect of successful security performances, then, is the appearance of
the state as a unitary, continuous actor, and one who can claim legitimacy
over those "internal" to it. An additional effect of successful security performances is the constitution of the state as an actor who is hierarchically
dominant to certain other international actors, frequently states. Both of these
can be accomplished by performing security in accord with the norms of the
hegemonic masculinity. The relational quality of gender ensures that any
performances that give the state the appearance of personhood will necessarily
position its personhood in relation to other states. Any gendered construction
of the state, even if it does not live up to masculine ideals, will be "socially
defined in contradistinction from some model (whether real or imaginary) of
femininity;"[57] thus, the gender norms that make a state intelligible as a subject
also situate it relationally to other actors.

This argument may be operationalized by first determining the dominant
form of masculinity that operates among states, and then observing states'
efforts to perform security in ways that align with it. For the first step, there is
good reason to believe that a model of masculinity centered on protection has

achieved dominant, if not hegemonic, status. While the question of its hegemonic status will have to be settled empirically, protection appears to be both
clearly masculine and sufficiently widespread. And although studies of the
idea of protection are dwarfed by studies of the idea of security within IR,
there is enough work that has been done on its normative force, evolving
meaning, and the growing range of performances that it regulates to merit
consideration. Work on these different aspects of protection could be usefully
combined to reveal an overarching process—one through which feminist
Security Studies can study the gendering of the state that takes place at a
systemic level.

Over the past few decades, only a few feminist scholars have theorized
protection as a masculinizing performance. Judith Hicks Stiehm and Iris
Marion Young, in particular, have offered important formulations of its logic
and effects.[58] From these works, protection emerges as a pervasive model of
masculinity. Although they are not cast in the language of performativity,
these works take performances that embody this ideal (i.e. the giving of protection) to be constitutive of relational identities that privilege masculine
subjects and subordinate feminine subjects. Stiehm focuses principally on
protection at the hands of male-dominated militaries, and her conceptualization of the protector and the protected remains mostly at the level of individuals (officials, soldiers, and so on). Her central argument is that men have
reserved the role of protector for themselves, relegating women to the status
of dependents—a move that not only subordinates women but leaves them
vulnerable to the dangers posed by masculine protectors. Building upon
Stiehm's analysis, Young uses the same logic to characterize the security state
as the protector and the citizenry as the protected. Importantly, she maintains
that these roles are naturalized through their connection to the protector/pro-
tected relationship that defines the patriarchal household. In her words:

> An exposition of the gendered logic of the masculine role of protector in
> relation to women and children illuminates the meaning and effective
> appeal of a security state that wages war abroad and expects obedience
> and loyalty at home. In this patriarchal logic, the role of the masculine
> protector puts those protected, paradigmatically women and children, in
> a subordinate position of dependence and obedience. To the extent that
> citizens of a democratic state allow their leaders to adopt a stance of
> protectors toward them, these citizens come to occupy a subordinate
> status like that of women in the patriarchal household. We are to accept a
> more authoritarian and paternalistic state power, which gets its support
> partly from the unity a threat produces and our gratitude for protection.[59]

The strength of both these models is that they allow for an analysis of protection that transverses conventional levels of analysis and highlights the
variety of arenas in which protection is performed. Moreover, they capture
performances that occur in myriad sites throughout the world, yet are united

by a common logic. As Young claims, every state is at least partially a security state, and the legitimacy it derives from performances of protection can be explained by the fact that the same logic legitimates unequal relationships in the personal lives of men and women everywhere.

In this formulation, protection does not have any essential meaning. In fact, both authors emphasize that the protection offered, while beneficial in specific instances, is a bad arrangement for the protected. Protection is, therefore, less about what is provided than it is about the effects of the performances undertaken in its name. This is evident today as states form policies for the protection of trafficked women. On that issue, protection may entail practices as divergent as temporary asylum, abolitionist policies toward sex work, educational campaigns, operations targeting transnational organized criminal networks, border control, and deportation. A significant effect of the performances, regardless of what forms they take, is the production of unequal, gendered identities in the form of protector and protected.[60] With protection stripped of its essentialized meaning, it follows that the identities of protector and protected do not describe accurately any traits possessed by the state or the citizens. Instead, the identities are relational, established by the performances of protection even though they appear to precede those performances. "What matters," Young explains, "is the gendered meaning of the positions and the association of familial caring they carry for people."[61]

Protection does not have an essential meaning, but it does have a political rationality, a plan that provides overall coherence to the various forms that protection takes and the meanings that it acquires. Didier Bigo's work has sought to understand this rationality, as well as the different meanings of protection and the technologies of governance that are guided by it.[62] To accomplish this, he proposes studying protection at the point of application, namely within the field of security professionals. In so doing, he finds three etymologies of protection to be informing the technologies in use, each of which serves as an ideal-type and, though Bigo fails to observe it, each of which gathers its meaning (at least partially) through a connection to gender. The first of these etymologies, *tegere*, represents a non-passive form of protection, one in which the protected both desires protection and maintains her/his sovereignty as an active subject. The protector acts out of a "sacred duty;" the subject is grateful for the protection she/he receives. Within the other etymologies, *praesidere* and *tutore*, the asymmetry is more pronounced. *Praesidere* invokes the guaranteeing of security and survival by someone else. This is a meaning of protection that is familiar to security scholars in IR, as it is often reflected in understandings of sovereignty, security, and borders. It is also the kind of protection that the military provides within Stiehm's framework. *Tutore* is a form of protection that is carried out through profiling: monitoring and surveillance, the identification of risks, the obedience of the protected. The protector operates not out of obligation, as in *tegere*, but out of love. Young, in observing the internal surveillance that characterizes the protection offered by the security state, references this etymology of protection. It merits mention that each of these meanings that protection can acquire is dependent upon an asymmetric relationship between the protector and the protected. Among these, *tegere* characterizes those performances of protection that are the least constitutive of unequal relations—the best case scenario for protection. Within Bigo's analysis, however, *tegere* appears also as the least relevant for the contemporary forms that protection takes. Instead, protection tends to take on less desirable forms, where "the protected has difficulty overcoming the relation to regain voice and the capacity of acting politically."[63]

Bigo does not consider that the rationality of protection may be better understood if it is posited in relation to gender norms. Following Young's argument, one could deduce that rationality to be the reproduction of gendered identities through the unequal relations that produce them. Bigo's silence on gender is a missed opportunity. If his work explored how technologies of security, reflecting the different meanings that protection can take, establish *gendered* identities in the form of protector and protected, Bigo's analysis would have a more complete picture of the systemic incentives that perpetuate these performances, as well as the identities that are at stake in the outcome.

That such analysis would be worthwhile is underscored by the similarities between the meanings of protection that Bigo provides and the qualities reflected in the models of masculinity described by Charlotte Hooper. The Judeo-Christian ideal of masculinity, which centers on responsibility, ownership, and paternal authority, is featured prominently in protection when protection is performed as either *praesidere* or *tutore*. The silencing of agency, the restriction on movement, the claiming of knowledge about threats that the protected does not possess—when viewed in relation to dominant forms of masculinity, it is apparent that such performances establish not only asymmetric relations, but relations that are asymmetric *because of* their relations to gender norms. Additionally, the bourgeois rationalist model, recognizable as the dominant model of the modern era, is manifest in Bigo's characterization of *tutore*. With its idealization of "calculative rationality in public life," that model of masculinity lends gendered meaning to those performances of protection that occur through the profiling of risk. These similarities suggest that a newly hegemonic masculinity may be operating as the regulative ideal of security performances. Combining elements of earlier hegemonies, it appears not as a rupture in the symbolic structure of gendered meaning, but as a continuation of that structure. Reflecting its continuation with earlier models, it may be best termed a "rational protector" model. If such a model is now dominant, then those wishing to examine the masculinizing performances of states can start with the assumption that states have strong motivation to perform security in ways that approximate this ideal.

Conclusion

Bigo's discussion of protection suggests that this model of masculinity can be studied usefully through the technologies deployed as states strive to emulate it. And it suggests how central the concept of protection is becoming to the production and reproduction of the state. But his work also shows, unintentionally, the necessity of incorporating gender into Security Studies. As performances of protection increasingly come to characterize the way a state "does" security, the connection of those performances to dominant masculine ideals must be taken into account. Yet, even for scholars who are amenable to process-oriented ontologies, gender is omitted. Those within IR whose theoretical innovations have paved the way for a processual relational account of identity—Wendt, Campbell, Jackson and Nexon, to name a few—must go further by considering gender as a central component of those processes. They operate with frameworks well adapted to theories of performativity, yet stop short of applying the insights of Butler, Weber, and other feminists. Remedying this shortcoming by integrating gender is a necessary step. Still, an even larger hindrance to a more complete incorporation of gender into the field of Security Studies is the reluctance of the field to move away from its substantialist foundation, to get to a point where gender can be studied as an identity-constituting system of meaning, with effects that go beyond shaping the secondary identity of an already-existing entity. Until more scholars move in this direction, there will be little recognition that the personhood of the state—its "body" and "life"—is itself a product of performances read through gendered norms of intelligibility. And until that is recognized, most within Security Studies will continue to view the state as a genderless being. One danger of such a view is apparent: With the state's masculine identity masked, the protection it offers may seem like a good deal.

Notes

1 Alexander Wendt, "The State as Person in International Theory," *Review of International Studies* 30, no. 2 (2004): 289–316.
2 See Johanna Kantola, "The Gendered Reproduction of the State in International Relations," *The British Journal of Politics & International Relations* 9, no. 2 (2007): 270–83; Cynthia Weber, "Performative States," *Millennium: Journal of International Studies* 27, no. 1 (1998): 77–96. For what it means to study world politics through a "gender lens" (alternatively, a "gender-sensitive lens" or "feminist lens"), see V. Spike Peterson and Anne Sisson Runyan, *Global Gender Issues, Dilemmas in World Politics* (Boulder, CO: Westview Press, 1993); Jill Steans, *Gender and International Relations: An Introduction* (New Brunswick, NJ: Rutgers University Press, 1998).
3 Laura Sjoberg, Introduction, in this book.
4 Ronnie D. Lipschutz, "Negotiating the Boundaries of Difference and Security at Millennium's End," in *On Security*, ed., Ronnie D. Lipschutz (New York: Columbia University Press, 1995).
5 Barry Buzan, Ole Wæver, and Jaap de Wilde, *Security: A New Framework for Analysis* (Boulder, CO: Lynne Rienner Publishers, 1998); David Campbell, *Writing Security: United States Foreign Policy and the Politics of Identity* (Minneapolis: University of Minnesota Press, 1992); Roxanne Lynn Doty, "Foreign Policy as Social Construction: A Post-Positivist Analysis of U.S. Counterinsurgency Policy in the Philippines," *International Studies Quarterly* 37, no. 3 (1993): 297–320; Jef Huysmans, *The Politics of Insecurity: Fear, Migration, and Asylum in the*

E.U. (New York: Routledge, 2006); Ole Wæver, "Securitization and Desecuritization," in *On Security*, ed. Ronnie D. Lipschutz (New York: Columbia University Press, 1995); Jutta Weldes *et al.*, eds., *Cultures of Insecurity: States, Communities, and the Production of Danger* (Minneapolis, MN: University of Minnesota Press, 1999).

6 Judith Butler, *Gender Trouble: Feminism and the Subversion of Identity*, 10th Anniversary ed. (New York and London: Routledge, 1999), p. 33.

7 Iver B. Neumann, "Beware of Organicism: The Narrative Self of the State," *Review of International Studies* 30, no. 2 (2004): 259–67, at 265.

8 Patrick Thaddeus Jackson and Daniel H. Nexon, "Relations before States: Substance, Process and the Study of World Politics," *European Journal of International Relations* 5, no. 3 (1999): 291–332, at p. 291. Jackson and Nexon are paraphrasing a definition offered in Mustafa Emirbayer, "Manifesto for a Relational Sociology," *American Journal of Sociology* 103, no. 2 (1997): 281–317.

9 J. Ann Tickner, *Gender in International Relations: Feminist Perspectives on Achieving Global Security* (New York: Columbia University Press, 1992), p. 41. See also, Rebecca Grant, "The Sources of Gender Bias in International Relations Theory," in *Gender and International Relations*, eds., Rebecca Grant and Kathleen Newland (Bloomington, IN: Indiana University Press, 1991). V. Spike Peterson points out that the consolidation of the state and the gendering of the state were concomitant processes. That argument parallels closely the one made here. The anthropomorphization of the state is tied inextricably to these processes, simultaneously reinforcing them and resulting from them. Given that, the personhood of the state should be investigated rather than assumed.

10 Neumann, "Beware of Organicism: The Narrative Self of the State," pp. 265–6.

11 Alexander Wendt, *Social Theory of International Politics* (New York: Cambridge University Press, 1999), p. 194.

12 Ibid., p. 197. Others, too, have found Wendt's use of quotations puzzling. Iver Neumann exclaims: "[T]he inverted commas [quotations] must be lapses, for he insists that he is not discussing the state *as if* it had a body and a life ... the metaphorical distance implied by the use of inverted commas is explicitly done away with, and it should therefore be a correlate that Wendt should have done away with the inverted commas as well." (Neumann, "Beware of Organicism: The Narrative Self of the State," p. 261)

13 Wendt, *Social Theory of International Politics*, p. 198.

14 Ibid., p. 202.

15 Alexander Wendt, "Anarchy Is What States Make of It: The Social Construction of Power Politics," in *Theory and Structure in International Political Economy: An International Organizational Reader*, eds., Charles Lipson and Benjamin J. Cohen (Cambridge, MA: MIT Press, 1999), p. 86.

16 Wendt, *Social Theory of International Politics*, p. 197.

17 Campbell, *Writing Security: United States Foreign Policy and the Politics of Identity*, p. 8.

18 Jacqueline Berman, "(Un)Popular Strangers and Crises (Un)Bounded: Discourses of Sex-Trafficking, the European Political Community and the Panicked State of the Modern State," *European Journal of International Relations* 9, no. 1 (2003): 37–86, at p. 59.

19 J. Ann Tickner, *Gendering World Politics: Issues and Approaches in the Post-Cold War Era* (New York: Columbia University Press, 2001).

20 Kristin Hoganson, *Fighting for American Manhood: How Gender Politics Provoked the Spanish American and Philippine-American Wars* (New Haven, CT: Yale University Press, 1998), pp. 144–5.

21 Jean Bethke Elshtain, "Sovereignty, Identity, Sacrifice," in *Gendered States: Feminist (Re)Visions of International Relations Theory*, ed., V. Spike Peterson

(Boulder, CO: Lynne Rienner Publishers, 1992). Importantly, Elshtain notes that both masculine and feminine gender roles are created and reinforced in the sacrifices of war.

22 Ralph Pettman, "Sex, Power, and the Grail of Positive Collaboration," in *The "Man" Question in International Relations*, eds., Marysia Zalewski and Jane Parpart (Boulder, CO: Westview Press, 1998), p. 174.

23 Campbell, *Writing Security: United States Foreign Policy and the Politics of Identity*, p. 91.

24 Catherine V. Scott, "From Saving Children to Tough Guy Nostalgia: Masculinity and Foreign Policy from Clinton to Bush," paper presented at the 43rd Annual ISA Convention, New Orleans, LA, March 24–27, 2002.

25 Quoted in Scott, "From Saving Children to Tough Guy Nostalgia: Masculinity and Foreign Policy from Clinton to Bush."

26 Cynthia Weber, *Simulating Sovereignty: Intervention, the State, and Symbolic Exchange* (New York: Cambridge University Press, 1995), p. 125.

27 Wendy Brown, *States of Injury: Power and Freedom in Late Modernity* (Princeton, NJ: Princeton University Press, 1995), p. 183. See also Catharine A. MacKinnon, *Toward a Feminist Theory of the State* (Cambridge, MA: Harvard University Press, 1989); Carole Pateman, *The Sexual Contract* (Stanford, CA: Stanford University Press, 1988).

28 Tickner, *Gender in International Relations: Feminist Perspectives on Achieving Global Security*.

29 Most notably, see R. B. J. Walker, *Inside/Outside: International Relations as Political Theory*, Cambridge Studies in International Relations (Cambridge: Cambridge University Press, 1993).

30 Valuable contributions include Brown, *States of Injury: Power and Freedom in Late Modernity*, Grant, "The Sources of Gender Bias in International Relations Theory"; Steve Niva, "Tough and Tender: New World Order Masculinity and the Gulf War," in *The "Man" Question in International Relations*, eds., Marysia Zalewski and Jane Parpart (Boulder, CO: Westview Press, 1998).

31 This approach requires, however, moving from "why" questions to "how" questions, and abandoning causal theory in favor of constitutive theory. See Roxanne Lynn Doty, *Imperial Encounters: The Politics of Representation in North–South Relations* (Minneapolis: University of Minnesota Press, 1996).

32 Specifically, Butler's focus is on a heterosexual matrix, which provides "standards of intelligibility" for performances of gender.

33 Butler, *Gender Trouble: Feminism and the Subversion of Identity*, p. 2.

34 It is worth noting that the shared ontologies of Butler and Jackson/Nexon come despite differences in their beliefs about the role of theory. Whereas Butler employs theory as a political tool for destabilizing dichotomous identities and promoting new hybrid ones, Jackson and Nexon approach theory as "explanatory through ideal-typifying moral and ethical commitments." For this point, the author is indebted to Patrick Thaddeus Jackson.

35 Judith Butler, *Bodies That Matter: On the Discursive Limits Of "Sex"* (New York: Routledge, 1993), p. 2.

36 Butler, *Gender Trouble: Feminism and the Subversion of Identity*, p. 33.

37 Ibid., p. 23.

38 "The audience" may be either what comes to be labeled "domestic" or "foreign." The distinction itself is an outcome of the process; the creation of the audience is intrinsic to the process of state formation.

39 Jackson and Nexon, "Relations before States: Substance, Process and the Study of World Politics," p. 316. With this point, the authors are drawing upon Nicholas Rescher, *Process Metaphysics: An Introduction to Process Philosophy* (Albany, NY: State University of New York Press, 1996).

40 Jackson and Nexon, "Relations before States: Substance, Process and the Study of World Politics," p. 316.
41 Cynthia Weber, *Faking It: U.S. Hegemony in a "Post-Phallic" Era* (Minneapolis, MN: University of Minnesota Press, 1999). On applying Butler's theory of performativity to International Relations, in general, and to the concept of sovereignty in particular, see Weber, "Performative States."
42 Jutta Weldes, *Constructing National Interests: The United States and the Cuban Missile Crisis* (Minneapolis, MN: University of Minnesota Press, 1999), p. 211.
43 Iris Marion Young, "The Logic of Masculinist Protection: Reflections on the Current Security State," *Signs: Journal of Women in Culture and Society* 29, no. 1 (2003): 1–25.
44 Kantola, "The Gendered Reproduction of the State in International Relations," p. 278.
45 To avoid sacrificing a key component of Butler's theory of performativity, it should be noted that there are other ways in which these performances may be read, so that a state can perform in ways that complicates its identity to norms of masculinity and femininity.
46 R.W. Connell, "Masculinities and Globalization," *Men and Masculinities* 1, no. 1 (1998): 3–23.
47 Of course, masculine/feminine is not the only binary oppositional pair established among states. Others can include parent/child, white/colored, and Western/non-Western. See R.W. Connell, *Gender and Power: Society, the Person, and Sexual Politics* (Stanford, CA: Stanford University Press, 1987); Doty, *Imperial Encounters: The Politics of Representation in North–South Relations*; Michael H. Hunt, *Ideology and U.S. Foreign Policy* (New Haven, CT: Yale University Press, 1987); and Edward W. Said, *Orientalism* (New York: Vintage, 1979).
48 Additionally, one risks reinforcing stereotypes of "masculine" and "feminine."
49 Connell, *Gender and Power: Society, the Person, and Sexual Politics*; R.W. Connell, "Hegemonic Masculinity: Rethinking the Concept," *Gender & Society* 19, no. 6 (2005): 829–59.
50 Charlotte Hooper, *Manly States: Masculinities, International Relations, and Gender Politics* (New York: Columbia University Press, 2001), p. 62.
51 Connell, "Hegemonic Masculinity: Rethinking the Concept," p. 841.
52 Carol Cohn and Cynthia Enloe, "A Conversation with Cynthia Enloe: Feminists Look at Masculinity and the Men Who Wage War," *Signs: Journal of Women in Culture and Society* 28, no. 4 (2003): 1187–207, 1192.
53 Charlotte Hooper, "Masculinist Practices and Gender Politics: The Operation of Multiple Masculinities in International Relations," in *The "Man" Question in International Relations*, eds., Marysia Zalewski and Jane Parpart (Boulder, CO: Westview Press, 1998), p. 46.
54 Kenneth N. Waltz, *Man, the State, and War: A Theoretical Analysis*, 2nd ed. (New York: Columbia University Press, 2001), p. 179. Of course, Waltz does not view this unity as an effect of the representational practices enabled by the discursive context of war.
55 Tickner, *Gendering World Politics: Issues and Approaches in the Post-Cold War Era*, p. 41.
56 The term "security performances" is not intended to imply that any performance is inherently "about" security. Rather, a performance *becomes* a security performance only if it is interpreted as such, which will depend upon the discourses through which the performance is interpreted.
57 Connell, "Hegemonic Masculinity: Rethinking the Concept," p. 848.
58 Judith Hicks Stiehm, "The Protected, the Protector, the Defender," *Women's Studies International Forum* 5, no. (1982): 367–76; Young, "The Logic of Masculinist Protection: Reflections on the Current Security State." See also, V.

Spike Peterson, "Security and Sovereign States: What Is at Stake in Taking Feminism Seriously?" in *Gendered States: Feminist (Re)Visions of International Relations Theory*, ed., V. Spike Peterson (Boulder, CO: Lynne Rienner Publishers, 1992).

59 Young, "The Logic of Masculinist Protection: Reflections on the Current Security State," p. 2. For further explanation and application of this argument, see Jonathan D. Wadley, "Sex Trafficking and the Reproduction of Europe: Identities, Integration, and the Politics of Protection" (Dissertation, University of Florida, 2009).

60 Even when protection is rejected, the process is constitutive. For example, a woman who rejects the bargain offered by the security state becomes a "bad woman." The state, in that case, often becomes a "threat."

61 Young, "The Logic of Masculinist Protection: Reflections on the Current Security State," p. 13.

62 Didier Bigo, "Protection: Security, Territory and Population," in *The Politics of Protection: Sites of Insecurity and Political Agency*, eds., Jef Huysmans, Andrew Dobson, and Raia Prokhovnik (London: Routledge, 2006); Didier Bigo, "When Two Become One: Internal and External Securitisations in Europe," in *International Relations Theory and the Politics of European Integration: Power, Security, and Community*, eds., Morten Kelstrup and Michael C. Williams (London: Routledge, 2000).

63 Bigo, "Protection: Security, Territory and Population," p. 93.

Part II
Gendered security theories

4 Gendering the cult of the offensive

Lauren Wilcox

Offense–defense theory in international Security Studies asserts that war is more likely when offensive military strategies and technologies are at a relative advantage over defensive strategies and technologies. The offense–defense balance is, in short, "the relative ease of attack and defense."[1] This insight has led scholars to try to calculate and understand the components of the "offense–defense balance" at different times throughout history in order to understand and predict the occurrence of war. According to offense–defense theorists, the variables determining the offense–defense balance include geographical, doctrinal, and societal aspects, but the overall state of military technology is generally considered to be the most important factor.[2]

While several scholars have noted the difficulty in determining whether offense or defense has the military advantage and what the correct conceptualization of the offense–defense balance is/should be, most analyses of the offense–defense balance presume that the offensive or defensive bias of the system can be rationally known. However, these same theorists are equally cognizant that the offense–defense balance is frequently misunderstood, and in fact, offensive capabilities are commonly overestimated. One prominent scholar of offense–defense theory, Stephen Van Evera, notes that perceived offensive dominance is widespread, but real offensive dominance is rare: "Offensive dominance is more often imagined than real, however. Thus the more urgent question is: How can illusions of offense dominance be controlled? Answers are elusive because the roots of these illusions are obscure."[3]

Van Evera argues that illusions of offensive dominance have caused wars. One of the times that Van Evera contends that these illusions have been most influential is in the initiation of World War I. He explains that "during the decades before the First World War a phenomenon which may be called a 'cult of the offensive' swept through Europe."[4] These "mythical or mystical arguments [about offensive dominance] obscured the technical domination of the defense" in military strategy and security policy-making.[5] As a result, Van Evera reasons, "the belief in easy conquest eventually pervaded public images of international politics" and "the cult of the offensive was a mainspring driving many of the mechanisms which brought about the First World War."[6]

This chapter critiques a missing link in offense–defense theory: though Van Evera effectively presents the argument that misperceived offensive dominance caused World War I, and notes that it is therefore important to learn the "roots of these illusions" that cause states to be preoccupied with offense even in times of defense dominance, offense–defense theory does not present a convincing explanation of the source of the perception of offensive dominance. I demonstrate that insights from feminist scholarship point to several different ways in which gender is relevant in constituting the "roots of these illusions": the overestimation of offense dominance and the resulting propensity to war. Specifically, I suggest three pathways that gender constitutes the roots of the illusion of offense dominance: the gendered perceptions of technology, gendered nationalism, and definitions of citizenship and honor based on the gendered concept of protection—and that, therefore, gender is the missing link in explaining the cult of the offensive.

Perception in traditional accounts of the offense–defense balance

Offense–defense theorists argue that the offense–defense balance changes the probability of war by affecting the severity of the security dilemma.[7] The security dilemma will be more severe if the balance favors the offense, while the destabilizing effects of anarchy can be lessened substantially if the defense is dominant, assuming offense dominance and defense dominance can be distinguished.[8] While there is much debate about the precise factors that constitute the offense–defense balance, the most frequently cited predictor of the (actual) offense–defense balance is military technologies, which are important insofar as they contribute to making offensive or defense strategies easier.[9] While some offense–defense theorists argue some weapons are inherently offensive or defensive, others argue that is it the overall state of military technology that defines the offense–defense balance. Regardless of the precise measurement of the offense–defense, offense–defense theorists share an assumption that the offensive or defense advantages of other technologies may depend upon the era, but can be objectively determined.

Offense–defense theorists note, however, that it is often not the actual or material dominance of offense or defense that influences states' strategic choices, but instead states' (often mistaken) perceptions of the offense–defense balance. Military and political doctrines can override the existence of defensive predominance in military technologies to result in offensive strategies.[10] Ted Hopf has argued that "strategic beliefs" are more important than military capabilities in causing instability in war.[11] These beliefs encompass ideas about the intentions of other states and fears of bandwagoning and domino effects. Lynn-Jones goes further to specify that it is perceptions of the offense–defense balance that give the theory its explanatory power.[12] As Van Evera notes, "Real offense dominance is rare in modern times, but the perception of offense dominance is fairly widespread. Therefore, if perceived offense dominance causes war it causes lots of war, and offense–defense theory explains much of international history."[13] There are, however, few if any accounts of the cause or constitution of perceived offensive dominance in offense–defense theory.

Some notion of the "objective" offense–defense balance is necessary, however, for there to be a notion of a cult of the offensive which overestimates the ease of conquest. There can be no "misperception" of the offense–defense balance without some notion of an "objective" balance, no matter what quantifiable or unquantifiable variables. Whatever this "objective" balance may be is outside the scope of this piece,[14] but it seems likely that absent social and political factors contributing to perceptions of the ease and desirability of aggressive strategies, there would be fewer wars. In this chapter, I focus entirely on the sources of perception of offense dominance and the conditions underpinning the cult of the offensive that encourages aggressive military strategies. The remainder of this chapter argues that gender analysis demonstrates the centrality of gender to understanding perceived offensive dominance, both generally and in specific, the cult of the offensive.

Feminist analyses of offense–defense theory

As discussed in the introduction, IR feminists use gender as a category of analysis to questions of framing and possibility in global politics. A feminist analysis of offense–defense theory asks what assumptions about gender (and race, class, nationality, and sexuality) make it possible that belligerents consistently exaggerate offensive capabilities and therefore engage in counter-productive offensive military strategies. Rather than coming up with an alternative causal explanation of why wars occur (or of why a specific war has occurred), I theorize the role of gender to the offense–defense balance as one of constitution. Gender is constitutive of the offense–defense balance if gender is necessary for establishing certain perceptions of offensive or defensive capabilities.

Constitutive theorizing differs from causal theorizing in a number of ways. As explained by Alex Wendt,[15] constitutive theorizing involves asking "how possible" and "what" questions rather than the "why" of causal theorizing. Constitutive theorizing recognizes that social entities are constructed and imbued with characteristics derived from external or internal social structures. Thus, to say that X is constitutive of social kind Y is to argue that Y exists "in virtue of" X. Sjoberg, in the Introduction to this edited volume, quotes Wendt on constitutive theorizing: "what we seek in asking these questions is insight into what it is that instantiates some phenomenon, not why that phenomenon comes about."[16] This is a different logic than the assumptions of causal theory that X and Y exist independently, and that one precedes the other in time. In constitutive theorizing, there is no way to distinguish an independent and dependent variable and thus the argument is logical, rather than based on specific causal mechanism that can be represented in a covering law. Constitutive theorizing strives to "account" for the effects of social structures, in the "instantiation" of phenomena. In this chapter, I use constitutive theorizing to argue that gender, as a social structure, is constitutive of perceptions of the offense–defense balance in terms of perceptions of technology, nationalism and offensive military doctrine, and the "protection racket."

This type of analysis is subject to counterfactual tests: in a world in which gendered ideologies were different, perceptions of the offense–defense balance would be different. In order to understand whether gender is constitutive of the offense–defense balance, it is necessary to understand what influence gender would have and how it would function to be constitutive. Constitutive gendering is not a matter of individual characteristics of men or women, but rather a structural feature of social and political life.[17] V. Spike Peterson defines gender as performing several related functions: "in one sense, gender is a socially imposed and internalized lens through which individuals perceive and respond to the world. In a second sense, the pervasiveness of gendered meanings shapes concepts, practice and institutions in identifiable gendered ways."[18] Gender constitutes, then, by serving as a lens for individual identity and perception of the world and by shaping meaning and political practice.

Another defining feature of gender as a constitutive factor is that it is dynamic—gender does not just constitute identities and meanings once in a readable and constant manner. Instead, gender identities and meanings are constantly reproduced by processes of identity construction in which gender functions as means of encoding power.[19] This encoded power not only distinguishes between values associated with masculinity and values associated with femininity, but creates a hierarchy *among masculinities* based on an ideal-typical, or hegemonic, vision of masculine virtue. The concept of hegemonic masculinity describes the dominant version of ideal male characteristics defined in relation to subordinate masculinities associated with racial, sexual, or class others. Gender is a primary way of signifying relationships of power, such that other hierarchical relationships such as class, sexuality or race become "gendered" in that they are justified by appeals to supposedly natural relationships between men and women. Hegemonic masculinity therefore does not have a fixed definition; rather, it is the masculinity that occupies the hegemonic position in a given set of gender relations. It is therefore historically contingent and contestable.[20]

The remainder of this chapter contends that there are three ways that gender constitutes a (mis)perception of offense–defense balance. First, I argue that the gendered perceptions of the meaning and uses military technology are at the root of perceived offense dominance. Second, I demonstrate that nationalism, as a gendered ideology, underpins the belligerent perception of the power of offense and the desirability of offensive strategies. Third, I explain that a phenomenon feminists have identified as a "protection racket," in which war is the heroic activity of male soldiers saving the lives of innocent women and at the same time earning full citizenship in their polities,[21] constitutes gendered identities that promote conflict-seeking behavior in men and states looking to live up to dominant or hegemonic understandings of masculinity.

Gender and military technology

The question of perception of technology is a well-established issue in the offense–defense literature. Jervis notes that the offense–defense balance depends upon the whether offensive weapons are distinguishable from defensive weapons. If they are not distinguishable, or the same weapons can be advantageous to both the offense and defense, then the offense–defense balance of military technology cannot mitigate the dangers of war caused by the security dilemma.[22] The offensive or defensiveness of a particular technology or system of technologies can be seen as a social construct. In other words, whether a technology favors the offense or defense depends upon what meanings that technology holds in to particular actors in particular contexts. The process through which individuals estimate or use a weapon system's capabilities is not necessarily "rational"; in many cases, gender discourse and identities can play a role in assigning certain meanings to different technologies.

Many feminists have argued that the quest for technological development is inherently based on masculine or patriarchal values. This argument is based on a view of gender in which "gender" does not refer to individual bodies or representations of men and women but rather a dichotomous system of thought that has been reproduced in many ways throughout Western culture. This symbolic structure has arisen from Enlightenment epistemologies that position men alone as rational, as legitimate "knowers" and as producers of knowledge.[23] Scientific ideology can be seen as based on masculine projects of control over nature and built upon the gendered Western dichotomies of mind/body, culture/nature, rational/emotional, control/dependence, and objectivity/subjectivity. In each case, the first term is privileged over the second and associated with masculinity, while the second is subordinated and associated with femininity. Science and technology are considered inherently masculine, as they are associated with the masculine values of domination, control, and objectivity.[24] The "harder" the technology, the more masculine it is. However, from this view, it would be difficult to ascertain why certain technologies have been considered "feminine" while some have been considered "masculine" at different points in history. It is more useful to examine how and in what ways technology has been gendered throughout history.

Studies of scientific and technological practices highlight the ideological work that has gone into building and sustaining technology as a masculine domain and rejecting technologies on the basis of their incompatibility with masculine ideal-types. Military technology has not always been considered "masculine," in the same way, and at times has not even been considered masculine at all. In fact, many defensive developments in military technology have been seen as "emasculating" as they lessen the importance of traditional warrior values of personal courage, physical strength, and honor in warfighting.[25] Since bravery is a key component of militarized masculinity, it is emphasized in gendered evaluations of military technologies. Those technologies which enhance the strength and bravery of warriors are seen as positively

associated with manliness and masculinity. On the other hand, those technologies which make it strategically advantageous for soldiers to lie in wait, to
hold back, and to defend are seen as negatively associated with manliness and
masculinity, because, if employed, they would not require soldiers to display
the heroism associated with courage, strength, honor, and manhood. In times
(like World War I) where military technologies favor a defensive image of
soldiering, belligerents tend to downplay the role of technology and overestimate the importance of the spirit and honor of offensive war-fighting.
Thus, to understand how the perceptions of technologies change, we should
look to the discourses of gender that understand technologies as suitable or
not to dominant definitions of masculinity.

Innovations in military technology perpetuate these gendered perceptions
of the offense–defense balance by entrenching the association of soldiering
and manliness. Rachel Weber gives an example of this phenomenon in her
study of the design of military cockpits. Weber uses the example of military
cockpits to demonstrate that military technologies are not inherently masculine, but rather their masculinity has to be constructed. In building cockpits
to the specifications of men's bodies, the Pentagon built in a bias against
women's bodies into military technologies. The technology of military aircraft
has been marked as masculine through engineering specification and design
guidelines. This bias has wide-ranging implications for gender equality in the
military not only providing a tangible reason for arresting women's advancement but also as a symbolic marker of a masculine social space.[26] Gender-based
assumptions about whether men or women make better pilots cause the planes
to be built in a certain way, but once they were built, they served to reinforce the
exclusion of women from certain military roles. The ultimate honor of being a
fighter pilot and the maleness of fighter pilots are then tied together by the technological developments that favor male bodies *and* masculine characteristics.

When technological developments fail to favor either male bodies or masculine characteristics (e.g., when the developments favor the defense), they are
likely to be ignored or underestimated by belligerents in conflict. In fact,
technologies have fallen in and out of favor on the basis of their perceived
relationship with chivalry and honorable soldiering. For example, in the 1899
Hague Peace Conference, delegates were concerned with the unchivalrous
nature of the use of airplanes in combat. Belgium's Auguste Beernaert, pre-
siding over the Commission on Arms Limitations, proclaimed, "to permit the
use of such infernal machines, which seem to fall from the sky, exceeds the
limit." He added, "As it is impossible to guard against such proceedings, it
resembles perfidy, and everything which resembles that ought to be scrupu-
lously guarded against. Let us be chivalrous even in the manner of carrying
on war." At this point, the "perfidy" is linked to the asymmetry of such
attacks and the difficulty in effective protection against them. The thought of
"infernal" bombs being dropped in a "perfidious" attack positions the tactic
of aerial bombardment as feminine and unchivalrous in a discourse of
betrayal and treachery. The link to notions of "betrayal" and "chivalry"

signal linkages to appropriate masculine behavior, to what is honorable as opposed to what is base, or uncivilized, unmanly types of violence. This demonstrates that whether or not the use of certain technologies is considered appropriately "manly" or not varies. World War I is a good example of ideas about gender affecting how certain technologies were used.

Because the use of planes to drop projectiles was considered "unchivalrous," planes were flown in World War I mostly for reconnaissance, for support of ground troops, and more prominently, to destroy the planes of the other side. Even though combat planes were at the forefront of technological advancement of the time, their contribution to the outcome of the war was minimal: their greatest use was as the heroic symbols they were made to be by the press. The pilots had extremely short life-expectancies in the war (sometimes less than a week), but came to symbolize the ultimate in masculinity: risk-seeking, individualistic, "knights of the air" and "lone wolves." The British and French stuck with the "single combat" model in their air combat against the Germans, though the German method of flying in squadrons was more effective in battle and less risky for inexperienced pilots. From the British perspective, the German method was seen as "cowardly" and "bullying."[27] For the British, the "lone wolf" method of combat was popular in promoting the virtuous nature of the war as it best approximated the one-on-one combat of chivalric times, a mode of warfare that differed drastically from the mass carnage of the land war. Even though the German method of using combat planes was more effective, its perception as less manly led to a lengthy delay in its emulation by Entente Powers. In other words, the use of airplanes in World War I was associated not with their actual technological advantages, but with the ability of the planes to be used in ways that supported the bravery and strength of soldiers without impugning their chivalry.

The gendering of technology can also be linked to the cult of the offensive in World War I. There is a consensus among offense–defense theorists that in 1914, military technologies favored the defense, but all of the belligerent states, unaware of or determined to ignore the actual offense–defense balance, developed military doctrines that assumed the dominance of offense.[28] Gender, class, and racial ideologies combined to create a situation in which defensive technological developments such as the machine gun and barbed wire were underestimated and the cavalry charge was still considered to be the primarily strategic tool for winning wars. Military leaders were aware of new developments in technology, such as barbed wire and machine guns that the "knightly" cavalry would have to overcome, but dealt with those technologies much like they dealt with airplanes—by valuing boldness, bravery, strength, and chivalry over defensive positioning, patience, balancing, and calculation. Gendered perceptions of technology are evident even in Van Evera's descriptions of the cult of the offensive leading up to World War I, even if he does not identify them with gender. For example, Van Evera explains that:

> British and French officers suggested that superior morale on the attacking side could overcome superior defensive firepower, and that this superiority

in morale could be achieved simply by assuming the role of attacker, since offense was a morale-building activity. One French officer contended that "the offensive doubles the energy of the troops" ... in short, mind would prevail over matter; morale would triumph over machine guns.[29]

In other words, technologies that required mundane fighting rather than bravery and excitement would be defeated by morale and courage. As a result, military and political leaders in World War I interpreted clearly defensive technologies as offensive. Van Evera recounts Foch's understanding that "any improvement in firearms is ultimately bound to add strength to the offensive" and the French President's observation that the "offensive alone is suited to the temperament of French soldiers."[30] Continental military leaders downplayed the significance of machine guns in Britain's victories in Africa as these battles were not fought against "civilized" foes, and the British themselves downplayed the implications of these victories for the ease of conquest and defense.[31] German military dogma was bolstered by a belief that single-mindedness of purpose could overcome technological and logistic limitations.[32] In the popular German literature, technology was imagined contributing to the "adventure" of war, rather than to mass killings and the industrialization of warfare.[33] Technologies, then, were interpreted as offensive or defensive *not* on their material contribution to offensive or defensive strategies of fighting, but instead on their relationship to idealized images of soldiers' masculinity bound up in strength, bravery, and chivalry. Given that values associated with the hegemonic masculinity of heroic combat overwhelmingly favor aggressiveness and offense (e.g., bravery, strength, courage, control) and rarely favor military restraint, developments in military technology are overwhelmingly interpreted as offensive or their defensive value is downplayed as outside of traditional associations of soldiering and masculinity.

Gendered nationalism as an inspiration for the cult of the offensive

The cult of the offensive entails more than faulty perceptions of the military implications of the balance of technology: it is also based on inappropriately aggressive military strategies. In his 1984 book, Snyder argues that the offensive strategies of the French, German, and Russian militaries in the run-up to World War I cannot be explained by a rational calculation of interests, but rather are the result of doctrines that had more to do with the organizational values of the militaries than with the technological limitations and the defensive nature of the military balance.[34] Similarly, Van Evera has argued that World War I was caused by the glorification of offensive strategies in Europe's militaries, ignoring the lessons of recent prior wars about the defensive advantages to the technology.[35] While Germany, France, Belgium, Britain and Russian armies were all professing offensive strategies, they believed that superior morale would overcome the disadvantages due to the machine gun. As reasons for this cult of the offensive, Snyder suggests that the duties and training of the military officers force them to concentrate on threats to the state and to view war as an ever present possibility, taking the hostilities of others for granted. Taking the hostility of others for granted leads to a bias towards offensive plans such as preventative wars and pre-emptive strikes. Due to this bias towards the offensive, "defensive plans and doctrines will be considered only after all conceivable offensive schemes have been decisively discredited."[36] From a feminist perspective, arguments about military culture are bound up in connection between nationalism and masculinity. Gender may be said to constitute nationalism, in that these ideologies are inextricably tied to gendered discourse. Thus, gender provides the backdrop that makes the cult of the offensive possible.

Some scholars have argued that men are more likely to make war than women, because men are naturally aggressive. Wars break out because men are in positions of political and military power. Francis Fukuyama's 1998 *Foreign Affairs* article is an example of this type of reasoning.[37] If this logic were true, it could be argued that men are likely to misinterpret the actual offense–defense balance because their aggressive tendencies inspire them to seek out conflict. The relationship between gender and aggression, however, is more complicated. Claims of "natural" aggression in men are politically suspect because they imply it is impossible for men to be otherwise, and therefore ignore the many men who do not behave aggressively. Joshua Goldstein finds little evidence that increased levels of testosterone in men fuel wars, or that biological factors explain the near-monopoly men have had on warfighting throughout history.[39]

Instead of blaming men's biological composition for state aggressiveness, feminists in IR have identified military training and the installment of martial values in men as a source of aggressive policies.[39] Cynthia Enloe draws attention to the myriad strategies associating nationalism and masculinity that military recruiters have used around the world and through time to encourage men to enlist, from promises of a fast-track to "first-class citizenship" for racial minorities, to presumptions of cultural superiority for groups already privileged.[40] In the case of World War I, a "crisis of masculinity" in Britain was incited by the physical ineligibility of much of the working classes for military service, resulting in widespread government intervention to produce a nation of men more suited for the rigors of war deemed necessary to maintain Britain's colonial empire and place in the world.[41] Anxieties over the ability of men to defend the nation prompted attempts to reshape gender relations throughout society to encourage the reinvigoration of traditional gender roles. This evidence indicates that rather than being inherently masculine, the military serves as an important site for the creation and maintenance of gender identities in society. As Enloe points out, "If maleness, masculinity, and militarism *were* inevitably bound together, militaries would always have all the soldiers they believed they required."[42] Viewing gender as an identity, as "a socially imposed and internalized lens through which individuals perceive and respond to the world,"[43] does a better job at explaining the underestimation of the costs of war than theories of men's innate aggression.

Gender identity can help to explain the roots of this romanticization of offensive warfare. Understanding militaries as institutions that mold men into the values of warrior masculinity can help to explain the disproportionate prevalence of offensive doctrines given the offense–defense balance. Barry Posen describes the attractiveness of offensive doctrines to militaries as resulting from the military as an organization's drive to increase its own autonomy and self-image.[44] Snyder explains the offensive bias in the Germany military establishment as partly due to their interests in promoting war as a "beneficial social institution."[45] Likewise, David Englander argues that the offensive spirit in the British military leading up to World War I expressed the military's position as the vanguard of a virile, manly nation.[46] Feminists argue that military socialization not only shapes men's bodies in terms of desired levels of fitness, but military service serves as an important rite of passage in making men out of boys. The cultural and institutional training of the military has taken the masculine virtues of stoicism, detachment, aggression, strength and resolve and worked to install them into the individual characteristics of men. Training men for war, even outside of the institutional setting of the military, has taken place through sports, "adventure stories" and movies.[47] Men have to be trained to be willing to kill, to perform under the immense stress and gruesome horror of battlefield conditions, and to endure the psychological trauma by suppressing their emotions. This training begins at an early age and is supported by women in many ways.[48] In other words, it is not men that cause war so much as war makes men. The possibility of war creates a perceived necessity to instill certain characteristics in men, forming the basis for certain types of masculine gender identity.

Conceptions of gender that are concerned with symbolic structure of gender, rather than the appropriate roles of men and women, argue that 'offense' has been gendered masculine, while "defense" has been gendered feminine. This is due to the associations of "the offensive" with activity, aggression, strength, and boldness (concepts considered masculine in Western culture) as well as the association of "defensive" with passivity, weakness, and victimhood (considered feminine). "Offensive" strategies are preferred because of the association with positive, masculine attributes, while defensive strategies are considered "wimpy" and unmanly. Carol Cohn describes the importance of "the wimp factor" in her experiences at working with defense intellectuals in the 1980s.[49] When certain strategic actions, such as withdrawal from territory, are interpreted as "wimpy," no matter how "rational," they are delegitimized. Playing a simulated war game with a group of defense intellectuals, Cohn's team "lost" by withdrawing troops from some areas and refusing to retaliate from a nuclear strike, even though her "homeland" and its civilian population had remained safe. Such actions become "unthinkable" in the discourse of international security even though they may be strategically beneficial and consistent with other value systems. In this way, aggression and "offense" in the international arena are legitimized through gendered discourses. Gender as a discourse defines the boundaries of acceptable options and serves as a "preemptive deterrent" to certain strategic options.[50] Gender thus constitutes offense/defense by assigning values more value to the offensive posture than the defensive posture. This is one way in which feminists would attempt to explain the puzzle of why decision-makers have the propensity to overestimate the strategic advantages of the offensive; there is a heavy "gender deterrent" against the passive, weak, "defensive" position, even if, as military balance theorists allow, the defense usually has the objective advantage in war, and disasters like World War I can occur if the balance is misinterpreted.

The militarization that is linked to offensive policies is closely connected to nationalism. The literature on offense–defense balance indicates that nationalism can affect the balance by making people more willing to fight.[51] Nationalism is also a source of militarism and offensive strategies, as it usually entails perception by elites and military planners that conquest will be easier because of the superiority of their own soldiers. Van Evera lists nationalism as a mechanism through which the cult of the offensive can be developed, but does not explore how it is possible for nationalistic sentiment to be shaped in the direction of favoring the offensive. Though offense–defense theorists note that belligerents tend to attribute a more coherent, grand and evil scheme to their enemies than is often the case,[52] to believe that their adversaries are more unified than is the case,[53] and to assume that opponents' policy inconsistency is a result of duplicity or treachery rather than confusion,[54] they do not provide a way for scholars to understand these consistent misperceptions as a matter of the gendered practices of identity and nationalism. Feminist analyses would argue that nationalism and militarism are constituted by gender discourses in both the processes of "othering" other nations as well as in the presentation of a national identity and chauvinism that exist by promoting particular ideologies about gender roles.

The process of dehumanizing or "feminizing" enemies is such a means of understanding this misperception. David Campbell, for example, argues that state identity is secured by discourses about the threats others pose: "for the state, identity can be understood as the outcome of exclusionary practices in which resistant elements to a secure identity on the 'inside' are linked through a discourse of 'danger' with threats identified and located on the 'outside.'"[55] These outside threats are constructed in terms historically associated with the feminine, such as irrational, dirty, chaotic, and evil. As others are constructed as inferior through a feminizing discourse, their abilities are underestimated, while somewhat paradoxically, the threat they pose is overestimated. For example, the United States and Britain underestimated the military capabilities of the Japanese during World War II because of beliefs in the inferiority of Japanese. The Japanese were considered "subhuman" and "illogical," and their military capabilities were downgraded prior to the outbreak of war.[56] Military officials in both the United States and Britain ignored evidence of Japanese military successes and the potential threat they posed on the assumption that the Japanese simply could not be capable of such achievements.[57] Thus, the belief that wars will be quick and easy because "our men" are superior in strength, resolve and technological capability has its roots in a process of "othering" in which one's own identity is buttressed by the distancing from and disparagement of a different national or racial group. The feminization of enemies is a reflection of masculinized nationalism—states tell stories about their valorized masculinity in relation to their opponents' devalued femininity, or subordinate masculinity.

The subordinate masculinity that encouraged Britain, France and the US into the war was that of Germany's barbarism. The discourse of "barbarism" which was applied to the Germans in World Wars I and II, and to the Japanese in World War II as well, has had a double meaning in the West: it is considered the opposite of "civilization," while can be either a good thing or a bad thing. "Barbarism" is good when it involves a rejection of the feminized "civilization" of commerce, industry, and domesticity for the more strenuous pursuits of hunting and war. However, it is considered negative, a lower form of masculinity when it refers to racial others. This subordinate masculinity is associated with uncontrolled aggression, a "hypermasculinity" that is to be feared and tamed. In British discourse, Germans were "huns" who stood for despotism and militarism as opposed to British individualism and civilized values and accomplishments. While denigrating the Germans, this construction also entails a fear that the Germans were a more vital people who might succeed in overtaking the British Empire, a fear which led some to call for British men to emulate what was seen as a more "virile race."[58]

The role of this sort of national "myth-making" in increasing the likelihood of war plays a prominent role in Van Evera's list of results of perceived offensive dominance. However, Van Evera denies the centrality of myth-making to the concept of nationalism:

> [M]yth is not an essential ingredient of nationalism: nationalism can also rest on a group solidarity based on truth, and the effects of nationalism are largely governed by the degree of truthfulness of the beliefs that a given nationalism adopts; as truthfulness diminishes, the risks posed by the nationalism increase.[59]

Here, Van Evera mistakenly equates "myth-making" with "falsity." It is these "myths" that create the nation though the hope of a common future, and despite the relatively recent invention of nationalism, the figuration of the nation with a common, distant, origin.[60] These myths about national greatness may be argued to be constitutive of aggressive wars, as such myths play a crucial role in the "othering" and dehumanization of the enemy along gendered lines such that the extreme violence of war becomes fathomable, and a viable policy option. Feminist scholars have examined these myths and their causes and consequences in terms of gendered ideologies and found them to be influential in remaking gender roles.

Rather than seeing the relationship between nationalism and the entrenchment of certain gender identities as a matter of coincidence, feminists have theorized the ways in which national identity is produced though the use of gender discourses. Nationalism, which was at a high point in the build-up to World War I, is a set of discourses about who "we" are and who belongs in the political community. As such, it reproduces the inside/outside logic of the state system, in which those "inside" the state or nation are superior to those "outside." Nationalism therefore depends upon "national chauvinism," such that members of other nations, or racial, sexual, or ideological "others" inside the nation are constructed in terms of femininity or subordinate masculinity. They are weak and inferior, or they are hyper-masculine: beast-like in brutality and sexuality. Feminist have argued that the boundaries between the "self" and "other" are produced by discourses of gender and sexuality.[61]

Feminists have demonstrated that nationalist discourses that constitute the identity of the nation are dependent upon discourses of gender that reproduce traditional gender roles. Feminists argue that nationalists need gendered ideologies to gain support for their cause.[62] For example, Anne McClintock writes, "All too often in male nationalism, *gender* difference between women and men serves to symbolically define the limits of *national* difference and power between *men*."[63] The "imagined community" of the nation depends upon the homosocial relations of men to protect the nation-as-women's-body against foreign incursion.[64] Symbolic gender imagery serves not only to construct the boundaries of national identities, but reproduces gender identity as well. Propaganda and recruitment campaigns frequently held up the volunteer soldier as the only acceptable man—those who did not volunteer were seen as weak, effete and cowardly.[65] The war also dampened the feminist movement in Britain, as many feminists as well as non-feminists supported traditional gender roles for men and women despite women working outside the home in large numbers during the war.[66] As an example of how nationalist passions frequently prevail over attempts to reform traditional gender roles, the feminist magazine *The Suffragette* changed its name to *Britannia* to symbolize patriotic unity and its support of the war effort despite its critiques of the political and legal order.[67]

As gender is a relational concept, hegemonic definitions of masculinity necessarily entail hegemonic definitions of femininity. Nira Yuval-Davis has categorized several ways in which women function in nationalist ideologies, symbolically or in their actions.[68] Women are constructed as the biological reproducers of the nation, as well as the cultural reproducers. After all, "group reproduction—both biological and social—is fundamental to nationalist practice, process, and politics."[69] Under nationalist regimes, women are often expected to bear and raise young men who will fight on behalf of the nation. The nation is therefore dependent upon women in traditional roles as mothers and caretakers to reproduce itself. The entire nation may be symbolized by a woman who must be fought and died for. Indeed, nationalist discourses often present the nation as a woman, a guardian and symbol of the nation's values, such as Germania, Britannia, or France's Marianne, or the cult of Queen Louise of Prussia. These symbolic women were Madonna-like in their image as chaste mothers of the nation.[70] Rape, then, becomes a metaphor for national humiliation, as in "the rape of Belgium" or "the rape of Kuwait" as well as a tactic of war used to symbolically prove the superiority of one's national group.

Not only do nationalist projects construct gender identities that prescribe different spheres for men and women, but this production of gender identities has been a necessary condition of nationalism as women have symbolically figured as the markers of the nation who must be protected by the men who run the state (or are trying to create one). Nationalism is naturalized, or legitimated, though gender discourses that naturalized the domination of one group over another through the disparagement of the feminine and the constitution of separate and unequal spheres for men and women. Gender is constitutive of nationalism, which is factor in the promotion of offensive military doctrines and the cult of the offensive. Nationalism in terms of the assertion of the superiority of *our* men over *their* men often legitimates war in terms of a "protection racket," in which offensive wars are fought in order to defend "women and children" from potential or actual threats. This "protection racket" extends the logic of nationalism to allow for offensive policies to be legitimated as defensive.

Protection as offensive military doctrine

Rather than a unified, aggressive and warlike nature that gender essentialists like Fukuyama imagine, the hegemonic masculinity of World War I calls upon men to be courageous protectors of those less strong and capable: a chivalrous version of masculinity that has more frequently accompanied "offensive warfare" than a dominating, conquering bloodlust (although the former may resemble the latter from certain vantage points). These gendered constructions of identity can make offensive military strategies appear to be defensive, enabling wars to take place. Often, the gendered ideologies that constitute nationalism contribute to forming offensive doctrines. "Chivalric" masculinity is not solely about men, but rather gendered relations of power. In particular, the just war narrative involve "good guys" or "just warriors" who fight against "bad guys" for just and valorous reasons.[71] In order to produce the chivalric masculinity of the "just warrior, a 'beautiful soul" and a malevolent other are needed.[72] As Iris Marion Young explains,

> The gallantly masculine man faces the world's difficulties and dangers in order to shield women from harm … Good men can only appear in their goodness if we assume that lurking outside the warm familial walls are aggressors, the "bad" men, who wish to attack them.[73]

Not only does this "protection racket" legitimate war, but it may be said to legitimate the constitution of the state as the provider of security of outside threats as well.

Feminist scholarship in International Relations has described the various ways in which this ideal of chivalric masculinity has formed the basis of the national security state as well the principles behind just war theory. For example, Jean Bethke Elshtain has described "just warriors" and "beautiful souls" as gender identities that legitimate war. Masculine "just warriors" are only reluctantly violent, but violent nonetheless as they wage war on behalf of the pure and feminine "beautiful souls" who are "too good for this world yet absolutely necessary to it."[74] While seemingly benign, such chivalric discourses require helpless, feminized victims: not full and equal citizens capable of defending themselves. The protector and the protected cannot be equal to one other. "The male protector confronts evil aggressors in the name of the right and the good, while those under his protection submit to his order and serve as handmaids to his efforts."[75] Without this discourse of "protection," many of the offensive military doctrines that resulted in war would not have been possible, as this discourse enables men to take violent action with the narrative that makes their actions seem moral, even commendable. Even so, specifics of time and place shape the specific forms this form of hegemonic masculinity takes.

Prevailing gendered constructions of identity in the form of chivalric myths in the upper classes contributed to offensive strategies and the cult of the offensive in the British military in World War I. Tropes of "defending civilization" or "civilized values" as a reason for mounting offensive military campaigns have a long history. The resonance of such discourses, such as World War I as a crusade to defend civilization against the barbarity of the Germans, is based on gendered discourses in which medieval knights saved damsels or madonnas from cruel beasts.[76] War would provide an escape for young men, a chance to gain honor, as well as a purge and regeneration of society.[77] That war would cure societies of the weakness, decadence, and emasculation of peace was a prevailing cultural assumption among the upper-class members of the political elite across Europe, a fear linked to Social Darwinism and the threat of "racial degeneration."[78] Alarmed at the lack of physical fitness of urban volunteers for the Boer War, Britain began a campaign of encouraging hunting and other sports to increase the physical fitness and virility of British youth, a task seen as essential to maintaining the British imperial holdings and racial dominance. The Scouting Movement, begun by Lord Baden-Powell and emphasizing outdoor expeditions, action over reflection, and developing the skills for war, was linked to concerns over military fitness and colonial expansion.[79] In Baden-Powell's *Scouting for Boys* and in many popular adventure books of the time, boys and young men were encouraged to conduct themselves in accordance with the chivalrous values of bravery, sacrifice, honor, and loyalty to the nation and religion.[80]

While this image of the just warrior as defender of civilization at first glance seems to favor the defensive (and, would therefore *not* contribute to the cult of the offensive), a closer look shows that the discourse of the protection racket is actually offensive in three distinct ways. First, it leads states to value offense in order to be the best possible protectors, since offense is associated with increased chance at victory and a perception of an active approach to protection. Second, it allows militaries aspiring to the idealized or hegemonic masculinity to identify those in need of protection outside of its borders, and to start aggressive wars to protect those in need.[81] Third, insomuch as protection is a performance rather than an actual service, the appearance of boldness and bravery in actions taken on behalf of this chivalrous ideal brings attention to the protecting which is being done. In these ways, the protection racket can be associated with the increased likelihood of pursuing offensive military strategies.

The chivalric codes in vogue at the turn of the century identified the vulnerable female body as the main cause for war. The enemy was cast as an inhuman, sexual predator. Propagandists described German attacks on Belgium towns in late summer, 1914 as the "rape of Belgium." The famous World War I propaganda poster illustrates this melding of race and gender: a large brown gorilla-like creature with a bloodied bat labeled "kulter" grasps a half-naked white woman who appears to have fainted. "Destroy this mad brute: Enlist," the poster demands. Posters in Britain encouraging men to volunteer evoked women and children as defenseless targets of war and drew upon chivalric discourses of honor and protection, declaring, "Your rights of citizenship give you the privilege of joining your fellows in defence of your Honour and your Homes," and "There Are Three Types of Men: Those who hear the call and Obey, Those who Delay, and—The Others."[82] Discourses of chivalrous masculinity served not only make offensive approaches to international politics in World War I possible but also to constitute a set of gendered power relations that posited white men as protectors of the nation against racialized others who threaten the purity of naïve and defenseless women.

Examples of the influence of the protection racket on perceived offensive dominance and the cult of the offensive are common in present-day politics as well. This chivalric narrative has been resurrected in the post-Cold War era, and gendered identities have not only legitimated but also promoted wars. The various humanitarian wars of the 1990s are read as a narrative in which NATO, and other actors re-invent themselves as masculine, heroic, rescuers of weak and passive victims.[83] Farmanfarmaian describes how the reports of the Iraqi army raping women in Kuwait were used to construct Iraq as a barbaric enemy so that war was not only thinkable, but necessitated.[84] This new American masculinity was "tough and tender," capable of awesome military prowess but also compassion and empathy.[85]

The mission of "liberating" Afghan women was used to garner public support for the invasion of Afghanistan, and served also to silence feminist protests against the war.[86] Two and a half years later, this same discourse of "liberation" was used to fuel support to overturn the Iraqi regime of Saddam Hussein, represented in racialized terms as an inhuman despot when the evidence against weapons of mass destruction turned out to be fabricated or exaggerated. This narrative of rescuing the Iraqi people (as "damsels in distress") from the clutches of an evil man may help to explain why many people in the US and its allies came to believe, with little evidence, that the invading forces would be "greeted as liberators." These rescue narratives demonstrate that the protection racket encourages offensive military policies even when it is couched in the language of defense and protection. The protection racket is a gender discourse that produces the gender identities of just warriors and beautiful souls. It is also the backdrop that allows for offensive military policies to be viewed as defensive, thereby gaining traction and legitimating war by enabling offensive wars to take place under the mantle of "protection." The existence of discourse of protection can therefore help us understand the occurrence of offensive policies in the light of an ostensible defensive dominance.

Conclusion

One of the conclusions of the offense–defense literature is that states perceive themselves to be much more insecure than they really are. Van Evera writes, "The prime threat to the security of modern great powers is ... themselves. Their greatest menace lies in their own tendency to exaggerate the dangers they face, and to respond with counterproductive belligerence."[87] While states have been more or less been secure, these feelings of insecurity have led to great insecurity for *people* worldwide. Tens to hundreds of millions of people were killed in wars in the twentieth century alone, to say nothing of those who were injured, lost loved ones, or had their lives disrupted by war.

Van Evera goes on to write, "The causes of this syndrome pose a large question for students of international relations."[88] Feminists have to much offer in regard to this question. Focusing on how gender discourses and gender identities provide a necessary condition under which many of the factors of the offense–defense balance can thrive, feminists offer a way to think about many of the issues related to the causes of war that have been neglected by most scholars of Security Studies. For scholars interested in the offense–defense balance as a way of explaining why wars occur, feminist analysis can contribute to both defensive realists who consider wars to begin because of the perceptions of the offense–defense balance, as well as scholars who support the offensive realist position that states start wars regardless of their calculations of the offense–defense balance. Thus, despite the recent debate between Lieber and Snyder about whether or not a cult of the offensive was the key factor in Germany's offensive war plans,[89] feminist analysis of nationalism and the protection racket provides insights into the underlying conditions that make preventative or pre-emptive wars possible in terms of anxieties over gender and racial identities and gendered discourses of military strength and the benefits of war. Feminists argue that offensive wars are based on similar concerns over gender relations and the nation, making offensive wars appear to be legitimately "defensive." As Snyder argues, "The belief in the feasibility and necessity of offensive strategy entices both fearful and greedy aggressors to attack [and] erases the distinction between security and expansion,"[90] the gendered constitution of the cult of the offensive applies to states acting out of fear or expansion. The feminist analyses of the role gender plays in constituting the perception of technology, the gendered ideologies of nationalism, and the gendered "defensive" logic of the protection racket support this view of the erasure of the distinction between security and expansion. A feminist analysis would understand gendered ideologies and identities to be at the root of both strategies, with their particular historical manifestations leading to variation in the specific forms that militarism takes.

Far from being only concerned with the status of women, feminists use the concept of gender to analyze the workings of power through gendered discourses and identities. Gender matters in the ways in which technologies are perceived and used, as well as in formulating offensive military strategies. Gendered perceptions of technology, gendered discourses of nationalism, and the "protection racket" are three related ways in which offensive wars are legitimated, and thus enabled. By explaining the impact gender has on issues related to the perception of offense–defense balance, feminist analysis shows how gender discourses and the production of gender identities are not confined to individuals and the private realm, but rather are a pervasive fact of social life on an international scale. International Relations theorists concerned with determining the causes of war would do well to consider the ways in which gender can shape the conditions under which wars occur.

Notes

1 Stephen Biddle, "Rebuilding the Foundations of Offense–Defense Theory," *Journal of Politics* 63, no. 3 (2001): 741–74.
2 See, for example, Robert Jervis, "Cooperation under the Security Dilemma," in *Offense, Defense, and War*, eds., Michael E. Brown *et al.* (Cambridge, MA: MIT Press, 1998), pp. 3–65; George Quester, *Offense and Defense in the International System* (New York: John Wiley & Sons, 1977); Jack Levy, "The Offensive/ Defensive Balance of Military Technology: A Theoretical and Historical Analysis," *International Studies Quarterly.* 28(2) (June 1984); Charles Glaser and Chaim Kaufmann, "What is the Offense–defense Balance and Can We Measure It?" in *Offense, Defense and War*, eds., Michael E. Brown *et al.* (Cambridge, MA: MIT Press., 1998); Stephen Van Evera, "The Cult of the Offensive and the Origins of the First World War," in *Offense, Defense, and War*, eds., Michael E. Brown *et al.* (Cambridge, MA: MIT Press, 1998), pp. 69–118; Stephen Van Evera, "Offense, Defense and the Causes of War," *International Security* 22 no. 4 (1998); and *Causes of War: Power and Roots of Conflict* (Ithaca, NY: Cornell University Press, 1999); Stephen Biddle, "Rebuilding the Foundations."
3 Van Evera, "Offense, Defense and the Causes of War," p. 263.
4 Van Evera, "The Cult of the Offensive," p. 69.
5 Ibid., p. 72.
6 Ibid., pp. 73, 77.
7 The security dilemma describes a situation in which means taken by one state to increase its security render other states more insecurity. Jervis, "Cooperation Under the Security Dilemma," p. 169.
8 Ibid., pp. 46–50.

9 Lynn Jones, "Offense–defense Theory and Its Critics," pp. 675–7.

10 Jack Snyder, *The Ideology of the Offensive: Military Decision Making and the Disasters of 1914* (Ithaca, NY: Cornell University Press, 1984); Van Evera, "Offense, Defense, and the Causes of War," p. 228; Keir A. Leiber, *War and the Engineers: The Primacy of Politics over Technology* (Ithaca, NY: Cornell University Press, 2005).

11 Ted Hopf, "Polarity, Military Balance, and War," *American Political Science Review* 85, no. 2 (June 1991): 475–93.

12 Lynn-Jones, "Offense–defense Theory and Its Critics," p. 681.

13 Van Evera, "Offense, Defense and the Causes of War," p. 263.

14 The existence of an objective offense–defense balance is problematic from a feminist perspective for a number of reasons. First, it assumes that there is a context in which it is "rational" to go to war, such as in certain "windows of opportunity." The main problem is in properly discerning the most and least advantageous times. Feminists have challenged the legitimacy of the realist assumptions that underpin this logic (see, for example, Ann Tickner, *Gender in International Relations* (New York: Columbia University Press, 1992), pp. 27–66; Ann Tickner, *Gendering World Politics* (New York: Columbia University Press, 2001)).

15 Alexander Wendt, *Social Theory of International Politics* (New York: Cambridge University Press, 1999), pp. 77–91.

16 Alexander Wendt, "On Constitution and Causation in International Relations," *Review of International Studies* 24, no. 1 (1998): 105.

17 V. Spike Peterson and Jacqui True, "'New Times' and New Conversations," in *The "Man" Question in International Relations*, eds., M. Zalewski and J. Parpart. (Boulder, CO: Westview Press, 1999), p. 16.

18 V. Spike Peterson, "Transgressing Boundaries: Theories of Knowledge, Gender, and International Relations," *Millennium: Journal of International Studies* 21, no. 2 (June 1992): 194.

19 B. Locher and E. Prügl, "Feminism and Constructivism," *International Studies Quarterly* 45, no. 1 (2001): 123–4.

20 See R.W. Connell, *Masculinities* (Berkeley, CA: University of California Press, 1995), p. 76; and Charlotte Hooper, *Manly States: Masculinities, International Relations, and Gender Politics* (New York: Columbia University Press, 2001), pp. 53–6.

21 See, for example, Iris Marion Young, "The Logic of Masculinist Protection: Reflections on the Current Security State," *Signs: Journal of Women, Culture and Society* 29 no. 2 (2003): 15–35.

22 Jervis, "Cooperation Under the Security Dilemma," p. 35.

23 Feminist work in IR that takes up this critique includes Ann Tickner, "What is Your Research Program? Some Feminist Answers to International Relations Methodological Questions," *International Studies Quarterly* 49, no. 1 (2005): 1–20, Tickner, "You Just Don't Understand: Troubled Engagements Between Feminist and IR Theorists," *International Studies Quarterly* 41, no. 4 (1997): 619–23; V. Spike Peterson, "Transgressing Boundaries," and Locher and Prügl, "Feminism and Constructivism". See also Brooke Ackerly, Maria Stern and Jacqui True, eds., *Feminist Methodologies for International Relations* (Cambridge: Cambridge University Press, 2006).

24 The feminist literature on the masculine underpinnings of science and technology is quite vast. A few influential works include Evelyn Fox Keller, *Reflections on Science and Gender* (New Haven, CT: Yale University Press, 1985); Sandra Harding, *The Science Question in Feminism* (Ithaca, NY: Cornell University Press, 1986); and *Whose Science? Whose Knowledge?* (Ithaca, NY: Cornell University Press, 1991); Carolyn Merchant, *The Death of Nature: Women, Ecology and the Scientific Revolution* (San Francisco: Harper & Row, 1980).

25 Max Boot, *War Made New: Technology, Warfare, and the Course of History, 1500 to Today* (New York: Gotham Books, 2006), pp. 22, 59, 88.

26 Rachel N. Weber, "Manufacturing Gender in Military Cockpit Design," in *The Social Shaping of Technology*, eds. Donald MacKenzie and Judy Wajcman, (Philadelphia, PA: The Open University Press, 1999), pp. 372–81.

27 See Linda Robertson, *The Dream of Civilized Warfare: World War I Flying Aces and the American Imagination* (Minneapolis: University of Minnesota Press, 2003), pp. 324–6.

28 For the use of World War I and offense–defense theory, see Van Evera, "The Cult of the Offensive"; Jack Snyder, "Civil-Military Relations and the Cult of the Offensive, 1914 and 1984," in *Offense, Defense and War*, ed. Michael E. Brown *et al.* (Cambridge, MA: MIT Press, 1998), pp. 119–57.

29 Van Evera, "The Cult of the Offensive," p. 71.

30 Ibid., pp. 72, 71.

31 Michael Howard, "Men Against Fire: Expectations of War in 1914," in *Military Strategy and the Origins of the First World War*, eds., S.E. Miller, S. M. Lynn-Jones; and S. Van Evera (Princeton, NJ: Princeton University Press, 1991), p. 8, see also John Ellis, *The Social History of the Machine Gun* (Baltimore, MD: The Johns Hopkins University Press, 1975), pp. 79–111.

32 Jack Snyder, *The Ideology of the Offensive: Military Decision Making and the Disasters of 1914* (Ithaca and London: Cornell University Press, 1984), pp. 137–8.

33 Mark Hewitson, *Germany and the Causes of World War I* (New York: Berg, 2004), pp. 94–5.

34 Snyder, *The Ideology of the Offensive.*

35 Van Evera, "The Cult of the Offensive," p. 72.

36 Jack Snyder, "Civil-Military Relations and the Cult of the Offensive, 1914 and 1984," in *Offense, Defense and War*, eds., Brown *et al.* (Cambridge, MA: MIT Press, 1998), p. 130.

37 Francis Fukuyama, "Women and the Evolution of World Politics," *Foreign Affairs* 77, no. 5 (1998): 24–40.

38 Joshua Goldstein, *War and Gender: How Gender Shapes the War System and Vice Versa* (Cambridge: Cambridge University Press, 2001), pp. 143–58.

39 See Francine D'Amico and Laurie Weinstein, *Gender Camouflage: Women and the US Military* (New York: New York University Press, 1999), p. 5; Jean Bethke Elshtain, *Women and War* (Chicago: University of Chicago Press, [1987] 1995), Hooper, *Manly States*, pp. 81–2.

40 Cynthia Enloe, *Maneuvers: The International Politics of Militarizing Women's Lives* (Berkeley, CA: University of California Press, 2000), p. 237.

41 Johanna Bourke, *Dismembering the Male: Men's Bodies, Britain and the Great War* (Chicago: University of Chicago Press, 1996).

42 Enloe, *Maneuvers*, p. 245.

43 Peterson, "Transgressing Boundaries," p. 194.

44 Barry Posen, *The Sources of Military Doctrine* (Ithaca, NY: Cornell University Press, 1984).

45 Snyder, *The Ideology of the Offensive*, p. 123. See also Hewitson, *Germany and the Causes of World War I*, p. 97.

46 David Englander, "Discipline and Morale in the British Army," in *State, Society and Mobilization in Europe During the First World War*, ed., John Horne (Cambridge: Cambridge University Press, 1997), p. 126.

47 Hooper, *Manly States*, pp. 80–7; see also Adams, *The Great Adventure: Male Desire and the Coming of World War I* (Bloomington, IN: Indiana University Press, 1990).

48 Goldstein, *War and Gender*, Chapter 5.

49 Carol Cohn, "War, Wimps and Women: Talking Gender and Thinking War," in *Gendering War Talk*, eds., M. Cooke and A. Woollacott (Princeton, NJ: Princeton University Press, 1993) pp. 227–46; and Carol Cohn, "Sex and Death in the Rational World of Defense Intellectuals," *Signs: Journal of Women in Culture and Society*, 12, no. 4 (1987): 687–718.
50 Cohn, "War, Wimps and Women," p. 232.
51 See, for example, Glaser and Kaufmann, "What Is the Offense–defense Balance?," pp. 288–9.
52 Robert Jervis, *Perception and Misperception in International Relations* (Princeton, NJ: Princeton University Press, 1976), pp. 319–21.
53 Ibid., pp. 323–6.
54 Ibid., pp. 338–42.
55 David Campbell, *Writing Security: United States Foreign Policy and the Politics of Difference* (Minneapolis: University of Minnesota Press, 1998), p. 68.
56 See John Dower, *War without Mercy: Race and Power in the Pacific War* (New York: Pantheon Books, 1986), pp. 94–7.
57 Ibid., pp. 99–117.
58 George Robb, *British Culture and the First World War* (Basingstoke, Hampshire: Palgrave, 2002), p. 8; Susan Kingsley Kent, *Gender and Power in Britain, 1640–1990* (London: Routledge, 1999), p. 239.
59 Stephen Van Evera, "Hypotheses on Nationalism and War," *International Security* 18 no. 4 (1994): 27 fn 42.
60 Nira Yuval-Davis, *Gender and Nation*, p. 43.
61 Joane Nagel, "Ethnicity and Sexuality," *Annual Review of Sociology*, 26 (2000): 107–33.
62 For further examples of the ways in which feminists have interrogated nationalism, and for greater detail about the differences between anti-colonial, postcolonial, settler-state and other types of nationalisms, see Jan Jindy Pettman, *Worlding Women: a Feminist International Politics* (New York: Routledge, 1996), pp. 45–63; and Jill Vickers, "Feminists and Nationalism," in *Gender, Race and Nation: Global Perspectives*, eds., J. Vickers and V. Dhruvarajan (Toronto: University of Toronto Press), 2002.
63 Anne McClintock, "Family Feuds, Gender, Nationalism and the Family," *Feminist Review* 44 (Summer 1993): 62.
64 V. Spike Peterson, "Sexing Political Identities/Nationalism as Heterosexual," *International Feminist Journal of Politics*, 1, no. 1 (1999): 48–9; see also Carole Pateman, *The Sexual Contract* (Stanford, CA: Stanford University Press, 1988).
65 Robb, *British Culture and the First World War*, pp. 32–6; Ilana R. Bet-El, "Men and Soldiers: British Conscripts, Concepts of Masculinity, and the Great War," in *Borderlines: Genders and Identities in War and Peace, 1870–1930*, ed., Billie Melman (New York: Routledge, 1998), pp. 73–94.
66 Susan Kingsley Kent, "The Politics of Sexual Difference: World War I and the Demise of British Feminism," *The Journal of British Studies* 27, no. 3 (1988): 232–53.
67 Elshtain, *Women and War*, pp. 111–12.
68 Nira Yuval-Davis, *Gender and Nation* (London: Sage, 1997) and Floya Anthias and Nira Yuval-Davis, *Women-Nation-State* (New York: St. Martin's Press, 1989).
69 Peterson, "Sexing Political Identities," p. 39.
70 George L. Mosse, *Nationalism and Sexuality* (Madison, WI: The University of Wisconsin Press, 1985), pp. 90–100.
71 Laura Sjoberg, *Gender, Justice, and the Wars in Iraq* (Lanham, MD: Lexington Books, 2006), p. 35.
72 Elshtain, *Women and War*, pp. 3–13.
73 Iris Marion Young, "Feminist Reactions to the Contemporary Security Regime," *Hypatia* 18, no. 1 (Winter 2003): 224.

74 Elshtain, *Women and War*, p. 140.

75 Young, "Feminist Reactions to the Contemporary Security Regime," p. 230.

76 See Robertson, *The Dream of Civilized Warfare*, pp. 115–54; Leo Braudy, *From Chivalry to Terrorism: War and the Changing Nature of Masculinity* (New York: Alfred A. Knopf, 2003), pp. 288–90,

77 Adams, *The Great Adventure*; Goldstein, *War and Gender*, pp. 275–6; and Braudy, *From Chivalry to Terrorism,*pp. 281–4.

78 See, for example, Adams, *The Great Adventure*; Holger Herwig, "Germany," in eds., Richard F. Hamilton and Holger Herwig, *The Origins of World War I* (Cambridge: Cambridge University Press, 2003), pp. 150–88; Susan Kingsley Kent, *Gender and Power in Britain, 1640–1990* (London: Routledge, 1999), pp. 236–42; and Pat Thane, "The British Imperial State and the Construction of National Identities," in *Borderlines: Genders and Identities in War and Peace, 1870–1930*, ed., Billie Melman (New York: Routledge, 1998), pp. 30–1.

79 Angela Woollacott, *Gender and Empire* (Basingstroke: Palgrave Macmillan, 2006), pp. 75–7; and Cynthia Enloe, *Bananas, Beaches and Bases* (Berkeley, CA: University of California Press, 1990), pp. 48–51.

80 Bet-El, "Men and Soldiers," pp. 78–9, Kent, *Gender and Power in Britain*, pp. 237–9.

81 For example, the legitimation of the US war in Afghanistan to protect Afghan women from Afghan men.

82 Ilana R. Bet-El, "Men and Soldiers," p. 82.

83 Anne Orford, "Muscular Humanitarianism: Reading the Narratives of the New Interventionism," *European Journal of International Law* 10, no. 4 (1999): 679–711.

84 Abouali Farmanfarmaian, "Did You Measure Up? The Role of Race and Sexuality in the Gulf War," in *The Geopolitics Reader* ed., G. Tuathail (London: Routledge, 1998), pp. 286–93.

85 Steve Niva, "Tough and Tender: New World Order Masculinity and the Gulf War," in *The "Man" Question in International Relations*, eds., Marysia Zalewski and Jane Parpart (Boulder, CO: Westview Press, 1998), pp. 109–28.

86 See, for example, Zillah Eisenstein, "Feminisms in the Aftermath of September 11," *Social Text* 72, vol. 20, no. 3 (Fall 2002): 79–99; Hilary Charlesworth and Christine Chinkin, "Sex, Gender and September 11," *The American Journal of International Law* 96, no. 3 (July 2002): 600–5.

87 Van Evera, *Causes of War*, p. 192.

88 Ibid.

89 Lieber, "The New History of World War I"; and Jack Snyder and Kier Lieber, "Defensive Realism and the 'New' History of World War I," *International Security* (Summer 2008): 174–94.

90 Snyder, "Defensive Realism and the 'New' History of World War I," p. 177.

5   Gendering power transition theory

Laura Sjoberg

According to Douglas Lemke, "in recent decades, America's power advantage over China has diminished substantially."[1] While some predict that "short of a catastrophic nuclear war or domestic disintegration, one cannot but anticipate the emergence of China as the largest and most productive nation in the international system,"[2] others "suggest that Chinese under-development means that it will take more time before the GDP transition can be translated into a relative power advantage."[3] In this time of uncertainty about China's development as a superpower, power transition theorists contend that, "the choice between China as a 'strategic partner' and China as a 'strategic competitor' looms large" because it could make the difference between a peaceful transition between satisfied powers and a war-like one.[4]

One of the major approaches to the "China question" in political science is the power transition research program.[5] Power transition theory (PTT) argues that China is rising to challenge US hegemony, and that the question of whether or not there will be a conflict turns on whether China is satisfied with the existing international order at the time of the transition. This chapter examines the PTT research program and its predictions about China from a feminist perspective.

Feminist work has argued that research programs that fail to consider gender as a causal variable and a constitutive element lack explanatory power and empirical validity. Specifically, the omission of gender from PTT gives it a partial conceptual and empirical view of international security. The chapter begins with an introduction to the central tenets of PTT. The second section uses feminists' insights to ask how PTT contains, reproduces, and reflects gender relations, gender stereotypes, and gender subordination.[6] This section critiques PTT's concept of power, its choice of actors, and the omission of gender-based variables. The third section presents a feminist analysis of the core hypotheses of the power transition research program. The chapter concludes with a brief feminist (re)evaluation of the major empirical prediction of PTT: that China is likely to overtake the US as the dominant state in global politics.

The power transitions research program and the rise of China

PTT has been heralded as "one of the most successful structural theories of world politics."[7] Scholars within the power transition research program tout both their causal explanations and "specific management tools" to ensure peace.[8] Like realism, PTT contends that states are self-interested, rational, unitary actors that seek relative gains against competitors.[9] Unlike realism, however, "power transition theory describes a hierarchical system"[10] in which "one state has already established an edge in relative power over the others."[11] The dominant nation "shapes the 'international order' in which relations between states are stable and follow certain patterns and even rules of behavior promoted by the dominant power."[12]

PTT sees hegemony as a peaceful equilibrium, and threats to dominance as the major source of conflict. PTT characterizes a state as dominant when it has "the ability to impose on or persuade [any] opponent to comply with demands."[13] As Rapkin and Thompson explain, according to power transition theorists, "around the time that the bigger fish catches up to the smaller fish and establishes parity, conflict between the challenger and the once-dominant power becomes more likely."[14] As such, "the probability of war between the rising challenger and the dominant state peaks near the point of power transition between them."[15] Transitions are especially dangerous when the challenger is dissatisfied with the status quo.

Power transition theorists see satisfaction as the linchpin that determines whether or not war occurs during transition.[16] The dominant state, which created the international order, is by definition satisfied. Other states, however "have grown to full power after the existing order was fully established and the benefits already allocated."[17] In such an order, "jointly satisfied nations are expected to be the most cooperative and to face the lowest probability of conflict" because they have a mutual interest in the preservation of the status quo.[18] On the other hand, dissatisfied nations are more likely to risk conflict to change their unfavorable lot with policies "dominated by attempts to maximize relative gains"[19] whenever they can "reasonably anticipate military success."[20] However, war is not inevitable. Instead, it should be "the principal objective of the dominant power and its closest allies ... to expand satisfaction in the international arena."[21] If the dominant state can alter the structure of the system substantially enough to bring the challenger into a position of satisfaction, a peaceful transition could occur.

In sum, the three major hypotheses generated by the power transitions research program are:[22]

(H1) The higher the position of a nation in the international hierarchy, on the basis of national capabilities, the more often that nation will go to war.

(H2) The greater and more stable the concentration of power in the international system, the more peaceful that system will be.

(H3) Major war is more likely when a great power's external and internal capabilities are overtaken by those of another great power. Speedy transitions are more likely to cause wars than slow ones. War is most likely at the time the internal and external capabilities of two great states are equally distributed.

Organski and Kugler found support for "the hypothesis that the combination of parity and transition is conducive to major war."[23] Power transitions theorists have found that "among those states capable of contending for global leadership, no wars take place without a transition; in addition, half of the observed transitions were followed by the outbreak of war."[24] Several empirical studies have characterized PTT hypotheses as "robust" and identified the combination of dissatisfaction and parity as a leading identifier of great power war.[25]

According to power transition theorists, the US is dominant but in decline.[26] Power transition theorists contend that the US should attempt to "co-opt" challengers by reinforcing commitments to the status quo.[27] Certainly, "if rates of economic growth and military modernization ... are extrapolated into the future, not too many more decades will pass before China is able to mount a significant challenge to the predominant position of the U.S."[28] In this situation, Efird, Kugler, and Genna explain that:

If the U.S. and China are satisfied with the *status quo*, then high levels of cooperation are possible by 2050, avoiding the possibility of conflict. If, on the other hand, the two nations are dissatisfied with each other, a major war between these two nuclear powers remains a distinct possibility.[29]

In light of a "series of militarized disputes" between the two states, it is not impossible "to imagine how a U.S.–China war could begin."[30]

Because of these potential dangers, PTT recommends that the US either look for peaceful transition strategies or prepare for conflict.[31] PTT offers "policy prescriptions that [power transition theorists] hope the U.S. will employ to successfully manage its long-term decline relative to China,"[32] including the suggestion that the US co-opt China as a strategic partner.[33] Lemke explains "the United States can encourage reforms within China that could make it a satisfied state,"[34] or try to convince China that its interests mirror US interests.

Toward a feminist perspective on PTT

A feminist approach suggests several critiques of the PTT research agenda which question the accuracy of its causal explanations, the normative value of its definitions, and the appropriateness of its empirical predictions. Feminists argue that gender expectations and assumptions are a constitutive and causal force in global politics.[35] PTT's failure to acknowledge gender in global politics is reflected in its definition of power, its normative commitment to elitist assumptions about the relevant actors in global politics, and the variables used to explain empirical phenomena.

Power in power transition theory

Power transition theorists see power as "the ability to impose one state's will on another."[36] Feminists identify this interpretation as "power-over"[37] and critique its conceptual narrowness and gendered content.[38] Power-over means that ideologies "suit the changing interests of those in power, and not those whose lives are controlled by them."[38]

This is particularly evident in PTT's explanation of how a state obtains power(-over). PTT explains the acquisition of power as having three dimensions: population, productivity, and political efficiency.[40] As Tammen *et al.* explain, "population is the sine qua non for great power status" because it is "the potential resource pool that a nation can begin to mobilize for its economic development" and "ultimately determines in the long run which nations will remain major powers."[41] Power transition theorists seem unaware that women's rights vary inversely with population increases.[42] The same is true of labor productivity. States that increase labor productivity do so by augmenting the export sector. Women fill these new jobs, which are underpaid and risky. Women who had previously been in the household are often still expected to fulfill their household functions.[43]

PTT's view of power also sets up future conflicts. Power-over means that the accumulation of power is necessarily competitive *and* zero-sum, making conflict likely if not necessary. Viewing power as zero-sum also presumes a stark distinction between self(state) and other(state) where the advantages of accumulated power can be confined to its accumulator. Some states (even "great states") are not primarily or even secondarily concerned with the competitive acquisition of power.[44] In a globalized world, not all power acquisitions are zero-sum. Presuming the necessity of competition puts global politics on a path towards conflict, and assuming that power acquisitions can be contained misrepresents the distribution of gains.

Feminists argue that people and states without power-over are not powerless. As Allen argues, "To think about power solely in terms of domination neglects the power that women do have ... empowerment."[45] In fact, "the need to theorize power that women retain in spite of masculine domination" has led feminists to explore different sources and manifestations of power. Two important results are understandings of power which Allen categorizes as "power-to" and "power with."[46] Power-to is "the capacity of an agent to act in spite of or in response to power wielded over her by others" (i.e., rebellion or revolt).[47] Power-with is the ability to act in concert with other weak actors to match the strength of the dominant power.[48] In this interpretation, "by emphasizing plurality and community ... [feminist theory] consciously seeks to distance power from domination" and understands power "collaboratively."[49]

PTT's inability to see power-to and power-with decreases its explanatory value. PTT cannot explain why the weak start wars they cannot win (power-to),[50] or gather international political capital to find a mutual and peaceful solution (power-with).[51] Power-to or power-with "represent analytically distinguishable features of a situation."[52]

Given this, it is incumbent on power transition theorists to look at power *as a whole* in order to understand the role of power. This means observing and analyzing power-to and power-with and looking at the ways in which these different facets of power come to be mapped onto international politics. A feminist understanding of power demonstrates that power is a scaffolding of "multiple and overlapping power relations."[53] A feminist critique notes the narrowness of the PTT's definition of power and draws attention to the omission of gender.

The primacy of the great state in power transition theory

PTT focuses on great states to explain the dynamics of international security. Power transition theorists explain that PTT "attacks the central issue of world politics—great power stability."[54] Great power stability matters because the dominant state defines the structure of the international system. Feminist perspectives question both the state-centrism of PTT and its focus on big states.

First, feminists interrogate the state-centrism of PTT. PTT assumes that the state is unitary with definable interests. Feminists define security in broad terms. In these terms, a "secure" world would be one without physical, structural,[55] or ecological violence.[56] Security threats are also found in threats to individual lives at the margins of global politics, such as hunger, disease, sexual violence, and small arms.[57]

Feminist research has shown how those at the political margins can become insecure even while states are becoming more secure. Women's bodies have been considered the means to an end in debates over the US security force in South Korea, the prevalence of and possible solutions to AIDS, and debates about refugee camp composition, to name a few.[58] These threats are often more vicious than the threat of great power war.[59]

Because many feminists see individual security as central, they critique the hierarchy that PTT values. Feminist theorizing, as a "commitment to understanding the world from the perspective of the socially subjugated," recognizes that the least fortunate are the people who are excluded from the consideration of decision-makers and grand theorists.[60] Feminist theorists have been critical of hierarchy for the pressure that it puts on the "bottom."

PTT does not share this interest. In PTT, "the international system is viewed as a pyramid-shaped hierarchy" where "at the very top tier is the system's dominant power. The next tier contains the great powers, followed by the medium and small powers."[61] PTT's policy prescriptions demonstrate that power transition theorists not only see the model as *accurate*, they believe it is *beneficial*. Tammen *et al.* characterize small powers as irrelevant because they "pose no threat to the dominant nation's leadership in the international system."[62] PTT suggests that a dominant nation should convince challengers to live in a world stacked against their interest, because "a dominant nation that successfully co-opts potential challengers ensures that the international status quo will be preserved."[63] In other words, PTT has a normative investment in a hierarchical international system.

Rather than endorse domination, some feminist theorists argue that empathy and care should be seen as alternatives to domination. Christine Sylvester explains that "empathy rests on the ability and willingness to enter into the feeling or spirit of something and appreciate it fully. It is to hear ... and be transformed in part by our appreciation."[64] An empathetic approach "enables respectful negotiations with contentious others because we can recognize involuntary similarities across difference as well as differences that mark independent identity."[65] As such, "there is no arrogance of uniqueness" and "precious little committed defensiveness."[66] Instead of an international structure which excludes most citizens of the world, some feminists suggest connectedness as an alternative structure.[67]

Explanatory variables in great power politics

Gender dynamics also act on the empirical phenomena PTT studies. Even taking the subject matter of PTT (great power competition) on its own merits, feminist analyses question the causal mechanisms that PTT uses. PTT considers power parity and dissatisfaction. These variables cannot explain the events of interest to PTT for two major reasons. First, while the power transition scenario envisions a possibility that a peaceful power transition takes place where the challenger is satisfied, the internal logic of PTT makes that a contradiction in terms. Elsewhere, PTT explains that other states are dissatisfied with the status quo international order because it was put in place by the hegemon for its own benefit.[68] Challengers are, by definition, dissatisfied. Second, parity of material power-over can be very different depending on the influence of power-to and power-with.

Additional forces may be acting on the propensity of great powers to come into conflict. One such force is international system patriarchy. Patriarchy is "the structural and ideological system that perpetuates the privileging of masculinity."[69] Feminists have identified "patriarchy as a principal cause for so many of the world's processes [such as] empire-building, globalization, modernization."[70] Enloe details:

> Patriarchal systems are notable for marginalizing the feminine. That is, insofar as any society or group is patriarchal, it is there that it is comfortable—unquestioned—to infantilize, ignore, trivialize, or even actively cast scorn upon what is thought to be feminized.[71]

In an international system of patriarchy, one would expect that dominance would be the ultimate place of honor, and states would strive to approximate that position. Feminist work suggests that international system patriarchy could be a key explanatory component of great power (and other) conflict in the international arena.[72] PTT's research question might be rephrased to ask why, at the moment of equality, great powers are most likely to engage in conflict. Feminists might suggest that relatively equal great powers come to blows because of state masculinity.

States compete to prove their masculinity, irrespective of power parity. For example, as Ann Tickner explains, "The 1991 Persian Gulf War was frequently depicted as a personal contest between Saddam Hussein and George H. W. Bush and described in appropriate locker-room or football language."[73] In states' competitions, the winner's masculinity is affirmed, while the loser's masculinity is subordinated. In the dominant narrative of the First Gulf War, the US' "tough but tender" ideal-typical masculinity saved Kuwait's helpless femininity from Iraq's "hypermasculinity."[74] The masculinity of the US was affirmed and valorized while Iraq's masculinity was called into doubt.[75]

Feminist theorists have used the term "hegemonic masculinity" as an analytical tool to understand this competition. According to Charlotte Hooper, "Hegemonic masculinity is constructed in relation to a range of subordinated masculinities in opposition to femininity."[76] In describing a state's hegemonic masculinity, feminists argue that "the state organizational practices are structured in relation to the reproductive arena."[77] An ideal-typical masculinity establishes cultural hegemony through moral persuasion and consent, entrenched ideological ascendency, and an ethos of coercion.[78] Hegemonic masculinity consists of the attributes that "are most widely subscribed to—and least questioned—in a given social formation: the 'common sense' of gender as subscribed to by all men save those whose masculinity is oppositional or deviant."[79] Each hegemonic masculinity is the set of standards to which men are expected to aspire.

Hegemonic or ideal-typical masculinities have been linked to states' contextual understandings of heroism on the battlefield. Feminists have argued that "some men fight wars while other men *could* fight wars; war-fighting is always tied to the image of masculinity."[80] Judith Gardam has explained that, often, "the social construct of what it is to be male ... is represented by the male warrior, the defender of the security of the state."[81] In these models, "masculinity, virility, and violence have been linked together."[82]

Feminists have long argued that hegemonic masculinities and subordinate masculinities play a role in ordering the international system.[83] For example, Steve Niva describes the hegemonic "tough but tender" US masculinity during the First Gulf War as valuing bravery on the battlefield and sympathy and care for civilians.[84] A number of feminist scholars have noted that, sometimes, a state's hegemonic masculinity becomes reactionary or "hypermasculine" in response to threat.[85] Feminists have identified elements of state hypermasculinity in the US in the post-9/11 era, as well as in the Spanish-American War and the beginning of the Cold War.[86]

Feminists argue that variations in the characteristics and salience of a state's hegemonic masculinity over time influence state behavior. Feminist research suggests that the question of whether two powerful states come into conflict as they reach "power parity" might result from the characteristics of the ideal-typical masculinity in that state at the time. In such a scenario, conflict becomes more likely when states' hegemonic understandings of masculinity involve conquest, war heroism, competition, aggressiveness, or fighting; or some sense of racial or cultural superiority vis-à-vis a challenger. On the other hand, conflict would be less likely when states' hegemonic understandings of masculinity involved tenderness, stoicism, restraint, or responsibility.

Feminist evaluations of power transition hypotheses

A feminist analysis of PTT needs to reformulate the PTT hypotheses.[87] This section applies the feminist critiques of the mechanism (power), the object (great states), and the variables (power parity and dissatisfaction) that PTT uses to explain international conflict to the reformulation of the major PTT hypotheses. It posits alternative explanations and alternative possible solutions and futures (Table 5.1).

Relative position, state hegemonic masculinity, and bellicosity

Power transition theorists found that "occupation of a high position in the international hierarchy is associated with war involvement, irrespective of other attributes (ideology, etc.) of the state occupying that position."[88] Even if those states at the top of the international hierarchy are more likely to be involved in wars,[89] feminists question the assumption that this is because nations with the capacity to fight wars are necessarily more likely to fight.

Feminist reformulation (R1) (see Table 5.1) posits that the content and salience of a state's hegemonic masculinity will be a factor in its bellicosity. The feminist argument is that the more competitive a state's hegemonic masculinity, the more likely that state is to make war; this risk is compounded by high salience. In World War II Germany, a competitive form of masculinity was very salient. George Mosse's study of the ideal German man[90] in the 1930s reveals him as:

> Tall and muscular, he has no fat on his body and no hair anywhere but on his head. His broad, contoured shoulders narrow to a thin waist. He has a fine colorless chiseled face with a strong prominent square jaw. He is the flawless man ... , not only did he embody the older aristocratic vlues of bravery, courage, and chivarly, but mirroring bourgeois values, he was also disciplined, orderly, and restrained ... The perfect man, therefore, was committed to sacrifice and heroism, in other words, soldierly values that put the nation ahead of the individual.[91]

This German masculinity "increasingly came to be linked to ideas about nationalism."[92] This idea of masculinity became increasingly salient as "the

Table 5.1 Feminist reformulations of power transition hypotheses

Power transition hypothesis	Feminist reformulation
H1) The higher the position of a nation in the international hierarchy, on the basis of national capabilities, the more often that nation will go to war.	R1) The higher the position of a nation in the international hierarchy, combined with the content and salience of the hegemonic masculinity of that nation, will determine how often that nation will go to war. States where the hegemonic masculinity is less aggressive and/or less salient (or even absent) are less likely to engage in conflict than states where the hegemonic masculinity is aggressive or even hypermasculine.
H2) The greater and more stable the concentration of power in the international system, the more peaceful that system will be.	R2) A greater and more stable concentration of power in the international system may lead to less wars between great powers, but will increase international conflict and internal unrest outside of the center of power. Great power competition is likely to draw attention away from the world's worst humanitarian problems.
H3) Major war is more likely when a great power's external and internal capabilities are overtaken by those of another great power. Speedy transitions are more likely to cause war than slow ones. War is most likely when the internal and external capabilities of two great states are equally distributed.	R3) In a patriarchal international system, equality breeds conflict. In an empathetic international system, equality breeds peace.

nationalist press often portrayed Jewish men as the exact opposite of the manly ideal in looks and behavior ... jittery, restless, greedy, selfish, and ... ugly—nearly deformed."[93] In the 1930s, "German fascists ... took the notion of masculinity to its awful, ghastly, and seemingly logical extreme."[94]

Perhaps this can be contrasted with the case of a rising China. Kam Louie, a scholar of Chinese masculinities, explains that while "Western stereotypes of the 'real man' have described the Occidental male as forming his notion of male-self within images of toughness, courageousness, and decisiveness, ... in the Chinese case, the cerebral male model tends to dominate the macho, brawny male."[95] The Communist Revolution in China has further demilitarized Chinese masculinity,[96] since, while "the core meaning of *wen-wu*[97] still revolves around cultural attainment and martial valour ... [ideal-types of masculinity have been shaped by] Communist insistence that able-bodied citizens work [which] ... has generated idealized images of workers and peasants" rather than soldiers.[98] Louie suggests that the current Chinese hegemonic masculinity is less aggressive and militaristic, and that it is both more open and less salient now than it has been previously.[99]

Given these two examples, the feminist reformulation (R1) would expect bellicosity from 1930s Germany rather than contemporary China. The same empirical evidence that PTT uses could instead support a feminist argument that Germany's level of interest in aggressive masculinity made Germany a belligerent state, and that a dissatisfied China would have less interest in war than the 1930s Germany. A feminist reinterpretation would expect that Germans' hypercompetitive hegemonic masculinity in the 1930s would motivate German leaders and citizens to try to subordinate other masculinities, while the Chinese government, following their more cerebral hegemonic masculinity, would place less priority on competition with other states.

Hegemony and peace

PTT claims that the greater and more stable the concentration of power, the more peaceful that system will be. PTT associates peace with the absence of armed conflict between great powers. As such, the world can still be "at peace" if dozens of civil wars are going on in countries outside of the class of "great powers."[100] The dominant/challenger dichotomy means that PTT ignores all but the most powerful states. Instead of limiting the discourse on security to the concerns of the dominant global power and the (few or even only one) challenger(s), feminists pay attention to the entire global political community.

The PTT understanding of "peace" obscures terrible atrocities and conceals a crucial and contradictory effect of the concentration of power in the international arena. Feminist work has consistently shown that, as the powerful wield more power, the weak feel more pressure. This pressure is manifested not only in the form of interstate war, but also in civil war and structural violence.[101] Feminists' interrogation of state centrism suggests that lack of war between great states does not automatically create peace within them,[102] and that the marginalized citizens of great states should be a topic of concern in global politics. Feminists' interest in gender subordination shows that women's security and their lives are constantly at risk.

As such, the feminist reformulation (R2) predicts that concentrated power is a net negative, empirically, normatively, and epistemologically. Empirically, it is likely to increase international conflicts and internal unrest outside of the center of power, and to draw attention away from the world's worst humanitarian disasters. As Ann Tickner notes, much of the violence in the world is outside of great power war and, as theorists, "we in the west can no longer afford to privilege a tradition of scholarship that focuses on the concerns and ambitions of great powers."[103] Feminists reject the dominance of the strong over the weak as a mechanism of control in favor of empathy and connectedness. Epistemologically, feminists note different social experience produces different knowledges.[104] A theory of international security that excludes most people also leaves out important knowledge.[105] An empathetic approach might increase the inclusiveness of knowledge about global politics.

These insights mean that a feminist perspective would draw attention to the security of the people on the margins rather than focusing on an improbable conflict between the US and China. Feminist insights suggest it is important to recognize that in a world where the US and China compete for dominance, more than four billion other people neither compete nor dominate. Decisions made by states with the preponderance of power-over reverberate around the world. If the US and China decided to fight a nuclear war, their decision would be felt around the world. Even less severe decisions by powerful states have wide-ranging impacts on individuals' lives. For example, the US government's decision to condition continued military presence in South Korea on mandatory STD testing in Korean prostitution villages impacted the social and economic dynamic between Korean prostitutes.[106]

Neither the US nor China provides its poorest citizens adequate humanitarian aid to avoid death from starvation or preventable disease.[107] Yet the US and China are the two biggest military spenders in the world.[108] In real terms, the most marginalized citizens of each nation lose when strategic posturing inspires them to focus on military readiness. Feminists have documented how militarization of women's lives decreases freedoms and changes economic and social patterns.[109] Because of the these threats, feminists problematize the assumption that entities called the US and China legitimately merit more consideration than the most marginal citizens within those states or the citizens of states that their dominance subordinates.

International system patriarchy, great state equality, and the risk of war

PTT has found empirical support for the prediction that war is more likely surrounding a power transition between two great states, and most likely when their capabilities are equally distributed.[110] A feminist approach suggests that states' resistance to equality comes from the patriarchal nature of the international system. In such a forum, the dominant masculinity wins by exposing the latent femininity in subordinate masculinities. In a system that values superiority and patriarchy, or a "war system,"[111] violence is the norm and not the exception.

The argument that international system patriarchy is a permissive and instigative cause of great power war is difficult to test because the international system has always been patriarchal. The hypothesis predicts the same result as power transition analysis. Still, the two theories' predictions can be distinguished in times when the challenger does not start a war with the hegemon. The feminist hypothesis places primary emphasis on states' jockeying for position in a hierarchical system. Since jockeying for position can occur without military conflict, the feminist hypothesis expects gendered competition between great powers even when they do not go to war.[112]

The Cold War gives a good example of the distinction made above. It has been said that PTT could not predict the occurrence of the Cold War.[113] PTT would have expected the Soviet Union, approaching equality with the US in the 1950s or 1960s, to start a war in order to reorganize the international system in its interests.[114] The feminist reformulation (R3) suggests that the US and the Soviet Union would compete for the coveted position of apparent (masculine) dominance regardless of the organization of the international system or whether a war occurs. Anecdotal evidence for such a supposition can be found in Carol Cohn's reports that a "well-known academic security adviser was quoted as saying that 'under Jimmy Carter the United States is spreading its legs for the Soviet Union'"[115] or in John F. Kennedy's campaigns for office "promising to halt America's decline into flabbiness and impotence against the threat of a 'ruthless' and expanding Soviet empire."[116] Cynthia Enloe links this competition not to immediate dissatisfaction with the international system, but instead to "the inherent nature of states ... [and] the masculine character of the state elite" competing in a patriarchal international system.[117]

Additional evidence that the feminist explanation is more likely comes from *how* great states come into conflict when they do. The PTT scenario is one where the challenger's dissatisfaction comes from the international system being shaped by the hegemon against the interest of the challenger. The challenger, then, starts a conflict rationally in order to reshape the international system. A war caused by challenger dissatisfaction, then, should be anticipated, started rationally, and fought for goals stated in terms of advancement of national interests in the international system. The scenario that (R3) suggests, however, pictures very different genesis of conflict. The conflict brought about by position-jockeying in a patriarchal system could begin with a series of mistakes or miscommunications. It could be caused by states' mutual unwillingness to step down first, or triggered by some insult to a nation's status, capabilities, or masculinity. An example of such a scenario can be found in the genesis of World War I, which has been described as an accidental war which resulted from competitive national pride and (individual and state) jockeying for position in a hierarchy defined by hegemonic masculinity.[118] Feminist scholars have also noted the relationship between the competition in the Spanish-American War and "US and European male codes of honour" including state "competitiveness, independence, and persistence."[119] These examples suggest the plausibility of the feminist supposition that the patriarchal atmosphere of the international system could have something to do with why states fight wars when they reach relative power parity.

If (R3) is correct, then it is possible to envision great state equality without war in a non-patriarchal international system. In a system that values care and empathy, actors would be interested in the collective security of the world's citizens. Such a system would prioritize understanding, communication, and community. A feminist perspective might imagine challenging great powers to engage in empathetic cooperation, and suggest that major powers take unilateral steps to transgress the cycle of violence in international politics.[120] Each power would engage in purposive compromise of values and interests in order to create peace between them.

In PTT's scenario of potential conflict between the US and China, then, the US should not fear a dissatisfied China or attempt co-option. Instead, it should attempt to understand the interests, values, and needs of those challengers. If challengers took a similar approach, they would not have to choose between unattainable satisfaction and perpetual dissatisfaction. Along these lines, feminists suggest that the US should include China in deliberative dialogues, treat the Chinese government and people with empathy and understanding, and show China and other potential challengers by example that the strong can defy international system patriarchy unilaterally and stop the cycle of violence.[121]

Feminists have argued that inclusive understanding is key to peaceful coexistence. Spike Peterson clarifies that "feminists argue that the domination of women, nature, and all who are constructed as 'other' is not a matter of 'essential,' atemporal qualities but of socially constructed, historically contingent."[122] In other words, the voices of marginalization could serve as a bridge between hostile and masculinized states. In these terms, a dialogue which promoted understanding between the US and China (and their differentiated citizens) would go a long way towards decreasing the potential for conflict between the two great states.

Analyzing the Chinese "overtaking" through gendered lenses

These feminist reformulations of PTT's key hypotheses provide both alternative understandings of the potential for conflict between the US and China and alternative futures. PTT suggests that the question of whether or not that rising will cause conflict between the two states depends on China's satisfaction or dissatisfaction as it approaches parity with the US. A feminist approach suggests that a good deal of the possibility for conflict between the US and China might be explained by gender-related variables. The patriarchal nature of the international system provides an incentive for the US to attempt to maintain dominance. Such a system also gives China a motivation to seek not parity but supremacy. In addition, the cultural salience of masculinity in each society is manifested in each state's desire to compete with the other.

This alternative explanation for the potential competition between the US and China suggests alternative solutions. Realists like Mearsheimer suggest a combined strategy of economic containment and military presence,[123] and power transition theorists suggest attempts to co-opt China into satisfaction with the existing order. Some International Relations scholars outside of the realist paradigm have suggested strategies like GRIT (graduated reciprocation of tension reduction) in order to establish trust between the US and China.[124] If gendered competition and international system patriarchy underlie the competition between the two states, however, none of these strategies will be successful. Mearsheimer's containment strategy will incite more competition; power transition theorists' co-optation strategy is misdirected since dissatisfaction is endemic and would not be China's main motive for making war; and trust-building solutions without the deconstruction of the masculine competition for superiority would just be read as weakness. Seeing gender-as-power both helps explain the potential for conflict between the US and China and provides a theoretical and practical alternative to that competition in recasting the genderings of the state and the international system.

Some feminists prescribe the strong need to unilaterally deconstruct the cycle of violence and masculinized competition between great powers in the international arena. States would need to recognize conflict's basis in competition, posturing, and subordination under patriarchy and deconstruct *that* in order to head off violence. Feminist theorists suggest that the US and China could come to terms with the gendered nature of their competition by dealing with each other in empathy and in dialogue to try to find a deeper sense of understanding if not common ground. The path to an empathetic reconstruction of the relationship between the US and China could begin with the rejection of PTT's claim that hegemonic domination is empirically and normatively valuable. Domination and the resulting subordination, at the international level as well as at the personal level, are normatively problematic. Therefore, even if hegemonic dominance did decrease great power warfare, a feminist approach asks if that would be a sort of peace that the international arena would truly thrive under.

Feminist work has consistently read more content into "peace" than the cessation of great power hot wars. As discussed above, a feminist approach to the rise of China recognizes the contingencies of the entities of the US and China and the limits of focusing on those two states where "others" outnumber them several times over and where their competition makes people within their borders insecure even as the state becomes more secure. A feminist perspective therefore suggests that the US and China (along with other actors traditionally marginalized in global politics) engage in dialogue about what a peaceful and just international system might be, and that the US begin to reshape the international arena *not* to co-opt China but to decrease the pressure of consolidated power in the international arena on those least powerful against it. In doing so, the US and China would need to come to understand themselves and each other as imperfect, non-omnipotent, gendered actors in an imperfect, gendered world—without more right to decide than anyone else simply because they have more power-over.

If the gendered concept of power-over was replaced *both in theory and in practice* with a more inclusive understanding of power including power-to and power-with, different resources could be drawn upon both in the comparative measuring of state power and in redressing the consequences of international hierarchy and subordination at the political margins. A feminist engagement with PTT suggests that great states, small states, and non-states look for places in the complicated scaffolding of international power where non-zero sum, anti-systemic, and even emancipatory uses of power could benefit those at the margins of global politics. Employing a feminist understanding of security could lead the way to creative solutions of resistance and empowerment in the face of a competitive and hierarchical international system. Feminist complex and multilayered understandings of power could not only provide explanatory leverage for great power conflicts, but also for conflicts that defy the logic of PTT.[125]

Conclusion

Feminist theory critiques of PTT's concept of power, its focus on great states, and its omission of gender-based variables inspire reformulations of the hypotheses of the power transition research program which provide alternative accounts of the empirical phenomena that power transition theorists observe and normative critiques of the exclusionary nature of their original critiques. By suggesting alternative causal mechanisms and constitutive factors, a feminist reinterpretation of PTT presents a unique explanation of great power conflict alongside a convincing case that these conflicts should not be the exclusive focus of international security analyses. With its alternative explanatory framework, a feminist approach suggests both that conflict between the US and China is not inevitable and that, if it comes, it will be on different terms and for different reasons than suggested by PTT. As such, a feminist approach to the Chinese "overtaking" of the US both produces a new set of policy recommendations and envisions alternative futures— making a distinct contribution not only to the power transition research program but to international security theory as a whole.

Notes

1 Douglas Lemke, "Investigating the Preventative Motive for War," *International Interactions* no. 29 (2003): 276.
2 Roland L. Tammen, Jacek Kugler, Douglas Lemke, Allan C. Stam III, Mark Abdollahian, Carole Alsharabati, Brian Efird, and A. F. K. Organski, *Power Transitions: Strategies for the 21st Century* (London: Chatham House Publishers, 2000), p. 59.
3 David Rapkin and William R. Thompson, "Power Transition, Challenge, and the (Re)emergence of China," *International Interactions* no. 29 (2003): 321.
4 Brian Efird, Jacek Kugler, and Gaspere Genna, "From War to Integration: Generalizing Power Transition Theory," *International Interactions* no. 29 (2003): 308.
5 See Tammen *et al.*, *Power Transitions*.
6 V. Spike Peterson and Anne Sisson Runyan, *Global Gender Issues*, 2nd edn (Boulder, CO: Westview Press, 1999).
7 Douglas Lemke and Ronald L. Tammen, "Power Transition Theory and the Rise of China," *International Interactions* no. 29 (2003): 269.
8 Tammen *et al.*, *Power Transitions*, p. 4.
9 See, e.g., Inis L. Claude, *Power and International Relations* (New York: Random House, 1962); John J. Mearsheimer, *The Tragedy of Great Power Politics* (New York: W.W. Norton, 2001); Hans J. Morgenthau, *Politics Among Nations* (New York: Alfred A. Knopf, 1948); Kenneth N. Waltz, *Theory of International Politics* (Reading, MA: Addison-Wesley, 1979); Quincy Wright, *A Study of War* (Chicago: University of Chicago Press, 1965).
10 Tammen *et al.*, *Power Transitions*, p. 6. See also Jonathan Dicicco and Jack Levy, "Power Shifts and Problem Shifts: The Evolution of the Power Transition

Research Program," *Journal of Conflict Resolution* 43, no. 6 (1999): 675–704, at p. 679.

11 Rapkin and Thompson, "Power Transition," p. 321

12 Dicicco and Levy, "Power Shifts," p. 681. See also A. F. K. Organski, *World Politics* (New York: Alfred A. Knopf, 1958), pp. 313–16.

13 Tammen *et al.*, *Power Transitions*, p. 7.

14 Rapkin and Thompson, "Power Transition," p. 322.

15 Dicicco and Levy, "Power Shifts," p. 681.

16 Woosang Kim, "Power Transitions and Great Power War from Westphalia to Waterloo," *World Politics* 45, no. 1 (1992): 153–72, at p. 157; Tammen *et al.*, *Power Transitions*, p. 27.

17 Kim, "Power Transitions," p. 157, citing Organski, *World Politics*, p. 366.

18 Tammen *et al.*, *Power Transitions*, p. 11.

19 Ibid., pp. 25, 110.

20 Lemke, "Investigating the Preventative Motive," p. 276.

21 Tammen *et al.*, *Power Transitions*, p. 35.

22 H1 is derived from the research program's claimed centrality of great power politics, and from Tammen *et al.*, Chapter 1. H2 is explicitly stated in Henk Houweling and Jan G. Siccama, "Power Transitions as a Cause of War," *Journal of Conflict Resolution* 32, no. 1 (1988): 89; H3 is a combination of three hypotheses explicitly stated in Kim, "Power Transitions," p. 158.

23 A. F. K. Organski and Jacek Kugler, *The War Ledger* (Chicago: University of Chicago Press, 1980).

24 Dicicco and Levy, "Power Shifts," p. 682.

25 Brian Efird, Jacek Kugler, and Gaspere Genna, "From War to Integration," p. 304.

26 As Houweling and Siccama explain, "the immediate relevance of the power transition hypothesis for the present time should be sought in the demise of American hegemony" while other major powers "might be competing for the succession of US leadership in the world" (in "Power Transitions," pp. 101, 102).

27 Tammen *et al.*, *Power Transitions*, pp. 123, 127.

28 Rapkin and Thompson, "Power Transition," p .316.

29 Ibid., p. 308.

30 Ibid., p. 316.

31 Lemke, "Investigating the Preventative Motive," p. 277.

32 Ibid., p. 277.

33 Efird *et al.*, "From War to Integration," p. 308; Tammen *et al. Power Transitions*, p. 123.

34 Lemke, "Investigating the Preventative Motive," p. 288.

35 J. Ann Tickner, *Gender and International Relations: Feminist Perspectives on Achieving Global Security* (New York: Columbia University Press, 1992).

36 Tammen *et al.*, *Power Transitions*, p. 7.

37 Amy Allen, "Rethinking Power," *Hypatia* 13, no. 1 (1998): 21–40.

38 Elisabeth Prügl, *The Global Construction of Gender: Home-Based Work in the Political Economy of the 20th Century* (New York: Columbia University Press, 1999), p. 6.

39 Peterson and Runyan, *Global Gender Issues*, p. 42.

40 Tammen *et al.*, *Power Transitions,* p. 7.

41 Ibid., p. 19.

42 Ibid., p. 19; S. Correa and R. Reichmann, *Populations and Reproductive Rights: Feminist Perspectives from the Global South* (London: Zed Books, 1994).

43 For detailed analysis, see Naila Kabeer and Simeen Mahmud, "Globalization, Gender, and Poverty: Bangladeshi Women Workers in Export and Local Markets," *Journal of International Development* 16, no. 1 (2003): 93–109.

44 See, e.g., analysis of Britain's "good international citizenship" foreign policy in the late 1990s by Nicholas Wheeler and Tim Dunne, "Good International Citizenship: A Third Way for British Foreign Policy," *International Affairs* 74, no. 4 (1998): 847–70.
45 Amy Allen, *The Power of Feminist Theory: Domination, Resistance, and Empowerment* (Boulder, CO: Westview Press, 1999), p. 122.
46 Ibid., p. 24.
47 Ibid., p. 34.
48 Ibid, p. 35; Jean Bethke Elshtain, "Reflections on War and Political Discourse: Realism and Feminism in a Nuclear Age," *Political Theory* 13, no. 1 (1985): 39–57.
49 Allen, "Rethinking Power," p. 36.
50 For example, to the extent that the Arab states surrounding Israel together or the Palestinian community alone has antagonized Israel, that cannot be explained by even a regionalized version of power transition theory—because the Arab states/ the Palestinians are not coming into equal power with Israel and do not have a reasonable hope of "winning" the war in a traditional sense.
51 The Landmines Treaty is an example of the weak using power-with or empowerment in order to gain widespread support for a cause that those who possessed power-over would have neglected.
52 Allen, *The Power of Feminist Theory*, p. 129.
53 Ibid., p. 129.
54 Lemke and Tammen, "Power Transition," p. 270. There are some exceptions to this great-power focus (see, e.g., Chapter 3 of Tammen *et al.*, *Power Transitions*; Woosang Kim, "Power Parity, Alliance, Dissatisfaction, and War in East Asia, 1860–1993," *Journal of Conflict Resolution* 46, no. 5 (2002): 654–71; Gaspere Genna and Taeko Hiroi, "Power Preponderance and Domestic Politics: Explaining Regional Economic Integration in Latin America and the Caribbean, 1960– 97," *International Interactions* 30 no. 2 (April 2004): 143–64), but it is still the dominant derivation of PTT.
55 Structural violence includes economic deprivation, social repression, household violence, and other threats to individual well-being. See Johan Galtung, "Violence, Peace, and Peace Research," *Journal of Peace Research* 6, no. 3 (1969): 167–91.
56 J. Ann Tickner, *Gendering World Politics* (New York: Columbia University Press, 2001).
57 Critical security theorists have also argued for a critical re-evaluation of the subject and object of security. The feminist approach, however, is unique for its understanding that *subordination* is the factor on which human *insecurity* turns.
58 On military-related prostitution, see Katharine Moon, *Sex Among Allies* (New York: Columbia University Press, 1997); on AIDS, see H. Amaro, "Love, Sex, and Power: Considering Women's Realities in HIV Prevention," *American Journal of Psychology* 50, no. 6 (1995): 437–47; on refugee camps (and DDR), see M. J. Toole and R. J. Waldman, "The Public Health Aspects of Complex Emergencies and Refugee Situations," *Annual Review of Public Health*, 18 (1997): 283–312.
59 This is not to argue that great power war does not threaten women's security. Women's security is imperiled by war. Still, the exclusive focus on warfare between great powers neglects many of the women in the world, as well as many of the security threats that most women face. For more information the work of the WomanStats project, see www.womanstats.org.
60 Sarah Brown, "Feminism, International Theory, and the International Relations of Gender Inequality," *Millennium: Journal of International Studies* 17, no. 3 (1988): 461–75, at p. 472.
61 Rapkin and Thompson, "Power Shifts," p. 317. Tammen *et al.* depict the "classic power pyramid" on p. 7 of *Power Transitions*.

62 Tammen *et al.*, *Power Transitions*, p. 6.
63 Ibid., p. 123.
64 Christine Sylvester, *Feminist Theory and International Relations in a Postmodern Era* (Cambridge: Cambridge University Press, 1994), p. 96; Jill Bystudzienski, *Women Transforming Politics: Worldwide Strategies for Empowerment* (Bloomington, IN: Indiana University Press, 1992); Sara Ruddick, *Maternal Thinking: Towards a Politics of Peace* (New York: Houghton-Mifflin, 1989).
65 Christine Sylvester, *Feminist International Relations: An Unfinished Journey* (Cambridge: Cambridge University Press, 2002), p. 119.
66 Ibid., p. 120.
67 Fiona Robinson, *Globalizing Care: Ethics, Feminist Theory, and International Relations* (Boulder, CO: Westview Press, 1999), p. 49.
68 While, in their policy prescriptions, power transition theorists suggest that declining hegemons re-shape the international order to include challengers, they do not give evidence that declining hegemons have ever been able to realize their interest in doing so and successfully include the challenger in the status quo international order.
69 Cynthia Enloe, *The Curious Feminist: Searching for Women in a New Age of Empire* (Berkeley, CA: University of California Press), p. 4.
70 Ibid., p. 6.
71 Ibid., p. 5.
72 Ibid., p. 4.
73 Tickner, *Gender and International Relations*, p. 9.
74 Steve Niva, "Tough and Tender: New World Order Masculinity and the Gulf War," in *The "Man" Question in International Relations*, eds., Marysia Zalewski and Jane Parpart (Boulder, CO: Westview Press, 1998).
75 See, for a similar argument, Laura J. Shepherd, "Veiled References: Constructions of Gender in the Bush Administration Discourse on the Attacks on Afghanistan post-9/11," *International Feminist Journal of Politics* 8, no. 1 (2006): 19–41.
76 Charlotte Hooper, "Masculinist Practices and Gender Politics: The Operation of Multiple Masculinities in IR," in Zalewski and Parpart, eds., *The "Man" Question*, p. 34.
77 R. W. Connell, *Masculinities* (Berkeley, CA: University of California Press, 1995), p. 73.
78 Hooper, "Masculinist Practices," p. 34.
79 John Tosh, "Hegemonic Masculinity and Gender History," in *Masculinities in Politics and War: Gendering Modern History*, eds., Stefan Dudink, Karen Hagemann, and John Tosh (Manchester: Manchester University Press, 2004), p. 55.
80 Sjoberg, *Gender, Justice, and the Wars in Iraq*, p. 97.
81 Judith Gardam, "Gender and Non-Combatant Immunity," *Transnational Law and Contemporary Problems* 3 (1993): 345–70, p. 348.
82 Jill Steans, *Gender and International Relations: An Introduction* (New Brunswick, NJ: Rutgers University Press, 1998), p. 81.
83 Charlotte Hooper, "Masculinities in Transition: The Case of Globalization," in Marianne H. Marchand and Anne Sisson Runyan, eds. *Gender and Global Restructuring* (New York: Routledge, 2000), p. 70.
84 Niva, "Tough and Tender."
85 Jennifer Maruska's work on state hypermasculinity has been key to my understanding of this concept; see, e.g., Chapter 12 of this book.
86 Maruska, this volume; Charlotte Hooper, *Manly States: Masculinities, International Relations, and Gender Politics* (New York: Columbia University Press, 2001), pp. 66, 72.
87 See J. Ann Tickner, "What is Your Research Program? Some Answers to International Relations' Methodological Questions," *International Studies Quarterly* 49, no. 1 (2005): 1–22; Sjoberg, *Gender, Justice, and the Wars in Iraq*.

88 Houweling and Siccama, "Power Transitions," p. 90.

89 Though some credible evidence from liberal peace theory (e.g., J.R. Oneal and Bruce Russett, "Assessing the Liberal Peace with Alternative Specifications," *Journal of Peace Research*, 36 no. 4 (1999): 423–42), democratic peace theory (e.g., Bruce Russett, *Grasping the Democratic Peace* (Princeton, NJ: Princeton University Press, 1993)), and other theorists, rebuts this hypothesis, this chapter is more interested in the critique of its causal logic if it is, as power transition theorists claim, an accurate description of global politics.

90 George Lachmann Mosse, *The Image of Man: The Creation of Modern Masculinity* (Oxford: Oxford University Press, 1996).

91 Bryant Simon, "Review of *The Image of Man*," *Journal of the History of Sexuality* 8, no. 3 (1998): 534–6.

92 Ibid., p. 535.

93 Ibid., p. 535.

94 Ibid., p. 536.

95 Kam Louie, *Theorizing Chinese Masculinity: Society and Gender in China* (Cambridge: Cambridge University Press, 2002), pp. 7–8.

96 This is not to say there is *a* single Chinese masculinity; instead, it indicates that this section is researching and discussing the ideal-typical, or hegemonic, notion of masculinity in Chinese culture.

97 Louie (*Theorizing Chinese Masculinity*) explains Chinese idealized masculinity as bound up in the dyad of *wen-wu* (cultural attainment and martial valor). She explains, however, that while the *wen-wu* label has remained constant, the content of the dichotomy has changed over time – that, for example, in present times, *wen* can be a wide range of things from literary attainment to musical ability, and *wu* can be a variety of things as well, including physical readiness for work (ibid., p. 162).

98 Ibid., p. 161.

99 Ibid., p. 162, where Louie explains that traditional understandings of Chinese masculinity were race-specific, but "this system began to disintegrate in the twentieth century. Chinese Central Television now regularly shows foreign students who have mastered the traditional *wen-wu* arts."

100 Depending on the definition of civil war which is used, civil wars are going on in 2008 in Afghanistan, Algeria, Senegal, Russia (Chechnya), Chad, Colombia, the Ivory Coast, Sudan, Georgia, Israel (Palestine), Iraq, Somalia, Sri Lanka, Ethiopia, the Democratic Republic of Congo, and Uganda – wars which, in their duration, have produced hundreds of thousands if not millions of casualties, but fall outside of the realm of "great power conflict" and are thus largely outside the interest of power transition theory.

101 Brigit Brock-Utne, *Feminist Perspectives on Peace and Peace Education* (New York: Pergamon Press, 1989), p. 44.

102 For example, the fact that Russia is not at war with any other great powers does not make it a state "at peace," and looking into Russia shows a civil war in Chechnya where many of the most marginalized people within Russia's borders face serious security risks.

103 Tickner, *Gender in International Relations*, p. 33. Tickner observes that "faced with a gap in living standards between the rich and the poor that some observers doubt will ever be overcome ... the health of the global economy depends on the health of all of its members."

104 J. Ann Tickner, "Hans Morgenthau's Principles of Political Realism: A Feminist Reformulation," *Millennium: Journal of International Studies* 17, no. 3 (1988): 429–40.

105 Sandra Harding (*Is Science Multicultural?* (Bloomington, IN: Indiana University Press, 1998)) argues for a more inclusive "strong objectivity" which incorporates marginalized perspectives.

106 Moon, *Sex Among Allies*, p. 13.
107 Thomas Pogge, "Priorities of Global Justice," *Metaphilosophy* 32, nos 1–2 (January 2001): 6–24.
108 Concerning China, see Robert Hartfiel and Brian Job, "Raising the Risks of War: Defence Spending Trends and Competitive Arms Processes in East Asia," *Pacific Review* 20, no. 1 (March 2007): 1–22. Concerning the US, see Pavel Yakovlev, "Arms Trade, Military Spending, and Economic Growth," *Defence and Peace Economics* 18, no. 4 (August 2007): 317–48. These are measured in absolute terms; the SIPRI Military Expenditures Database records the US military budget as $528 billion, and the Chinese at $55 billion in 2006. The two powers are also in the top ten military spenders in the world per capita.
109 See Cynthia Enloe, *Bananas, Beaches, and Bases: Making Feminist Sense of International Politics* (Berkeley, CA: University of California Press, 1990); Cynthia Enloe, *Maneuvers: The International Politics of Militarizing Women's Lives* (Berkeley, CA: University of California Press, 2000); Moon, *Sex Among Allies*.
110 Woosang Kim and James D. Morrow, "When do Power Shifts Lead to War?" *American Journal of Political Science*, 36, no. 4 (1992): 896–922.
111 Betty Reardon, *Sexism and the War System* (New York: Teacher's College Press, 1985).
112 For example, arms races, taunting, propaganda wars, brinksmanship.
113 Richard Ned Lebow, "The Long Peace, the End of the Cold War, and the Failure of Realism," *International Organization*, 48, no. 2 (Spring 1994): 249–77.
114 Some suggest that, if the Soviet Union had started a war then rather than relying on economic competition where it was weaker, it might have won (T. W. Wolfe, "Soviet Military Policy" *Survival* 10, no. 1 (January 1968): 2–27; J. K. Mackintosh, *Strategy and Tactics of Soviet Foreign Policy* (Oxford: Oxford University Press, 1962)).
115 Carol Cohn, "Wars, Wimps, and Women: Talking Gender and Thinking War," in *Gendering War Talk*, eds., Miriam Cooke and Angela Wollacott (Princeton, NJ: Princeton University Press, 1993), p. 236.
116 Robert D. Dean, "Masculinity as Ideology: John F. Kennedy and the Domestic Politics of Foreign Policy," *Diplomatic History* 22, no. 1 (1998): 29–53, at p. 30, citing John F. Kennedy, "Are We Up to the Task?" in *The Strategy of Peace* (New York, 1960).
117 Cynthia Enloe, *The Morning After: Sexual Politics at the End of the Cold War* (Berkeley, CA: University of California Press, 1993), p. 46.
118 Michael C. C. Adams, *The Great Adventure: Male Desire and the Coming of World War I* (Indianapolis: Indiana University Press, 1990); Paul F. Lerner, *Hysterical Men: War, Psychiatry, and the Politics of Trauma in Germany, 1890–1930* (Ithaca, NY: Cornell University Press, 2003).
119 See, e.g. Joane Nagel, "Masculinity and Nationalism – Gender and Sexuality in the Making of Nations," in *Nations and Nationalism: A Reader*, eds., Philip Spencer and Howard Wollman (New Brunswick, NJ: Rutgers University Press), p. 113.
120 Jean Bethke Elshtain, ed., *Just War Theory* (New York: New York University Press, 1992).
121 Elshtain, *Just War Theory*; Reardon, *Sexism*; the argument is that war is not only an event, but a constitutive process of a gendered international system, which needs to be interrupted before it is possible to think of "peace."
122 V. Spike Peterson, ed., *Gendered States: Feminist (Re)visions of International Relations Theory* (Boulder, CO: Lynne Rienner Publishers), p. 203.
123 Mearsheimer, "The Future of the American Pacifier," pp. 61–2.
124 For example, Alan R. Collins, "GRIT, Gorbachev, and the End of the Cold War," *Review of International Studies* 24 (1988): 201–19.
125 For example, civil wars, conflicts outside of the center of global politics, terrorism, unwinnable wars, etc.

6 The genders of environmental security

Nicole A. Detraz

Largely since the end of the Cold War, environmental security has come to represent a way for scholars and policy-makers to link the concepts of traditional security scholarship[1] to the environment. Within academia, there are a number of different conceptions of the relationship between the environment and security.[2] Even given the diversity of current work on the environment and security, there has been little systematic work done that examines the intersection between environmental security and gender.[3] This chapter will address the necessity of including gender in the approaches on the environment and security. The environmental security debate exhibits gendered understandings of both security and the environment, and these gendered assumptions and understandings benefit particular people and are often detrimental to others. Examining environmental security through a gender lens gives insight into the gendered nature of global environmental politics and provides crucial redefinitions of the concept that are more useful, both empirically and analytically. Since the various environmental security perspectives have important, unexplored gender dimensions, then these must be uncovered so that the security of humans and the environment can be better protected.

This is an important area of study for several reasons. First, there exists a significant literature on both the gendered impacts of conflict and war,[4] as well as a literature on the intersection between gender and the environment,[5] however, the ideas of these scholars are rarely incorporated into current environmental security perspectives. If there are specific gendered aspects of both security and the environment, it seems logical that the intersections between the two would be explored under the umbrella of environmental security. Second, environmental security has been a topic of discussion recently in major international policy venues. If specific gender implications are not acknowledged, then the policy-making process is not being informed by all the relevant information. Third, if it is found that there are particular gender implications of environmental change for either women or men and these implications negatively impact daily life, then it is important to reveal them to improve strategies of humanitarian aid.

In order to explore gender in environmental security, I will first examine the current scholarly debate on environmental security through gendered lenses, using three categories to outline views of the relationship between the environment and security in the literature and feminist criticisms of these perspectives. Next, I suggest reformulating environmental security approaches from a gender-based perspective, arguing that this approach provides more conceptual leverage and empirical validity than either approach separately. The chapter concludes with two case studies: an exploration of gender in the case of concerns over the Ganges–Brahmaputra–Meghna river system, and an examination of gender in the case of wildlife management in Tanzania. These cases demonstrate the new questions and issues that arise when gender becomes incorporated into discussions of security and the environment.

The current debate on security and the environment

The argument that the environment should be considered a security issue in IR arose, like feminist arguments, in the midst of the "Third Debate" in the discipline and the end of the Cold War. Among those who argue that the environment should be securitized, I recognize three distinct viewpoints that combine security and the environment: *environmental conflict*, *environmental security*, and *ecological security*, described briefly in Table 6.1 and in more detail in the sections below.

Environmental conflict

The *environmental conflict* perspective is the approach that most clearly links traditional security concerns to the environment. Most authors who examine environmental conflict focus on the possibility that groups within society will engage in violent conflict as natural resource stocks diminish due to environmental degradation. These conflicts are understood to threaten the stability of

Table 6.1 Three security and environment perspectives

	Main object of focus	Primary concern	Relationship to traditional security scholarship
Environmental conflict	Human beings	Potential for violent conflict over resources	Most closely related to security; adding environmental elements to security
Environmental security	Human beings	Negative impacts of environmental degradation for humans	Further removed from security than environmental conflict; closer to human security than military security
Ecological security	Ecosystems	Negative impacts of human behavior for the environment	Advocates a revision of security; sees security as damaging the environment

the state. There are several broad trends that are identified as increasing the likelihood of environmentally induced conflicts, "including: expanding and migrating human populations; water, arable land and other resource and environmental scarcities; ... globalisation which brings people (and disease) into closer proximity; and increasing recognition of the injustice of Northern-induced underdevelopment of the South."[6] Central to these discussions is the concept of scarcity. Thomas Homer-Dixon identifies resource scarcities as being potentially so severe that they can seriously undermine human well-being. He identifies three types of scarcities: supply-induced scarcity, demand-induced scarcity, and structural scarcity.[7] The main argument is that some types of scarcity, coupled with other factors, can contribute to violent conflict.[8]

Given the similarities between the environmental conflict approach and "mainstream" security, a number of feminist criticisms of the environmental conflict approach can be read into the core feminist work in Security Studies.[9] Specifically, feminist theories would criticize the environmental conflict approach's narrow definition of security, its state-centrism, its focus on scarcity, and its neglect of gender as a possible cause for environmental conflict. First, feminists argue that the environmental conflict approach holds an inadequate understanding of what security is. Environmental conflict scholars are focused on the potential for environmental degradation and scarcity to cause violent conflict, rather than looking at what happens to people and their environment during wars. To term something a "security" issue and then to leave important elements of insecurity untouched is problematic. Including gender means including the assessment of potential insecurities during wartime as well, given that women often face particular security risks during times of conflict.

A second problematic element of the environmental conflict literature from a gendered perspective is its state-centrism. Feminists often engage in a multilevel analysis, with particular attention paid to individuals and groups within societies.[10] Environmental conflict scholars typically restrict their attention to the level of the state, again demonstrating the close links between this approach and traditional Security Studies.[11] Feminists contend that it is necessary to pay attention to security at levels above and below the state in order to understand how women participate in and are affected by international security issues.

Third, ecofeminists will take issue with the assertion of a link between environmental conflict and scarcity because they see that treatments of scarcity in this literature are largely anthropocentric, suggesting that the environment is made up of resources for human consumption. Authors like Carolyn Merchant call for the acknowledgement of a dynamic relationship between human and nonhuman nature, with each having a degree of power over the other.[12] To use terms like "scarcity" implies that the environment is something of a stockroom of resources for humans that may become depleted, which disregards the deeper relationship between the two entities.

Finally, feminists, in their concern for the gender-differential impacts of international politics, express concern that environmental conflict scholars' proposed causes of conflict are themselves gendered. The factors often put forward as potentially contributing to resource scarcity and conflict in environmental conflict literatures include population growth, human migration, globalization, and unequal resource distribution. Each of these topics has particular implications for gender analysis that are largely unaddressed within this literature. For example, environmental conflict scholars argue that increases in human populations can directly contribute to both supply-induced and demand-induced scarcities, which could result in violent conflict.[13] This tells us very little if we do not consider where these populations are located and who they are made up of. Also, the issue of population has specific gendered implications. Impacts may be different if populations have "youth bulges" typically made up of young males. This group disproportionately engages in crime, commits suicide, or joins militias, all of which are important security concerns.[14] Additionally, by identifying population increase as a contributor to environmental conflict, these authors are automatically making women the potential target of "solutions" because of their role as child bearers. When issues are securitized, certain actions are seen as justifiable—and it is likely that men and women will experience these actions differently.[15] Similar arguments can be made for a number of the other causal factors privileged in the environmental conflict approach. These instances of male/female differential impacts have implications for the security of particular individuals, if security is conceptualized broadly.

Environmental security

The *environmental security* approach is concerned with the negative impacts of environmental degradation for human beings. While environmental conflict can still directly be linked to military security, environmental security is much more closely linked to notions of "human security."[16] In other words, environmental security is a broader notion than environmental conflict, because it is concerned not only with those directly susceptible to environmental conflict, but instead with all of humanity. In environmental security, the security referent is people and threat is located in negative consequences of environmental damage.[17] Some of the main themes in this body of work include the environmental impact of accelerating globalization, concerns over population increases, the spread of disease, and the potentials for sustainable development.

There is much more conceptual affinity between feminist approaches to security and the environmental security approach. Like feminist approaches, it argues for a much broader definition of security. Still, while the environmental security approach takes account of many of the complexities of the relationship between humans and their environment, it omits both the gendered nature of making that dichotomy to begin with and many of the gendered impacts of its key constitutive factors.

First, the environmental security approach fails to take note of the gendered content of the human/nature dichotomy. A caution from ecofeminists would be the potential to de-link humans and the nonhuman environment in this approach. Merchant recognizes that humans have a degree of control over nature through human behaviors, however, nature also has the power to destroy and evolve with or without humans in many cases. She therefore calls for "an earthcare ethic, which is premised on this dynamic relationship, [and] is generated by humans, but is enacted by listening to, hearing, and responding to the voice of nature."[18]

Second, environmental security authors typically fail to recognize the gender dynamics that would transform their analyses. For example, environmental security scholars pay substantial attention to sustainable development as a way to combat environmental degradation and human insecurity simultaneously.[19] Feminists have pointed out that many sustainable development programs have not been gender-sensitive.[20] Since different paths to development often have survival implications for its population, a gender-sensitive approach to sustainable development that takes into account the needs of women, the ecosystem, and future generations within a particular setting appears necessary to ensure security. This means that if sustainable development or sustainability are advocated as providing security, then the specific needs of women also need to be addressed within that framework.

Feminist have also expressed concern that advocates of sustainable development remain entrenched in current (gender-subordinating) social and political structures.[21] Feminists have expressed concern that a sustainable development approach to environmental security maintains the state-centric and top-down foci of the environmental conflict approach, masking it under a broader definition of who merits security.

Ecological security

Finally, *ecological security* is a perspective that focuses on the negative impacts of human behaviors on the environment. The entity whose security is of concern in this approach is the environment. Katrina Rogers explains that ecological security refers to "the creation of a condition where the physical surroundings of a community provide for the needs of its inhabitants without diminishing its natural stock."[22] This definition says nothing explicitly about the position of human beings. This reflects the idea that human beings constitute one part of the environment, but are not necessarily present in all ecosystems. That being said, it is important to note that ecological security scholars are not totally unconcerned with the fate of human beings. Human beings are seen as an essential part of ecosystems. However, ecological security scholars do not privilege humans as the most important species. In this approach species and ecosystems are preserved for their own sake, not for their value to humans.[23]

The ecological security approach is the farthest removed from traditional Security Studies, as can be seen in Table 6.1. The scholars who use this framework are interested in the security of the environment, which includes human beings, largely from the threats presented by human activities. In this respect, many ecofeminists will be pleased with the acknowledgement of a close relationship between human and nonhuman nature and the rejection of the idea that humans are justifiably dominant over nature. From an ecological security viewpoint, items like water, fertile soils and fossil fuels are seen as parts of the total environment rather than as "resources" available for human consumption. This rejection of the idea of exploitation of resources mirrors ecofeminists' rejection of the dominating relationship that patriarchal structures in society set up between humans and nature. However, the fact that ecological security does not address the differential impacts of environmental degradation for men and women will be a concern that needs to be addressed.

One area of overlap between several feminist scholars and ecological security scholars is their tendency to highlight the destruction to the environment that has historically stemmed from the traditional conceptions of security. Rather than the traditional Security Studies scholars' propensity to examine the causes of war or conflict and stop at that, both of these literatures concern themselves with the goings on during wars and impacts of them. Matthew Paterson addresses the environmental effects of war by claiming that "the environment has been an instrument and a casualty of warfare itself, as strategists have used and abused ecosystems to give themselves military advantage."[24] For centuries, military personnel have directly targeted the environment during combat, usually at an extremely high price to surrounding ecosystems. Likewise, women have been targeted by strategies of wartime rape for centuries.[25] Additionally, since military service has traditionally involved men, thus women and children have often been the casualties of collateral damage or other forms of insecurities either during or after wars. This instance of similarity demonstrates that while ecological security does not currently include a systematic gender analysis of the impact of war on men and women, there is some precedent for the undertaking.

Towards a feminist environmental security perspective

The above discussion has demonstrated that there remains a high degree of debate over the best way to conceptualize the link between the environment and security, and that all three perspectives securitizing the environment have uneasy relationships with feminist approaches to security. The addition of gender to the environmental conflict perspective would be a transformative force. The environmental security perspective is more compatible with feminist scholars' understandings of the referents of and threats to security, but still neglects gender. While the ecological security approach has an overlap with various feminisms, it is ecocentric where feminists are fundamentally concerned with gender subordination. This chapter argues that a feminist approach is an appropriate alternative discourse. Based on the analysis of the intersections between the current approaches to security and the environment and various feminisms, I assert that environmental security perspectives that incorporate gender analysis and build on elements of the existing debate will be a fruitful addition to international environmental politics and International Relations in general. Perspectives securitizing the environment might be the right entry vehicle for feminist approaches, and feminist approaches might clarify debates between perspectives about the environment and security.

As there are multiple approaches to the environment and security, there are also multiple feminisms, each of which would have different contributions to perspectives of the environment and security.[26] Here, rather than setting up a debate between different feminisms, I offer some suggestions about how some of the various feminist traditions can be used to inform the environmental security debate and what a gender-focused environmental security perspective might look like. The gender-focused environmental security approach that I envision will in some respects look similar to current approaches to security and the environment, particularly the environmental security approach and the ecological security approach, however, there will be important differences between the approaches as well.

A gender-focused environmental security perspective will begin with a multi-level analysis of security and the environment, paying particular attention to individuals and groups in society who face insecurities. These insecurities can take various forms and are best conceptualized as incidents that increase one's likelihood of experiencing danger, injury, or a decline in personal well-being. Examining these insecurities will involve valuing the contributions of local knowledge as well as other forms of knowledge such as scientific ones. Likewise, the notion of the environment that this approach uses is one that includes human and non-human nature as well as attention to the places where people live. To think of the environment as some distant, external entity masks the close relationships that exist between humans and non-human nature as well as the severity that many environmental issues have for the livelihoods of much of the world's population, including both women and men.

Conflict stemming from environmental change must be examined from a gender-focused environmental security perspective, but with specific attention paid to contextual and historic factors that contribute to violence and the impacts that violence has for members of the population in question. Rather than assume that scarcity is an unproblematic notion, it must be examined in order to determine how assessments of scarcity and plenty are arrived at, and for the benefit of whom. Power dynamics must be assessed if one is to fully understand the potential for conflict as well as all of the implications involved. Additionally, scarcity must not be thought of only in terms of a lack of access to a resource for human consumption. The needs of the environment to function productively must also be taken into account in order to determine scarcity in a given case. This reflects the fact that humans and non-human nature are inextricably linked and the insecurity of one has implications for the insecurity of the other. A detailed examination of scarcity will also bring to light the dominant relationship that humans most often claim over nature, which has links to other dominant relationships in society: North/South, elite/non-elite, and most importantly for this analysis. men/women. This can provoke the questioning of the "normalcy" of these relationships and hopefully invite alternative understandings of the relationships.

This brings us to the issue of the potential causes of environmental insecurity. It must be acknowledged that by pointing to a factor as causing environmental insecurity, that factor also becomes the subject of proposed solutions. These factors must therefore be examined with specific attention being given to the gender differences embedded within them. Issues of increased consumption often associated with accelerating globalization, growing population, and migrating populations are all cited as phenomena contributing to environmental degradation by scholars concerned with the environment. What must be realized is that while these factors might in fact produce environmental insecurities, they must not be taken as straightforward targets for solutions if these solutions do not examine any potential imbalanced impacts that they may have for segments of the population—women in particular. Thus far, none of the perspectives on security and the environment have engaged in determining the particular impacts that solutions targeting the above-mentioned issues may have on women. This is a necessary task for gender-focused environmental security perspectives.

An environmental security perspective that includes gender will also be amenable to solutions that reject the dominant institutional or societal structures. While sustainable development and environmental peacemaking may provide increased security for both the environment and some individuals in society, they do nothing to challenge the patriarchal structures that allow for the continuation of valuing male-ness over female-ness, thus they cannot be the final solution to insecurity. Through the analysis of environmental issues that directly impact people's lives, feminist environmental security scholars can both determine particular gender-differentiated impacts, responses and contributions to environmental degradation as well as call attention to the gendered assumptions in society through which these issues are typically understood.

In sum, some of the issues that are brought to light when gender is included as a fundamental aspect of environmental security are as follows:

- Multilevel analysis of security and the environment are essential.
- Broad and critical conceptualizations of security, environment, and scarcity are necessary.
- Particular attention must be paid to the unique security situations of women.
- A close relationship between humans and non-human nature must be acknowledged.
- What happens during times of conflict as well as their causes must be examined.
- The impacts of militarization on both the environment and human beings must be examined.

- The causes of environmental insecurity must be critically assessed as well as their potential impacts for segments of the population.
- Attention must be given to multiple sources of knowledge.
- Potential solutions that reject the dominant institutional or societal structures must be entertained.

An environmental security perspective with a gender focus can use these issues to build on the existing debate over security and the environment and to revise some aspects and add gender analysis.

The two case studies below make this point. Both cases demonstrate how perspectives that combine security and environment appear in discussions of a real-world environmental issue. Additionally, the cases highlight the contributions of a gender-focused environmental security perspective across two different environmental issue-areas: water and wildlife conservation. The first case, hydropolitics in the Ganges–Brahmaputra–Meghna water basin, shows the absence of gender concerns within an important environmental issue and the contributions of a gender-focused environmental security perspective in addressing this absence. The second case, wildlife management in Tanzania, highlights the range of gender concerns that are open for discussion when a gender-focused environmental security lens is used to view the topic.

Gender, water, and the Ganges–Brahmaputra–Meghna river system

The Ganges–Brahmaputra–Meghna (GBM) river system is one of the largest hydrologic regions in the world. This large basin is constituted mainly by the two tributary basins of the Ganges and the Brahmaputra, originating from the water sources in the Himalayan mountain range. A smaller rainfed tributary called Meghna Barak, originating in the Naga hills of north-east India, joins the Ganges–Brahmaputra near Dhaka and the total outflow drains into the Bay of Bengal as the Meghna.[27] The total drainage basin of about 1.75 million km is shared by 5 countries: Bangladesh, Bhutan, India, Nepal, and the People's Republic of China. The estimated population of the basin region is more than 600 million.

Countries in the GBM basin have a long history of interactions and international negotiation or hydro-diplomacy. More attention is given here to Bangladesh, India, and Nepal due to their longstanding roles in coordinating basin management. The populations in these three countries are growing at an average rate of about 2 percent a year.[28] The countries of this region remain heavily reliant on agriculture, with the majority of their populations depending on it for their living—meaning that water issues are livelihood issues for many in the area.

> Water is a resource on which there is complete dependency and for which there is no substitute. As the demand for water has surpassed supply, with rival demands by various economic sectors, provinces, and sovereign states, this has led to increased competition, tension, and disputes.[29]

The issue of India and Bangladesh sharing the waters of this basin goes back to partition in 1947. Canals and other irrigation systems that had been operating under a single entity now had to be separated into multiple new states. At independence, India was already consuming a larger share of Ganges waters than was East Pakistan, later Bangladesh.[30] This strain reached boiling point when India decided to unilaterally build the Farakka Barrage in order to divert water from the Ganges to flush the port of Calcutta to prevent silting.[31] After the barrage came online in 1975, several adverse impacts stemming from the new flow of the Ganges were said to afflict Bangladesh,[32] contributing to strained political relations.[33] Because India is upstream from Bangladesh, it has been in a position to act unilaterally with water diversion schemes, thereby straining relations between the two countries. Upper riparian countries like Nepal and Bhutan are largely concerned with their hydropower potential, which can be exploited in collaboration with India. Both currently have favorable ratios of per capita water availability, and thus have no major water-related problems with India. Bangladesh, on the other hand, is in the position of being uniquely dependent on the rivers that make up the GBM basin, and at the end of the line in terms of water use.[34] Most recently, India signed water-sharing treaties in 1996 with both Nepal and Bangladesh.

Scholars have considered the GBM basin in terms of the environment and security from an environmental conflict perspective (focusing on issues of allocation/scarcity, power dynamics, and the potential for interstate war or domestic conflict),[35] an environmental security perspective (focusing on cooperation and human security concerns such as poverty and food insecurity),[36] and ecological security (emphasizing ecosystem function).[37] In general, the connections between gender and water have not gotten nearly as much attention by scholars as have issues of water-conflict.[38] This is unfortunate, because the fact is that men and women tend to experience water issues differently. In most societies, women are disproportionately responsible for the tasks of water provisioning.[39] Because of this, the harmful consequences of water insecurities tend to fall on the shoulders of women.[40] Recognition of these unique experiences has led some scholars and policymaking bodies to explore the connections between gender and water in order to better understand how water can be provided and managed in fair ways.

Despite this recognition of gender–water connections, content analysis of various sources focused on management of the GBM basin showed that gender was rarely included in the discussion—either narrowly discussing the situation of women or broadly considering gender relations. This is consistent with my earlier claim that gender infrequently emerges as a fundamental aspect for analysis within perspectives on security and the environment. Despite an acknowledgement by many scholars of the unique relationship between women and water in many societies, this is seldom (if ever) included in discussions of water management in this particular basin.

Although there is very little discussion of gender in the existing literature on hydropolitics in the GBM basin, we can identify possible contributions that gender could make. Because this case is largely discussed in either the environmental conflict or environmental security perspective at present, there are shifts that are possible. For example, there would likely be a level of analysis shift from almost exclusively focusing on the level of the state, as is currently the case in both of these perspectives. Scholars who study gender tend to focus on the causes and outcomes of insecurity, but also what happens during times of insecurity.[41] For example, in the case of the GBM basin, it is essential that scholars uncover what happens to populations within states who experience water insecurity. Conca argues that:

> The most common form of international water conflict today is not the interstate "water war" foreseen by many prognosticators, but rather the increasingly transnationalized "local" conflicts between river developers and their opponents. These are triggered by the enormous financial, social, and ecological costs of large water-infrastructure projects, the often highly skewed distribution of benefits, the tendency of river-development advocates to oversell benefits and understate costs, and the trail of victims such projects often leave in their wake.[42]

This suggests that there are very real threats associated with water management schemes to populations at a local level. If scholars and policymakers merely focus on the state level of analysis, then these threats may go unaddressed for both men and women.

Research that incorporates analysis of these types of struggles into the larger picture of GBM basin management is essential if we are to understand and address all types of insecurity. This focus is particularly important in order to understand the specific ways that men and women in the region experience water insecurity. Wallace and Coles feel that understanding the ways gender shapes who has control of water, who gets access, the differing needs and positions of women and men, is crucial for understanding issues of poverty and development.[43] The current economic paradigm has definite impacts of the connections between gender and water. The World Water Forum claims that:

> [Women's] subordination and the consequent barriers to their active involvement in influencing water programmes are barely addressed. There is limited attention to women's rights to water and what these would mean in practice in poor communities where women's status is often very low, although the need to do more to realize women's empowerment is acknowledged.[44]

Tied to this is the idea that we must be reflexive about the labels that we use to understand conflict. An overview of the GBM literature that is situated in the environmental conflict perspective suggests that populations can easily be labeled as "conflict-prone" without digging deeper to determine whether other factors are at play. When discussing water conflict in India, Myers claims that "constant clashes have erupted in Punjab, where Sikh nationalists claim too much of their water has been diverted to the Hindu states of Haryana and Rajasthan."[45] When discussing the same conflict, Shiva claims that the above is an example of where "a water war is presented as a religious war," which diverts "much-needed political energy from sustainable and just solutions to water sharing."[46] Whichever view is correct, this apparent disagreement implies that these types of water tensions need to be understood for their complexity rather than attempt to have them fit into a water-conflict mold.

Incorporating gender would lead us to ask different questions when exploring the management of the GBM basin. For example, rather than accepting that cooperation in the basin is good and the mechanisms for this cooperation are desirable, we need to understand the gender components of these issues. A case in point is the Joint Rivers Commission (JRC), created in 1972 by the governments of India and Bangladesh to help facilitate water discussions. The JRC statutes establish a range of functions: including aiding in flood control, and maximizing the benefits of common rivers. As mandated in its statutes, the JRC has a set number of engineers at all times—two of the four members of the commission team from each country must be engineers.[47] This leads to broader questions about the issue of expertise, and typically male expertise. Strang argues that moves toward technological management at the hands of experts have shifted the relationship between humans and water to women's disadvantage.[48] Wolf explores a similar topic by examining indigenous water management techniques in two drylands regions, suggesting that rather than being content to see water knowledge determined by some type of scientific "expertise"—there is much to learn from those with historically close ties to water.[49] Deferring to the unique water knowledge of women represents a similar situation. There is evidence to suggest that currently women's participation in water supply projects in India is extremely limited.[50] This means that there is less of a chance that their unique knowledge is being used to find appropriate management schemes.

Additionally, if gender were more fully incorporated into discussions about international basin management, there would possibly be more of a focus on the environment for its own sake and less of treating it as a "resource" for human consumption. The fact that there are only scattered references to protecting the security of the environment as a goal in and of itself demonstrates the way that "the environment" is conceptualized in the current literature on GBM management. The waters of the basin are typically seen either a possession or as a means of ensuring human security. Although most feminisms also tend to focus their concern at the level of humans, ecofeminists tell us that regarding the environment as an entity that humans can dominate has important parallels for other relationships based on domination, including male domination over female.[51] Using this insight to examine the GBM basin case will lead to envisioning the environment as an entity that has the right to exist for its own sake.

Finally, there would likely be a more nuanced understanding of the basin states and more of a focus on alternative forms of development—less focused on economically defined development. Biswas presents a discussion of international water management that assumes that economic development is desirable and a high priority goal for states. He says:

> Since all exclusively national sources of water that could be used economically have already been developed, or are in the process of development, there would be tremendous pressure to develop international water bodies, which are often the only new sources of water that could be used cost-effectively.[52]

This presents basin states as poor, backward, and typically reliant on outside help to "develop" the watercourse. On the other hand, Vandana Shiva presents an alternative view for the future of basin states, and India in particular.[53] She argues that water management schemes were more sustainable before they were tied to things like expertise and pricing.[54] She identifies the sacred tie to water that Indians have traditionally experienced as a more desirable way to value water and use it in sustainable ways. For her, conducting water management schemes at the level of the state and based on "modern" modes of relating to water mask the important relationship between humans and the environment that they rely on. These different perspectives demonstrate that we must ask a range of questions about how local water users, many of whom are women, relate to their environment and want management schemes to be carried out.

This case shows that different perspectives that combine security and environment are currently being used to discuss existing environmental issues. What is missing from these discussions, however, is an incorporation of gender concerns. A gender-focused environmental security perspective is a way for these concerns to enter the debate and offer a more encompassing look at security concerns in the GBM basin.

Gender and wildlife conservation in Tanzania

Like the previous discussion of hydropolitics in the GBM basin, examining the case of wildlife conservation in Tanzania provides an example of the value added when gender becomes a fundamental element of the perspectives on security and the environment. This particular case exhibits multiple security issues, which would be the focus of different security and environment approaches. These security issues range from security forces violently conflicting with resource users (environmental conflict) to human security issues like access to agricultural land in order to grow enough food (environmental security) to the security of biodiversity in Africa (ecological security). Tanzania is a country with one of the highest number of wildlife conservation areas in the world. According to the Tanzanian Ministry of Natural Resources and

Tourism (MNRT), "Tanzania has 19 percent of her surface area devoted to wildlife in [protected areas] where no human settlement is allowed ... and 9 percent of its surface area to [protected areas] where wildlife co-exists with humans."[55] This amounts to a vast deal of land in a country whose total area is 945,087 sq km.

Additionally, Tanzania is one of the world's poorest countries, ranking 164 out of 177 countries in the UN Human Development Report 2005. The Swedish International Development Cooperation Agency (SIDA), an organization heavily involved in contributing aid to Tanzania, explains that "poverty continues to plague the country and many live off very limited resources. The most vulnerable groups are farmers, nomads, the landless, young people, women-led households and urban dwellers who work for the 'informal sector'."[56] This means that individuals facing desperate financial situations are limited in their use of natural resources for their livelihoods if they live near wildlife reserves, often creating volatile security situations.

According to Roderick Neumann, wildlife conservation and violence often go hand in hand in the practice of state-directed wildlife conservation in Africa. He offers three main reasons why this is so: (1) it is often the case that weapons are in the possession of parties involved in disagreements over wildlife laws either due to being officially sanctioned or due to the necessity of their self-preservation from animals; (2) historical reasons such as the process of modern state formation in Africa involving gaining control over natural resources that were vital to rural livelihoods; and (3) geographical reasons such as the fact that areas of wildlife concentration are remote from towns and cities, thus making violating laws easier to get away with and also reflecting the unequal patterns of development in much of Africa with rural areas being relatively poor.[57] Each of these points holds true for Tanzania. The three main types of violence that appear in the course of wildlife conservation are displacement, increased vulnerability to natural hazards, and person-to-person violence—each of which have gendered implications for local populations.

Wildlife conservation in Tanzania has been enthusiastically undertaken by the state government, in large part for the ecotourism revenues that it offers the country. According to statements by the Director General of Tanzania National Parks (TANAPA), Lota Melamari, the country's wildlife resources offer a potential avenue for increased tourism in the coming decades. "Tanzania envisages that the number of tourists will be in the 1 million range by the year 2010, and that the proceeds from the tourism industry are projected to increase from the current average of 8.1 percent to an annualised average growth rate of 10 percent by 2005."[58] The tourism industry currently contributes to 14 percent of the GDP of the country.[59]

The Tanzanian government considers illegal use of wildlife resources to be the greatest threat to protected area networks and wildlife population. Therefore, wildlife authorities are considered to be a type of police force—an example of the environment being militarized. The Ministry of Natural

Resources and Tourism describes the wildlife authorities' goals and supply needs in military terms.[60] There have been numerous documented incidents of violent clashes between wildlife agents and local resource users in and around many of Tanzania's wildlife reserves over the years that have resulted in injuries and deaths.[61]

This situation of wildlife protection has particular gender implications in Tanzania. Like most countries in Africa, there are significant differences between the living situation of men and women in Tanzania.[62] This is particularly the case in the rural areas of the country. According to the 2004–5 Tanzania Demographic and Health Survey, women in rural areas of the country had lower levels of maternal and child health, lower levels of treatment for malaria and other diseases, and higher prevalence of female circumcision than did women in urban areas of the country.[63] Many of the initiatives put into place by the Tanzanian state to address gender inequality, such as the quota system where women are allocated a percentage of political seats in local government and political parties, tend to benefit urban-based elite women over rural women.[64] This is of particular interest for the case of wildlife conservation due to the fact that those most impacted by wildlife conservation live in rural areas of the country. Although we must be cautious about making generalizations on the experiences of women in these rural areas, we must also be aware that they may face unique security challenges due to their living situations.[65]

While environmental conflict scholars examine violent conflict over resources, a gender analysis of wildlife conservation looks at instances of person-to-person violence that specifically involve women. Roderick Neumann describes firsthand reports of villagers around the Arusha National Park complaining about abuses by wildlife authorities, including instances of beatings and rape of village women.[66] The penalties for rape in Tanzania are fairly strict, with imprisonment ranging from a minimum of 30 years to a maximum of life.[67] However, the paramilitary wildlife guards are often protected from punishment for wrongdoing. According to Tanzania's Ministry of Natural Resources and Tourism, one of the strategies for protecting wildlife against illegal use is "protecting the wildlife staff from liabilities resulting from injuries and death of suspects during their official duties."[68] The reports of rape and other abuses of women around Arusha National Park are one example of a particular insecurity faced by female resource users around wildlife protection areas. A gender-focused environmental security perspective brings these particular insecurities to light and asks how the gendered structure of wildlife management serves to worsen these insecurities.

These accounts serve to support the claim that the militarization of environmental issues can have unintended negative consequences.[69] This issue of rape around wildlife conservation areas can be linked to the militarization of the security force and discussions of militarized rape. Wildlife guards represent security forces with a degree of control over the locals, and women in particular. This example demonstrates that wildlife conservation can increase the insecurity of women who are forced to interact with guards in the course of their daily routine. If wildlife areas are expanded, it will mean that women have to go further to collect water and fuelwood, thus increasing their chances of insecurity. Additionally, if the government decides to expand wildlife areas and this decision results in displacement and forced migration, women's insecurity as in the form of a lack of physical safety could increase.

A report by the Tanzania Gender Networking Programme claims that "[W]hile women are the daily managers and users of natural resources, largely for the benefit of others, women are not involved in the major decisions that affect these resources and the environment."[70] The customary laws of the country have given men more power over resources and decision-making processes. This is led to widely differing levels of access to resources. Even in instances of community-based wildlife management, which are intended to empower local communities, women are typically underrepresented, and often suffer unequal burdens due to conservation policies than do men. Through an examination of the Selous Conservation Programme, Alexander Songorwa concludes that "The programme's negative impacts on women were in the form of increased loss of crops to wildlife, reduced access to land, and increased work burden to those whose husbands volunteered for the programme."[71] Women's typical role as food producers for the household means that issues of loss of food security due to crop destruction by wildlife impact them explicitly. This is also the case of reduced access to land. Women are forced to produce household food on smaller and smaller amounts of land as protected areas grow. The final issue, increased workload, reflects both the enlarged burdens on women and the lack of representation of women in community-based conservation (CBC) projects. Women are explicitly forbidden to hold some wildlife management positions because of the traditional association of wildlife-related business, especially hunting, as men's work. While this assessment is based on a CBC project surrounding just one game reserve, it likely reflects larger trends across the country. Tanzania's economy depends a great deal on agriculture, with around 80 percent of the able-bodied population engaged in agriculture. Women constitute the majority of the individuals involved in agricultural work. This is even true for pastoralist groups who tend to practice shifting agriculture.[72] The implications of this is that since crop destruction due to wildlife activity is an acknowledged problem for locals around wildlife reserves,[73] and since women are heavily engaged in agriculture, an assessment of environmental security needs to take the particular situation of these women into consideration.

This issue of a lack of gender sensitivity in CBC projects has implications for discussions of both environmental security and ecological security. In terms of environmental security, women face particular forms of insecurity based on their traditional household roles. Their position as food producers and gatherers of fuelwood has implications for food security, economic security, and physical security—all elements of human security. In Tanzania's rural setting, women work more than 14 hours per day, compared to men's typical 10 hours per day, undertaking physically demanding activities which include domestic chores, family care, and farm work.[74] Additionally, a recent study indicates that women reported a fear of animal attacks more often did men—likely due to their household tasks and role as caregivers for other household members.[75] This means that because wildlife conservation policies often result in increased hardship for locals, and women often bear a larger share of those hardships, an analysis of security and wildlife conservation is incomplete without an examination of the situation of women.

In terms of ecological security, CBC projects are presented as a way to involve the local communities and increase their awareness of the necessity of conservation in order to better maintain biological diversity.[76] The problem is that many CBC projects have been strictly top-down and villagers often end up resenting the projects and the lack of benefits that they receive from them.[77] Katherine Homewood and Daniel Brockington claim that:

> Conservation in Africa has been dominated by exclusion of people from resource use and decision making in protected areas. Current political and economic realities, and awareness of the needs and aspirations of rural African populations, make it clear this may not be optimal management policy, however attractive to hardline conservationists.[78]

This is particularly the case for women who face added burdens because of their family's involvement with the projects, as evidenced by the Selous case. This will likely mean that locals continue to have a contentious relationship with wildlife conservation projects and may contribute to ecological insecurity in the form of poaching or other forms of illegal resource use. Additionally, the top-down nature of the projects typically results in a lack of attention to local knowledge,[79] which many feminists would regard as continuing a dominant relationship between the state and rural locals and discounting alternate perspectives. Although women are sometimes targeted groups for some form of inclusion in wildlife management schemes,[80] it is unclear how much participation actually goes on.

Conclusion

The cases presented here demonstrate that a gender-focused environmental security perspective highlights specific insecurities that would largely go unexplored in the current security and the environment perspectives. We see that discussions of hydropolitics in the GBM basin include each of the security and environment perspectives, but no systematic examination of gender impacts and concerns. We also witness the contributions that a gender-focused environmental security perspective make to this particular case, namely, asking different questions and regarding the relationship between humans and the environment in a more holistic way. In turn, the case of wildlife management in Tanzania demonstrates that women experience wildlife conservation policies and programs in ways that often contribute to their insecurity, be that through physical abuse at the hands of wildlife guards or through increased difficulty providing food for their families because of reductions in crop lands. The exercise of viewing cases like these is particularly valuable if it can be incorporated the process of policy formation. When environmental policies are formed, it is important that all facets of the story are uncovered and people's unique security experiences are taken into account.

A gender-focused environmental security perspective allows for more reflexive scholarship and policymaking due to its recognition that not everyone experiences environmental insecurity in the same ways. By encouraging scholars to ask different questions and examine issues from a different point of view, this gender-focused environmental security perspective aids in our understanding of important livelihood issues. These cases represent just two in a line of cases that would benefit from examining environmental insecurity in this way.

Scholars can employ a gender-focused environmental security approach by conducting gender-sensitive investigations of widely discussed environmental concerns. In this endeavor, gendered assumptions about the way these issues are studied and the solutions most often proposed can be brought to light, thus aiding in both the understanding of environmental issues as well as the process of finding policy solutions to them. Site-specific explorations will be important both for conducting gender analysis of environmental concerns and for highlighting the particular situation of women and environmental degradation. Feminist scholars from other disciplines have undertaken projects similar to this, and these studies will be valuable for feminist environmental security scholars to draw on and integrate into a gender-focused environmental security framework.[81]

Including gender as a fundamental element of analysis in an approach to security and the environment represents an important opportunity for scholars to gain an essential perspective on the security of both humans and the environment. Some important steps have been made thus far by scholars in terms of highlighting connections between security and the environment. It is now time to bring out the gendered elements both of these scholarly debates, as well as gendered elements of the topic of security and the environment itself for people's daily lives. Humans cannot live independently of the environment, and such environmental security represents an elemental livelihood issue for everyone on the globe. If we are to understand the ins and outs of environmental security, gender must be a focus of analysis due to its ever-present impact on how environmental security is understood and its impacts on how environmental insecurity is experienced.

Notes

1 Traditional security scholarship is conceptualized as "the study of the threat, use, and control of military force" as discussed by Joseph Nye and Sean Lynn-Jones, "International Security Studies," *International Security*, 12, no. 4 (1988): 5–27.

See also Stephen Walt, "The Renaissance of Security Studies," *International Studies Quarterly* 35, no. 2 (1991): 212.

2 See Jon Barnett, *The Meaning of Environmental Security: Ecological Politics and Policy in the New Security Era* (New York: Zed Books, 2001); Larry A. Swatuk, "Environmental Security," in *Palgrave Advances in International Environmental Politics*, eds., Michelle Betsill, Kathryn Hochstetler and Dimitris Stevis (New York: Palgrave Macmillan, 2005), pp. 203–36.

3 For an early discussion of the intersections between gender and environmental security, see J. Ann Tickner, *Gender in International Relations: Feminist Perspectives on Achieving Global Security* (New York: Columbia University Press, 1992).

4 See Cynthia Enloe, *Bananas, Beaches and Bases: Making Feminist Sense of International Politics* (Berkeley, CA: University of California Press, 1990); Christine Sylvester, *Feminist Theory and International Relations in a Postmodern Era* (Cambridge: Cambridge University Press, 1994); Lene Hansen, "The Little Mermaid's Silent Security Dilemma and the Absence of Gender in the Copenhagen School," *Millennium: Journal of International Studies* 29, no. 2 (2000): 285–306; J. Ann Tickner, *Gendering World Politics: Issues and Approaches in the Post-Cold War Era* (New York: Columbia University Press, 2001); Cynthia Cockburn and Dubravka Zarkov, eds., *The Post-war Moment: Militaries, Masculinities, and International Peacekeeping* (London: Zed Books, 2002); Laura Shepherd, "Victims, Perpetrators, and Actors Revisited: Exploring the Potential for a Feminist Reconceptualisation of (International) Security and (Gender) Violence," *British Journal of Politics and International Relations* 9, no. 2 (May 2007): 239–56.

5 See Carolyn Merchant, *Earthcare: Women and the Environment* (New York: Routledge, 1996); Karen J. Warren, ed., *Ecofeminism: Women, Culture, Nature* (Bloomington, IN: Indiana University Press, 1997); Karen J. Warren, *Ecofeminist Philosophy: A Western Perspective on What It Is and Why It Matters* (Boulder, CO: Rowman & Littlefield, 2000).

6 Barnett, *The Meaning of Environmental Security*, p. 50.

7 Supply-induced scarcity arises through a decrease in the supply of a key resource, demand-induced scarcity arises through an increase in demand for a key resource, and structural scarcity occurs through a change in the relative access of different groups to a key resource. Thomas Homer-Dixon, *Environment, Scarcity, and Violence* (Princeton, NJ: Princeton University Press, 1999).

8 While the literature that focuses on environmental scarcity tends to be the best known, there are several other scholars who stress the situation of the abundance of resources leading to conflict. This view highlights the increase in likelihood of conflict when differing actors see a benefit in capitalizing on a particular, valuable resource. Additionally, several scholars stress the issue of dependence on resources leading to conflict. The issue of dependence and scarcity as discussed here are closely related. See Paul Collier, *Economic Causes of Civil Conflict and Their Implications for Policy* (Washington, DC: World Bank, 2000); James Fairhead, "The Conflict Over Natural and Environmental Resources," in *The Origins of Humanitarian Emergencies: War and Displacement in Developing Countries*, eds., E. Wayne, Frances Stewart Nafziger, and Raimo Väyrynen (New York: Oxford University Press, 2000); Philippe Le Billon, "The Political Ecology of War: Natural Resources and Armed Conflicts," *Political Geography* 20 (2001): 561–84; Ian Bannon and Paul Collier, eds., *Natural Resources and Violent Conflict: Options and Actions* (Washington, DC: World Bank, 2003); Philippe Le Billon, "The Geopolitical Economy of 'Resource Wars'," *Geopolitics* 9, no. 1 (2004): 1–28.

9 According to Lene Hansen and Louise Olsson: "The goal of feminist security analysis has been twofold: to critique the field of Security Studies for its inherent male biases and to trace how particular political practices *produce* collective conceptualizations that constrict or enable what can be recognized as legitimate

problems of the individual." (Hansen and Olsson, "Guest Editors' Introduction," *Security Dialogue*, 35, no. 4 (2004): 405–9)

10 Tickner, *Gendering World Politics.*

11 For a notable exception to this trend, see Olivia Bennett, ed., *Greenwar: Environment and Conflict* (Washington, DC: The Panos Institute, 1991).

12 Merchant, *Earthcare.*

13 Homer-Dixon, *Environment, Scarcity, and Violence.*

14 Urdal claims that "Youth bulges provide greater opportunities for violence through the abundant supply of youths with low opportunity costs, and ... stronger motives for violence may arise as youth bulges are more likely to experience institutional crowding, in particular unemployment," Henrik Urdal, "A Clash of Generations? Youth Bulges and Political Violence," *International Studies Quarterly* 50 (2006): 607.

15 Lene Hansen, *Security as Practice: Discourse Analysis and the Bosnian War.* (New York: Routledge, 2006).

16 For a discussion of the potential problems that the notion of "human security" has for masking gender differences, see Heidi Hudson, "'Doing' Security As Though Humans Matter: A Feminist Perspective on Gender and the Politics of Human Security," *Security Dialogue* 36, no. 2 (2005): 155–74.

17 Simon Dalby, *Environmental Security* (Minneapolis: University of Minnesota Press, 2002).

18 Merchant, *Earthcare*, p. xix.

19 See Barnett, *The Meaning of Environmental Security*; Dennis Clark Pirages and Theresa Manley DeGeest, *Ecological Security: An Evolutionary Perspective on Globalization* (Boulder, CO: Rowman & Littlefield Publishers, Inc., 2004).

20 Wendy Harcourt claims that "[F]eminists involved in the ecological and women's movements are concerned that the complex social, cultural, economic and political relations, which inform women's lives and gender inequalities, are not being addressed by the mainstream debate [on sustainable development]." Wendy Harcourt, "Negotiating Positions in the Sustainable Development Debate: Situating the Feminist Perspective," in *Feminist Perspectives on Sustainable Development*, ed., Wendy Harcourt (New Jersey: Zed Books Ltd., 1994), p. 2.

21 Donald Worster, "The Shaky Ground of Sustainability," in *Deep Ecology for the 21st Century: Readings on the Philosophy and Practice of the New Environmentalism*, ed., George Sessions (Boston: Shambhala, 1995), pp. 417–27.

22 Katrina Rogers, "Ecological Security and Multinational Corporations," *Environmental Change and Security Project Report* no. 3 (1997): 30.

23 Karen T. Litfin, "Constructing Environmental Security and Ecological Interdependence," *Global Governance* 5, no. 3 (1999): 359–78.

24 Matthew Paterson, *Understanding Global Environmental Politics: Domination, Accumulation, Resistance* (New York: Palgrave, 2001), p. 44.

25 See Katherine Moon, *Sex among Allies: Military Prostitution in US–Korea Relations* (New York: Columbia University Press, 1997); Roland Littlewood, "Military Rape," *Anthropology Today* 13, no. 2 (1997): 7–17; Cynthia Enloe, *Maneuvers: The International Politics of Militarizing Women's Lives* (Berkeley, CA: University of California Press, 2000).

26 See the Introduction to this book.

27 Jayanta Bandyopadhyay, "Water Management in the Ganges–Brahmaputra Basin: Emerging Challenges for the 21st Century," in *Conflict Management of Water Resources*, eds., Manas Chatterji, Saul Arlosoroff, and Gauri Guha (Burlington, VT: Ashgate Publishing Company, 2002), pp. 179–218.

28 Jayampathy Samarakoon, "Issues of Livelihood, Sustainable Development, and Governance: Bay of Bengal," *AMBIO: A Journal of the Human Environment* 33, no. 1 (2004): 1–12.

29 Hamir K. Sahni, "The Politics of Water in South Asia: The Case of the Indus Waters Treaty," *SAIS Review*, XXVI, no. 2 (2006): 155.

30 Stephen Brichieri-Colombi and Robert W. Bradnock, "Geopolitics, Water and Development in South Asia: Cooperative Development in the Ganges–Brahmaputra Delta," *The Geographic Journal* 169, no. 1 (2003): 43–64.

31 Surya P. Subedi, "Hydro-Diplomacy in South Asia: The Conclusion of the Mahakali and Ganges River Treaties," *The American Journal of International Law* 93, no. 4 (1999): 953–62.

32 These negative impacts include loss of up to 90 percent of the previous water flow during the dry season, which leads to a shortened agricultural cycle and a reduced harvest. Stephan Libiszewski, "International Conflicts over Freshwater Resources," in *Ecology, Politics and Violent Conflict.*, ed., Mohamed Suliman (New York: Zed Books, 1999), pp. 115–38.

33 Libiszewski, "International Conflicts over Freshwater Resources"; Brichieri-Colombi and Bradnock, "Geopolitics, Water and Development in South Asia: Cooperative Development in the Ganges–Brahmaputra Delta."

34 Islam M. Faisal, "Managing Common Waters in the Ganges–Brahmaputra–Meghna Region," *SAIS Review* XXII, no. 2 (2002): 309–27.

35 Jayanta Bandyopadhyay, "Water Management in the Ganges–Brahmaputra Basin: Emerging Challenges for the 21st Century." See also Peter H. Gleick, "Water and Conflict: Fresh Water Resources and International Security," *International Security* 18, no. 1 (1993): 79–112; Sandra Postel, *Last Oasis: Facing Water Scarcity* (New York: W.W. Norton & Company, 1997); Aaron T. Wolf, Shira B. Yoffe, and Mark Giordano, "International Waters: Identifying Basins at Risk," *Water Policy* 5 (2003): 29–60; Faisal, "Managing Common Waters in the Ganges–Brahmaputra–Meghna Region;" Asit K. Biswas, "Management of International Waters: Opportunities and Constraints," *International Journal of Water Resources Development* 15, no. 4 (1999): 429–41; Shlomi Dinar and Ariel Dinar, "Negotiating in International Watercourses: Diplomacy, Conflict and Cooperation," *International Negotiation* 5 (2000): 193–200; Pirages and DeGeest, *Ecological Security*, p. 63.

36 Pirages and DeGeest, *Ecological Security: An Evolutionary Perspective on Globalization*, p. 63; Faisal, "Managing Common Waters in the Ganges–Brahmaputra–Meghna Region," p. 311; Brichieri-Colombi and Bradnock, "Geopolitics, Water and Development in South Asia: Cooperative Development in the Ganges–Brahmaputra Delta."

37 Samarakoon, "Issues of Livelihood, Sustainable Development, and Governance: Bay of Bengal," p. 40.

38 R. Maria Saleth, Madar Samad, David Molden and Intizar Hussain, "Water, Poverty and Gender: An Overview of Issues and Policies," *Water Policy* 5 (2003): 385–98.

39 Ken Conca, "Global Water Prospects," in *From Resource Scarcity to Ecological Security: Exploring New Limits to Growth*, eds., Dennis Pirages and Ken Cousins, (Cambridge, MA: The MIT Press, 2005), pp. 59–82.

40 Green Cross International, "National Sovereignty and International Watercourses," ed., Green Cross International (The Hague: Green Cross International, 2000).

41 Tickner, *Gendering World Politics*.

42 Conca, "Global Water Prospects," p. 75.

43 Tina Wallace and Anne Coles, "Water, Gender and Development: An Introduction," in *Gender, Water and Development*, eds., Anne Coles and Tina Wallace (New York: Berg, 2005), pp. 1–20.

44 Gary Chamberlain, *Troubled Waters: Religion, Ethics, and the Global Water Crisis* (New York: Rowman & Littlefield Publishers, Inc., 2007), p. 126.

45 Norman Myers, *Ultimate Security: The Environmental Basis of Political Stability* (Washington, DC: Island Press, 1996), p. 52.
46 Vandana Shiva, *Water Wars: Privatization, Pollution and Profit* (Cambridge, MA: South End Press, 2002), p. xi.
47 Ainun Nishat and Islam M. Faisal, "An Assessment of the Institutional Mechanisms for Water Negotiations in the Ganges–Brahmaputra–Meghna System," *International Negotiation* 5, no. 2 (2000): 289–310.
48 Veronica Strang, "Taking the Waters: Cosmology, Gender and Material Culture in the Appropriation of Water Resources," in *Gender, Water and Development*, eds., Anne Coles and Tina Wallace (New York: Berg, 2005), pp. 33–4.
49 Aaron T. Wolf, "Indigenous Approaches to Water Conflict Negotiations and Implications for International Waters," *International Negotiation* 5, no. 2 (2000): 357–73.
50 Linda Stalker Prokopy, "Women's Participation in Rural Water Supply Projects in India: Is It Moving Beyond Tokenism and Does It Matter?" *Water Policy* 6 (2004): 103–16.
51 Warren, *Ecofeminism: Women, Culture, Nature.*
52 Biswas, "Management of International Waters: Opportunities and Constraints," p. 429.
53 Vandana Shiva, *Water Wars: Privatization, Pollution and Profit* (Cambridge, MA: South End Press, 2002); Vandana Shiva, *India Divided: Diversity and Democracy Under Attack* (New York: Seven Stories Press, 2005).
54 Shiva, *Water Wars: Privatization, Pollution and Profit.*
55 Ministry of Natural Resources and Tourism, *The Wildlife Policy of Tanzania* (Dar es Salaam, Tanzania: United Republic of Tanzania, 1998), pp. 3–4.
56 Swedish International Development Cooperation Agency (2006), "Why Does Sweden Provide Support to Tanzania?" Available at: www.sida.se/sida/jsp/sida.jsp?d = 401& language = en_US.
57 Roderick P. Neumann, "Africa's 'Last Wilderness': Reordering Space for Political and Economic Control in Colonial Tanzania," *Africa: Journal of the International African Institute* 71, no. 4 (2001): 641–65.
58 Lota Melamari, "Experience of Tanzania National Parks on Planning, Development and Management of Ecotourism," paper presented at the Regional Prepatory Meeting for the International Year of Ecotourism, Maputo, Mozambique: 2002.
59 United Republic of Tanzania, *Tourism* (Dar es Salaam, Tanzania, 2006).
60 Ministry of Natural Resources and Tourism, "The Wildlife Policy of Tanzania," p. 10.
61 Roderick P. Neumann, *Imposing Wilderness: Struggles over Livelihood and Nature Preservation in Africa* (Berkeley, CA: University of California Press, 1998); Dan Brockington, *Fortress Conservation: The Preservation of the Mkomazi Game Reserve Tanzania* (Indianapolis: Indiana University Press, 2002).
62 United Nations Statistics Division (2006), "Millennium Indicators of Development: Tanzania." Available at: www.unstats.un.org/unsd/mi/mi_resultsd.asp; Tanzania Gender Networking Programme, *Beyond Inequalities: Women in Tanzania* (Dar es Salaam, Tanzania, 1997).
63 Tanzania National Bureau of Statistics, *2004–5 Tanzania Demographic and Health Survey* (Dar es Salaam, Tanzania, 2005).
64 Tanzania Gender Networking Programme, *Beyond Inequalities: Women in Tanzania.*
65 Chandra Talpade Mohanty, *Feminism Without Borders: Decolonizing Theory, Practicing Solidarity* (Durham, NC: Duke University Press, 2003).
66 Neumann, *Imposing Wilderness*, p. 189.
67 US Department of State, *Tanzania: Country Reports on Human Rights Practices, 2004*, ed., Human Rights Bureau of Democracy, and Labor (Washington, DC, 2005).

68 Ministry of Natural Resources and Tourism, *The Wildlife Policy of Tanzania*, p. 11.
69 Daniel Deudney, "The Case against Linking Environmental Degradation and National Security," *Millennium: Journal of International Studies* 19, no. 3 (1990): 461–76; Ole Wæver, "Securitization and Desecuritization," in *On Security*, ed., Ronnie D. Lipschutz (New York: Columbia University Press, 1995), pp. 46–86.
70 Tanzania Gender Networking Programme, *Beyond Inequalities: Women in Tanzania*, p. 1.
71 Alexander N. Songorwa, "Is Wildlife Management Gender Sensitive?" *Uongozi Journal of Management Development* 11, no. 2 (1999): 151.
72 United Republic of Tanzania, "The United Republic of Tanzania: National Website," accessed March 23, 2006.
73 Ministry of Natural Resources and Tourism, *The Wildlife Policy of Tanzania*.
74 Tanzania Gender Networking Programme, *Beyond Inequalities: Women in Tanzania*.
75 Bjørn P. Kaltenborn, Tore Bjerke and Julius Nyahongo, "Living with Problem Animals: Self-Reported Fear of Potentially Dangerous Species in the Serengeti Region, Tanzania," *Human Dimensions of Wildlife* 11 (2006): 397–409.
76 Ministry of Natural Resources and Tourism, *The Wildlife Policy of Tanzania*.
77 Alexander N. Songorwa, "Community-Based Wildlife Management (CWM) in Tanzania: Are the Communities Interested?" *World Development* 27, no. 12 (1999): 2061–79.
78 Katherine Homewood and Daniel Brockington. "Biodiversity, Conservation and Development in Mkomazi Game Reserve, Tanzania," *Global Ecology and Biogeography* no. 8 (1999): 309.
79 Mara Goldman, "Partitioned Nature, Privileged Knowledge: Community-Based Conservation in Tanzania," *Development and Change* 34, no. 5 (2003): 833–62.
80 Ministry of Natural Resources and Tourism, *Reference Manual for Implementing Guidelines for the Designation and Management of Wildlife Management Areas (WMAs) in Tanzania* (Dar es Salaam, Tanzania, 2003).
81 See Vandana Shiva, *Staying Alive: Women, Ecology, and Development* (Atlantic Heights, NJ: Zed Books, 1988); Sally Sontheimer, ed., *Women and the Environment: A Reader* (New York: Monthly Review Press, 1991); Penny Newman, "Killing Legally with Toxic Waste: Women and the Environment in the United States," in *Close to Home: Women Reconnect Ecology, Health and Development*, ed., Vandana Shiva (London: Earthscan Publications Ltd, 1994), pp. 43–59. Most of these types of studies have been more involved in calling attention to women's position rather than challenging gendered assumptions.

Part III
Gendered security actors

7 Loyalist[1] women paramilitaries in Northern Ireland

Beginning a feminist conversation about conflict resolution

Sandra McEvoy

> The question [of why I committed acts of paramilitary violence] was put to me umpteen times at different places ... And I turn around and says, "Me and my kind were there so that you and your kind could go to bed at night and sleep. That is why we were there. That's why we, the women, were there at that time, so that you and your kind ... You want to go in and close your doors and close blinds and go to your bed and sleep while me and the like of me are out?" ... It was something that you felt you had to do. You were there. It was your duty. It was your duty to do it.[2]

The sense of fear, frustration, concern and duty that "Lynn" expresses in our interview in April, 2006, succinctly summarizes the sentiments of many politically violent Loyalist women with whom I spoke. Lynn's response to my inquiries about her participation in a Loyalist paramilitary organization (LPO) also affirms her belief that, in part, women were responsible for defending their communities from armed Republicanism.

Utilizing data collected by the author in a 2006 empirical study of women's participation in LPOs, the aim of this chapter is to reframe the security debate by taking a deeper and more thoughtful look at the threat that women combatants already pose to security and to solidify the connection between this threat and processes of conflict resolution. Analysis of the insights, experiences and responses of Protestant women members and supporters of three paramilitary organizations in Northern Ireland to "peace" legislation proposed by the British government will reveal the importance of incorporating women combatant voices in these processes. The empirical nature of the study provides a unique starting point from which the chapter then engages in both the practical and theoretical implications of excluding politically violent women from Security Studies and International Relations (IR) scholarship.

Gendering security

As Sjoberg and Gentry[3] convincingly argue, analysis of women's uses of politicized violence in global politics is needed if women's experiences of war and conflict beyond their status as victims are to be recognized. A growing field of feminist International Relations provides key tools to explore the role that female combatants play in conflict and conflict resolution practices. Feminist political scientists Cynthia Enloe, Ann Tickner, V. Spike Peterson and Christine Sylvester (to name only a few) question what field of knowledge International Relations could rightly lay claim to without consideration of the role that gender plays in the workings of the state.[4] As Enloe asserts:

> Feminist-informed investigations by academic and activist researchers have revealed that many forms of public power and private power are dependent for their operation, legitimation and perpetuation upon ... controlling popular notions of femininity and masculinity. It therefore follows that if we do not become seriously interested in the conditions and lives of women, we are likely to craft analyses of international power dynamics that are at best incomplete, at worst faulty and unreliable.[5]

In fact, it is the "control" of "popular notions of femininity and masculinity" that makes inquiry of women's threat to security all the more important. It is important not only because such inquiries make us smarter about those women who wield political violence but about the male heads of state, generals, diplomats, social commentators, religious leaders and others who facilitate, encourage or deny it. Moreover, embracing the reality of women's diverse participation in armed political conflict and incorporating these insights about combatant women into the dialogue about security may help to reduce the widespread "understanding that women are irrelevant to the making and fighting of wars."[6]

A gender-informed examination of security also complicates our understanding of power relationships previously considered straightforward, especially the relationship between the public and private sphere. For example, in the case of women combatants we might ask whether women's manufacturing of petrol bombs in their homes for the use of paramilitary organizations is a public or private activity. Further, is the use of her home to conceal bombs and other munitions of public or private concern? Feminist inquiry allows us to appreciate the "causal link *between* power in private spaces and power in public spaces" further revealing the complexity of women's lives in areas living with conflict.[7] Women who wield violence, even as mothers, sisters, aunts, nieces, and grandmothers, can be seen not as paradoxes but as complex actors in a complex world.

When some women are "threats" to international security

When women (and especially mothers) are examined as perpetrators of political violence, the focus of observers and analysts typically is on the seemingly unnatural[8] or surprising idea that someone that has the ability to bring a life into the world would have the desire to take a life. Scholars' gendered assumptions about women's relationship to armed conflict permeate their work; in many portrayals, women are stripped of their agency and fashioned into ruthless and crazed killers or unthinking, easily manipulated and overly emotional.[9] For example, Russian popular media has labeled women perpetrators in the Russian/Chechen conflict as "zombies" and "black widows," characterizing them as deadly, but at the same time easily manipulated and not in control of their decisions.[10]

The apparent confusion among observers over why women wield political violence is evident in a survey conducted in 2003 by the Public Opinion Foundation of the All-Russia Center for the Study of Public Opinion.[11] The survey found that 84 percent of Russians surveyed believed that female suicide bombers were controlled by someone else; only 3 percent believed that the women acted independently. These public opinions run counter to research suggesting that women have at least some if not full agency in their suicide attacks.[12] Still, Stack-O'Connor rightly notes that such viewpoints are consistent in the West where women are again perceived to be "forced" into terrorism rather than rational political actors who make independent decisions to participate in armed groups.[13]

Whatever the motivations attributed to them, however, the visibility of women suicide terrorists has increased substantially in recent years. For example, in a December 13, 2005 editorial in the *Baltimore Sun*, Farhana Ali, Associate International Policy Analyst at the RAND Corporation stated, "Two recent attacks by female suicide bombers have put the world on notice that Muslim women are playing an increasingly important role in this form of terrorism." Ali estimates that between 2000 and 2005 about fifty women from Palestine, Iraq, Chechnya, Jordan and Uzbekistan have carried out such attacks and that the number is growing.[14]

Still, in both the policy and academic arenas, attention to women's violence seems to be associated with their actions in the Middle East and for causes related to radical Islamic terror groups. Women's participation in political violence is not limited by geography or religion, however; women have engaged in violence throughout history and across diverse political conflicts. One place where women's participation in political violence has been notable but neglected is in Loyalist paramilitary organizations in Northern Ireland. The lack of scholarly attention to Protestant women's participation in the conflict in Northern Ireland appears all the more curious given the intense scrutiny scholars of comparative politics and International Relations have used in looking at a number of other facets of that political situation.

Investigating Loyalist women as threats to security

Investigations of men's long-time participation in Loyalist paramilitary organizations (LPOs) in Northern Ireland are extensive. Examinations of men's participation in LPOs range from investigations of their experiences of imprisonment,[15] to those of their reintegration to society following imprisonment,[16] to their motivations for paramilitary participation,[17] to their roles as founders of LPOs,[18] to their processes of identity formation within Loyalist groups.[19] However, there is a glaring absence of Loyalist women's presence in LPOs. While a few authors[20] acknowledge that women did take part in Northern Irish Loyalist paramilitaries, even then, those women's actions, motivations, social networks and political analysis are not studied in depth. As a result, information about the nature of, and degree to which, women historically participated in LPOs is highly limited.

This study aims to begin to fill the knowledge gap about women's participation in Loyalist paramilitary organizations using the reflections of women participants in LPOs concerning their experiences as combatants and their ideas about the British government's attempts to negotiate agreements to bring an end to the conflict in Northern Ireland.

I collected these reflections through interviews with women participants in LPOs. My initial success in reaching women who participated in LPOs was limited and I learned quickly that access to these women was highly regulated by Loyalist men. In the early stages of the fieldwork I was told by men affiliated to LPOs that "the women were never there." When I asked if I could talk to any of the women that "might have been there," the response was frequently, "what women are you talking about?" Convincing male members of LPOs and their associates that I was trustworthy was crucial to obtaining interviews with women participants.

One asset in my ability to access and be trusted by my participants is my familial connections to Northern Ireland and numerous visits to Belfast. This background provided a familiarity with the history, streets and vernacular of the city. The fact that my parents lived in Loyalist areas before their immigration to the United States and that my grandfather was a member of a number of Orange Lodges and a former member of the disbanded Ulster Specials Constabulary or "B. Specials"[21] made my credibility in Loyalist areas all the more reliable. "Snowball" sampling was used to locate interviewees and was particularly important method of locating potential study participants.[22]

Even after I located women participants, the challenges of conducting research into the presence and participation of women in LPOs were considerable, especially in light of the sensitive nature of the research questions that I hoped to pose to the participants and the difficulties I experienced as a result of conducting fieldwork in a low-intensity conflict zone. Challenges to the participants included:

1 acknowledgment of their participation in illegal activities or organizations;
2 hesitancy on the part of women to speak about their experiences in LPOs may be considered disloyal to their current or former group;
3 the potential that recalling such participation may be emotionally or psychologically traumatic.

Further complicating the collection of information were concerns by the participants that I was a reporter or a member of the security forces. Still, I was able to perform 30 interviews with women participants.

The interview protocol consisted of approximately 50 open-ended questions that inquired into three general themes including:

1 women's motivations to participate in Loyalist paramilitary organizations;
2 internal group dynamics;
3 where applicable, women's experiences of their participation in relation to their status as mothers.

Sample questions include; "What motivated you to become active in the group?," "Was there a particular moment or event that inspired you to join?" and "What risks (if any) were involved in becoming part of the group?"

Interviews were tape-recorded, transcribed, and edited to remove identifying information about individuals. The recordings were listened to again while proofreading the accompanying transcript and then analyzed using thematic coding.

The participants in the study ranged in age from 34 to 65 and were affiliated to three different Loyalist paramilitary groups. Four women lived in rural areas and the remaining 26 in or around the city of Belfast. All women held at least a high school equivalency with smaller numbers of the sample holding technical or secretarial training and a few with some college training. Twenty-five of the women were married and five were either single or divorced. All but one participant had children. In one case a mother and her daughter were interviewed which provided a unique intergenerational perspective to the questions posed by the study. All of the interviewees came from the working class.

Several common themes emerged in the conversations with Loyalist women paramilitaries. The first was the rejection of a widely held stereotype that as a group, Protestants live among the comfortable middle-class population in Northern Ireland. Objections to this stereotype were mentioned in every interview, and often repeated more than once. Participants linked these objections to their disapproval of Unionist leaders like Ian Paisley who lend credibility to the conception that Protestants are from the middle to upper-middle class. In almost every case, participants in the study viewed Paisley protecting middle-class interests while ignoring the needs of Loyalist paramilitaries, which come almost exclusively from the working class.

Another common theme in the interviews was respondents' anger and frustration at the British government's successive attempts to formalize peace legislation in the province. It was common during the interviews for the women to express their anger and frustration with the government or the impact of the legislation on them and their families even when the questions posed were intended to illicit information seemingly not related to agreements. At the completion of the study coding of the data revealed that every respondent commented on the agreements on at least one occasion. In some cases, women mentioned the agreements more than once. Given the common stereotype that women have an interest in peaceful and negotiated settlements to conflicts, these women's objections to the British government's attempts to make and formalize peace were a particularly unexpected but significant finding.

The third common theme across the interviews was the women's active participation in LPOs. Throughout the interviews, participants discussed their varied contributions to the LPO they supported. While a number of smaller LPOs developed in the 30-year period of the Troubles, two main organizations have dominated the political landscape: the Ulster Defense Association (UDA) and the Ulster Volunteer Force (UVF). Although their methodology was often different, both groups have had generally the same aims:

1 to defend Protestant communities from Irish Republican Army (IRA) violence;
2 to act as mouthpieces for working-class Protestants and Loyalists;
3 to defend the union between the United Kingdom and Northern Ireland.

The largest LPO (and legal until 1992) is the UDA. Formed in 1971, its membership was originally made up of a number of vigilante groups or "defense associations." Ongoing Republican violence, the disbanding of the Royal Ulster Constabulary in 1970, and the disarming of the police force soon thereafter, hastened the development of the group. In 1972, it was estimated that the group had as many as 40,000–50,000 members.[23]

Th0e second main LPO is the much smaller, more violent and secretive Ulster Volunteer Force (UVF). Many members of the UVF trace their roots to the 36th Ulster Division, a battalion of Northern Irish soldiers who fought for the British during World War II and in large measure the group considers itself an extension of that brave fighting force. Estimates of the group's total membership are difficult to substantiate but were generally understood to have about 1,500 members in 1972.[24]

Women joined these organizations in smaller numbers compared to their male counterparts. My fieldwork revealed that in the case of the UDA, that women formed their own units in Protestant communities throughout Northern Ireland. This study documented approximately two dozen active women's units at various times throughout the conflict with a combined membership as high as 3000 women. Alternatively, there does not appear to be any evidence of a formal separate women's unit in the UVF. Women in this LPO worked secretly and in small numbers alongside male counterparts. Estimates are that at most women accounted for 2 percent of the UVF membership over the 30-year conflict.[25]

Women's tasks in these all-volunteer groups included: transporting arms, munitions and intelligence in baby carriages, purses, cars, and on their bodies; conducting surveillance; cleaning crime scenes and destroying evidence of paramilitary crimes; storing arms and munitions in their homes; transporting LPO contraband into and out of detention facilities; serving as funeral honor guards; carrying out punishment beatings on behalf of the organization; and armed robbery.

Northern Irish Loyalist women combatants' reflections on peace agreements: 1974, 1985, 1998, and 2007

As mentioned above, one of the surprising findings in these interviews was that women members of LPOs found the agreements intended to bring peace to Northern Ireland problematic and objectionable. These interviews demonstrated that women's historic and continual exclusion from formal politics in Northern Ireland should not be read as an indictor that women did not have ideas and beliefs related to the successive peace agreements. Instead, women *and* their opinions were left out of the bargaining processes. This is especially true within extreme Loyalism. Though I never specifically asked any interviewee for an opinion about any agreement, the interviewed women consistently expressed strong opinions about each of the agreements in response to more general questions. These women viewed the existence and content of these agreements as central to their involvement in paramilitary groups, despite (or perhaps because of) their having been systematically left out of the negotiating process.

Between 1974 and 2007, the British and Irish governments made four separate attempts to bring political stability and reduce armed conflict in Northern Ireland.[26] The primary avenue for that endeavor was through a variety of cross-border initiatives or agreements that at various times intended to devolve power, create a power-sharing executive and reform Northern Ireland's social and political structures. From the perspective of the majority of the Loyalist population, these agreements (often referred to as "disagreements") were unacceptable compromises that served to reward Republicans for violence against the British state. In over 30 years of conflict, senior policy scholars and political party leaders have either excluded such women wholesale, from their thinking on conflict and its resolution or have assumed that their views mirrored that of their male counterparts. The material from my interviews reveals that women not only objected to each of these agreements, but went to substantial lengths in order to prevent their passage and/or interrupt their implementation.

The Sunningdale Agreement, December 1974

Between 1968 and 1974, six years of bloody conflict between Republican and Loyalists/British troops which later came to be known as "the Troubles" took their toll on the Northern Irish population and drained the political will of the government of the United Kingdom. Policy-makers in the Heath government were finding the conflict in the province expensive and politically costly for its elected officials. With tensions continuing to rise, the British and Irish governments attempted to devolve government in Northern Ireland which they hoped would bring some measure of peace to the province.[27] Designed to allow Unionists, Social Democrats and the Alliance Party to share power, terms of the proposed agreement were discussed at a conference at a Civil Service College at Sunningdale in December 1974. This new political framework, intended to establish an "Irish Dimension" between Britain and the Republic of Ireland, set forth a series of articles related to the future governance of Northern Ireland. In sum, the articles sought to codify the idea that if the majority of the province expressed a desire to become a united Ireland it could be realized and supported by the governments of the United Kingdom and the Irish Republic. From this cross-border relationship a new "Council of Ireland" would be established comprised of representatives from both governments that would address a diverse range of cultural, social and public interests common to both countries.[28]

The proposal to invite the Irish Republic into the affairs of Northern Ireland was confusing to many Loyalists and it become clear that "without a doubt the British and Irish states aimed to dilute their claims of sovereignty regarding Northern Ireland."[29] Loyalists were incensed and immediately opposed Sunningdale. A notable feature to their opposition was the 14-day strike in May of 1974. Over two weeks the City of Belfast, and in many of its surrounding areas, Loyalists shut down the power station at Ballylumford, Belfast's aircraft and shipyard factories, and even small businesses bringing production in Northern Ireland to a halt. Ultimately the pressure placed on Unionist leaders to withdraw from the negotiations was so great that the conference was dissolved, signifying Loyalist unity against cross-border initiatives.

For some Protestant women, the agreement served as a motivator to become involved in paramilitary organizations. One woman who was concerned with the toll that the agreement would take on her rural community joined the local unit of the Women's UDA which served a central role in protecting and providing basic necessities to Protestant communities throughout the Troubles. In her twenties, married and with children when she joined the organization in 1974, she recalled:

> *Respondent*:
> That was the time whenever they tried to force that other agreement, not the Anglo-Irish one ... the ...
>
> *Interviewer*:
> Sunningdale?
>
> *Respondent*:
> Yes, because that was the reason why I got involved.[30]

Notably, this woman uses the term "force" as she references the Sunningdale Agreement. That is, she saw the "agreement" *not* as an agreement, but as a solution imposed by outsiders. Mentioning another agreement, "the Anglo-Irish one," she suggests that the many agreements that that government has proposed seem to merge together in her mind in the sense that she perceives that each has been imposed upon the population rather than agreed to by its citizens. What the interviewee does state with clarity is that it was because of the agreement and its effects on her Loyalist community that she chose to join the Women's UDA.

Throughout other interviews women consistently expressed their sense of perceived threat that the agreements posed to themselves as well as their communities. During an interview with another former member of the Women's UDA, a woman I call "Chloe" was asked why she and other women participated in supporting paramilitary activities during the period before and after the Sunningdale Agreement. She responded:

> As I say, because we felt at risk, you know? We felt hard done by. You could see your whole culture and your whole way of life just going down the drain and becoming a united Ireland. You know? You could just see that. You can see that to this very day we are all still very, very frustrated. You could see that then, you can still see it.[31]

Chloe repeatedly states her fear of her Protestant culture being degraded by further advances by Republicans to form a united Ireland under a Dublin lead government and saw Sunningdale as just a first, but decisive step in this process. Interviewees like Chloe felt overwhelmingly that this possibility was not only real but with the passing of each agreement that a united Ireland was gradually becoming a reality. During our interview it appeared that her concern that a united Ireland could be realized was as present for her then in July 2006 as they were during the period of the Sunningdale negotiations in December 1974. In almost a refrain, she states, "You could just see that. You could see that then and you can still see it … " and, "You can see that to this very day" suggesting that the position of threat that this Loyalist woman sees has not shifted in the 32 years since the agreement was first proposed. As my discussions with Loyalist women combatants continued throughout 2006, I would come to understand that this perspective was consistent across women and across agreements.

The mobilization of Loyalist women to oppose a cross-border relationship of the British government with the Irish government was one response to these two governments' attempt to pass yet another agreement in 1985 called the Anglo-Irish agreement. What is also clear is that the government's attempts to bring peace to Northern Ireland via the negotiation of the Sunningdale Agreement were a failure. The testimony of these women reveals that women members of paramilitary organizations played an important but often overlooked role in this failure.

The Anglo-Irish Agreement, November 1985

Some ten years following the stunning failure of the Sunningdale conference and with the Troubles continuing to rage in Northern Ireland, in November of 1985 the British and Irish governments again attempted to bring some form of political settlement to Northern Ireland that they hoped would bring a resolution to the conflict. Again, the British and Irish governments sought to solidify an official relationship with one another. Negotiated by British Prime Minister Margaret Thatcher and Irish Taoiseach (Prime Minister) Garret FitzGerald, the Anglo-Irish Agreement (AIA) contained a series of 13 articles designed to address cross-border co-operation and political, security and legal matters between Northern Ireland and the Republic of Ireland. Although Sunningdale proved that Loyalists' all-male leadership would not tolerate any negotiation with, or inclusion of, the Republic of Ireland in the political future of Northern Ireland, a number of the articles were of particular concern to major sectors of the Loyalist community. Articles 5 and 6 mirrored the aims of the previous agreement which stated that the two governments of Britain and Ireland would support any future wish by the people of Northern Ireland to enter into a united Ireland. Not surprisingly, many Nationalists in both the North and the South saw this as an important development. However, Unionists (those Protestants who wish to maintain the union between Northern Ireland and Britain) were outraged with the terms of the agreement and began a long campaign to have the AIA withdrawn. For many Loyalists the signing of the AIA marked the second official occasion in which their government would concede to Republican violence which in essence proved that "violence pays."[32]

The extent to which AIA failed to bring peace or stability to Northern Ireland is reflected in the increase in violence following its passage.[33] Much of this violence in 1985 and early 1986 was attributed to Loyalists, who, in response to AIA, began to form groups, some of these new groups had affiliations to existing Loyalist paramilitary organizations and took as their missions opposition to the agreement. The spokesman for the Ulster Clubs called for a "people's army to make this country ungovernable to bring this government to its knees."[34] In addition to paramilitary violence an estimated 100,000 people gathered in protest against the agreement at Belfast City Hall on November 23, 1985. Chanting the slogan for the anti-agreement movement "Ulster Says NO!," many Protestants were certain that further attempts by the British government to push through the agreement would be abandoned. One former member of the Women's UDA and member of the Ulster Clubs expressed her anger with British Prime Minister Margaret Thatcher who negotiated the agreement on behalf of Northern Ireland in poetry which she read aloud to me during the interview.[35] The poem references the campaign against the agreement, emphasizing that Ulster *still* says no, and shaming the British government for its lack of support of Loyalists.

The respondent highlights a largely overlooked sentiment among these Loyalist women related to their feelings of almost disbelief that their government would betray them by again entering into talks with "Dublin" and "selling" Northern Ireland. As this respondent looks retrospectively at Unionist reaction to the AIA, she again conveys a sense of despair in the proposed agreement. Like their response to the Sunningdale conference before it, Unionists and Loyalists organized a massive a widespread general strike called the "Day of Action" where again factories and shops were closed and public transportation and air travel was interrupted. By February 1987, the articles proposed under the AIA were still not formalized. Unknown to Unionists at the time, many of these same provisions would be carried over and implemented in the next agreement posed by the British government, the Belfast Agreement of 1998.

The Belfast/Good Friday Agreement,[36] May 1998

Just as Sunningdale and the Anglo-Irish Agreement before it, the Belfast Agreement was designed by the British and Irish governments to create devolved democratic institutions for Northern Ireland and further consolidate the role of the North–South Council. However, unlike the two previous agreements, the Belfast Agreement sought to decommission all paramilitaries weapons, reform Northern Irish policing and to release political prisoners. Widely reported as a new beginning for the province, the referendum passed with over 71 percent of voters voting "yes." Still, some were dubious about the results:

> Somewhat peculiarly, the vote was not broken down by electoral ward as is commonplace in elections. The suspension of this practice was under-taken owing to fears that any such spatial breakdown would indicate that the majority of unionists had voted against the agreement. At best 51 percent of unionist electorate supported the Agreement. It was also assumed that a vote breakdown would have indicated that there was a small but significant rejectionist vote within certain republican-dominated communities.[37]

It would appear that the fears of British government ministers and other political leaders that should detailed information regarding the specific sectors/ communities within various Unionist parties that did not support the refer-endum be revealed, it could jeopardize the agreement. Indeed, in my own research in Loyalist communities in Northern Ireland, many Loyalists report that the "agreement" did not represent the interests of their community. Rather than unifying the population in a combined sense of hope for the future, for many Loyalists the agreement assured future division "the Belfast Agreement copper-fastened the importance of groups."[38] The agreement also filled many on the ground with the sense the British government had failed its "loyal" citizens. For example, one Loyalist woman community worker who was interviewed in a study of Loyalist explained that they had "been kicked in the teeth, not once but twice; once by the perpetrators and the second time by our own government."[39]

In another interview, a woman who was a former member of the Ulster Volunteer Force, referenced the intense sense of anger and disappointment that she feels toward elected Unionist politicians. She felt so mistreated by the Northern Irish/British government that she is unwilling to fly the Northern Irish / Ulster flag. She felt that Unionist political representatives have historically failed to protect Protestant/Loyalist interests. In the following exchange the respondent specifically names David Trimble (the former leader of the Ulster Unionist Party and chief negotiator for Protestants in the 1998 Belfast Agreement talks) as being responsible for abandoning Loyalist interests in Northern Ireland. Her anger toward both Britain and Unionist politicians combined with her sense of disappointment and frustration was unmistakable. Out of this anger she now believes that Northern Ireland should voluntarily separate itself from the United Kingdom and become an independent state. She stated:

> The Ulster flag? Well, the way that I look at it, Trimble, he was the man that was standing for us and look what he has worked us into now. And I am not part of that. I believe in Ulster going on her own if she could, but she couldn't. But I think she should try it anyway.[40]

An especially notable and gendered element of this respondent's account of the Ulster flag and her idea that Northern Ireland separate itself from Britain is that she refers to Ulster as female in stating her own belief that "Ulster should go on her own" and that while it is unlikely that such a political arrangement would be realized "she should try it anyway."[41] From the field of political psychology, Winter discusses the ways in which it has traditionally been seen as men's role to protect the gendered nation and it is generally depicted as vulnerable and "defenseless."[42] However, in this respondent's description of Ulster, a woman, in this case a combatant woman, has taken the responsibility to protect "her." In other words, traditional nationalist discourse characterizes a state as a woman being fought for by its men. In this discourse, the state is a woman being fought for by its women.

For other women members of LPOs interviewed for the study there was a sense of confusion about what effect the Belfast Agreement would have on their lives. The complete restructuring of the police force (the Protestant-dominated Royal Ulster Constabulary or RUC) was one such unintended result:

> [People] like me, they didn't understand all the implications. I knew the police force was going to get a good shake-up. But I didn't realize how much and that we would lose the RUC altogether and that they would be discredited all over the world. After thirty years we had had enough, and most moderates voted for the GFA [Good Friday Agreement], but we didn't realize the price we would have to pay.[43]

Another respondent took issue with the ways that the agreement invited members of Sinn Fein (the largest nationalist party in Northern Ireland) Gerry Adams and Martin McGuinness to take seats in a power-sharing government given their background as leading members of the paramilitary organization the Provisional Irish Republican Army. The interviewee "resented" the invitation and made an analogy to the US War on Terror to illustrate her point to her American interviewer. When asked about the agreement she stated:

> We resented the fact that they were being brought into government. And they were still out there murdering and killing British soldiers and the British population—and the British government expected us to sit. You know, and take it and sit on government like. Can you imagine Bush and the likes sitting on the government with Al Qaeda after the 9/11? But that's what they expected us just to do to sit down and say "Carry on." You know?[44]

The St. Andrew's Agreement, March 2007

Despite the optimistic news reports related to the signing of the St. Andrews agreement on March 26, 2007, and the withdrawal of British troops on July 31, 2007, for many in Northern Ireland, the political and religious conflict in the province continues. So while news bulletins no longer report bombings, shootings and riots with the same frequency, the degree of discontent (particularly at the street level) remains, and sustained peace in Northern Ireland has not yet been fully realized. For example, on July 31, 2007, Roman Catholic and Protestants clashed over Republican plans to march through the largely Protestant community of Ballymena.[45] In a separate incident outside of Belfast, two hundred members and supporters of the UDA staged a massive riot in response to police searches of homes of some of its members.[46] While this type of Loyalist paramilitary violence is mundane compared to the level and scope of violence during the height of the Northern Irish conflict, sectarian tensions still do remain.

Although my fieldwork in Northern Ireland concluded in August 2006, the signing of the St. Andrews Agreement by the British and Irish governments in March of 2007 has been part of ongoing discussions between me and one of the study's key informants in Northern Ireland. When asked about her reaction to the signing of the agreement, this former member of the Women's UDA's sense of disdain and disappointment with the most recent agreement was consistent with her feelings about the three previous "disagreements." Characterizing the agreement as "just another paper," she said:

> The St. Andrews agreement? No one really knew anything about it, or paid much attention even though it was on the news. It was just another

paper, another way for the British Government to threaten it better work or else all power would be taken from us for the foreseeable future. We know Paisley did a double take so he could become First Minister, although he lost some votes because of it, there really wasn't any decent Unionist to vote for against his party … Like most people here, I have no faith in the different groups and no faith in the politicians. All spin, we don't know what the truth is any more.[47]

Here this interviewee expresses a cumulative sense of distrust, despair and failure that all of the women engaged in the study stated that they felt. This is palatable in this respondent's assertion that "I have no faith in the different groups and no faith in the politicians" and "we don't know what the truth is any more."

It is out of such despair that arguably a degree of radicalization developed in these women and sustained their participation in LPOs and further complicated and compromised these agreements. The testimony of women combatants may also suggest a realization that their government is not prepared to reward Loyalists for their fight against armed Republicanism by guaranteeing the continued union with Northern Ireland.[48]

In response to this perceived abandonment some women interviewed were motivated to join LPOs. When asked why she participated in her local branch of the Women's UDA, one woman affirmed her belief that not only was the group something that she believed in, but the social welfare that the group provided was essential given the "injustices" being wrought against Protestants not only by the IRA, but also by the British government. Another interviewee emphasized that it was not only the Republican population that suffered political and economic isolation in Northern Ireland in the 1970s and 1980s, but large portions of the Protestant population as well. In her view, this economic suffering is not something that some outside of Northern Ireland wanted to acknowledge, adding to her anger toward the British government and further alienating her from their political maneuvering related to peace agreements. She stated:

I just, I just found it fighting for something that I believed in. And the injustice that went on, and it did. I mean, everybody said "Oh, this happened to the Republicans, and that happened to the Republicans." They did not see what was happening to us. And they did not even want to know what was happening to us.[49]

These women's perspectives not only illustrate the central role of the LPOs in their lives and their communities, but also the significant role that women played in these organizations over the period of the Troubles.

Locating "women" in the dialogue on conflict

Within the last decade, feminist scholars of IR have documented the many ways in which women's concerns, ideas and hopes have been habitually excluded from many of the places and spaces where male political leaders and representatives conduct peace negotiations.[50] Feminists have noted "In *most* conflict-ridden societies, male dominance and advantages over women are issues rarely ever found on the negotiating agenda."[51] That is, the dominance of male visions of post-conflict society frequently trumps women's concerns or ideas about how a society might take shape following conflict, a dynamic that has consequences for the post-conflict distribution of resources as well.[52]

Azza Karam, Senior Policy Research Advisor at the United Nations Development Program, outlines nine ways that women's lives are "reshaped" by conflict including:

1 sudden accession to becoming household head with limited resources;
2 mobilized as soldiers in patriarchal militaries;
3 subjected to increased medical and social vulnerability;
4 have to shoulder increased security risks in disintegrating polities;
5 must confront increased sexualized violence;
6 must negotiate family disruptions;
7 become disadvantaged refugees;
8 experience increased violence against women in "domestic" space;
9 suffer war-structured sexual work.[53]

On the basis of these diverse ways that women experience conflict, Karam argues that sustainable peace projects cannot rationally exclude significant portions of any population that suffers under conflict (read women) and that their inclusion must go beyond token efforts for women's appeasement. For Karam, the inclusion of women in peace processes is a logical and moral imperative, one that goes beyond the symbolic inclusion of a few high profile women at the negotiation table to an "integral part" of even the most diverse societies, even allowing such societies the opportunity to "evolve."

This emphasis on including women in peace processes has affected the peace negotiations around the conflict in Northern Ireland. Some women were present at the negotiation table. One of the most prominent women present in the negotiations surrounding the Good Friday Agreement (GFA) in 1998 was Mo Mowlam, then the United Kingdom Secretary for State for Northern Ireland. Mowlam has often been considered an important broker of the GFA and she was central to facilitating conversations between representatives from the United Kingdom, Northern Ireland and the Republic of Ireland.

Also, the non-partisan but short-lived political party, the Northern Ireland Women's Coalition (NIWC), did contribute to disrupting the highly patriarchal politics at play in the negotiation of the GFA. Still, the NIWC served as a buffer between Unionists and Republicans and therefore had little opportunity or support to advance their own progressive, women-centered political agenda.

In other words, there were two distinctive features of representation of women at the peace negotiation table for the GFA. The first is that it was non-partisan, peace-brokering women who were included rather than partisans and combatants. The second is that the women who participated were either unwilling or unable to seriously pursue the consideration of women's issues by the negotiators. The remainder of this chapter argues that the conflict in Northern Ireland serves as a theoretical and practical example of a serious flaw in both feminist analysis and policy work that encourages the inclusion of women in peace-building processes. A crucial question that neither feminist theorists nor policy-makers have really addressed, however, is whether the women being included in peace processes are representative of all women, or if they are a particular *type* of women.

Many of the theoretical arguments and policy provisions for women's inclusion justify it by linking femininity and peace. For example, United Nations Security Council Resolution 1325 recommends women be included in peace-building processes "because women are key to international peace and security," implying that it is women's peacefulness that makes them a useful addition to negotiations. This assumed link between femininity and peacefulness creates a selection effect for the *sort* of women who are allowed to participate in peace processes. Women included in peace processes are often those women who play roles traditionally associated with femininity, advocating for and brokering peace agreements rather than invested in the conflict.

In Northern Ireland, combatant women are being systematically excluded from peace processes. The exclusion of combatant women from peace processes reifies gender stereotypes, while marginalizing a part of the population that feminists have sought to empower. Gender subordination, however, is not the only impact of the exclusion of combatant women from peace processes. The absence of combatant women at the bargaining table, as the Northern Ireland conflict demonstrates, risks the negotiation of unrepresentative and untenable agreements.

Combatant women as key to gaining security: the impacts of leaving LPO women out

One key feature of the exclusion of combatant women in the Northern Ireland peace process is that they were not only excluded by the British government, their opponents, and/or the formal organizers of peace talks. Their role in the conflict was denied by their own male LPO comrades. In this context it became routine to deny politically violent women recognition of their contributions to the "defense of Ulster." Even though the women I interviewed played crucial roles in a conflict which has dominated their lives for decades, the denial of their existence by their own partisans provides a structural barrier to the representation of any unique interests they might have. Further, regardless of their unique interests, the exclusion of these women is a relic of the patriarchy not only of the governments at the table but also of the political parties and paramilitary organizations that they participate in. The inclusion of these women, then, can disrupt the patriarchy both of "high" politics and of armed non-state groups, providing not only alternative pathways to women's liberation but also alternative pathways to peace.

The exclusion of women, in this view, is symptomatic of hierarchal and masculinized norms and practices that in themselves reaffirm women's feminized and subservient position in scholarly and policy thinking about solutions to conflict. In this understanding, investigations about conflict and conflict resolution must start with a consideration of gender and power if, as Sjoberg suggests in the Introduction to this book, we are to be more "descriptively accurate and predictably powerful" in our understanding of global politics.

This is clear from the other consequences of excluding LPO women. From the evidence gathered in my interviews, it appears that the exclusion of LPO women in consecutive peace-building and conflict resolution processes in Northern Ireland was a missed opportunity for the governments of Britain and the Republic of Ireland. Despite there being little change in the views of the majority of Loyalists regarding their desire to remain part of the United Kingdom, the British government pressed forward with the attempt to develop an "Irish dimension" in the future governance of the province. In a very tangible way these agreements failed to address the needs of a sometimes violent and critical constituency in the province. Instead of gaining benefits, security or confidence via the agreements, the widespread feeling among these LPO women was one of loss. Without the recognition of these issues, the conflict and tension in the province continue. Not only between opposing Loyalist and Republican communities but *also within* Loyalist communities whose future political path has become clouded since the signing of the GFA. Shirlow and Murtagh reinforce this idea, stating:

> [T]he failure to resolve ethno-sectarian tensions at the ground level and within the most marginalized and deprived communities in Belfast is indicative of a continual refusal to tackle the nature of underlying tensions and realities ... Beliefs and practices ... [and] inequality both in materials and cultural terms [remain] as an ever-present force that shapes the reality of wider divisions.[54]

In other words, the exclusion of LPO women created an addition fractionalization within Northern Ireland, and an additional constituency that felt disenfranchised not only by their own government and the British government, but also by their own "representatives" in the peace process.

A second issue that the inclusion of LPO women in the peace and conflict resolution processes would have revealed was the critical role that class alienation played in fomenting Protestant and Loyalist opposition to the agreements. As those most likely to bear the financial burden of war on the home, women would have been excellent barometers of the social and economic conditions

Protestant Northern Ireland. As stated earlier, working-class Loyalists were at the center of ongoing efforts to mobilize strikes against Sunningdale and Anglo-Irish Agreements, while middle- and upper-class Unionists represented their cause at the peace table. The particular sensitivity that Loyalist women have to issues of class could have given negotiators foresight into a potential pitfall with the agreement. The remarkable influence of working-class Loyalists over a large majority of the Northern Irish community and their control of powerful LPOs was not fully appreciated or recognized by British negotiators. As interviewees testified, British apathy toward working-class Protestants (particularly hard-working Protestant families) was an insult that could not be overlooked by politically violent Loyalists. As each of the peace agreements were negotiated and as these Loyalist women continued to feel excluded, the class and gender conflicts remained unresolved.

Finally, and along those lines, the inclusion of LPO women *both* in the peace negotiations and in the study of the success or failure of the agreements that came out of them would have produced substantially different results. The LPO women I interviewed would have objected to all four agreements as they were negotiated. Whether or not they would have successfully altered the agreements or prevented their passage, these women's opinions would have altered the discourse in the peace negotiations substantially, and brought issues to the table that were not centrally featured in the negotiations without their voices. Further, the interviews I conducted indicate that the common claims that the agreements have successfully brought peace to Northern Ireland are, to a large extent, erroneous. As the testimonies of these LPO women affirm, that four consecutive attempts were made by the governments of Britain and the Republic of Ireland is in many ways indicative of the failure of this legislation versus its success.

Conclusion

The feminist question "where are the women?" in peace negotiations has inspired substantial effort in the scholarly and policy worlds to put women at the table at peace negotiations. However, this chapter argues that it is important not only to ask where the women are, but to ask where the *combatant* women are during the peace-building process. Three key arguments suggest that this is an important intervention. First, combatant women are a violent constituency capable of disrupting the success of any negotiated peace. They, like any other combatants, are a security threat that needs to be included efforts to de-escalate the conflict. Second, combatant women may have unique insights (e.g., the class conflict issue) and interests (e.g., in gender rights) useful to the negotiation of a representative and effective peace agreement. Third, the inclusion of combatant women in peace negotiations interrupts gendered stereotypes of women as necessarily peaceful, as well as patriarchal traditions of their governments and their political and paramilitary organizations.

Ultimately, the utility of contributing the perspectives of women comba-tants in conflict resolution processes is untested—combatant women have not been tangibly included in the peace negotiation processes in Northern Ireland or elsewhere in the world. However, the potential benefits are promising. The research and curiosity of feminist scholars have cautioned that the incor-poration of women's voices is not a panacea. Simply considering women does not in itself resolve conflict without an acknowledgment of the many ways that masculine politics has sown distrust and political alienation among this segment of the Northern Irish population. Interviews with women members of LPOs have revealed what scholars have previously been hesitant to acknowl-edge: where women stand on the multiple and complex issues surrounding political conflict has an impact on peace *and* security.

The testimony of Loyalist women who have wielded political violence in Northern Ireland has not only exposed the fatal error that British negotiators committed in omitting the ideas and perspectives of women combatants in the 30 years of the Troubles, but also gives notice to other negotiators—male and female—that there is a gendered dimension to security. More thoughtful considerations should also serve to make us all smarter about what role women played in the Hamas takeover of the West Bank in June 2007, the ongoing role women are playing in the violent separatist campaigns in Chechnya and Sri Lanka, and how women may have shaped the deadly out-come of the siege of the Red Mosque in Pakistan in July 2007. As women continue to register their political perspectives through the use of political violence, there is now hope that peace-building and security community will have new tools from which they can draw to reduce and better understand the violence—and perhaps avoid it all together.

Notes

1 The concept of Loyalism and those who identify as "Loyalists" is a hotly con-tested term within Northern Irish Protestantism. Here the term is used to refer to those people and groups who support or are affiliated to Loyalist paramilitarism and affirm Northern Ireland's connection to the United Kingdom. For more on Loyalist identity, see Arthur Aughey, "The Character of Ulster Unionism," in *Who Are "The People?" Protestantism, Unionism and Loyalism in Northern Ireland*, eds., Peter Shirlow and Mark McGovern (London: Pluto Press, 1997), pp. 16–33.
2 Interview with the author, Belfast, April 2006.
3 Laura Sjoberg and Caron E. Gentry, *Mothers, Monsters and Whores: Women's Violence in Global Politics* (London: Zed Books, 2007).
4 See Cynthia Enloe, *Does Khaki Become You? The Militarization of Women's Lives* (London: Pluto Press, 1983); Cynthia Enloe, *Bananas, Beaches and Bases: Making Feminist Sense of International Politics* (Berkeley, CA: University of California Press, 1989); Cynthia Enloe, *Maneuvers: The International Politics of Militarizing Women's Lives* (Berkeley, CA: University of California Press, 2000); Cynthia Enloe, *The Curious Feminist: Searching for Women in a New Age of Empire* (Berkeley, CA: University of California Press, 2004); Ann Tickner, *Gender in International Relations* (New York: Columbia University Press, 1992); Ann Tickner, *Gendering World Politics* (New York: Columbia University Press, 2002);

V. Spike Peterson, ed., *Gendered States: Feminist (Re)Visions of International Relations Theory* (Boulder, CO: Lynne Rienner Publishers, 1991); Christine Sylvester, *Feminist Theory and International Relations in a Postmodern Era* (Cambridge: Cambridge University Press, 1994); Christine Sylvester, *Feminist International Relations: An Unfinished Journey* (Cambridge: Cambridge University Press, 2002).

5 Cynthia Enloe, "Feminist International Relations: How to Do it; What We Gain," in *International Relations for the 21st Century*, ed., Martin Griffiths (New York and London: Routledge, 2007), p. 6.

6 Laura Sjoberg, "Gendered Realities of the Immunity Principle: Why Gender Analysis Needs Feminism," *International Studies Quarterly* 50, no. 4 (December 2006): 897.

7 Enloe, "Feminist International Relations," p. 1. Emphasis in the original.

8 Sara Ruddick, *Maternal Thinking: Toward a Politics of Peace* (Boston: Beacon Press, 1995).

9 See Eileen MacDonald, *Shoot the Women First* (New York: Random House, 1991) and Barbara Victor, *Army of Roses: Inside the World of Women Suicide Bombers* (New York: Rodale Press, 2003).

10 Alisa Stack-O'Connor, "Picked Last: Women and Terrorism," *Joint Forces Quarterly* 44 (1st Quarter 2007): 95–100.

11 Stack-O'Connor, "Picked Last," p. 97.

12 Sjoberg and Gentry, *Mothers, Monsters, Whores*, Chapter 5.

13 Stack-O'Connor, "Picked Last," p. 96.

14 Ibid., p. 96.

15 Roy Garland, *Gusty Spence* (Belfast: Blackstaff Press, 2001).

16 Jim Crothers, *Reintegration: The Problems and the Issues: Ex-Prisoners Information Center Research Document, No. 2* (Belfast: EPIC Print Press, 1998).

17 See Jim Cusack and Henry McDonald, *UVF* (Dublin: Poolbeg Press, 1997); David Boulton, *The UVF 1966–73: An Anatomy of a Loyalist Rebellion* (London: Torc Books, 1973); Steve Bruce, "Turf War and Peace: Loyalist Paramilitaries Since 1994," *Terrorism and Political Violence* 16, no. 3 (Autumn 2004): 501–21; Derek Lundy, *The Men that God Made Mad: A Journey Through Truth and Terror in Northern Ireland* (London: Jonathan Cape Press, 2006).

18 Ian Wood, *God, Guns and Ulster: A History of Loyalist Paramilitaries* (Christchurch: Caxton Editions, 2004).

19 Peter Taylor. *Loyalists* (London: Bloomsbury Press, 2000).

20 See Miranda Alison, "Women as Agents of Political Violence: Gendering Security," *Security Dialogue* 35, no. 4 (2004): 447–63; Eileen Fairweather *et al.*, *Only the Rivers Run Free: Northern Ireland: The Women's War* (London: Pluto Press, 1987); Rachel Ward, *Women, Unionism and Loyalism in Northern Ireland: From "Tea-Makers" to Political Actors* (Dublin: Irish Academic Press, 2006).

21 The Ulster Special Constabulary or "B. Specials" were a Northern Ireland-based police unit organized by the British government charged with anti-terrorism duties in the province.

22 Snowball sampling is a chain of referrals whereby one person involved in the study referred another person to me so that ultimately a series of participants may be developed from one initial contact.

23 Sydney Elliot and W.D. Flackes, *Northern Ireland: A Political Directory 1968–1999* (Belfast: The Blackstaff Press, 1999), p. 474.

24 Ibid., p. 474.

25 Interview with UVF member, July 26, 2006.

26 At the time of my 2006 interviews, three agreements were negotiated between the United Kingdom and the Republic of Ireland. At the time of this writing an additional agreement, the St. Andrews Agreement (2007) has also been negotiated between these two governments.

27 See John Leavy, *Political Thinking Behind Sunningdale* (Dublin: Talbot, 1973); and Rhoda Margesson, *Changing Perceptions about Resolving Conflict in Northern Ireland: The Failure of the 1974 Sunningdale Agreement and its Implications for Settlement in the 1990's* (Cambridge, MA: Harvard Law School, 1991).
28 Elliott and Flackes, *Northern Ireland*, pp. 460–1.
29 Peter Shirlow and Brendan Murtagh, *Belfast: Segregation, Violence and the City* (London: Pluto Press, 2006), p. 32.
30 "Gloria," interview with author. Rural County Antrim, June 2006.
31 Interview with author, Belfast, June 2006.
32 Alan Bairner, "The Battlefield of Ideas: the Legitimation of Political Violence in Northern Ireland," *European Journal of Political Research* 14, no. 5–6 (Nov., 1986): 642.
33 Ibid., p. 32.
34 Alan Wright, "Hoping for the Best but Preparing for the Worst." *Fortnight* 233 (1986): 5.
35 Interview with the author, June 2006. In the poem the interviewee uses the term "Ulster" to refer to province of Northern Ireland. This reference is frequently used as a synonym by traditional Northern Irish Protestants within Unionism and especially among Loyalists.
36 As a further indicator of the ongoing divisions between Republicans and Unionists, each group refers to the agreement by a different name. For Protestants, the agreement is referred to as the Belfast Agreement while Republicans refer to it as the Good Friday Agreement.
37 Shirlow and Murtagh, *Belfast: Segregation*, p. 37.
38 Ibid., p. 5.
39 Bill Rolston, "Dealing with the Past: Pro-State Paramilitaries, Truth and Transition in Northern Ireland," *Human Rights Quarterly* 28, no. 3 (August 2006): 666.
40 Interview with the author, July 2006.
41 Interview with the author, July 2006.
42 David G. Winter, "Circulating Metaphors of Sexuality, Aggression, and Power: Otto Rank's Analysis of 'Conquering Cities' and 'Conquering Women.'" *Internationale Zeitschrift für arztliche Psychoanalyse,* 2 (2001): 54.
43 Email correspondence with the author, Belfast, July 2007.
44 Interview with author, June 2006. Rural County Antrim.
45 "Loyalists to Oppose Republican Parade Through Ballymena," *Belfast Telegraph.* Available at: www.belfasttelegraph.co.uk/news/local-national/article2820519.ece, accessed 1 August 1, 2007.
46 "Orde Hits Out at UDA Over Rioting," *British Broadcasting Corporation.* Available at: www.news.bbc.co.uk/2/hi/uk_news/northern_ireland/6928004.stm, accessed 1 August 2007.
47 Email correspondence with author, April 2007.
48 Rolston, "Dealing with the Past," pp. 661–2.
49 Interview with the author, June 2006. Rural County Antrim.
50 See Cynthia Cockburn, *The Space Between Us: Negotiating Gender and National Identities in Conflict* (London: Zed Books, 1998); Cynthia Cockburn, *The Line: Women, Partition and the Gender Order in Cyprus* (London: Zed Books, 2004); Cynthia Cockburn, *From Where We Stand: War, Women's Activism and Feminist Analysis* (London: Zed Books, 2007); Karen Turner, *Even the Women Must Fight: Memories of War from North Vietnam* (New York: Wiley and Sons Publishers, 1999); Mary Ann Tetreault, "Women and Revolution in Vietnam," in *Global Feminisms Since 1945: Rewriting Histories,* ed., Bonnie Smith (London and New York: Routledge, 2000), pp. 45–64; Martha Ackelsberg, *Free Women of Spain: Anarchism and the Struggle for the Emancipation of Women* (Oakland, West Virginia and Edinburgh: AK Press, 2005); Azza Karam, "Women in War

and Peace-building: The Roads Traversed, the Challenges Ahead," *The International Feminist Journal of Politics* 3, no. 1 (April 2001): 2–25; Laura Shepherd, "'Victims, Perpetrators and Actors' Revisited: Exploring the Potential for a Feminist Reconceptualisation of (International) Security and (Gender) Violence," *British Journal of Politics and International Relations* no. 9 (2007): 239–56.

51 Karam, "Women in War," p. 10.
52 For Vietnamese women's post-conflict experiences, see Tetreault, "Women and Revolution in Vietnam." For women's experiences in post-conflict Russia, see Linda Racioppi and Katherine O'Sullivan, "Organizing Women Before and After the Fall: Women's Politics in the Soviet Union and Post-Soviet Russia," in *Global Feminisms Since 1945: Rewriting Histories,* ed., Bonnie Smith (London and New York: Routledge, 2000), pp. 205–34.
53 Karam, "Women in War," pp. 4–5.
54 Shirlow and Murtagh, *Belfast: Segregation*, p. 2.

8 Securitization and de-securitization

Female soldiers and the reconstruction of women in post-conflict Sierra Leone

Megan MacKenzie

Sierra Leone is recovering from over 11 years of civil war and decades of corrupt governance. After the signing of the Lome Peace Accord in 1999, international organizations and development institutions began implementing a variety of peace, development, and reconstruction programs. In particular, the disarmament, demobilization, and reintegration (DDR) process was initiated to help former soldiers transition from "soldiers to citizens." Following Sierra Leone's conflict, nearly 75,000 soldiers were received at dozens of centers for disarmament.[1] The reintegration phase of the program for adults and children officially ended in 2002 and 2005 respectively; however, there is evidence that frontline workers and citizens of Sierra Leone still feel reintegration and rehabilitation are not complete.[2]

Numerous sources have described the disarmament process as a key element in achieving security and sustainable peace.[3] Specifically, the DDR program in Sierra Leone was touted as a fundamental element of the country's transition out of civil conflict.[4] I argue that the DDR is a prime example of Mark Duffield's account of the radicalization of development, or the coalescence of development and security policies.[5] The three phases of the DDR were designed with the understanding that peace will not result merely from the removal of guns from the hands of combatants; rather, a regimented process of rehabilitation and societal reconstruction is a prerequisite for a secure nation.

This chapter examines the inconsistencies within post-conflict programming—particularly the DDR—in the treatment of male and female soldiers. I argue that the exclusion and silencing of women in the post-conflict context in Sierra Leone are representative of the systematic and historical omission of women from post-conflict planning and development activities. The DDR in Sierra Leone is one of many humanitarian and development policies and programs that serve to construct natural, peaceful female subjects in contrast to securitized male soldiers.[6] The case of Sierra Leone demonstrates that the failure to address gender as a factor in post-conflict programming has not only sacrificed gender equality, but also the overall effectiveness of the DDR process and the chances for a true and lasting transition from conflict to peace.

Focusing on the example of Sierra Leone, I argue that despite the low numbers of female participants in the DDR process, women and girls were major players in the civil conflict in Sierra Leone. Using the Copenhagen School's conception of security as constructed through speech acts and prioritized above non-securitized or "normal" politics, I point out that even when women participate in the activities of "high politics" or sectors traditionally categorized as security priorities such as conflict, they are effectively shuffled out of the public political sphere and into the domestic realm through post-conflict development policies. The valorization of traditional issues of "high politics" (men and states with guns) relies on the devaluation of "low politics" (sex, domestic work, childbirth and the family).[7] In effect, securitizing post-conflict development, or the ranking of development issues from securitized to "normal politics" to the "domestic realm" requires both that a domestic realm exists and that it be relegated to the margins. The DDR program in Sierra Leone effectively (re)constructed female soldiers as "wives," "camp followers," or "sex slaves" in order to both distinguish them from "men with guns" and to justify the attention and resources directed at the securitized male soldier subject. The DDR in Sierra Leone, like similar failed programs in countries such as Angola and the Democratic Republic of Congo, was inadequate primarily because it was based on the assumption that female soldiers are not a security concern in the same way that male soldiers are.

The Copenhagen School's approach to security can used to explain the tendency for actors to highlight particular security concerns while neglecting others.[8] The Copenhagen School's rendering of securitization as a speech act places the securitizing actor and the audience as the central players in the construction of security. Those parties capable of raising an issue to a securitized status are said to be bestowed with a "particular legitimacy."[9] In this way, securitization is a strategic practice aimed at swaying a targeted audience to accept their interpretation of a threat. Securitization is an intersubjective process in the sense that it is only when the audience accepts a securitizing actor's speech act that an issue will become securitized.

Mark Duffield's work on the "radicalization of development," or the merging of security and development, is useful in conceptualizing the prioritization of perceived security issues that takes place in the post-conflict development context. The radicalization of development is a declaration that there is no distinct line between development and security: "achieving one is now regarded as essential for securing the other."[10] Duffield argues that the underdeveloped South has increasingly been viewed as a source of international instability "through conflict, criminal activity and terrorism."[11] For Duffield, the securitization of development has produced shifts in the priorities and approaches to development. Under this new security regime, development issues that are classified as security matters are prioritized above issues that may be considered "everyday politics."

Work on securitization generally and the securitization of development specifically lays the groundwork for understanding the DDR's treatment of male combatants as security issues and women combatants as part of "everyday politics." Still, the Copenhagen School (and critical Security Studies generally) have not systematically included gender as a category of analysis. This chapter, then, extends and applies those analyses to consider imperative questions associated with gender and power relations in post-conflict Sierra Leone, the construction of the subject, and the spaces of silence in so-called intersubjective policy dialogue.

This chapter begins with an evaluation of the DDR process in Sierra Leone as reliant on gender stereotypes which assume that men experienced the conflict as active participants, including as soldiers; while women experienced it as victims or non-combatants. Using material from more than 50 personal interviews with female former soldiers, the second section demonstrates that, contrary to these stereotypes, many women experienced the conflict in Sierra Leone as soldiers. Next, I develop an account of the gendered DDR process and the resulting policy failures. The chapter concludes by analyzing what the successful securitization of male soldiers in contrast to the de-securitization of female soldiers reveals about the social limits placed on the notion of soldier, perpetrator, and victim.

Engendering the DDR: why women were overlooked

The DDR process in Sierra Leone was advertised as a success and has been recommended as a model for future programs.[12] Despite its praises, one of the "lessons learned" from the DDR has been drawn from its treatment of women and girls. The exact number of women and girls involved in the fighting forces is unknown, however, estimates range from 10 up to 50 percent for the number of women and girls in various armed factions.[13] These numbers are not reflected in DDR statistics. Of the approximately 75,000 adult combatants disarmed, just under 5000 were females.[14] The number of girls that went through the children's DDR was abysmal; of the 6845 child soldiers disarmed, 92 percent were boys and only 8 percent were girls. UNICEF has admitted, "DDR programmes have consistently failed to attract female combatants ... Sierra Leone was no exception."[15]

Along with a growing body of research that critically examines gender and the DDR process in Sierra Leone, one of the most common explanations for the low numbers of females in the DDR is the argument that women and girls were not "real" soldiers; rather, they were primarily abductees, camp followers, domestic workers and sex slaves. In some cases, the attention given to the widespread use of sexual violence by all warring parties during the civil war in Sierra Leone has eclipsed investigations into female soldiers and female perpetrators. The international humanitarian response to Sierra Leone's conflict has also tended to concentrate on female victims. There are numerous examples of internationally supported programs directed at female victims of conflict, however, there are few programs (in fact almost none) that are directed at former female combatants. Unfortunately there are also numerous media accounts of the conflict that depict women and girls solely as victims.

Another report identified women as the "worst losers" of Sierra Leone's war. This article claimed: "Women [are] the symbol of love, kindness, mercy and spend her life in coping with sexual and mental abuses done by one or more men in countries dealing with war like situation [*sic*]."[16]

Susan McKay and Dyan Mazurana argue that having "DDR processes planned and implemented by military officials has resulted in a bias against those the military does not consider 'real soldiers' (i.e. men with guns)."[17] Mazurana and Khristopher Carlson have also determined that in Sierra Leone there was an "over-classification of girls and young women abducted by the RUF, AFRC, and SLA as 'camp followers,' 'sex-slaves,' and 'wives' by some within the international community and the Sierra Leone government."[18] They argue that this over-classification led to a disarmament process that did not address the "actual lived experiences" of girls and women.[19]

Another justification given to explain the low numbers of women in the DDR was that women and girls were simply overlooked. For example, in UNICEF's report on the lessons learned from the DDR, they cite the consideration of gender and the inclusion of girls as a major shortcoming of their programming. In fact, one of the major programs initiated in response to criticisms about the inclusion of girls and women in the DDR process was called "The Girls Left Behind." According to UNICEF, this program was created to target "young girls and women who were either still living with their captors or who had been abducted (before the age of 18) and had been released or escaped."[20] The program was designed to be a short-term intensive intervention "for abducted girls and young women to ensure their protection and reintegration and to offer them basic education and skills training."[21]

Both of these explanations deny any agency on the part of females during the war. There is an assumption that women and girls were either victims caught up in the fray of a male-dominated conflict or that they were left behind by programs that likely would have benefited them in the same way they benefited male soldiers. These explanations ignore how socially constructed ideas about the roles and place of women and men during war impact policies, depictions, and our ability to accept and acknowledge violent female soldiers with agency. My interviews with female soldiers and an investigation of the discourses used to construct males as securitized subjects in contrast to de-securitized female victims disrupt these stereotypes of women and girls as exclusively passive victims of the conflict.

Women, violence and war

One only has to peruse the literature on conflict to find evidence of the gendered assumption that men make war, women make peace.[22] War, in general, has been described as "a masculine endeavour for which women may serve as victim, spectator, or prize."[23] Women's peaceful nature and their perceived aversion to risk[24] are sometimes described as stemming from their "natural" capacity as mothers.[25] Instead of soldiering, women's primary roles during conflict tend to be described as "wives, girlfriends, and mothers, waiting for their soldiers to return and caring for wounded."[26]

Certainly there are a growing number of researchers who have been challenging assumptions about the "natural" qualities of men and women—particularly from radical, post-modern and post-structural feminists, critical Security Studies, post-colonial and development studies. Feminist International Relations scholars such as Christine Sylvester and Laura Sjoberg in particular have highlighted the historical contributions of women during war.[27] In Africa specifically there is evidence that women "have had a long history of participation in the liberation struggles of their continent" including organized resistance movements, protests, and bearing arms.[28] Despite this burgeoning research, the message that "men are natural soldiers and women are not" remains prominent in many mainstream messages about war, including the media and government and NGO reports.

Women as soldiers in Sierra Leone

Although it is indisputable that women and girls as well as men and boys experienced trauma, abuse, malnourishment, fear, and neglect, the manner in which females are consistently and continually portrayed as victims—often helpless victims—must be critically examined. Interviews with a group of former female soldiers in Sierra Leone help to shed light on the multiple roles and activities of women during the 11-year civil conflict. Every woman responded positively to the question: "Would you define yourself as a former soldier?" Women were quick to point out which armed group they were a part of, what rank they held, and what roles they carried out. For example, one woman identified herself as a commander with the RUF; another woman specified that she was a soldier "because [she] was given one week training on how to fire a gun and subsequently became active;"[29] another woman identified as a soldier because she "took part in most of the horrible activities of the evil conflict in SL;"[30] and, several women admitted that they voluntarily joined a particular faction. Women even reported going to places like Burkina Faso for military training.[31]

One soldier, Mary,[32] was one of the few women interviewed who went through the DDR process. She participated in the war as a soldier for two years. Her reported activities included fighting and killing. When she went to the demobilization center she was held for two months and given a small amount of money; however, after the program she could not find her mother and discovered that her father had died during the conflict. Mary concluded that the counselling she was given "not to do bad" was useful but argued that she needed help with the children she gave birth to from the rebels. She noted that men had the advantage of being able to leave behind their children while women were left to care for them. Mary's most provocative report was that there were at least 100 women fighting alongside her in her group: "all had guns."[33]

The duties carried out by this group of women were incredibly diverse. When asked "What were your role(s) during the conflict," over 75 percent of the women I interviewed declared that they were involved in active combat duties. The variety of responses to this question indicates the range of the roles carried out by women during the war. These responses include: "leading lethal attacks," "screening and killing pro-rebel civilians," "combatant," "poison/inject captured war prisoners with either lethal injection or acid," "I trained with [the AFRC] bush camp how to shoot a gun," "killing and maiming pro-government forces and civilians," "gun trafficking," "killing," "planning and carrying out attacks on public places," "do execution on commanders of my age group," "fighting," "murdered children," "weapon cleaner."[34] Although a significant number of the women admitted to acting as sex slaves, the vast list of duties carried out by these women defied any strict gendered notions about the roles of women during conflict. In fact, Edward Anague from a local community development organization in Freetown reported "some of the most vicious soldiers and commanders were women."[35] From these interviews it becomes clear that women and girls participated in all facets of war including active combat, commanding, and military training.

Beyond gendered stereotypes

My interviews with female soldiers in Sierra Leone not only demonstrate that women were actively involved in combat but also that the answer to the question "Why did so few women and girls go through the DDR?" requires a more in-depth answer than "they were left behind." Women's explanations for why they did not go through the DDR ranged from "I had escaped and was trying to find my parents,"[36] to "I had [another] mission in the Ivory Coast."[37] No women I spoke with indicated that they felt "left out" of the DDR and very few women indicated that they thought the DDR would have been helpful for them.

To begin with, a significant number of the women I interviewed had an incredibly negative perception of the DDR process and did not see it as an attractive option for them post-conflict. For example, descriptions of the program included "a trap to screen anti-government combatants."[38] Some women claimed that they were not convinced that the program benefited anybody other than international NGOs including Sonia[39] who reported, "We were used as everything for them [NGOs/international aid community] to have and be everything they want to be in their war and political ambitions."[40] The program was also described as a tactical "use of ex-combatants as tools for fund raising" for NGO workers to "enrich themselves."[41] Another woman commented, "All I saw was expensive vehicles being used by those NGOs and so much bureaucracy."[42]

An additional concern expressed by former female soldiers was their distrust of the promises made by the Sierra Leone government and the organizations involved in the DDR. Some witnessed the first phases of the DDR while they were still involved with the fighting forces and concluded that the "flamboyant promises"[43] made to ex-combatants were not fulfilled. This distrust also stemmed from accusations of corruption with "funds [being] directed to families of program officials"[44] in the program. These testimonies demonstrate that negative perceptions impacted women and girls' decisions not to participate in the DDR. In these cases, these women did not feel "left out" of the process; rather, they chose to avoid it because they were critical of the program and the way it was implemented.

In addition to negative perceptions of the DDR, women listed various other reasons why they did not participate in the process. A frequent response was that women believed that they needed to have a gun to be eligible for the DDR and they either did not possess a gun, or no longer had one in their possession at the time of the DDR. Initially, the disarmament process for adults required soldiers to present a gun to be eligible for benefits; during the last phases of the DDR the possession of a gun was not required. For children, the possession of a gun was never a requirement; however, many children were not clear on this fact. DDR procedures for children defined eligibility as follows "aged 7 or above; have learned to 'cock and load'; have been trained; have spent 6 months or above in the fighting forces."[45] Despite this, the primary understanding of the DDR for a striking number of the women interviewed was that it was "just about men with guns"[46] or that it was a "gun for money"[47] program directed at male rebels.

Given that the conflict in Sierra Leone lasted over 11 years, involved various armed factions, and erupted in several phases, each individual combatant did not necessarily possess his/her own weapon. The types of weapons used to fight were diverse and included machetes. These weapons were acquired, lost or stolen, and transferred from one area and faction to another. This made the DDR policy of each combatant turning in a gun for eligibility unreasonable and ineffective. Although numerous women I interviewed admitted to carrying and using guns; several admitted that they had their guns taken away from them before the DDR while others told me they left their weapons behind when they escaped from their armed group. In some of these cases, commanders or comrades deliberately took weapons from women and girls before the disarmament process so they would not be eligible for the program. In addition, both males and females who performed support roles during the conflict including domestic tasks, acting as spies or messengers, and looters may or may not have ever possessed a gun.

Saphie was one of the women who explained that she did not participate in the DDR because she did not have a weapon. Conscripted by the AFRC/RUF at the age of 14, Saphie's roles during the conflict included fighting, gun trafficking, acting as a "bush wife," and acting as a spy. Despite her role as a fighter, she reported that her commander deliberately prevented her from participating in the DDR: "I was excluded by my commander as they [*sic*] took my gun from me—the symbol to guarantee me to be part of the reintegration program." For Saphie, the strengths of the program included the huge amount of international support; however, she felt that the program did not fulfill its promises to ex-combatants. She also felt that most reintegration initiatives ended prematurely and heard about embezzlement of program funds by officials. Saphie reported that she finds her current situation frustrating as she is "just trying to survive" despite poverty.[48]

Of the 50 women I interviewed in Makeni, 44 had escaped from the armed group they were associated with. Women who had escaped from their armed group avoided the DDR not only because they did not have a weapon but also because they had returned to their families and had begun to disassociate themselves from the armed groups. For example, Fatima explained that she did not see herself as eligible for the disarmament process because she had escaped and "wasn't with the rebels any longer."[49] Another woman told me that her priority upon escaping was on finding her parents rather than going to the DDR.

In a way, escapee women left the DDR "behind" because they no longer saw themselves as soldiers or no longer wanted to be connected with armed forces. In order for the DDR to have met the needs of the large number of women and girls who escaped from the armed forces, the DDR should have specifically targeted "escapees" by making efforts to inform them that they were eligible for the DDR and that their safety would be ensured during the process.

Escapees also mentioned the fear of stigmatization that kept them away from disarmament facilities. The shame associated with going through the DDR and being connected to the armed forces was mentioned by a number of women. The stigma associated with the DDR was a result of both local attitudes about the armed groups and the actual process of the DDR. Although the people of Sierra Leone have done a remarkable job "forgiving and forgetting" the atrocities that took place during the war and accepting the former rebels and soldiers back into communities, former soldiers—particularly women—faced stigma through their association with armed groups. Also, some women were anxious to start a new life and to break ties with their lives as soldiers. Their association with programs designed for former soldiers meant that they were continually identified with the conflict. This was not an option for women who "didn't want people to know that [they] took part in [the] mad war."[50]

Stigmatization was a major source of insecurity for former female combatants. One woman told me she did not want to be "seen publicly as an ex-combatant" out of "fear of retaliation"[51] from community members or other rebel factions. Similarly, a young woman told me she had reason to believe that if she showed up at the DDR, she would be killed by the Special Security Death Squad, a brutal specialized armed group. Given the fact that the DDR took place at the dubious end of a 11-year civil war, some women and girls were not convinced that the fighting was truly over and did not want to openly label themselves at the DDR out of concern for their security.

One soldier in particular, "Kadie," was recruited by the Kamajors before she was 12 years old. She reported that her duties as a soldier included spying, "toting property," and being used as a sex slave for her commander. She recounted that she did not go through the DDR: "the Kamajors prevented me because they have a taboo that they do not touch or come close to women—but that was a lie ... they use women as combatants." Kadie admitted she did not know the details of the DDR program, however, she had heard of the foreign involvement and the large amounts of money directed through the program. Kadie expressed frustration at how females were treated in post-conflict Sierra Leone: "All of us were combatants but treated as housewives and sex slaves."[52]

Pride was an additional theme in the responses given by women who were asked about their attendance at the DDR. Several women I interviewed indicated either that they had "better plans" for themselves than the DDR or that they felt the DDR was "below them" somehow. For example, one woman told me she avoided the DDR because she had been promised by the head of the Civil Defence Forces that she would be given "a lucrative house and educational support"[53] if she remained with the forces. Theresa told me she had money from the war and did not need the handouts offered at the DDR. A few women had made plans to go on missions in the Ivory Coast and Guinea or had hoped to travel to South Africa with the Executive Outcome Forces—an armed group from South Africa. These women were not left out of the DDR but had charted courses they saw as more attractive than participating in the process.

Perhaps what was most interesting about the answers the women gave me were the discussions I had with women who felt they were "above" the DDR. One woman explained to me that she thought her "looks would carry [her] a long way"[54] and that she did not need the resources offered by the DDR. Another informed me that she was "too popular"[55] to go to the DDR and that people would recognize her and target her and her family. After reading numerous accounts of the oppression and victimization of women during and after the conflict, it was surprising to hear the pride—even arrogance—women associate with their role as a soldier. For some women who had achieved higher ranks within the warring factions, the notion of attending the DDR with lower ranking soldiers was insulting. One woman explained, "I was not convinced to see myself parade before people I had authority over for years."[56] Several other women mentioned their disapproval of the "segregation within the command ranks" at the DDR.[57] The lessons learned from the DDR in Sierra Leone do not account for these shifts in power that occurred during the civil war (and numerous other wars) and the difficulty women had with losing this power.

These interviews indicate the complexities associated with women's decisions not to go to the DDR. Programs for female victims of the war, abducted girls and women, and girls "left behind" were developed in the absence of women's own accounts of what roles they took up during the war, how they perceived the DDR and why they did not participate in the DDR. Although these were "choices" made in extremely constrained circumstances; by ignoring women's accounts of why they made these decisions useful lessons to be derived from the DDR become buried. The decisions that female soldiers made in relation to the DDR should be seen as political decisions and must be taken into account when considering the effectiveness and impact of the DDR process.

Beyond followers and sex slaves: engendering representations

Even for the few women and girls who were recognized as playing an active role in Sierra Leone's conflict, a variety of titles were constructed to avoid calling them soldiers, including: "camp followers," "abductees," "sex slaves," "domestic slaves," or "girls and women associated with the fighting forces" and "vulnerable groups associated with armed movements". One of the facilitators of the DDR program admitted, "women were just seen as camp followers even though some were active combatants and some went through military training."[58] In fact, even major international organizations that helped oversee the DDR process have been reluctant to name women and girls as combatants. The program established by UNICEF to address women and girls that should have benefited from the DDR, "The girls left behind," makes little reference to the title "soldiers." In an hour-long interview with Glenis Taylor, a senior director at UNICEF Sierra Leone, she never used the term "soldier" to refer to these women and girls. Instead she identified them as "girls with the fighting forces" and "girls who were involved with the fighting forces."[59]

The logical maneuvering that categorizes females out of the rank of soldier goes something like this: most females acted in support roles for the fighting forces rather than in combat roles. Therefore females were primarily non-combatants, and non-combatants are not soldiers. This logic is fallacious both because of the problematic assumption that women and girls were not combatants and because it wrongly assumes that the support work carried out by females during conflict does not render them soldiers. Vivi Stavrou notes:

> Not labelling the work of non-combatant women soldiers as soldiering, continues the gender discrimination of the division of labour whereby critical work that is essential for survival, is simply considered a natural extension of women's domestic obligations and hence neither worthy of remuneration nor significant enough for women to qualify for training and livelihoods programs.[60]

Even though the term "soldier" refers to anyone who is a member of an armed group, questions and concerns over the distinction between *combatant* and *soldier* have been raised in relation to women and girls. A review of the capacities, ranks, and services of any army reveals that a variety of duties and contributions are required for almost all combat operations, however, typically there are few who question if male officers who fulfill support roles such as medical operations or communications are "real soldiers." When men act as porters, cleaners, domestic help, or messengers during war they are considered soldiers; there is little debate about the extent to which they deserve the soldier title. However, there has been extensive debate about the functions of female soldiers in Sierra Leone and the extent to which their work "counts" as soldiering. In effect, active female combatants became "de-securitized" through the process of being stripped of their title as soldier while male combatants were unquestionably categorized as soldiers and a security concern.

The manner in which male and female soldiers have been categorized post-conflict has had several interrelated impacts: first, stripping women and girls of their titles as soldiers by distinguishing them from "true" or "real" combatants depoliticized their roles during the conflict; second, as development grows ever more concerned with people and issues identified as security concerns, depoliticizing the role of women and girls during the conflict meant that they were not targeted as primary beneficiaries for the DDR program and other reintegration initiatives; third, politicizing and securitizing the DDR process for male soldiers and de-prioritizing and de-politicizing women has meant that the reintegration process for women has largely been seen as a social process, a "returning to normal" that would happen "naturally." In effect, the maneuvering to designate females as camp followers, victims, wives or any designation other than soldier should be seen as an example of the power relations at play in securitizing an issue and defining a securitized subject. Eliminating women from the category of soldier and security priority also removes them from significant policy discourses.

The new "normal"

For the case of Sierra Leone, the role of the development community in reshaping gender roles during the reintegration process cannot be overlooked. Organizations in Sierra Leone largely treated the reintegration of women and girls as a social process, a "returning to normal" that would either happen naturally, with time, or through sensitization—meaning talking to communities and families about the need to "take women and girls back." In particular, there was great concern about the "marriageability" of female soldiers largely because it was assumed that they had been raped, or they had given birth to children out of wedlock.[61] In some cases, grandmothers offered to raise the children of former soldiers so that they could marry without men having to worry about supporting "rebel children."[62] Some organizations even encouraged former female soldiers to marry their rape perpetrators in order to avoid shame and to blend into the community.[63]

Women were given few "choices" in their reintegration process: silence or stigma, limited training or nothing, isolation or marriage, motherhood, and returning to their families. Each of these "choices" was seen as an opportunity to hide their identities as soldiers and to "blend in" "naturally" to the community and family unit. Stevens argues, "to 'naturalize' is to express the necessity of a form of being or practice, to make something seem impervious to human intention and immutable."[64] Understood this way, "naturalizing" the process of reintegration for women and girls in Sierra Leone effectively de-securitized female soldiers and justified the limited attention given to them.

By encouraging women and girl soldiers to return to their "normal places" in the community, any new roles or positions of authority that they may have held during the conflict are stripped from them and any opportunities to rethink and reshape gender stereotypes and hierarchies are destroyed. "Normal women" become defined primarily as victims of the war while women and girls who were soldiers, who were perpetrators of violence and destruction, who volunteered to participate in conflict or who were empowered by the conflict, become categorized as deviants. In Hansen's reading of Derrida, she concludes:

> [T]he positive value ascribed to "women" is preconditioned upon women's acceptance of the subject position bestowed upon them. If "women" were to be constructed, or construct themselves, as less motherly, less caring, and less publicly passive, their supplementary privilege would in all likelihood be suspended.[65]

Implications of a gendered and securitized DDR

The interviews I did in Sierra Leone showed a different face of concepts such as "post-conflict," "reintegration," "rehabilitation," and "reconstruction." In the experiences of the 50 women who were interviewed for this project, these terms were not gender neutral. The overwhelming message my interviewees had was that there is no "post" conflict for many female soldiers in Sierra Leone. For a large number of the women interviewed different forms of violence such as forced marriage, sexual exploitation and isolation continue despite the cessation of formal conflict. In addition, female soldiers' social and political choices seem more constrained by notions of loyalty, duty, and identity in the "post-"conflict period than they were during the conflict.

In post-conflict Sierra Leone, international organizations, non-governmental organizations and aid agencies have funding, networks, and influence that garner them significant positions of power in comparison to Sierra Leone's shaky government. As a result of this power, these organizations possess the ability to selectively securitize issues and determine their priority. Given the radicalization of development, or the increasing attention to security as a major factor in development, NGOs and aid agencies have a particular stake in designating a societal phenomenon as a security concern requiring immediate attention. Due to the escalating emphasis placed on security by development actors and governments, securitizing an issue is an effective method of garnering funding; it indicates that an urgent response is required and that addressing this particular issue is central to stability and peace.

The radicalization of development in Sierra Leone has meant that issues understood as traditional security concerns, including disarmament, unemployed men, and male soldiers have been given significant attention in the post-conflict context. Moreover, matters relating to women, including sexual violence and female soldiers, continue to be categorized as domestic, social or private matters. Male soldiers continue to be securitized post-conflict in contrast to the "naturalization" and domestication of women. The reintegration process for men has been emphasized as vital to the transition from war to peace while the reintegration process for females has been deemed a "social concern" and has been moralized as a "return to normal." Post-conflict programs that assume women and girls are victims lacking agency have dismissed, isolated, and silenced a vast cohort of women and girls. The reluctance by international aid agencies, the United Nations, the World Bank and other international organizations to name female soldiers as soldiers rather than "females associated with the war," "dependants," or "camp followers" ignores and depoliticizes their roles during the conflict. In addition, this construction relegates them spatially to the private realm—well away from the attention given to securitized and politicized matters.

This research verifies the Copenhagen School's insight that security is a political category resulting in the prioritization of particular issues or events as significant over "everyday politics." In the case of post-conflict Sierra Leone, however, it is important to see that one of the political forces operating on the selection of security concerns is gender—male former combatants are securitized while female former combatants are marginalized. This understanding lends support to Lene Hansen's argument that "new" conceptions of security such as human security[66] do not free us from the hierarchy of policy priorities associated with traditional conceptions of security. Human security or individual security concerns still do not receive the same amount of attention and funding as so-called "hard" security matters. This means that, in patriarchal societies, security threats that typically concern women do not "make the cut" for securitization because women and "gender issues" largely remain in the domestic sphere rather than the political, international, or security sphere.

The relationship between notions of "stability," "peace," "victim," and "violent," "threatening," "conflict" to presumptions about femininity and masculinity must be unpacked in order to illustrate how security discourses not only continue to discount the role of women and girls in otherwise securitized activities but also contribute to the reconstruction of "normal" female subjects as benevolent, nurturing, or victims in contrast to violent and aggressive males. Women and girls have been victimized during conflict, however, they have also been active participants, including as soldiers. There are obvious limits to theorizing about violent women that must be deconstructed. Feminist scholars in particular can contribute a great deal by continuing to discover ways to intercept security discourses and to disrupt hegemonic characterizations of the female victim. Feminists also need to contemplate whether there is room within feminist work on violence, the state, and the political and domestic sphere to theorize about women who choose to be violent in the name of the state as well as women who choose to inflict sexual violence.

Further examination of the reordering that takes place through programs like the DDR in the name of development and security must be done in order to expose the canyons of silence that continue to surround women's and girls' experiences of war. As Carolyn Nordstrom has noted, "What we hear and do not hear about the world we occupy is no accident … Shaping knowledge, and a lack of knowledge, constitutes a basic element of power. Silences, spheres where knowledge has been kept from public awareness are undeniably political."[67] Sierra Leone's disarmament process should not be hailed as a success or exported as a model for other countries without accounting for women's and girls' own depictions of their roles and experiences during the conflict. Real attention to women's and girls' experiences would produce a more complicated understanding of women (who can be both victims and aggressors/agents) and of conflict (as consuming of the entire society and extending beyond the official timelines of war).

Such complicated notions of both women and the conflicts they participate in would bring new solutions and new questions to policy analysis in post-conflict reconstruction. One solution such an analysis offers is the argument that it is crucial to disarm, demobilize, and reintegrate female former combatants on the terms of their needs and their experiences in the conflict if the society is to transition from conflict to peace. Another important realization is that the needs of former female combatants cannot be determined solely by understanding the ways in which they have been victimized by the conflict—it is also important to consider the ways in which they have participated in the conflict as agents, as supporters, and as soldiers. A third important tool that this analysis provides is that the process of securitization is gendered and that the ultimate success of post-conflict policies and peace-building efforts depend on appropriate recognition of the broader security and development concerns that are muted or eclipsed as a result of this bias.

If the ultimate success of peace-building efforts relies on political decisions about what to securitize and what not to, this analysis brings up a number of new questions as well. The negative impacts of the DDR process in Sierra Leone on women suggest that there is a need to reconsider the positive association of "reintegration" and "reconstruction" with progress and development. In other words, if the reintegration process for females is called "a return to normal" guided by gender stereotypes and a return to pre-war limiting and oppressive understandings of women's capabilities, then the DDR process risks regressing women instead of bringing them forward and entrenching gender inequality. It follows that a truly progressive or developmental post-conflict reconstruction program would include more radical change in the area of women's status in society, both for its own sake and for the sake of the success of peace efforts.

What this analysis does make clear is that the time has come that the voluntary participation of women and girls in traditionally male-dominated activities such as war can no longer be overlooked. In Sierra Leone, the effectiveness of post-conflict programming, an inclusive transition from conflict to peace, and gender equality post-conflict have been compromised because of this omission; an error that will be repeated so long as reconstruction programs remain blind to the needs of women not only as victims but as participants in conflicts around the world.

Notes

1 Sanam Anderlini and Dyan Mazurana, "Boys and Girls Who Also Carried Guns: Forgotten in the Peace," *International Herald Tribune* op-ed, March 12, 2004.
2 Dehegue Shiaka, Sulay Sesay, Edward Abu, Joseph Momo, personal interview by Megan MacKenzie, Freetown, Sierra Leone, December, 2005.
3 WomenWarPeace. "Disarmament, Demobilization and Reintegration (DDR)," Women, War, Peace and Disarmament, Demobilization and Reintegration (DDR). Available at: www.womenwarpeace.org/issues/ddr/ddr.htm.
4 The disarmament processes in other African countries such as the Democratic Republic of Congo and Mozambique were very similar to the model used in Sierra Leone. In these cases, the DDR was also viewed as an essential element in the transition from war to peace.
5 Mark Duffield, *Global Governance and the New Wars: The Merging of Development and Security* (New York and London: Zed Books, 2001), p. 37.
6 See Charli Carpenter, *Innocent Women and Children: Gender Norms and the Protection of Civilians* (Aldershot: Ashgate, 2006).
7 See Laura Sjoberg, *Gender, Justice, and the Wars in Iraq: A Feminist Reformulation of Just War Theory* (New York: Lexington Books, 2006).
8 See Barry Buzan, Ole Wæver and Jaap de Wilde, *Security: A New Framework for Analysis* (Boulder, CO: Lynne Rienner Press, 1998); Barry Buzan and Ole Wæver, *Regions and Powers: The Structure of International Security* (Cambridge: Cambridge University Press, 2003).
9 Lene Hansen, *Security as Practice: Discourse Analysis and the Bosnian War* (London: Routledge, 2006), p. 35.
10 Duffield, *Global Governance and the New Wars*, p. 16.
11 Ibid., p. 2.
12 See World Bank. "The World Bank, Sierra Leone: Disarmament, Demobilization and Reintegration (DDR) in the World Bank's Engagement in Africa Region," Good Practice Infobrief Findings. Number 81, October 2002. Available at: www.worldbank.org/afr/findings/infobeng/infob81.pdf.
13 Sulay Sesay, Interviewees #1–50, interview by Megan MacKenzie, November 12–December 20, 2005. See also Anderlini and Mazurana, "Boys and Girls Who Also Carried Guns: Forgotten in the Peace."
14 Dyan Mazurana and Kristopher Carlson, *From Combat to Community; Women and Girls of Sierra Leone* (Washington, DC: Women Waging Peace, 2004).
15 UNICEF, "The Impact of Conflict on Women and Girls in West and Central Africa and the UNICEF Response." Available at: www.unicef.org/publications/files/Impact_final.pdf (New York: UNICEF, 2005).
16 We the Women. "Sierra Leone's War: Women the Worst Losers." Available at: www.wethewomen.org/entry/help-war-time-sexual-abused-sierra-leones-woman.
17 Susan McKay and Dyan Mazurana, *Where Are the Girls? Girls in Fighting Forces in Uganda, Sierra Leone and Mozambique: Their Lives During and After the War* (Ottawa, Canada: Rights and Democracy, 2004), p. 114.
18 Mazurana and Carlson, *From Combat to Community*, p. 21.

19 Ibid., p. 21.

20 UNICEF, "The Impact of Conflict."

21 Ibid., p. 17.

22 Jennifer Turpin. "Many Faces: Women Confronting War," in *The Women and War Reader*, eds., Lois Ann Lorentzen and Jennifer Turpin (New York: New York University Press, 1998), p. 32.

23 Francine D'Amico. "Feminist Perspectives on Women Warriors," in *The Woman and War Reader*, eds., Lois Ann Lorentzen and Jennifer Turpin (Albany, NY: New York University Press, 1998), p. 119.

24 See Rawwida Baksh, Linda Etchart, Elsie Onubogu and Tina Johnson, eds., *Gender Mainstreaming in Conflict Transformation: Building Sustainable Peace.* (London: Commonwealth Secretariat, 2002).

25 See Mary Daly, *Pure Lust: Elemental Feminist Philosophy* (London: The Women's Press, 1984); Sara Ruddick, *Maternal Thinking* (Boston: Beacon Press, 1989).

26 April Carter, "Should Women Be Soldiers or Pacifists?" in *The Woman and War Reader*, eds., Lois Ann Lorentzen and Jennifer Turpin (New York: New York University Press, 1998), p. 33.

27 See Christine Sylvester, *Feminist International Relations: An Unfinished Journey* (Cambridge: Cambridge University Press, 2002); Christine Sylvester and Swati Parashar, "The Contemporary 'Mahabharata' and the Many 'Draupadis,'" paper prepared for presentation at the 2008 Annual Meeting of the International Studies Association, San Francisco, CA, March 26–29, 2008; Laura Sjoberg, *Gender, Justice, and the Wars in Iraq* (New York: Lexington Books, 2006); Laura Sjoberg and Caron Gentry, *Mothers, Monsters, Whores: Women's Violence in Global Politics* (London: Zed Books, 2007).

28 Patricia T. Morris, "Women, Resistance, and the Use of Force in South Africa," in *Women and the Use of Military Force*, eds., Ruth H. Howes, and Michael R. Stevenson (Boulder, CO: Lynne Rienner Publishers, 1993).

29 Interviewee #28, interview by Megan MacKenzie, Makeni, Sierra Leone, December 15, 2005.

30 Interviewee #14, interview by Megan MacKenzie, Makeni, Sierra Leone, December 15, 2005.

31 Andrea Ferrero, interview by Megan MacKenzie, Makeni, Sierra Leone, November 30, 2005.

32 To protect the identity of the interviewees, all of the names used in reference to female soldier interviewees are fictional.

33 Interviewee #8, interview by Megan MacKenzie, Makeni, Sierra Leone, December 13, 2005

34 Interviewees #44, 12, 38, 9, 21, 22, 33, 4, 18, 39, 2, 25, 42, interviews by Megan MacKenzie, Makeni, Sierra Leone, December 13–15, 2005.

35 Edward Anague, interview by Megan MacKenzie, Makeni, Sierra Leone, November 28, 2005.

36 Interviewee #15, interview by Megan MacKenzie, Makeni, Sierra Leone, December 15, 2005

37 Interviewee #1, interview by Megan MacKenzie, Makeni, Sierra Leone, December 12, 2005.

38 Interviewee #42, interview by Megan MacKenzie, Makeni, Sierra Leone, December 11, 2005.

39 Interviewee #44, interview by Megan MacKenzie, Makeni, Sierra Leone, December 11, 2005.

40 Interviewee #37, interview by Megan MacKenzie, Makeni, Sierra Leone, December 12, 2005.

41 Interviewee #12, interview by Megan MacKenzie, Makeni, Sierra Leone, December 15, 2005.

42 Interviewee #8, interview by Megan MacKenzie, Makeni, Sierra Leone, December 14, 2005.
43 Interviewee #19, interview by Megan MacKenzie, Makeni, Sierra Leone, December 11, 2005.
44 Interviewee #25, interview by Megan MacKenzie, Makeni, Sierra Leone, December 15, 2005.
45 UNICEF, "The Impact of Conflict."
46 Interviewee #23, interview by Megan MacKenzie, Makeni, Sierra Leone, December 14, 2005.
47 Interviewee #17, interview by Megan MacKenzie, Makeni, Sierra Leone, December 14, 2005.
48 "Saphie," interview 49, interview by Megan MacKenzie, Makeni, Sierra Leone, December 15, 2005.
49 Interviewee #1, interview by Megan MacKenzie, Makeni, Sierra Leone, December 11, 2005.
50 Interviewee #25, interview by Megan MacKenzie, Makeni, Sierra Leone, December 11, 2005.
51 Interviewee #1, interview by Megan MacKenzie, Makeni, Sierra Leone, December 15, 2005.
52 Interview by Megan MacKenzie, Makeni, Sierra Leone, December 15, 2005.
53 Interviewee #42, interview by Megan MacKenzie, Makeni, Sierra Leone, December 15, 2005.
54 Interviewee #23, interview by Megan MacKenzie, Makeni Sierra Leone, December 15, 2005.
55 Interviewee #43, interview by Megan MacKenzie, Makeni, Sierra Leone, December 15, 2005.
56 Interviewee #42, interview by Megan MacKenzie, Makeni, Sierra Leone, December 15, 2005.
57 Interviewees #19, 42, 43, 26, interviews by Megan MacKenzie, Makeni, Sierra Leone, December 14–15, 2005.
58 Andrea Ferrero, interview by Megan MacKenzie, Makeni, Sierra Leone, November 30, 2005.
59 Glenis Taylor, interview by Megan MacKenzie, Freetown, Sierra Leone, December 2, 2005.
60 Vivi Stavrou, "Breaking the Silence: Girls Abducted During Armed Conflict in Angola," Final Report: Canadian International Development Agency and the Christian Children's Fund. Period covering September 2003–March 2005.
61 S. Shelper, "Les Filles-Soldats: Trajectoires d'après-guerre en Sierra Leone," *Politique Africaine* 88 (December 2002): 49–62.
62 Interviewee #42, interview by Megan MacKenzie, Makeni, Sierra Leone, December 26, 2005.
63 See Shelper, "Les Filles-Soldats," and Baldi Giulia and Megan MacKenzie, "Silent Identities: Children Born of War in Sierra Leone," in *Born of War*, ed., R. Charli Carpenter (London: Kumarian Press, 2007), pp. 78–94.
64 Jacqueline Stevens, *Reproducing the State* (Princeton: Princeton University Press, 1999), p. 22.
65 Lene Hansen, *Security as Practice*, p. 21.
66 United Nations Development Programme (UNDP), *Human Development Report 1994* (New York: Oxford University Press), p. 23. Available at: www.undp.org/hdro/1994/94.htm.
67 Carolyn Nordstrom, "Girls Behind the (Front) Lines," in *The Women and War Reader*, eds., Lois Ann Lorentzen and Jennifer Turpin (New York: New York University Press, 1998), p. 81.

9 Women, militancy, and security[1]

The South Asian conundrum

Swati Parashar

If the end of the Cold War permitted debates on security to focus on intra-state conflicts, another fundamental shift in security discourses took place in the wake of the September 11, 2001 attacks on the United States. This shift re-introduced the rhetoric of "us" vs. "them," "good" vs. "evil" and state vs. non-state actors is the new framework of security. "Terrorism" as a method, strategy or even tactics of political violence often employed by states and non-state actors in pursuit of an ideology is now being categorized as an ideology, much like Fascism, Nazism, and Communism, that liberal democratic states must defeat ideologically and militarily to preserve human values and precious human life.[2] In this new paradigm, the referent of security is the state, and the providers of security are courageous and strong male leaders and macho soldiers who are willing to lay down their lives in defense of civilized societies and states. These protectors "protect" from the enemy or the "other," "terrorists," with exclusivist and backward-looking ideologies and who generally have a sinister, violent and apocalyptic worldview.

The underlying assumption behind the "war on terror" is the view that a definite military victory against "terrorism" is possible, much like the way the other "isms" have been defeated. This idea sits uneasily, however, when the meaning of terrorism is explored more thoroughly. Most understandings of terrorism oversimplify it. Bruce Hoffman takes a first step, defining terrorism as

> [the] deliberate creation and exploitation of fear through violence or the threat of violence in the pursuit of political change. All terrorist acts involve violence or the threat of violence. Terrorism is specifically designed to have far reaching psychological effects beyond the immediate victim(s) or object of the terrorist attack.[3]

This explains the "what" of terrorism but there is no "why" or even "who" addressed here. I argue that definitions like this remain unable to capture the range of militant activities and political violence attributed to non-state actors. Ethnic, religious, political and cultural factors play an important role in the nature of violent tactics that militant groups adopt.

The challenge faced by "third world" theorists and feminist scholars of International Relations (IR) and Security Studies lies in deconstructing this "state-centric" discourse and dealing with the "why" question on "terrorism." The "why" question has other variants that include "who" and for "whom." These questions involve exploring issues of class, caste (in South Asia) and ethnic identities with gender as the common factor among them. The contours of "terrorism," or militancy as I prefer to use, therefore, cannot be mapped along the territories of nation-states alone.

The "war on terror" has been presented as a hyper-masculine war where virile and aggressive men, fighting for the honor of their nations, and freedom, lead the forces on either side. The Bush–bin Laden war of conflicting ideologies and worldviews strongly reinforces gendered understandings and identities and pushes women out of the IR theater. By engaging with two categories of militant women—in ethno-nationalist movements and in religio-political movements—through case studies of Sri Lanka and Kashmir, I attempt to highlight the multiple narrativisation taking place at the margins of the IR theater. However, these categories must not be understood as mutually exclusive as ethno-nationalist movements may draw inspiration from religious ideologies as is the case in Palestine and Chechnya. I merely wish to draw a distinction between movements which are driven by political demands for separatism against state-led majoritarian chauvinism and those that construct the "other" on the basis of religio-political interests. These two militant projects in South Asia use a range of violent tactics and women are engaged at logistical, ideological and even at combatant levels.

Gendered "terror" engendering in(security)

Gender and militancy[4] have an intimate relationship; the strategy of militancy is a "gendered" one. Gender matters in understanding 9/11 and other identity conflicts on various fronts. First, the largest numbers of victims of militancy, emanating from long-lasting conflicts are women and children, who suffer violent deaths, displacement, trauma, emotional and other physical problems as they reconstruct life in conflict zones. A gendered discourse has traditionally looked at women as hapless victims of conflicts and militant attacks, or as women's groups, which stand in opposition to conflict and militarization. Feminists have argued that a more peaceful world is possible only where women realize their full potential in an environment of equal opportunities. Feminist scholarship has brought into focus the notions of negotiation, good offices, mediation, articulation, multi-track diplomacy and other such methods of peaceful resolution of conflicts.

Second, women as cultural bearers of national identities become upholders of the key values of the conflicting sides. In other words, women's bodies and their gendered identities become the territories on which militants and counter-militants wage their war, and play out their ideologies. Religious fundamentalist groups target women as the potential bearers of their ideology by reinforcing religious symbols like the veil and by excluding them from public spaces. The Taliban's radical fundamentalist form of *Sharia*, Islamic rule in Afghanistan, banned women's education, activism and even physical presence in Afghan society. The misogynist ideology of the Taliban and Al Qaeda subjected women to extreme form of subjugation, indignities and private forms of violence.[5] States in their anti-militant operations, on the other hand, have the "emancipation" of women on their agenda, claiming the superiority of their democratic and liberal ideology as against the destructive and inhuman worldview of the militants. Such claims have been made in the justification of the recent US-led wars in Afghanistan and Iraq, as well as in many wars in the past.[6]

A third way and an important one in which militancy and gender are linked is the increasing militarization of women who participate in the "postmodern wars"[7] and support militant activities. Cynthia Enloe argues that women's gendered identities and bodies become marked territories on which both states and non-state militant groups wage their wars and construct national narratives.[8] These narratives incorporate gendered variables such as the ideology of masculinity, parades, alliances and weaponry resonated in the masculine high politics, terror tactics and armed attacks along with feminized concepts of patriotic motherhood, armed heroines, national sacrifice and sexualized female warriors in both state and non-state militant projects. Many contemporary ethno-nationalist and politico-religious armed militant movements against states and their institutions also rely upon a particular version of the idea of the "liberated woman," an ideological rhetoric that Enloe ascribes to state militaries.

Armed groups and non-state militant organizations, like state militaries, have traditionally been masculine domains. Though under-researched, women have performed different kinds of roles in non-state militant projects, challenging traditional notions of femininity and also in the process displacing the masculinist paradigmatic model of political violence. In a domain which has traditionally tested and certified the masculinity of men, the presence of women "contributes to the erasure of this symbolic feature" and destabilizes the gender hierarchy.[9] While women have participated in modern nationalist movements since the mid-nineteenth century (including anti-state subversive movements in Europe, Russia and Latin America), the state-run armed forces in the West opened to women in the 1970s to "restore legitimacy to the armed forces which in many countries were going through a deep crisis of public consensus."[10] In this vein, it can be argued that women's participation provides non-state militant movements with the much needed moral legitimacy and popular support base, a key contention in the remainder of this chapter.

Women's proximity to violence and terror is marked by a convergence of "ideology" and "nation" and this convergence is "suffused with both organized violence and selfless sacrifice."[11] Considering that women and their concerns are excluded from state practices and discursive ideologies and that states are gendered political constructs defined in terms of masculine values, it can be argued that non-state resistance movements, at the margins of the IR theater, offer scope for gendered maneuverings and shifting roles for men and women. Gendered roles and hierarchies are constantly being negotiated at the margins of global politics where non-state militant actors constitute "the other" for the states which occupy the center stage. Women militants being the "other within the other" have the onerous task of securing socio-political legitimacy for the resistance movement. These women in their multi-pronged roles as patrons, planners and perpetrators of militant violence, also expand the support network base of militant projects while their own status remains mired in ambiguity due to their perceived "deviant" social behavior that transcends conventional gender roles.

South Asia's en(gendered) wars

While wars and terror in popular South Asian discourse are easily classified as religious, political and economic, gender is never thought of as a category of analysis. Kashmir and Sri Lanka, in the Indian subcontinent, have witnessed long years of protracted conflict which are products of colonial and post-colonial politics. They have a history of organized armed militancy and guerrilla warfare. The secessionist demands in these two conflicts derive their moral and political legitimacy from constructions of the self as "victims" of the "oppressor" majoritarian state and its militaristic ideologies. While transnational networks have provided moral and material support to the Kashmiri (Indian) and Tamil (Sri Lankan) movements, internecine rivalries have undermined their political credibility.[12] The "everyday-ness" of violence has affected the lives of people, economy and infrastructure in both Kashmir and Sri Lanka.

However, despite these similarities, the two movements differ significantly in their methodology, propaganda, network and ideology. In Sri Lanka, the conflict is between two ethnic communities (majority Sinhala and minority Tamils) and the anti-state resistance by the Tamils has a distinct ethno-nationalist origin. The resistance itself has gone through several stages of political and violent engagements and the actors have transformed over the years. Pockets of resistance organized around several militant groups gradually crystallized around the Liberation Tigers of Tamil Eelam (LTTE), led by the charismatic Vellupillai Prabhakaran. The LTTE is engaged in a long guerrilla war[13] that also involves terror tactics like suicide bombings and political assassinations against the state and civilians.

Kashmir (in India) offers a much more complex conflict scenario, involving many actors and claimants to the nationalist discourse and representation. Many militant groups involved in the conflict are based in the territory of a neighboring state (Pakistan). The anti-state militancy is targeted against the Indian security forces and Indian citizens (Hindus, Muslims, and Sikhs) seen as the "other" who are soft targets in Kashmir as well as in other parts of India. Religious identity plays an important role in the militant separatist project in Kashmir.

Much has been written about the victimization of women in terror campaigns unleashed by the militant groups both in Kashmir and Sri Lanka. However, the lack of scholarly engagement with women's involvement in the militancy shows that International Relations and Security Studies continue to be gender-blind, excluding women from wars and conflicts and most importantly denying them their politics. In both conflicts, women are engaged at the logistical, ideological and even at the combatant levels.[14] Women facilitate and participate in violent activities that include guerrilla warfare, suicide bombings, and act as couriers of bombs, weapons, money and messages.

Against the state for a state

Ethno-nationalist political movements provide a theoretical framework for engaging with gender roles and experiences and aspirations of women. A careful study shows that anti-state separatist nationalisms provide more ideological and political space for women to participate as combatants than institutionalized state or pro-state nationalisms.[15] Nationalist political movements against perceived foreign "occupation" or political and economic "oppression" which rely on militant tactics are more likely to attract women as militants and potential suicide bombers than movements that are based on other kinds of religious and political ideologies.[16] It is the "political" as much as the "personal" that propels these women to become perpetrators and patrons of violence:

> In national liberation armies, where the hierarchical and organizational framework of the forces is much less formal, a strong common ideological stance might help to transcend some of the gendered prejudices and tensions, especially where women's emancipation is seen to symbolize the emancipation of the entire nation.[17]

Often, militant or combatant women transcend conventional roles only in order to reinforce them as the "ideal" that is lost in situations of conflict. The female body is the prime site for gendered politics in such nationalist projects. Women "sacrifice" their sons, fathers and brothers in the nationalist struggle. The "sacrificial" womb is also transformed into a weapon itself as suicide bombers detonate the explosive belts around their waist as part of their war against the hegemonic state for the creation of a political system that can meet their aspirations. They not only "reproduce" and "create" for the nation but are also prepared to embrace death for the cause of the nation. They are the upholders of the nation and the national values that validate their demands for a new state or an alternative political structure.

Valentine Moghadam has made a useful distinction between two kinds of revolutionary movements: one which uses women as a symbol of liberation and modernization, in which case women would be encouraged to participate actively in the military, and one which uses women as a symbol of the national culture and tradition which is to be reclaimed, in which case women are virtually excluded from formal participation, and the nature of their supportive roles is highly controlled.[18] The ethno-nationalist separatist movements would fall into the first category while religio-political movements can be better represented in the second category. The militant movement for a separate Tamil "Elam" (homeland for the Tamils) in Sri Lanka has often projected women's emancipation as an important revolutionary agenda and women are encouraged to take up arms against their oppressors, i.e. the Sinhalese people and the Sri Lankan state. The leadership in the Sri Lankan Tamil militancy movement has often argued that freedom, both economic and political, must translate into the emancipation of women and better conditions for their lives in both the private and public spheres.

In Sri Lanka, the LTTE includes within its cadres, men, women and even child soldiers for which it has been extensively criticized by the international community. One-fifth or about 20 percent of the LTTE's force consists of women who have performed deadly suicide bombings, especially of high profile targets like the former Indian Prime Minister, Rajiv Gandhi.[19] The LTTE began recruiting women into their fighting cadres in the mid-1980s. Women performed a range of logistical activities in the early stages. They participated in ideological propaganda, medical care, intelligence gathering, fundraising and recruitment. Gradually they began to be inducted in military training and turned into a "well organised, highly disciplined and experienced fighting force."[20] In 1983, the LTTE founded a special section for women called the Vituthalai Pulikal Munani or the Women's Front of the Liberation Tigers.[21] Women cadres began to increase after the 1990s and they have carried out a number of suicide bombings and armed attacks since then.

There is an intense debate among feminist scholars and also within the Tamil community in Sri Lanka about the status of LTTE's women cadres. One scholarly tradition traces their "victimhood" and inferior status within the patriarchal and conservative Tamil society which is then extended within the LTTE ranks. It is widely believed that most of these women were recruited when the LTTE had already lost a number of its male cadres. Radhika Coomaraswamy, the Director of the International Centre for Ethnic Studies in Colombo and former UN Special Rapporteur on Violence against Women (1994–2003) made headlines when she called the LTTE women "cogs in the wheel." To use her words, "They [the LTTE women] are not initiators of ideas, they are only implementers of policy made by someone else ... They are the consumers, not the producers of the grand political project."[22]

It can be argued that recruiting these women became indispensable for the movement and women were not always mobilized for their empowerment. In my interviews with ex-LTTE women combatants in Batticaloa,[23] many women mentioned not having a choice as they joined the ranks of the LTTE. The Tigers require every Tamil family to send one child to serve the Tamil cause through the LTTE; some families sent girls. The opportunities for women within the LTTE are generally limited and women have rarely occupied important positions. Akhila Akka has headed the women's wing but apart from selecting Dhanu and her companion Shuba, who were part of the Rajiv Gandhi death squad, there is little evidence to suggest she has had a major role in any decision-making. Women, thus, have never played key decision-making roles in the LTTE, and most of their activities have been under male subjugation and scrutiny. Their identity and their politics are reduced to their body and their sexuality.[24] It would seem to suggest that there is no possibility of emancipatory politics for women in the LTTE ranks or women who join any military formations.

Moreover, the LTTE is based on the divine iconography of its leader, Vellupillai Prabhakaran. It enforces collectivity, thereby suppressing any kind of an individual identity. Illegitimate sexual relations between cadres are banned and punished.[25] The onus of maintaining the discipline of the organization lies on the women who through their intensive military training "defeminize" themselves to become the "armed virgins," or the "birds of freedom" to uphold male honor and valor.[26] LTTE women have emerged out of the traditional domestic confines and stereotypical gender roles, but they experience subordination within the LTTE. The social taboos and subordinate status of women outside the LTTE are replicated within the militant organization. However, these women cadres of the LTTE have also negotiated new spaces for themselves in the Sri Lankan conflict. Senior LTTE leadership has often claimed that the respect women have gained militarily will give them the right to share leadership if peace can be achieved. Several sources have portrayed issues of women's subordination and liberation within the LTTE as more complex than they initially appear:

> Concepts such as empowerment and liberation are not static abstractions. Liberation is not a destination, but a life-long negotiation and struggle, perhaps without an achievable end. A female combatant may have been able to transcend various gendered roles on the battlefield, and may well be expected to regress to her former role in peace times. That, however, forms part of her negotiation with feminism. While the female Tigers may be part of a larger patriarchal nationalism, it does not mean that they are not negotiating their own agency within patriarchy on their own terms.[27]

Rita Manchanda, in an interview, cited positive developments for women in the LTTE, including anti-dowry policies and enforcement of domestic violence and rape prohibitions, as well as continued concerns about the masculinist structure of the LTTE.[28] Synthesizing these apparent contradictions, Darini Rajasingham-Senanayake characterizes the situation of LTTE women as "ambivalent empowerment," where, "while they may have broken out of the confines of their allotted domesticity and taken on new roles as fighters, it is indeed arguable that they are captive both to the patriarchal nationalist project of the LTTE leader Prabakaran and the history and experience of oppression by the Sri Lankan military."[29] Miranda Alison, in her study of the LTTE women, has extended Senanayake's argument, by stating that the reality of these women lies between the two binaries of agency and victimhood, liberation and subjugation, emancipation and oppression. She has suggested that "these binaries are unnecessary and unsophisticated forms of analytical tools"[30] My own field interviews corroborate the need for a middle ground that does not see the lives of these women within two binary constructs. The same woman who was forced to join, and had no choice even in leaving,[31] was able to realize her potential during the training, gain a sense of identity, and felt empowered due to her association with the LTTE.

The ethno-nationalist discourse provides strong justification for militant activities especially those undertaken by women. Traditional gender roles have been questioned at various levels and women have performed different roles in support of these militant ideologies. Feminist scholarship, in their efforts to study the role of these militant women in nationalistic projects, must consider the socio-cultural frameworks within which women are located. This implies a shift from the "binary-ism" that seems to have dominated the debate on women militants especially on the LTTE women cadres. An either–or debate on the status of these women will only serve to undermine ways in which these militant women are affecting and are being affected by these nationalistic projects and armed militancy.

For the love of men and God?

Fundamentalist religious ideologies with their exclusivist worldviews have used the strategy of militancy and terror to propagate their ideas and instill fear among those who are perceived as the "other" or enemies of the religion. Resistance movements against occupation have also deployed religious ideology and symbols to foster the sense of "nation" and to develop a national identity that is derived from religion.[32] Most of these religious based groups engaging in violence have kept women out of public spaces. Women have also been subjected to worst forms of violence both in public and private by the hyper-masculine and misogynist religious worldviews of men. Women's exclusion from public spaces is articulated on the basis that they are the bearers of the cultural honor and religious identity of the nation, and that "honor" is best kept covered at home. Ironically, this seems to suggest that there is something inherently wrong and "impure" about the public spaces that men inhabit and also that homes and families are devoid of any politics.

Identity is constantly being defined and redefined in religio-political conflicts. Not only is the "other" an amorphous category, but even the manner in which the "us" is constructed also frequently changes, influenced by local and global processes. Women are significantly affected by these identity issues and assume different roles in religio-political conflicts. In Kashmir, Palestine and Chechnya (now Iraq and Afghanistan too), the rhetoric of religion has always been used to back the nationalist struggle against "occupation." History bears

witness to the fact that religio-political militancy has been part of all organized religions in some form or the other (Christianity, Judaism, Hinduism,
Sikhism, Buddhism and Islam). In recent times radical Islamist groups have
hijacked the Islamic faith to suit their political agendas. Some of them, like the
Al Qaeda, are part of the radical pan-Islamist revivalist movement, which envisions a global *Khilafah* or Caliphate uniting Muslims of different nations; others
are more local in origin, aims and objectives like the Jemmah Islamiyah in
Indonesia, Islamic Jihad in Palestine, Lashkar-e-Toiba, and Jaish-e-Mohammed
in Kashmir.

One could argue that most theaters of conflict in the contemporary world
are witnessing some form of the "clash of civilizations."[33] Iraq, Palestine,
Chechnya, Kashmir and Afghanistan are places where religion forms the
basis of nationalism and women perform multiple roles in these theaters of
conflicts. My study on Kashmir highlights the participation of women as
planners, perpetrators and patrons of militancy in a society that is known for
its passivity and non-violence. The conflict in Kashmir has lasted more than
50 years and has both political and religious dimensions to it which are inse-
parable. Despite some recognition accorded to women in other conflicts as
participants in militant activities, women in the Kashmir conflict have had no
voice in the religious and nationalist discourse. Their silences have gone
unnoticed for far too long and their politics have not been acknowledged even
by feminists who claim to be speaking "of" and "for" marginalized women.

Militancy and terror tactics are not new in the context of the conflict in
Jammu and Kashmir in the Indian subcontinent. A significant number of
organized militant groups, operating from Indian and Pakistani parts of
Kashmir, have carried out a steady campaign of terror against the Indian
state, its security agencies and unarmed civilians for nearly two decades
now.[34] While popular support for the militancy seems to be waning, the
voices of radical women who articulate Kashmiri secession and/or harbor
pan-Islamic aspirations need to be engaged. Kashmiri Muslim women have,
in the past, provided logistical and ideological support to the Kashmiri militant groups and continue to do so as militancy takes newer and more innovative forms. They are apparently also undergoing religious indoctrination
and arms training in the *madrassas* and camps of various militant groups like
the Jaish-e-Mohammed and the Lashkar-e-Toiba.[35]

Militancy in the Kashmir Valley began in 1988–89, with the influx of *jihadi*
ideology from Afghanistan. The *mujahidins*, who had fought with the help of
the United States and Pakistan in Afghan *jihad* against the Soviets, now targeted the Indian-held Kashmir,[36] the northern frontier of India. They joined
forces with the disgruntled Kashmiri youth, instigating them for a *jihad*
against the Indian state for the creation of an independent Kashmir, or even
its accession to Pakistan. Though not much has been documented about the
role of women in the early phases of the militancy, there are references to
women participating in and leading public protests against the state and the
army. These women came out vociferously in favor of the militancy and

talked about *"azaadi,"* or independence. They sheltered militants in their homes, cooked for them and took care of them, all the while nurturing nationalist aspirations like the Kashmiri men.[37] Women's ideological and logistical support to the militancy started to decline in the late 1990s after the militants took to petty crimes in the Kashmir Valley and began to exploit the people for personal gains. By this time battle fatigue was clearly visible and several indigenous youth began to opt out of militancy and look for political solutions to the Kashmir issue. Militants also surrendered to the security forces in the Valley and many were even arrested in encounters.

However, the rise of the Taliban regime in Afghanistan and the political instability in Pakistan were once again reflected in the rise of militant activities in the Kashmir. Women's roles in militant activities and in the *jihadi* ideology in Kashmir resurfaced in 2004, when the all-women's "soft terror" outfit Dukhtaran-e-Millat (Daughters of Faith) became active. The group, founded by Asiya Andrabi in 1981, began as a reform movement to educate Muslim women about Islam and their rights.[38] Gradually, the group took to moral policing and advocating support for *jihad* in Kashmir for the cause of Islam. It has become increasingly active in the recent past and is said to be covertly supporting the *mujahidins* waging *jihad* in Kashmir. Since 2004, the Dukhtaran-e-Millat has been working with separatist and hard-line militant groups like the Lashkar-e-Jabber to enforce the Islamic code of conduct in the Valley. Asiya Andrabi told me in an interview in March 2007, "We believe in Muslim unity. There is no nation in Islam, and Muslims should not be divided into countries."[39] Andrabi has been arrested several times along with several members of her organization for alleged violations of the Public Safety Act.[40] Through their contacts with militants in Kashmir and Pakistan as well as with Islamic ideological leaders in other parts of the world, Andrabi and her group have had a substantial impact on Kashmiri society. Andrabi has created a niche for herself, paradoxically, in fundamentalist and also in feminist discourses, as a radical, outspoken, and yet ultra-conservative woman who is accepted by few and rejected perhaps by even fewer.

Apart from the Dukhtaran-e-Millat, there are other hard-line militant groups that have especially set up women's wings to train women and enlist their ideological and logistical support. Among the other groups, the Jammu Kashmir Liberation Front (JKLF), a hard-line separatist outfit, that was responsible for much militancy in the early years of the conflict, established a women's wing called Muslim Khwateen Markaz to enlist the support of women for their cause. The Markaz carried out covert activities to support the early militants and today is a political constituent of the All Parties Hurriyat Conference, a separatist entity made up of several political parties and factions. A former member of the Markaz, Zamruda Habib, was jailed by the Indian state for siphoning funds to major militant groups.[41] The Hizbul Mujahideen (HM) which later broke up into two separate militant groups, also established a women's wing, the Binat-ul-Islam, led by Umi Arifa, which would visit families of slain militants and help out with logistics.[42]

The Lashkar-e-Toiba, a militant group with links to Al Qaeda, according to the *Times of India*, has a full-fledged training camp for women militants situated 6 km from Muridke on GT Road between Lahore and Rawalpindi, with infrastructure to provide rigorous training to cadres in guerrilla warfare. The newspaper report claimed that women militants are given 21-day training in handling arms and ammunition, besides swimming and *jihadi* discourses. The special course, called Daura-e-Sofa, is provided to women cadres drawn from *madrassas* in Pakistan part of Kashmir and the Kashmir Valley in India.[43] In October 2005, a 22-year-old Kashmiri woman, Yasmeena, blew herself up at Awantipora on the Srinagar-Jammu highway. The Jaish-e-Mohammad militant group later claimed that Yasmeena was their suicide bomber. She was a member of the organization's women's wing, Banaat-e-Aaiyesha.[44] However, given that suicide bombing is not generally a tactic used in the Kashmir Valley, most Kashmiris believe that Yasmeena was not a suicide bomber and was instead acting as the courier for those explosives.

In addition to participating directly in the conflict, women in Kashmir have provided logistical support to militants. They have couriered arms, ammunitions, money, messages, etc. They have provided shelter to militants and cooked for them. Women have been involved in reconnaissance and intelligence gathering and have even been encouraged to use their "sexuality" to trap army officers and soldiers and to monitor troop movement and operations.[45] Organisations like the Dukhtaran-e-Millat and Muslim Khawateen Markaz, provide ideological support to the militancy. These women advocate the importance of an Islamic lifestyle and support the cause of *jihad*. They have even mentioned producing *mujahids* in the cause of Islam. Another way in which women's support is enlisted is through marriages between *mujahids* from Pakistan-held Kashmir and the Indian state of Jammu and Kashmir. Kinship networks, facilitated by inter-marriages, have helped the militant groups to expand their memberships and strategic capabilities.

Women are playing an important role in enforcing the fundamentalist Islamist ideology in Kashmir where predominantly a liberal-Sufi form of Islam had thrived for centuries. A visible trend of "purdah," sales of veils and "burqas" (cloaks) have gone up across the Kashmir Valley in the last few years and women have been sprayed with colored paint or acid or even shot in the legs for wearing western dresses. Separatist militant groups, with the support of women like Asiya Andrabi, have banned beauty parlors, cinema halls and wine shops and demanded that women adhere to the Islamic dress code. They have also ransacked internet cafes and restaurants for allowing young couples to meet privately.[46] Thus, while most women in Kashmir seem to be caught between the diktats of the fundamentalists and militants and the atrocities committed by the security forces, some women continue to support militant activities and articulate their political and personal aspirations within the ideology of militancy. They speak the language of violence and militancy and paradoxically serve to silence the voices of other women.

Narratives about motherhood also play a very important role in the mobilization of women by the militant groups operating in Kashmi, particularly by the group Lashkar-e-Toiba. The Lashkar chief, Hafiz Saed, has often been heard in conventions and rallies appealing to the sacrifices of the mothers in Islam in the cause of *jihad*. Motherhood provides greater justification for *jihad*, as appeals are made to the "mothers of Islam" to sacrifice their sons (in opposition to the traditional motherly duty to protect their children). The sacrifice of the mother is held greater than the monetary contribution in *jihad*.[47] These mother narratives paradoxically encourage women's political participation in *jihad* while invoking traditionally accepted norms of femininity.[48]

Women who perpetrate violence in the name of religion offer a complex understanding of "agency," and of gender, religious identity, nationalism and intersections between them. Religion does not offer the same emancipatory agenda for women as the nationalist discourses and secular movements do. Instead, often, women reinforce the masculine versions of the religious ideology even through their own violence. Women's *jihad* is advocated as inside the home and yet paradoxically there exist spaces for women to participate in traditional male activities like militancy and suicide bombings. Thus, modernity and fundamentalist conformity, speech and silence find a place in the discourse on women militants in religio-political movements. The "public" voices that some women like Asiya Andrabi, Zamruda Habib and Farida Behenji[49] have found in Kashmir or have been allowed as members of radical religious and militant groups, as their supporters and patrons, do not necessarily negate subjugation of many women to the very private space of family and home. In a rather complex understanding of gendered political subjectivities produced by these women and their actions, the silences speak, sometimes to reinstate the silences.

Between the margins and the mainstream

The tradition of women warriors is not new. In several parts of the world, they have been glorified in popular culture and historical texts. Women have been part of traditional state armies and combat units. As Joshua Goldstein has shown, in wars and combat, there has been a range from large-scale organized female participation to various types of gender integration through the participation of individual women.[50] Women can fight and they can kill.[51] Although today women represent a fraction of the militants worldwide, their significance is far-reaching. Women are responsible for approximately one-third of the suicide attacks perpetrated by the Tamil Tigers in Sri Lanka, and two-thirds of those by the Kurdistan Workers' Party. "Women have founded and led militant groups, hijacked planes, served on all-female tank units, blown up buildings and assassinated national leaders. What is new is that women are participating in attacks on behalf of organizations that promote Islamist causes."[52]

Feminists have been reluctant to "own wars" in the same way as they have owned other social institutions. As Christine Sylvester reminds us, "Feminists understudy war relative to other tranhistorical and transnational institutions, such as the family and religion."[53] Though there have been feminist critiques of "realist" wars on the grounds that they endanger the lives of women and alienate, exclude and marginalize women further from political and social frameworks, it has been difficult especially for IR feminists to theorize women who participate in these wars and who internalize, question, and displace patriarchy at the same time. Wars are the other, non-state actors are still the "other" and women who make wars remain the "other within the other" not merely in terms of how their gendered identities and relations may be constructed by these non-state actors, but also in terms of how mainstream as well as feminist IR view them as aberrations. While women are the *raison d'être* of specific national, ethnic and even religious projects, they are often excluded from the collective "we" of the body politic, and retain an object rather than a subject position.[54]

Feminist scholarship especially grapples with the "masculinity and militarization" dilemma. Some feminists have argued that wars and conflicts are direct manifestations of militarism traditionally identified with males.[55] Some feminists have rejected the idea of women fighting in men's wars claiming special affinity of women with peace.[56] Other feminists have acknowledged that women are the worst victims of wars and conflicts and yet they refuse to look beyond this "victimhood" that they ascribe to women.[57] There is a tension that exists for feminists—to reject "masculine militarization" and as a parallel process accept women's multiple roles and gender displacement in these militarized projects. As Miriam Cooke has suggested, "Recording women's presence and engagement at the front is crucial in order to counteract some of the distortions that have always been necessary to construct the age old story of war as men's business."[58]

If International Relations draws upon the discourse of "hegemonic masculinity"[59] that privileges male notions of militarism and statecraft, it also tends to create an ideal-typical femininity within which women are mostly seen as passive victims of male violence or agents of patriarchal institutional structures. Women's agency is expropriated and women are portrayed as having neither political ambitions nor any nationalist or religious aspirations.[60] I would argue that IR feminists need to draw upon their past theoretical advancements, focusing on people in IR instead of states[61] and recognize women as actors performing a multiplicity of roles, including the "not so nice" ones.[62] Systemic stability and balance of power at any given time in International Relations exist at the cost of peripheral conflicts and wars. These peripheral wars suggest that gendered hierarchies are displaced as well as entrenched in wars which are extensions of political processes that occur more at the local level than at the global level. Therefore, feminists can claim that the "high" politics should be replaced by "low" politics in war analysis. As women play important roles in the political processes at the local level, there is a crucial need to recognize the politics of women instead of reducing them to essentialized gender roles. The politics behind and around the militant women in Sri Lanka and Kashmir, for example, are the appropriate subject matter for "high" politics in IR. Far from being included only for the sake of inclusiveness, the study of women's militancy will offer better understandings not only of the individual participants in these conflicts but also of the conflicts in these regions writ larger than the national security discourses or realist "high" politics.

The "feminine niche" that is created wherein women's participation in traditional male activities is pushed into the realm of "personal" rather than the "political" space raises important questions for inquiry. Many accounts of women's militancy (including by feminists) seem to suggest that women are incapable of thinking and acting out politics. Feminism's primary agenda is to foreground the voices of women in discourses where women are conspicuously absent. If that is true, the discourses of ethno-nationalist and religio-political movements are ripe for feminist intervention. IR feminists discuss how developments in IR and the so-called "hard masculine" decision-making and policy framework impact and exclude about half of the world's population. Should the argument about including women's voices become subservient to concerns about which voices be privileged? Should the "choices" women make dominate the decisions regarding "voices" that should be made visible?

A useful framework for studying women militants has been laid out by Jessica West, in her study of the Chechen "black widows."[63] She argues that feminists should embrace their position at the margins of IR and the opportunities it provides to destabilize IR's hierarchies. In this view, feminist scholarship should be cautious about making value judgments about which women's voices should be privileged, and resist any attempts to essentialize or idealize women. Mainstreaming women's voices is always based on the politics of violence, exclusion and hierarchies. It is only in the margins of the discipline that feminism can achieve its end of a gender-sensitive framework of enquiry. West's concern is whether feminism remains "feminism" if it is not speaking from the margins.[64] I would further ask, with reference to the militant women, whether feminism is "feminism" if it does not speak "of" and "within" the margins. Perhaps the debate is less between our positionings at the margins or mainstream but more over further exclusions and scholastic violence on women whose actions affect us, inspire us and even terrorize us.

My proposition, therefore, would be to mainstream women's concerns and perspectives, which are quite diverse, and to problematize narratives which essentialize women as feminine. Masculine and feminine boundaries, private and public spheres, victimhood and agency notions should collapse into more flexible and porous frameworks. This would imply the introduction of new analytical tools, which could help in understanding global conflicts, including the crucial roles that ethnic membership, class, age, gender and ability play in determining who is included in and who is excluded in different conflict situations.[65]

Conclusion

Even as women militants struggle to find their space within the religious and nationalist movements that they claim to be part of, feminist and particularly

IR scholarship struggles to create an intellectual and policy discourse inclusive of them. Through the two case studies I have tried to establish that women participate in armed conflicts for a variety of reasons and in different ways, and an understanding of their politics and worldviews can provide valuable insights into conflicts as socio-political or even religious constructs. "Postmodern feminism"[66] that argues for the acceptance and validity of the diverse experiences of women may be the theoretical answer to the methodology of locating the voices of militant women. Sylvester provides a crucial insight: can we have meaningful categories of "women" and question them too?[67]

Feminist IR is a dynamic field where methodology is constantly evolving and "dialogue and diversity are seen as significant strengths."[68] The key feminist question I asked myself before I undertook research on militant women was whether I would be investigating the different marginalized "voices" or mapping the "silences." I would like to clarify that, like Bina D'Costa (who has worked on the raped women in the Bangladesh national war), I was also not under the impression that there were these "voiceless" women out there and I would be giving a voice to them through my research.[69] Their subject positioning at the margins and even the "silences" that are imposed on them within their communities as also in the scholarly discussions on gender and political violence, does not imply that women who support and participate in militant projects are "voiceless."[70] I was more interested in the multiple voices of these women and the political, social and cultural processes of silencing. I went into my fieldwork with the notion that women, like men, think and act politics, and there was a possibility that women's politics could be different and revealing. I wanted to interpret the "political" as much as the "social" and "cultural" in the lives of these women.

The identity of women militants is a multilayered one, constructed by the societies that they come from, by the militant and political extremist groups that they are part of, and the dominant media images that romanticize and feminize them.[71] It is in deconstructing the identities of women militants that an effective questioning and critique of the mainstream security and militancy discourse can be initiated by feminist scholars. I have argued for a more nuanced discourse on women militants and a shift away from binary representations of these women. The "public" voices of these women militants do not necessarily negate the very private space of family and home where women have traditionally played out their conventional roles and politics. In a rather complex understanding of gendered political subjectivities produced by these women and their actions, silences and speech exist in simultaneity. Armed militancy, therefore, is an opportunity for a few women, to have a public presence, and yet, it is an opportunity that seems to reinstate them further into the realm of the private. The reality is somewhere between and beyond the binaries of agency and victimhood, voice and silencing, as the case studies have demonstrated.

Finally, I have also argued that gendering security implies incorporating gender as a category of analysis in contemporary discourses on security and militant/terrorist movements. There is need for feminists to question the current masculinist discourse on militancy and political violence especially in the post-9/11 context, and at the same time, make space for diverse experiences and voices of women. It is imperative to locate the many voices of women who nurture personal, political, religious and nationalist aspirations within militant movements and whose gender identity in specific cultural and social contexts determine the exact nature of the roles they can assume in their efforts to fulfill their aspirations.

Notes

1 I am grateful to the women in Kashmir and Sri Lanka, who shared their experiences of armed resistance with me during my field trips in 2007 and 2008. I am especially grateful to Christine Sylvester for her inspiration and guidance and Nayanika Mookherjee for the valuable advice and support. Special thanks are also due to my husband, Ravi Bajpai, who has always traveled with me on the "road not taken," and has been a valuable but "unpaid" research assistant on my field trips. This chapter has further benefited from the insights of my feminist friends and colleagues, Laura Sjoberg, Megan McKenzie, Katherine Brown and Annick Wibben. An earlier version of this chapter was published in the *Cambridge Review of International Affairs*, June 2009.

2 Noted Indian security specialist, K. Subrahmanyam, makes this distinction between terrorism as a strategy and as an ideology in his chapter, "Can Terrorism Be Vanquished?" in *Terrorism in Southeast Asia: Implications for South Asia*, eds., John Wilson and Swati Parashar (New Delhi: Pearson Education Singapore, 2005), pp. 8–13.

3 Bruce Hoffman, *Inside Terrorism* (New York: Columbia University Press, 1998).

4 I prefer to use the term "militancy" instead of terrorism (the latter is more sporadic and fails to distinguish between a strategy or a tactic of terror and the ideological causes and the end motivations behind it). Militancy, on the other hand, is a term for armed resistance that non state actors themselves use. For example, in Kashmir, militancy is used in the common discourse to refer to the armed resistance by the militant groups, who take offense at being called terrorists. Militancy, therefore, is their language and not a term that I ascribe to them.

5 Amy Caiazza, "Why Gender Matters in Understanding 9/11: Women, Militarism and Violence," Institute for Women's Policy Research, Briefing paper. Available at: www.iwpr.org/pdf/terrorism.pdf (2001).

6 Nira Yuval-Davis, *Gender and Nation* (London: Sage, 1997).

7 Postmodern wars, according to Cooke, reveal the negotiability of war and of gender as one of its defining characteristics. This negotiation is conducted at the level of language, and it has the effect of blurring heretofore rigid boundaries between fact and fiction, between activism and writing, between experience and its recording. Women who are part of postmodern wars can easily articulate and therefore hold on to their participation. See Miriam Cooke and Angela Wollacott, *Gendering War Talk* (Princeton, NJ: Princeton University Press, 1993), pp. 177–204.

8 Cynthia Enloe, *Maneuvers: The International Politics of Militarizing Women's Lives* (Berkeley, CA: University of California Press, 2000).

9 Elisabetta Addis, Valeria E. Russo, and Lorenza Sebesta, eds., *Women Soldiers: Images and Reality* (New York: St. Martin's Press, 1994), p. xii.

10 Ibid., p. xiii.

11 I have borrowed Enloe's concept (which generally addresses women in state militaries) to include women in non-state militancy where "ideology" and the "nation" converge. See Cynthia Enloe, "The Politics of Constructing the American Woman Soldier," in Addis *et al.*, *Women Soldiers*, p. 82.

12 Swarna Rajagopalan, www.acdis.uiuc.edu/Research/S&Ps/2003-Su/S&P-Su2003.pdf.

13 While writing this chapter, the war between the Tamil Tigers and the Sri Lankan Army was still going on without any conclusive results. The Army claims that the LTTE have lost their core and senior cadres and has been routed, the LTTE is still persistent in its declarations that the war is far from over. Civilians are trapped between these two warring sides and large number of deaths have been reported in this ongoing war in the island nation.

14 Women combatants have been a significant force of the Tamil Tigers but there is only sporadic evidence to suggest that Kashmiri women have taken up arms as part of militant groups. They have been mostly involved at the logistical and ideological levels, which have had a significant impact on the militancy in Indian Kashmir. While writing this chapter, reports are pouring in about fresh infiltration in the Kashmir Valley with claims from the Indian Army that women were being trained across the Line of Control (in Pakistani territory). See the Indian Express Report. Available at: www.indianexpress.com/news/women-across-loc-being-trained-to-infiltrate-into-jk/446836/, accessed April 14, 2009.

15 Miranda Alison, "Women as Agents of Political Violence: Gendering Security," *Security Dialogue* no. 35 (2004): 447.

16 Several analysts have pointed out that the Iraqi and Afghan insurgencies that have witnessed the increasing role of women, especially as suicide bombers, were able to mobilize women from traditional patriarchal societies through claims of oppression and occupation by foreign forces. Religious norms can be subverted in order to justify women's participation based on claims of oppression and occupation. Farhana Ali, an analyst of Muslim women's roles in militant projects, has often said that unless the "occupation" ends in these countries, women will continue to become suicide bombers.

17 Yuval-Davis, *Gender and Nation*, p. 101.

18 Moghadam's arguments have been cited by Yuval Davis in *Gender and Nation*, p 103.

19 Rajiv Gandhi was killed in a suicide attack on May 21, 1991, in the southern state of Tamil Nadu. The attack was carried out by Dhanu, a Tamil woman, who had apparently suffered rape at the hands of the Indian Peace Keeping Forces (IPKF). The LTTE assassinated him for his decision to send the IPKF to Sri Lanka in 1987, on the request of the Sri Lankan government.

20 Adele Ann Balasingham, *Women Fighters of the Liberation Tigers* (Mahendra Veethy, Jaffna: Thasan Printers, 1993).

21 Ibid.

22 Radhika Coomaraswamy, "Tiger Women and the Question of Women's Emancipation," *Pravada* no. 4/9 (1996): 9.

23 I conducted these interviews on August 18, 2008, while on my visit to Eastern Sri Lankan towns of Trincomalee and Batticaloa. I met 17 former women cadres of the LTTE at a village, Kokkadicholai in Batticaloa.

24 The case of the pregnant LTTE woman, who carried out a suicide attack on the army headquarters in Colombo, which injured the Chief of Sri Lankan army, Sarath Fonseka, is of special significance. Unlike cases where women had pretended to be pregnant in order to carry out suicide operations, in this case the woman was actually pregnant, highlighting issues of sexuality, corporeality and militancy.

25 M. R. Narayan Swamy, *Inside an Elusive Mind: Prabhakaran* (Colombo: Vijitha Yapa Publications, 2003).

26 Defeminizing, therefore, is an important project within the LTTE. Related quotes from the LTTE women can be accessed at: www.focusasia.startv.com/indepth. php?CLIP_DATE = 20040725&CLIP_NO = 1

27 Tahira Gonsalves (2003), *Gender and Peacebuilding: A Sri Lankan Case Study.* Available at: www.idl-bnc.idrc.ca/dspace/bitstream/123456789/33539/2/Gonsalves_ Tahira_paper.doc.

28 This was also corroborated by my interviews with former women cadres of the LTTE in Batticaloa. Most of these women had left the LTTE but were unable to reintegrate into society and were facing a number of problems. See Dilys Ebert, personal interview with Rita Manchanga, November 2005, "Guerilla Movements Like LTTE Provide Opportunities for Women's Emancipation," available at: www.tamilcanadian.com/page.php?cat = 525& id = 3564, accessed 4/1/2009.

29 Darini Rajasingham-Senanayake, "Between Reality and Representation: Women's Agency in War and Post Conflict Sri Lanka," *Cultural Dynamics* no. 16 (2004): 141.

30 Miranda Alison "Cogs in the Wheel? Women in the LTTE," *Civil Wars* 6, no. 4 (2003): 37–54. Available at: www2.warwick.ac.uk/fac/soc/pais/staff/alison/ research/cogs_in_the_wheel/cogs_in_the_wheel.pdf.

31 The women I interviewed left because of the split in the LTTE leadership. Some of them also mentioned a constant fear that the LTTE would come after them since they had left without permission.

32 Wars of recent vintage in Afghanistan and Iraq, which are effectively against "occupation" have also used religious ideologies to organize their resistance. There has been a rise in religious militant groups in these states who are waging *jihad* against the infidel "occupiers."

33 Samuel Huntington, *The Clash of Civilizations and the Remaking of World Order* (New York: W. W. Norton, 1996).

34 For more details on militant groups in Kashmir, see Navnita Chadha-Behera, *Demystifying Kashmir* (Washington, DC: The Brookings Institution, 2006); Amir Mir, *The True Face of Jehadis: Inside Pakistan's Network of Terror* (New Delhi: Roli Books, 2006).

35 For details on women's roles in the Kashmiri Militancy, refer to Abhishek Behl, "Terrorists Use Women against Indian Army in Kashmir" *Merinews*, 31 July 2007. Available at: www.merinews.com/catFull.jsp?articleID = 125810, accessed 24 January 2009; CNN-IBN (29 May, 2008) "First Woman Terrorist Killed in Jammu and Kashmir." Available at: www.ibnlive.in.com/news/first-woman-ter-rorist-killed-in-jammu-and-kashmir/66173–3.html, accessed 24 January 2009; Manisha Sobhrajani, "Jammu and Kashmir: Women's Role in the post-1989 Insurgency," *Faultlines* no. 19 (April 2008). Available at: www.satp.org/satporgtp/ publication/faultlines/volume19/Article3.htm.

36 It must be clarified that Kashmir, as the status quo has been since 1949, is divided into two parts. Pakistan occupies part of the Kashmiri territory, calling it Azaad (independent) Kashmir. The other part remains with India and includes, Kashmir Valley, Ladakh and Jammu. The militancy that I mention here is within the Indian part of Kashmir and which for many years has not only included indi-genous Kashmiris resisting the Indian state but also includes militants (not ethnic Kashmiris) who are based in Pakistan.

37 See Sobhrajani, "Jammu and Kashmir: Women's Role in the Post-1989 Insurgency."

38 Much of the information about the DeM comes from Asiya Andrabi, the founder, whom I have interviewed twice in March 2007 and July 2008.

39 I met Asiya Andrabi at her residence in Srinagar in March 2007 and in July 2008 and in detailed interviews Asiya talked about the activities of her group, her political views and her life.

40 Sudha Ramachandran, "Women Lift the Veil on Kashmir Struggle," *Asia Times Online*, 7 March 2002. Available at: www.atimes.com/ind-pak/DC07Df01.html, accessed 4/1/2009.

41 I met Zamruda at her residence in Srinagar in July 2008. In a long interview which lasted for three hours, she denied that she had any role in the siphoning of funds and said that it was a conspiracy against her. However, Zamruda stated that without women's help and commitment (logistical and ideological), the militancy in Kashmir would not have lasted so long.

42 Muzamil Jaleel, "Spawning Militancy: The Rise of Hizbul," *The Indian Express* 22 May 2003.

43 Pradeep Thakur, "LeT Training Women Militants," *The Times of India*, 6 April 2007. Available at: http://timesofindia.indiatimes.com/NEWS/India/LeT_-training_women_militants/rssarticleshow/1862696.cms, accessed 4/1/2009.

44 "J& K: Woman Suicide Attacker Blown to Pieces," *The Indian Express*, 14 October 2005.

45 See Abhishek Behl (2007) "Terrorists Use Women against Indian Army in Kashmir."

46 See Sudha Ramachandran (2002) "Women Lift the Veil on Kashmir Struggle," *Asia Times Online*, 7 March. Available at: /www.atimes.com/ind-pak/DC07Df01. html.

47 A former militant (whose name I am unable to reveal in order to protect his identity) whom I interviewed in July 2008, said that he joined the armed militancy only after receiving encouragement from his mother. Mothers are important figures in Kashmiri society. I noticed how they are revered through songs dedicated to them. Mothers of young men killed by the security forces were honored and had a special place.

48 See Farhat Haq, "Militarism and Motherhood: Women of the Lashkar-e-Tayyaba," *Signs: Journal of Women in Culture and Society* (Summer 2007): 1023–46. For example, Asiya Andrabi in her interview with me also referred to the wife and mother narrative, referring to herself as a good mother and a faithful wife.

49 Farida Behenji is the head of Jammu and Kashmir Mass Movement, a separatist political outfit in Kashmir. She has also served a jail sentence for aiding militants. Her brother was a militant and is now settled in Pakistan.

50 Joshua Goldstein, *War and Gender* (Cambridge: Cambridge University Press, 2001).

51 Ibid., p. 127.

52 Jessica Stern, "When Bombers are Women," *Washington Post*, December 18, 2003. Available at: www.ksg.harvard.edu/news/opeds/2003/stern_women_bombers_wp1121803.htm, accessed 4/1/2009.

53 Christine Sylvester, "The Art of War/The War Question in (Feminist) IR," *Millennium: Journal of International Studies* 33 (2005): 855.

54 Yuval-Davis, *Gender and Nation*, p. 47.

55 Cynthia Enloe, *Does Khaki Become You?* (London: Pluto Press, 1983); Enloe, *Manuevers*; A. M. Chenoy, *Militarism and Women in South Asia* (New Delhi: Kali for Women, 2002).

56 For example, Sara Ruddick, *Maternal Thinking: Towards a Politics of Peace* (Boston: Beacon Press, 1989).

57 For example, Mia Bloom, *Dying to Kill: The Allure of Suicide Terror* (New York: Columbia University Press, 2005) and Barbara Victor, *Army of Roses: Inside the World of Palestinian Suicide Bombers* (New York: Rodale, 2003), however, make an attempt to examine women's roles in violent "terrorist" projects, and their women actors are often influenced by personal tragedies and hence 'victims' of situations and circumstances.

58 Cooke and Wollacott, *Gendering War Talk*, p. 177.

59 For a detailed discussion of this concept, refer to R. W. Connell and James W. Messerschmidt, "Hegemonic Masculinity: Rethinking the Concept," *Gender & Society* 19, no. 6 (December 2005): 829–59.

60 Chenoy, *Militarism and Women in South Asia*, pp. 17–21.

61 Cynthia Enloe, *Bananas, Beaches, and Bases: Making Feminist Sense of International Politics* (Berkeley, CA: University of California Press, 1990); Enloe, *Maneuvers*.

62 A beginning has been made in some of the recent works that explore the "not so nice" roles of women in international conflicts. Laura Sjoberg and Caron Gentry in *Mothers, Monsters, Whores: Women's Violence in Global Politics* (London: Zed Books, 2007) have, for example, looked at women in Iraq who engaged in prisoner abuses, like Lyndie England. Miranda Alison (in *Women and Political Violence* (London: Routledge, 2008) has also looked at women and political violence. Christine Sylvester and I argue that terrorism is a state-centric discourse and ignores women, flaws that reify each other and are responsible for avoidance of questions of difference. See Christine Sylvester and Swati Parashar, "The Contemporary 'Mahabharata' and the Many Draupadis: Bringing Gender to Critical Terrorism Studies," in *Critical Terrorism Studies: A New Research Agenda*, eds., Richard Jackson, Marie Breen Smyth, and Jeroen Gunning (London: Routledge, 2009).

63 Jessica West, "Feminist IR and the Case of the 'Black Widows': Reproducing Gendered Divisions," *Innovations (A Journal of Politics)*, no. 5 (2005).

64 Ibid.

65 Yuval-Davis, *Gender and Nation*, p. 96.

66 See Christine Sylvester, *Feminist Theory and International Relations in a Postmodern Era* (Cambridge: Cambridge University Press, 1994).

67 Ibid.

68 Brooke Ackerly, Maria Stern, and Jacqui True, eds., *Feminist Methodologies for International Relations* (Cambridge: Cambridge University Press, 2006).

69 Refer to D'Costa's footnote 7 on page 132 in Ackerly *et al*. D'Costa also acknowledges that the raped women she was writing about were not "voiceless."

70 Ackerly *et al.*, *Feminist Methodologies*, p. 126.

71 Sarala Emmanuel, "The Female Militant Romanticized," *Women in Action Newsletter*, no. 1 (2002). Available at: www.isiswomen.org/wia/wia102/femmilitant.htm, accessed 04/01/2009.

Part IV

Gendered security problematiques

10 Feminist theory and arms control[1]

Susan Wright

Although there is a rich feminist literature that addresses the gendered nature of war and preparations for war through weapons development, arms control has attracted relatively little attention from feminist theorists. At first glance, arms control negotiations might appear to have a very different character from that of warfare. In particular, negotiations aimed at disarmament would seem to be inspired by the goal of *ending war*, not pursuing it. The usually restrained and sometimes ritualized behavior on display at the Palais des Nations in Geneva during arms control negotiations appears as the polar opposite of the slaughter, brutality, and chaos of war. And yet, a well-known political scientist has called arms control "war by other means."[2] The main aims of this chapter are, first, to ask what kinds of insights feminist analysis can bring to the nature of the present dominant forms of arms control; and second, how these insights can be applied to a specific case: the development of the British proposal for an international convention banning biological weapons in the late 1960s.

In the first section, I will briefly discuss the evolution of feminist theory and the type of feminist theory used in this critique. The second section examines the main ideas and assumptions that supported arms control after World War II as the nuclear arms race between the two superpowers accelerated and focuses on the work of two theorists who are well known to political scientists: the American economist Thomas Schelling and the Australian-British political theorist Hedley Bull. In the third section, I show how Bull applied his views on arms control in a top secret study on chemical and biological weaponry for the British Foreign Office for which he worked as the first director of a new Arms Control and Disarmament Office from 1965 to 1967 before leaving to become a professor of International Relations at the Australian National University in Canberra. Finally, I will use feminist theory to examine and critique the IR theories used by Bull and Schelling and how assumptions forming the base of these theories affected Bull's approach to chemical and biological arms control and the later development of his approach in the British proposal for a Biological Weapons Convention.

A critical feminist approach to arms control

In the 1990s, I attended a series of conferences concerned with implementing the international conventions prohibiting chemical and biological weaponry. The majority of the participants were Western government officials, members of defense think tanks, and academics who did policy work related to arms control. Representation from non-Western countries was low: one or two people at most and there was a marked Western flavor to these meetings. Concern about "proliferation," the spread of weapons and knowledge relevant to weapons to countries that were not Western allies, was a significant theme; the implications of military use of the newer techniques of biotechnology in the West received much less attention. Over the course of several meetings, I found that certain kinds of questions—for example, questions related to the impacts of military activities on people—were not seen as central to the concerns of the organizers and most of the participants. If asked, such questions were quickly dropped or treated as naïve. To be taken seriously, one had to embrace the abstract language of arms control and to abandon moral and ethical concerns about the human side of the dangerous and disturbing possibilities that were being addressed. This experience raises interesting questions about the formation of the nature and norms of arms control as they have been practiced by Western states since World War II. Feminist theory provides important techniques for examining these questions.

Over the past 30 years, a wealth of feminist work on politics has recognized that women have been mostly absent from the main locations of power in the state and so have played little direct role in shaping the course of International Relations. They have almost always been far from the initiating end of the foreign policies of their states and, most often, on the receiving end of those policies. Feminist work has addressed the many and varied forms of discrimination that have kept women for the most part "hidden from international relations" except as victims of practices and laws that discriminated against them.[3] To this day, the shocking reality is that women can be treated as nothing more than chattel and can be subjected to the most horrific forms of abuse, and yet, much of this treatment falls outside the scope of international law.[4] These problems have been the focus of "liberal feminism," which addresses discrimination against women in its many forms and defines the removal of barriers to women's full participation in all levels of government as the fundamental way to address the problem.

Still, feminists have recognized that liberation is not simply a matter of "adding women and stirring" them into existing political and legal arenas and that discrimination is not only a matter of exclusion from political arenas based on their sex but that both are intrinsically related to the fundamental frameworks, assumptions, and concepts that work in these arenas to admit some and to exclude others, to hear some and to ignore others, to count some forms of knowledge as central and to marginalize others.

Considerable feminist work has focused on the political origins of these practices. A broad conclusion is that masculine political dominance in the

West originated in the division of ancient Greek society into the *polis,* the public realm of free (male) citizens where matters of governance and war were decided, and *oikos,* the private realm of the home and family occupied by those who were not free political agents: women, slaves, and children.[5] Thus the public sphere was marked originally as an exclusively male preserve and the private sphere of the home as that to which women were relegated. The practical implication is that "the two spheres are accorded asymmetrical value: greater significance is attached to the public, male world than to the private female one."[6]

Furthermore, feminist theorists have argued that the public and private spheres have been marked, supported, and legitimated by the use of gendered constructs: stereotypically masculine and feminine attributes used to characterize "normal" behavior in each sphere. They have concluded that, in the West at least, the formation of the state through war and the high value attributed to the willingness of men to die on behalf of the state have been fundamental for the formation of a binary system of opposing qualities.[7] The public sphere of the state has traditionally valued qualities such as competitiveness, aggression, autonomy and a goal-oriented form of rationality that overlooks human security whereas the private sphere of the home and child-rearing has valued such qualities as cooperation, affection, inter-dependency, and an empathic form of rationality focused on individual security and on means as much as ends.

Of course, there is nothing *essentially* weak, cooperative, empathic or dependent about real women any more than there is anything essentially strong, competitive, rational, or autonomous about "real" men. Nevertheless, these stereotypes are ingrained in Western society and culture and are deeply influential in defining male/female differences in all spheres of life. Especially relevant for this chapter is the argument that success in international politics is generally measured in stereotypically masculine terms that celebrate power over and control of the other that is deemed weaker.[8]

In this chapter, I use a "critical feminist" approach which addresses the social, cultural, and political conditions under which gender is constructed and deployed as a form of inequality. This approach assumes that political theories and concepts are constructed and used in specific historical circumstances and for specific, historically contingent purposes.[9] In the words of Robert Cox, "theory is always *for* someone and *for* some purpose."[10] In general, political and military claims of gender differences between men and women produce an inequality. According to Catherine MacKinnon: "Gender is the outcome of a social process of subordination that is only ascriptively tied to the body ... Femininity is a lowering that is imposed; it can be done to anybody and still be what feminine means. It is just women to whom it is considered natural."[11]

Within this framework, feminist methodological approaches will be used to analyze the assumptions underlying arms control as it was developed by Western governments in the 1960s. First, at the most general level, feminist approaches ask an *epistemological* question: "From whose perspective is IR knowledge constructed?" and examine the *ontological* assumptions associated with the answer.[12] For example, feminist theorists have pointed out that traditional IR theory takes the state as a discrete entity that requires no further deconstruction and reduces it to its government, also taken as a discrete entity. In this "billiard ball" model of the states, the humans who influence or who are affected by state behavior typically disappear from the analysis.[13]

A dramatic example of conventional IR ontology at work happened on February 6th, 2003 when then US Secretary of State Colin Powell presented the Bush Administration's case for invading Iraq to the UN Security Council before a shrouded tapestry reproduction of Picasso's *Guernica*. As Maureen Dowd of the *New York Times* commented: "Mr. Powell can't very well seduce the world into bombing Iraq surrounded on camera by shrieking and mutilated women, men, children, bulls, and horses."[14] Powell's speech provided the rationale for a war that would recreate those very conditions of human suffering and did so in terms that diverted attention from that suffering to the abstract requirements of the state.

Some of the most dramatic examples of the mind-numbing effects of nuclear strategic thinking draw on the billiard ball model's capacity to make humans disappear.[15] This was illustrated dramatically for me at one of the arms control conferences in the 1990s, when a former member of the US Arms Control and Disarmament Agency calmly opined that use of "small" nuclear weapons might be used to respond to the biological weapons activities of "rogue states" in the Middle East—a position later embraced by the George W. Bush administration but blocked by Congress.[16] The lack of response around the table was striking. On the assumption that silence signifies complicity, I responded that use of nuclear weapons was immoral, since it would inflict the most terrible suffering on civilian populations. The only explicit support was from a Middle Eastern participant who temporarily abandoned the state level of analysis to think in terms of the impact on his country's population. At that level, he warned that loose talk of using nuclear weapons in the Middle East was inadvisable given the potential to provoke nuclear escalation.

A related approach emphasizes the importance of exploring how gender in IR can *marginalize* or even *silence* concepts or approaches to the subject. Feminist theory poses the challenge of exploring the international implications of the stereotypically masculine, or "masculinist," qualities that typically inform traditional IR theory noted above—competitiveness, aggression, autonomy, achieving ends rather than addressing the effects of means, the distancing of the Self from the Other, and control over the Other. For example, Carol Cohn shows how the strength of a national security discourse is derived from the way in which its claims are positioned within a system of gendered codes that legitimizes statements that are seen as "tough, rational, logical" while marginalizing those seen as "emotional."[17] Annica Kronsell shows how the silence about gendered assumptions with respect to what is known in Sweden as "universal" conscription but is actually conscription exclusively for men is symptomatic of the wide acceptance of these assumptions in military discourse.[18] Borrowing Kronsell's language, one might argue that the most provocative act of feminist theory is to define "masculinist" qualities as a political category, which transforms them "from a universal nothing (in)to a specific something."[19] Studying such silences requires the analyst to use methods of deconstruction to analyze what is assumed in a text, or in other words, what is "written between the lines."[20]

Finally, it is essential to ask about the *legitimation* of knowledge that draws on gendered concepts and practices. How is this knowledge justified and made acceptable to all those who are excluded from its production?

These methods are used below to examine the conceptual underpinnings of the dominant forms of arms control practiced since the end of World War II. First, I will examine the theory of arms control developed in the 1960s under the shadow of the nuclear arms race, taking the work of the economist and strategic theorist Thomas Schelling and the political scientist Hedley Bull as representative of two strands of this theory that largely converged in terms of practice. I will then use the origins of the international convention banning biological weapons, the Biological Weapons Convention, as a source of empirical data for examining the practice of arms control within governments. This is an interesting example because the convention is often taken to be a "disarmament" agreement that goes beyond "arms control" whereas I will argue that the same strategic philosophy informs both practices. As a result of the openness of the British government beyond its 30-year secrecy rule, the rich documentary evidence of the arguments and actions pursued by the state under the utmost secrecy in the 1960s is now publicly available. The general argument I will develop here is that feminist theory explains rather precisely why "arms control" and "disarmament" are expressions of the same discursive practice, that is, the practice and legitimation of "war by other means."

Arms control after World War II: the contributions of Thomas Schelling and Hedley Bull

Following the carnage of World War II and the birth of the United Nations, there were extended efforts to launch negotiations for General and Complete Disarmament (GCD). There were moments—for example, from mid-1954 to the Geneva Summit Conference in July 1955—when it seemed that disarmament negotiations would be launched in earnest.[21] In 1959, the United Nations General Assembly adopted Resolution 1378 supporting "measures leading towards the goal of general and complete disarmament under effective international control ... in the shortest possible time," a goal endorsed by both Premier Nikita Khrushchev and President John F. Kennedy. It was also actively supported by non-governmental movements including the Women's International League for Peace and Freedom, which called for a "world truce," renunciation of war and armaments production, and use of the resources released by total disarmament to address hunger, disease, and illiteracy.[22] In Britain, a prominent advocate of GCD was the politician, diplomat, and Nobel Peace Prize recipient, Philip Noel-Baker, author of *The Arms Race: A Programme for World Disarmament.*[23] According to nuclear strategist Bernard Brodie, Noel-Baker viewed disarmament as "good for its own sake," a condition that would "automatically enhance international security"[24]—a view supported by several members of the Institute for Strategic Studies in London, of which Noel-Baker was also a member.[25]

At the same time, the Western powers, led by the United States, and the former Soviet Union, were embarking on the nuclear arms race, which led each side to a dance on the knife-edge of nuclear holocaust. The US bombing of Hiroshima and Nagasaki was followed by the Soviet development of the bomb, detonated in 1949, development of the hydrogen bomb and intercontinental ballistic missiles in the 1950s, and multiple independently targeted vehicles known as MIRVs and the "second-strike" capabilities that provided the basis for what became known as "mutual assured destruction" or MAD in the 1960s.

While Noel-Baker and others campaigned for GCD, other academics and strategic analysts formulated positions that accepted the existence of the bomb and saw nuclear weapons as playing a dominant role in strategy. In the United States, an influential group of strategic analysts associated with the RAND Corporation and the Hudson Institute and whose intellectual leaders included Herman Kahn, Samuel Huntington, Bernard Brodie, and Albert Wohlstetter, rejected the basic premises of GCD. These were people who attended the same conferences, read each other's work, and formed a rather strong "epistemic community." A prominent member of this group was Thomas Schelling. Schelling was an economist by training, not a political scientist or game theorist like many of the other members, and had worked in the late 1940s and early 1950s on allocating funds under the Marshall Plan in Europe. On his return to the United States, he became involved in the RAND Corporation's work on military strategy and emerged as an influential thinker on two areas he saw as closely related: nuclear strategy and nuclear arms control.[26]

In England, a young Australian, Hedley Bull, took a different route to nuclear strategy and arms control.[27] Trained in philosophy and history at the University of Sydney and in political theory at Oxford, Bull was appointed to a position in International Relations at the London School of Economics. In 1956, Bull worked briefly with Philip Noel-Baker, pursuing research for a book the latter was planning on the Disarmament Conference of 1932. But the collaboration fell apart over a fundamental disagreement on the value of disarmament as the path to peace. Bull traveled to Harvard in 1957, where he met Schelling and Henry Kissinger and experienced views on strategy and arms control that he found more congenial.[28] Despite their differences in intellectual background, the development of Bull's and Schelling's positions on strategy and arms control became closely connected. Each published articles and books on the subject in the same period and it is clear from cross-references that each read and critiqued the other's work.[29] In the end, important differences in intellectual orientation and recommendations would be outweighed by their shared conclusions about the nature and international role of arms control.

In what follows, I use Schelling's *Strategy and Arms Control*, written with his colleague Morton Halperin, and Bull's *The Control of the Arms Race*, both published in 1961, as examples of work in the emerging field of strategic analysis and arms control. According to Robert Ayson, Bull's text owed much to Schelling's earlier work, which Bull cited.[30] Schelling and co-author Halperin read an early draft of Bull's manuscript. The two books had a major feature in common: they responded to—and rejected—the arguments supporting "general and complete disarmament" being made in the United Nations and by Philip Noel-Baker, members of the Women's International League for Peace and Freedom, and others that only disarmament could provide a path to peace.

Both books were also responses to the accelerating nuclear arms race between the two superpowers. The launch of Sputnik in October 1957 was taken to demonstrate the vulnerability of the West to a surprise nuclear attack. Albert Wohlstetter in an article in *Foreign Affairs* argued that the "stability of the balance of terror" between the two superpowers had been fundamentally undermined.[31]

This precarious "balance of terror" was the frightening context in which Schelling and Bull developed their work on arms control and to which they applied rather different conceptual frameworks. As an economist, Schelling thought of states as a "system" of interacting units and strategies adopted by states as responses to "threats, commitments, and promises."[32] The state in its full complexity disappeared in this model. What was left was a point mass which moved according to certain forces, as in Newtonian physics. He used this model to develop a theory of strategy by examining how an adversary state (or "point") would be limited by "his expectation of the consequences of his actions." On this conceptual base, the problems that dominated *Strategy and Arms Control* were how to achieve what Schelling called the "stability" of the system through strategies that used weapons for deterrence and through arms control.[33]

Along with colleagues such as Bernard Brodie and Albert Wohlstetter, Schelling argued that one way to restore "stability" to the nuclear system was to protect the state's ability to deter a surprise attack by ensuring that the state's "retaliatory capability" would survive.[34] This meant that retaliatory forces had to generate a "stabilized deterrent" so that an adversary would know that the consequences of an attack would be disastrous.[35]

For Schelling and Halperin, arms control negotiations with the Soviet Union were a further way to stabilize deterrence by developing means to secure the whole system against misunderstanding, accidents, and so forth:

> Arms control can be thought of as an effort, by some kind of reciprocity or cooperation with our potential enemies, to minimize, to offset, to compensate or to deflate some of these [destabilizing] characteristics of modern weapons and military expectations. In addition to what we can do unilaterally to improve our warning, to maintain close control over our forces ... etc. ... to avoid accidents or mistaken decisions ... there may be opportunities to exchange facilities or understandings with our enemies, or to design and deploy our forces differently by agreement with our enemies.[36]

Thus arms control negotiations were seen as an adjunct to the fundamental role of nuclear weapons themselves in deterring and ultimately, according to their model, balancing interactions between the two superpowers. Although Schelling did not use the term, this approach provided the theoretical underpinnings for "mutual assured destruction."

Hedley Bull arrived at a similar conclusion but by a different conceptual route. Whereas Schelling's starting point was an abstract system of points (representing states), Bull saw states as entities that competed in an international society that was characterized by a certain degree of order. Hence the deliberately oxymoronic title of his well-known book, *The Anarchical Society*, which elaborated on his earlier work on arms control.

This view of International Relations provided a central reason for Bull's strong criticism of Philip Noel-Baker's advocacy of general and complete disarmament as the basis for world peace. In a critique of Noel-Baker's book, *The Arms Race: A Programme for World Disarmament*, Bull argued that the international system was "a society without a government" and that its justice was "crude and uncertain, as each state is judge in its own cause, and it gives rise to the recurrent tragedy in the form of war." However, Bull continued, "[this society also] produces order, regularity, predictability and long periods of peace, without involving the tyranny of a universal state."[37]

Thus, Bull, in contrast to Noel-Baker, attributed to armaments and war essential roles in achieving "order" in the "anarchical society" of states. While Noel-Baker saw the arms race as a major cause of international competition and war, Bull countered that there was no such cause–effect relation, that the arms race was both a cause and a consequence of international tensions. The competitive tensions among states as well as the fact that they could, nevertheless, have common interests and inscribe those interests into international law, were fundamental variables in both war and peace.[38]

Bull elaborated these arguments in *The Control of the Arms Race*. He saw the "balance of power" among states as fundamental for keeping international anarchy in check and, in one of the passages that must have been most shocking to advocates of disarmament, he argued that war was "one of the instruments by which [this] balance is maintained."[39] Indeed, for Bull, war was an integral part of the machinery for maintaining the balance of power:[40]

The chief function of the balance of power in international society has not been to preserve peace, but to preserve the independence of sovereign states from the threat of domination, and to preserve the society of sovereign states from being transformed by conquest into a universal empire: to do these things, if necessary, by war.[41]

Like Schelling, Bull saw the chief function of arms control as ensuring the stability of a balance of power, not achieving disarmament: "[T]here is no necessary presumption in favour of disarmament rather than rearmament in the design of a system of arms control."[42] Specifically in connection with mutual deterrence between the two superpowers, he wrote:

It is clear that the system of deterrence requires that each side has a strategic weapons system that is sufficient effectively to deter the other side. From this it follows that measures which reduced the strength of each side to a point below the level of sufficiency ... and undermined the nuclear stalemate without putting anything in its place, would not be a contribution to the stability of the balance of power. There are, then, minimum levels of [nuclear] armaments necessary for the continuance of the nuclear stalemate ... If it is the business of arms control to preserve and buttress the balance of power, it cannot be shaped by any such principle as that of the indiscriminate reduction of armaments.[43]

Bull went even further than this. He argued that "qualitative" change in armaments should not be stopped either, because it would "lead to less, rather than more, stability in the balance of power.".[44] Interestingly, because it underscores the historical contingency of his arguments, Bull pointed to the attempt to make strategic weapons invulnerable to destruction as an example of "qualitative change" that would "strengthen the strategic balance."[45]

Thus, both Schelling's and Bull's analyses converged on a single implication: acceptance of a world balanced on a nuclear knife-edge and operated on by the competing and cooperating forces of the two superpowers—with all of humanity hostage to the possibility of nuclear holocaust.

Case study in arms control: the origins of the 1972 Biological Weapons Convention

The view of arms control as an integral part of defense strategy, exemplified in the work of Schelling and Bull, has provided one of the main approaches to arms control since the 1960s. In this section, I show how this view influenced the decisions within the British government that resulted in its proposal to the Eighteen-Nation Disarmament Committee on 6 August 1968 for an international convention banning biological weapons. I will show how, even with respect to an international agreement that is widely seen to be about "disarmament," not "arms control," the official approach remained "war by other means."

There is a strong connection between Hedley Bull's views on arms control and the outcome of the British decisions. In 1965, Bull was invited to join the British Foreign Office as director of a new Arms Control and Disarmament Research Unit. He accepted, was given British citizenship in short order, and spent two years there, from 1965 to 1967, before returning to Canberra as a professor of International Relations at the Australian National University. What Bull accomplished for the Foreign Office was known only to certain civil servants and members of the UK government since it was covered by the Official Secrets Act. We now know that among his contributions was an analysis, classified "top secret," entitled "The Arms Control Implications of Chemical and Biological Warfare." The document went through two drafts before a final draft was shared with officials in the US Arms Control and Disarmament Agency in 1967. I use here the second draft, which was more detailed and frank that the final one.[46]

The context of Bull's work—and subsequently, of the process leading up to the British decision to propose a treaty banning biological weapons—was crucial for shaping assessments of the purposes and value of chemical and biological weapons (CBWs) at the time. The US was fighting in Vietnam and was using riot control agents, the incapacitant BZ, and herbicides as weapons. The UK was not involved directly, but it had an active chemical and biological warfare program and was bound by tripartite and quadripartite agreements for sharing information from its programs with the US, Canada, and Australia.[47] The UK had ratified the Geneva Protocol banning use of chemical and biological weapons, and had interpreted it broadly to cover riot control agents. The US had not ratified that treaty and so was not formally bound by it. The UK knew that, as a US ally, retaliation with lethal chemical weapons could be used against it. Most of this knowledge was secret, but small parts of it leaked out to the press. What British anti-war and pro-disarmament activists saw at the time were tips of a large military and arms control iceberg—enough to enable them to suspect UK complicity in American use of chemical weapons in Vietnam, call for transparency of activities at the British chemical and biological warfare facility at Porton Down, and press for chemical and biological disarmament. Documents of this period show a beleaguered UK Foreign Office worried about press reports and anti-war demonstrations in Whitehall.

In this context, Bull faced the challenge of addressing the question of possible new arms control initiatives for the UK government. Students of Hedley Bull's work would recognize his style in this report. It is an elaborate (to the point of being arcane) exposition of the conditions under which states might resort to using chemical or biological weapons, with possession or non-possession of nuclear weapons as a major variable in the analysis. This is followed by a detailed set of options for arms control. Clearly, Bull had broad access to military and intelligence information. In addition, he took into account the negotiations for the nuclear non-proliferation treaty that were in progress at that time. Of course, he was aware of pressures inside and outside the British Labour Party in favor of disarmament. All of these factors figure in his report, in addition to his own realist view of arms control.

Several important assumptions informed Bull's recommendations to the Foreign Office. While he viewed chemical and biological weapons as "not ideal deterrents," he argued that their use was conceivable in cases where "nuclear exchanges were inhibited" or in covert use by a non-nuclear state or in conflicts between non-nuclear states.[48] Although their possible use was largely "unnecessary" for nuclear powers, for non-nuclear powers, they represented a "destabilizing temptation."[49] Thus his analysis rested on a distinction between the nuclear-armed Self and the non-nuclear Other, which he depicted as the principal target of chemical and biological arms control. As Bull explained in a passage that resonated with the colonialism of the UK's recent past, the imminent conclusion of the Non-Proliferation Treaty (NPT) made consideration of the control of chemical and biological weapons important:

> [E]very success in exorcising the nuclear threat [through the NPT] must revive interest in other means of mass destruction, and every advance in chemical and biological knowledge in the underdeveloped countries will hasten their ability to make them; neither development is one that we would, or could, obstruct; so we must forestall their likely side-effects.[50]

And so:

> The time to strike [on arms control] is now, when those who can make CBW weapons have no need for them, except for mutual deterrence; while those who would like them are still ashamed to say so and cannot make them anyway.[51]

For Bull, the basic rationale for controlling chemical and biological weapons was *not* a universal need to prevent their possession and use but the need to prevent their *spread* before they became weapons of interest to non-nuclear, less technologically developed countries. An important feature of this analysis, then, is that it is developed from the perspective of the nuclear-armed, previously colonizing Self that is aligned with a powerful, nuclear-chemical-biological-armed state vs. the non-nuclear (and largely non-chemical/biological) Other that must be prevented from using biological and chemical weapons in the future.

A second important feature was his acceptance of *secrecy* for chemical and biological warfare preparations. The international non-governmental scientific organization Pugwash had called for transparency with respect to biological warfare activities. Its members had argued that the best way to reduce the biological weapons (BW) threat was to open BW defense laboratories for mutual inspections. As Bull put it, Pugwash wanted to "organize indiscretion" and to encourage "oaths of non-secrecy among a [scientific] profession already given to cooperativeness and solidarity."[52]

Bull dismissed the Pugwash proposal as naïve, citing Pugwash's "exceedingly frail assumptions about the cosmopolitanisms of scientists, ... the impracticality of military exploitation, and ... the implications of commercial secrecy with which so much microbiological work in the West is tied up."[53] Furthermore, he argued that it was impossible to guarantee "the permanence of our disinterest in a BW offensive capability ... [And] even aspects of research that appear purely 'defensive' could assist the enemy's offensive plans."[55] As such, "dismantlement of our own research facilites would merely make us more dependent on US work ... and more dependent on US defence aid with no guarantee that it would ultimately be given."[54]

In other words, secrecy for the defensive activities of the Self, including continuing technological innovation, was essential for protection from the Other. In view of these assumptions, it is not surprising that Bull's recommendations for chemical and biological arms control were weak and even regressive. For chemical weapons, he concluded that the most that could be achieved was to replace the existing practice of reservations to the Geneva Protocol's ban on all use with a formal no-first-use agreement. Moreover, given the certainty of American insistence on exempting "non-lethal" chemical weapons like the "riot-control" agents being used in Vietnam, he recognized that the UK and other European countries might have to back down from including "non-lethal" chemicals in the ban.

Third, Bull viewed biological weapons—in contrast to chemical weapons—as "militarily unnecessary and globally undesirable" and therefore dispensable.[56] He elaborated the well-known catalogue of militarily undesirable qualities—delayed action, ability to mutate, susceptibility to climatic conditions, possibility of rebound on the user, etc.

In summary, guided by the political philosophy of *The Control of the Arms Race*, Bull's report expressed a realist view of arms control cast largely in terms of what was militarily advantageous from the perspective of a nuclear-armed state. Once again, it was "war by other means." Because he recognized that the US would not accept a ban on riot agents and incapacitants, he proposed revising—and effectively weakening—the Protocol first, to make it a formal no-first-use agreement, and second, to limit the ban on use to "lethal" chemicals. From the perspectives of the international and national politics of the period, Bull's proposals were unworkable. Neither the Labour government, faced with anti-war activity inside and outside the ranks of the party, nor the United States, which hardly wanted to increase international attention to its use of chemical weapons in Vietnam through further debate in the UN General Assembly, was not likely to support the regressive revision of the Geneva Protocol which he proposed.

The proposal went nowhere. When the Bull report was shared with American officials in October 1967, their response was that the US was not about to ratify the Geneva Protocol or consider any modification of it.[57] Moreover, the top policy item at the time was completion of the NPT. Meanwhile, the anti-war movement continued to grow and questions about Britain's development and possession of chemical and biological weapons were constantly raised, in letters, in the media, and in Parliamentary Questions. On the other hand, the Americans were adamant in their opposition to revising the Geneva Protocol. The interest of the Minister of State for Foreign Affairs, Fred Mulley, in revising the Geneva Protocol, leaked to the press on June 16, 1968, caused a flurry of telegrams back and forth across the Atlantic attempting to discern the Minister's intentions and making clear American resistance to any British move to raise the issue. In the truncated language of a secret State Department instructions to the American embassy in London "US would not rpt not want possible UK redraft of [Geneva] Protocol introduced next session ENDC."[58]

Nevertheless, the Labour government felt compelled to respond to public pressure in some way. It dropped the idea of modifying the Geneva Protocol, dropped the idea of addressing chemical weapons, and instead proposed an international convention that would ban not only use but also possession of biological weapons.[59] By July 2, 1968, Mulley, and his trusted civil servant, Ronald Hope-Jones, were in Washington, meeting with the head of the US Arms Control and Disarmament Agency and other American officials. This time, a modest agreement was reached. Both sides viewed biological weapons as dispensable for the reasons that Bull had articulated in his report: each country could rely on nuclear weapons for deterrence. Both sides held that complete openness of the kind Pugwash called for could be a "real problem." The British deferred to the Americans in dropping any move to restrict chemical weapons and in agreeing to submit a working paper rather than a draft treaty to ban biological weapons (which would have indicated a higher level of commitment) to the Eighteen-Nation Disarmament Committee in Geneva.[60]

After Mulley and Hope-Jones returned to London, a rapid process of drafting and discussion of drafts ensued and was completed by August 1, when the final proposal went to Geneva. The Foreign Office was the lead government department for this process and several other government departments were involved in responding to briefs—notably the Ministry of Defence. A significant cleavage developed between the Foreign Office under Mulley, which wanted to move ahead with the proposal, and the Ministry of Defence under Dennis Healey, which resisted. The records show the Prime Minister, Harold Wilson and his chief science advisor, biologist Sir Solly Zuckerman, and the two senior Foreign Office civil servants deftly maneuvering around the MoD's objections. At the end of the day, the MoD was overruled, and Mulley, with the support of Wilson and his chief science advisor, prevailed.

But, to borrow its own metaphor, although the military may have lost the battle, it didn't lose the war. Its general goals still marked the text of the British proposal. First, the proposal was limited by the general requirement of maintaining strategic advantage. The most fundamental element of NATO doctrine, the ultimate reliance of the West on nuclear weapons for deterrence, was never questioned.[61]

Second, there was a strong perception of the significant defects of biological weapons from a military perspective. The chief science advisor, Sir Solly Zuckerman, was reported to have dismissed them as "a pain in the neck." Therefore they could be renounced without loss of strategic advantage. As Hope-Jones, echoing Hedley Bull's arguments, pointed out to American officials on July 30, 1968: "In forgoing BW, major powers would be giving up nothing since they had much more effective weaponry readily available and would not rationally contemplate using [biological weapons] against each other, for fear of nuclear retaliation."[62] This was an argument that also proved to be persuasive for President Richard Nixon, after the 1968 election. Following an extensive review of the US chemical and biological weapons policies in 1969, Nixon confided, crudely, to his speech writer, William Safire, "We'll never use the damn germs. So what good is biological warfare as a deterrent? If someone uses the germs on us, we'll nuke 'em."[63] On the other hand, as Hope-Jones, again echoing Bull, also reminded American officials, biological weapons "might have considerable attraction for smaller powers because of the cheapness and potential for off-setting in some degree [the] monopoly of nuclear powers enshrined in the NPT."[64] Renouncing biological weapons was seen as a way to protect military advantage, *not* as a step towards general and complete disarmament.

Third, there was the agreement with the United States *not* to address chemical disarmament even though chemical weapons were the more significant menace. They were being used as weapons in Vietnam, and both countries were involved in secret R&D on chemical incapacitants. Development of a ban on chemical weapons, which the eastern bloc and the neutral nonaligned countries would urge in response to the British proposal, would take 25 years.

Fourth, verification of compliance, which has figured as a large problem for the Biological Weapons Convention for almost 20 years, was not omitted from the proposal simply because it posed technical difficulties (the ease of hiding biological facilities, the dual-purpose nature of biological activities) or because the Soviet Union was averse to inspections. British and American officials understood that intrusive verification was undesirable from a *Western* perspective. As interactions show, the two governments were reluctant to reveal secrets regarding their defenses and anticipated that the pharmaceutical industry would be reluctant to reveal its commercial secrets.[65]

Finally, there was a fundamental ambiguity at the heart of the proposed ban, which was seen both as necessary for British military purposes and as a fundamental flaw, allowing research on biological weapons to continue. This was the lack of a clear distinction between "offensive" and "defensive" military research, development, and even production. The discussions in July 1968 show agreement among the various UK government agencies that production of biological agents for defense research would not be prohibited, and the three formulations of the proposed ban were written precisely to allow for that possibility.[66] While it can be argued that the BWC as it was eventually written does ban large-scale production of biological weapons, it does not unequivocally ban technological innovation, and judgments concerning pro-duction on a "small" scale and the distinction between "large" and "small" itself remain a matter of intention. Indeed, acute problems arising from that loophole have emerged during the past decade as US military and intelligence agencies have been allowed to respond to the lure of biotechnology and genetic engineering.[67]

A feminist deconstruction of arms control

In the second section of this chapter, I argued that despite differences in their conceptual frameworks, arms control played a similar role in Schelling's and Bull's theories of International Relations. For Bull, arms control, like war, was a means for "preserv[ing] and buttress[ing] the balance of power" and "it could not be shaped by any such principle as the indiscriminate reduction of armaments."[68] For Schelling, arms control was an integral part of strategy, another tool in strategic bargaining, like limited war. For both, arms control was "war by other means." In this section, I use feminist theory to analyze major dimensions of the Bull–Schelling conception of arms control and its application by the British government.

At a fundamental epistemological level, Bull and Schelling wrote in an Olympian voice that assumes absolute and universal standards of truth and objectivity, and that claims to rise above the chaos of International Relations (even while being obviously rooted in it). That Olympian voice was pervasive in academic work in the 1960s, even though change was in the air. Peter Novick has described the voices of the civil rights movement, the anti-war movement, the feminist movement, and the labor movement that were being raised in the 1960s and the challenges to the dominant empiricist and rationalist epistemology that would eventually deeply affect academic fields of all kinds.[69]

The Olympian epistemology was directly associated with the ontologies of the Bull and Schelling models of the international system. Schelling's model of the state system was almost Newtonian in conception: states were like mass points that interacted by exerting forces on each other.[70] In this case, the forces were those of military power and the ideal state of the system was "stability" achieved through deterrence and arms control to avoid an "imbalance" that would result in nuclear war. For Bull, similarly, the state was taken as an entity that required no further deconstruction and the goal was order in the state system achieved through "balance of power" exerted through diplomacy and arms control or if necessary through war. In each framework, arms control was depicted merely as an adjunct to the military machinery of deterrence and war.

A further fundamental concept used by Bull and Schelling is that of power in the voluntarist sense of "power over," achieved primarily by force or the threat of force.[71] The basic assumption in both views of arms control is that military power can be used to force another state—usually one seen as hostile—to do something it might not otherwise do. Military power vested in nuclear weapons was used by the United States and its nuclear-armed allies to deter the Soviet Union from contemplating any kind of attack on or incursion into the capitalist world. After the Soviet Union acquired nuclear weapons, the power game shifted to ensuring that neither state would attack the other, through each assuring the other of nuclear destruction. This was a stereotypically masculine form of power—power exerted over the behavior of the Other, linked in this case to an extreme form of violence in the form of a nuclear wrestling match.

"Power over" can also be expressed in Foucauldian terms. According to Foucault, power is expressed in the discursive practices of social institutions from the prison to the clinic to the school—and he could easily have added military and foreign policy institutions to that list.[72] Foucault saw power as a "productive network which runs through the whole social body."[73] No doubt in the present context, he would have argued that the state exerts its power through the practices and specific discourses that are linked to those practices. In Foucault's words:

> Truth isn't outside power or lacking in power ... truth isn't the reward of free spirits, the child of protracted solitude, nor the privilege of those who have succeeded in liberating themselves. Truth is a thing of this world. It is produced only by virtue of multiple forms of constraint.[74]

In Foucauldian terms, Bull and Schelling produced forms of "truth" that were readily incorporated by the "great powers" into the twin aspects of military strategy: weaponry and military training to use weapons on the one hand and arms control on the other. In their strategic discourses, the full complexity of the state with its factions, interests, processes, traditions, ethnicities, genders, and linkages across the world is reduced to a point source moved, primarily, by threats and coercion. Human beings appear in this picture as a passive, nameless mass protected by the armory of the state.

Bull and Schelling justify the use of "power over" states that are treated as adversaries, or potential adversaries, in several ways. First, violence in the state system, and therefore the need to defend against it, are taken as given. As Bull wrote:

> It is true that strategists take the fact of military force as their starting point ... The capacity for organized violence between states is *inherent* in the nature of man and the environment. The most that can be expected from a total disarmament agreement is that it might make armaments and armed forces fewer and more primitive.[75]

This claim of the inevitability of violence and the consequent need for military protection have been extensively analyzed by feminist theorists. If violence is inevitable, then someone or something is required to defend against it. Jean

Elshtain, Laura Sjoberg, and other feminist theorists have demonstrated the pervasive tradition of western political thought that claims that the inevitability of violence calls for the services of a Just Warrior (representing variously the state military apparatus or the soldier) who is "engaged in the regrettable but sometimes necessary task of collective violence in order to prevent some greater wrong" to the Beautiful Soul, representing variously *patria* or the homeland or innocent civilians.[76] Bull's political philosophy falls completely within this tradition.

A second feature that legitimates a state's exercise of "power over" another is the focus in both strategy and arms control on ends rather than means. Schelling and Bull are silent about the nature of the means used to exercise power over other states. The horrific effects of nuclear, chemical, biological, or of war in any form receive no attention except to dismiss those who focus on them. The ends, on the other hand—the security and survival of the state— are all important. As Bull commented:

> There is a sense in which strategic thinking does and should leave morality out of the account ... if what is being said is that strategic judgments should be coloured by moral considerations or that strategic inquiry should be restricted by moral taboos, this is something that the strategist is bound to reject.[77]

This moral silence is related to a further major feature of Bull and Schelling's work: the "psychic numbing" concerning the weapons assumed to guarantee the state's security. As Robert Jay Lifton and Richard Falk argue, human beings develop powerful psychic walls to protect them from contemplating the effects of extreme violence.[78] "Psychic numbing" is a defense mechanism that represses, denies and excludes contemplation of massive death and destruction. In their analysis of nuclear strategy and arms control, Bull and Schelling enlist this psychological mechanism by focusing on reassuring ends rather than on the weapons providing the means to get there. As Lifton, Falk and Carol Cohn have described in detail, the nuclear strategists' focus on ends is powerfully reinforced by their "domestication" of the weaponry through the use of abstract, familial, religious, or sexual language—radically different metaphors that have a single function: distracting the user and the listener from the reality of the subject matter.[79] Bull used this type of legitimation in his Foreign Office report through an exclusive focus on the strategic features of chemical and biological weapons and complete silence on their effects.

A third feature of Bull and Schelling's view of arms control is the distancing of states from each other, with the primary relationship being an adversarial one. Schelling might have argued that his model of strategy in International Relations was politically neutral, that he was concerned only with achieving strategic balance. Bull, on the other hand, explicitly identified with "strategists' greater sense of the moral stature of American and Western political objectives for which war and the risk of war must be undertaken."[80]

A fourth feature that justifies the Bull–Schelling approach to arms control is the claim that the approach is rational and undistorted by emotion. The rational/emotional dualism figures powerfully in *The Control of the Arms Race*. In the chapter on nuclear disarmament, for example, Bull wrote that the idea that measures for nuclear disarmament should be pressed as far as possible and that the more the better, "stems from a Luddite approach to the problem of security."[81] Thus, Bull dismissed the British campaign for nuclear disarmament led by people like Bertrand Russell (no mean logician) and the historian E.P. Thompson (no mean analyst of history). Using nuclear weapons as deterrents, Bull was implying, was rational; destroying them was an irrational, "Luddite" act. Again, this position draws on Bull's firm belief that "the physical capacity for organized violence is *inherent* in human society" and thus "the idea of absolute security from war emerging from [disarmament] is an illusion."[82]

Bull's Foreign Office report on chemical and biological arms control is essentially an application of the leading ideas of *The Control of the Arms Race*. First, the report shows no interest in universal chemical and biological disarmament. Bull would have rejected that goal. Rather, his interest is in achieving the dominance of technologically developed states by not only removing the motive for developing chemical and biological weapons on the part of less technologically developed states and but also in maintaining options for further development on the part of developed states.

Second, maintaining strategic advantage meant an imperative to continue technological innovation through research on chemical and biological weapons: "No one can guarantee the permanence of our disinterest in a BW offensive capability." Indeed, that imperative was protected in the British government's proposal in 1968 for an international convention banning biological weapons both by allowing BW research to continue and by defining the ban ambiguously, in terms of the intentions of its signatories.

Third, Bull aimed to protect chemical and biological innovation by enshrouding it in secrecy. In his view, arms control could *never* be about cosmopolitan sharing with countries other than close allies (as proposed by the Pugwash organization) because it was primarily about achieving and maintaining strategic advantage over potential adversaries. As noted earlier, that view would also be inscribed into the UK proposal for banning biological weapons by jettisoning a requirement for international inspections.

Finally, was not Bull's advice to the British Foreign Office to exert the power of the nuclear-armed Self over the non-nuclear, "under-developed" Other also an "emotional" act similar to the acts of the playground bully exerting control over smaller children? His dismissal of those committed to general and complete disarmament used the rational/emotional dualism to legitimate his own position.[83]

Conclusion

As Thomas Schelling and Hedley Bull clearly understood, arms control, as it has been practiced, is the other face of weapons development: both seek military advantage. The international treaty for which Bull prepared the foundations and that looks like a universal ban on a category of weaponry is no different in kind. But there is no imperative for arms control to be formulated or practiced in this way. It is the application of stereotypically masculine values of reducing the human complexity of the state to impersonal units, distancing the Self from the Other, exerting power over rather than power with the Other, seeking military advantage not the protection of human beings or of other species, that make it seem so. Since 1990, there has been much discussion among arms control and disarmament specialists about how to "strengthen" the Biological Weapons Convention. This treaty is most often portrayed by arms controllers as a path-breaking treaty that is—unfortunately—flawed. Feminist theory provides crucial tools for understanding those flaws as the results of acts of "power over" the Other and that account for the problems that arise later in its application. The next step in this research program is to look beyond the present, time-constrained, stereotypically masculine goals of the state to the timeless needs of humans and other species in attempts to re-vision, reformulate, and reconstruct arms control theory and policy.

Notes

1 Thanks to Robert Ayson, Hilary Charlesworth, Zia Mian, and the editor of this volume, Laura Sjoberg, for their stimulating responses to this chapter; to Brian Martin and the School of Social Sciences at the University of Wollongong for their generous hospitality and the opportunity for uninterrupted reading and reflection on feminist theory in 2007; and to the Institute for Research on Women and Gender at the University of Michigan for its support for research on gender and security.

2 Barry Posen, "Military Lessons of the Gulf War: Implications for Middle East Arms Control," in S. Feldman and A. Levite, eds., *Arms Control and the New Middle East Security Environment* (Jerusalem, Israel: Jaffee Center for Strategic Studies, 1994), p. 64.

3 Fred Halliday, "Hidden from International Relations: Women and the International Arena," in *Gender and International Relations*, eds., R. Grant and K. Newland (Bloomington, IN: Indiana University Press, 1991), pp. 158–69.

4 Hilary Charlesworth, Christine Chinkin and Shelley Wright, "Feminist Approaches to International Law," *American Journal of International Law* 85 (1991): 613–45.

5 Jean Bethke Elshtain, *Public Man, Private Woman: Women in Social and Political Thought* (Princeton, NJ: Princeton University Press, 1981), p. 12.

6 Charlesworth, *et al.*, "Feminist Approaches," 626, n.75.

7 V. Spike Peterson and Anne Sisson Runyan, *Global Gender Issues*, 2nd ed. (Boulder, CO: Westview Press, 1999); Laura Sjoberg, *Gender, Justice, and the Wars in Iraq: A Feminist Reformulation of Just War Theory* (Lanham, MD: Rowman & Littlefield, 2006).

8 J. Ann Tickner, *Gender in International Relations* (New York: Columbia University Press, 1992), pp. 6–7.

9 Sandra Whitworth, *Feminism and International Relations* (Basingstoke: Macmillan, 1994), Chapter 1.

10 Robert Cox, "Social Forces, States and World Orders: Beyond International Theory." *Millennium* 10, no. 2 (1981): 126–55, at p. 128.

11 Catherine MacKinnon, *Feminism Unmodified: Discourses on Life and Law.* (Cambridge, MA: Harvard University Press, 1987), p. 234, n. 6.

12 J. Ann Tickner, "Feminism Meets International Relations: Some Methodological Issues," in *Feminist Methodologies for International Relations*, eds., Brooke A. Ackerley, Maria Stern, and Jacqui True (Cambridge: Cambridge University Press, 2006), pp. 19–41, 21–5.

13 For example, John W. Burton, *World Society* (Cambridge: Cambridge University Press, 1972), pp. 28–9.

14 Maureen Dowd, "Powell Without Picasso," *New York Times*, February 5, 2003, A27.

15 See especially Carol Cohn, "Sex and Death in the Rational World of Defense Intellectuals," *Signs* 12, no. 4 (1987): 687–718.

16 G. Brumfiel, "Bush Buries US Bunker-Buster Project," *Nature* 438 (10 November 2005): 139.

17 Carol Cohn, "Wars, Wimps, and Women: Talking Gender and Thinking War," in *Gendering War Talk*, eds., Miriam Cooke and Angela Woollacott (Princeton, NJ: Princeton University Press, 1993), pp. 227–46, 237–8.

18 Annica Kronsell, "Methods for Studying Silences: Gender Analysis in Institutions of Hegemonic Masculinity," in Ackerly *et al.*, eds., *Feminist Methodologies for International Relations*, pp. 108–28, 113.

19 Ibid., p. 110.

20 Ibid., p. 115.

21 A. Myrdal, *The Game of Disarmament* (New York: Pantheon, 1974), p. 821; J. Goldblatt, *Arms Control: A Guide to Negotiations and Agreements* (Oslo: International Peace Research Institute, 1994), pp. 35–7.

22 G. Bussey and M. Tims, *Women's International League for Peace and Freedom, 1915–1965* (London: George Allen and Unwin, 1965), pp. 207–14.

23 P. Noel-Baker, *The Arms Race: A Programme for World Disarmament* (New York: Publications, c.1958).

24 B. Brodie, "Review of Hedley Bull, *The Control of the Arms Race*," *Annals of the American Academy of Political and Social Science* 341 (1962): 115–16.

25 R. O'Neill and D.N. Schwartz, eds., *Hedley Bull on Arms Control* (New York: St. Martin's Press, 1987), pp. 5–6.

26 R. Ayson, *Thomas Schelling and the Nuclear Age: Strategy as Social Science* (London: Frank Cass, 2004), pp. 13–14.

27 For a survey of the development of Bull's thinking on disarmament and arms control written by a close colleague, see Robert O'Neill, "Hedley Bull and Arms Control," in *Remembering Hedley*, eds., C. Bell and M. Thatcher (Canberra: Australian National University E Press, 2008), pp. 1–48.

28 O'Neill and Schwartz, *Hedley Bull on Arms Control*, pp. 4–6; J.D.B. Miller and R. J. Vincent, *Order and Violence: Hedley Bull and International Relations* (Oxford: Oxford University Press, 1990).

29 R. Ayson, "'A Common Interest in Common Interest': Hedley Bull, Thomas Schelling and Collaboration in International Politics," in Bell and Thatcher, *Remembering Hedley*, pp. 62–7.

30 Ayson, *Thomas Schelling and the Nuclear Age*, p. 76, n. 18.

31 Ibid., p. 27.

32 Ibid., p. 42.

33 Ibid., pp. 23–9.

34 Thomas Schelling, "The Role of Theory in the Study of Conflict, " RAND RM2515 (13 January 1960).

35 Thomas Schelling and M. Halperin, *Strategy and Arms Control* (New York: Twentieth Century Fund, 1961), pp. 58–60.

36 Ibid., pp. 3–4.

37 Hedley Bull, "Disarmament and the International System," *Australian Journal of Politics and History* 5 (May 1959), reprinted in O'Neill and Schwartz *Hedley Bull on Arms Control*, pp. 27–40.

38 As the arms race accelerated and nuclear weapons proliferated both vertically and horizontally, Bull may have eventually recognized some problems with his early insistence on the role of armaments as factors in achieving international stability (and the colonial posture that influenced them) but such doubts were nowhere to be found in his work in the 1960s, including his work for the British Foreign Office: see O'Neill, "Hedley Bull and Arms Control," pp. 41–3.

39 Hedley Bull, *The Control of the Arms Race* (New York: Praeger, 1961).

40 R. J. Vincent, "Order in International Politics," in Miller and Vincent, *Order and Violence*, pp. 38–64, 50.

41 Bull, *The Control of the Arms Race*, p. 39.

42 Ibid., p. 60.

43 Ibid., p. 61.

44 Ibid.

45 Ibid.

46 U.K. Foreign Office, Arms Control and Disarmament Research Unit, "The Arms Control Implications of Chemical and Biological Warfare: Analysis and Proposals," 4 July, classified "Top secret." FO , PRO, 1966.

47 Susan Wright, "The Biological Weapons Convention: Geopolitical Origins," in S. Wright, ed., *Biological Warfare and Disarmament: New Problems/New Perspectives* (Lanham, MD: Rowman & Littlefield, 2002), pp. 313–42.

48 U.K. Foreign Office, Arms Control and Disarmament Research Unit, "Draft Cover Note to Accompany CBW Paper," c. 4 July, classified "Top secret." FO , PRO, 1966, p. 2.

49 Ibid., pp. 3–4.

50 UK Foreign Office, "Arms Control Implications of Chemical and Biological Warfare," p. 58.

51 Ibid.

52 Ibid., p. 57.

53 Ibid.

54 Ibid.

55 Ibid.

56 UK Foreign Office, "Draft Cover Note to Accompany CBW Paper," p. 6.

57 Wright, "The Biological Weapons Convention: Geopolitical Origins," pp. 317–18.

58 U.S. Department of State. Telegram to U.S. Embassy London, 25 June. No. 192587, classified "Secret." RG59, POL 27–10, Box 2979, NA, 1968.

59 Wright, "The Biological Weapons Convention: Geopolitical Origins," pp. 326–29.

60 U.K. Foreign Office. "Record of a Conversation between the Minister of State for Foreign Affairs and the Director of the United States Arms Control and Disarmament Agency, Washington, 2 July," FCO , PRO, 1968.

61 U.K. Ministry of Defence, Chiefs of Staff Committee, "Chemical and Biological Warfare." Classified "Top secret U.K. Eyes Only," 15 December. COS , A-5–A-7; United Nations, 1968, UN document ENDC/231, 6 August 1967.

62 U.S. Department of State, U.S. Embassy London to State Department, 30 July 1968. Telegram London 11305. "UK Working Paper on Biological Weapons (BW)," classified "Secret." RG 59, POL 27–10. Box 2879, NA.

63 W. Safire, "On Language: Weapons of Mass Destruction," *New York Times*, April 19, 1998.

64 US Department of State, "UK Working Paper on Biological Weapons."

65 U.K. Cabinet, Defence and Oversea Policy Committee. Minutes, Meeting, 12 July 1968, OPD(68), CAB, PRO, classified "Secret;" W. Muth, "The Role of the Biotech and Pharmaceutical Industries in Strengthening the Biological Disarmament

Regime." *Politics and the Life Sciences* 18, no. 1 (March): 92–7; Susan Wright and D. Wallace, "Secrecy in the Biotechnology Industry: Implications for the Biological Weapons Convention," in S.Wright, ed., *Biological Warfare and Disarmament: New Problems/New Perspectives*, pp. 369–90.

66 This paper is the final version presented at the ENDC by the Minister of State for Foreign Affairs, Fred Mulley on 6 August 1968 The three formulations of the ban on "production of microbiological agents" proposed in this paper are: (1) "on a scale which had no independent peaceful justification;" (2) for hostile purposes; (3) "in quantities that would be incompatible with the obligation never to engage in microbiological methods of warfare in any circumstances." See U.K. Foreign Office. Working Paper on Chemical and Biological Warfare for Tabling at the Eighteen Nation Disarmament Committee, 30 July 1968. FCO , PRO.

67 Susan Wright, "Terrorists and Biological Weapons: Forging the Linkage in the Clinton Administration," *Politics and the Life Sciences* 25, nos (1–2) (2006): 57–115.

68 Bull, *The Control of the Arms Race*, p. 61.

69 A singular omission in Novick's analysis is the post-colonial voice which has so deeply affected the social sciences. See P. Novick, *That Noble Dream: The "Objectivity Question" and the American Historical Profession* (Cambridge: Cambridge University Press, 1988).

70 On this feature and others associated with nuclear strategic theory, see J. Falk, "The Discursive Shaping of Nuclear Militarism," *Current Research in Peace and Violence* 22, no. 2 (1989): 53–76.

71 For a review and discussion of the concept of power, see Stephen Lukes, *Power: A Radical View*, 2nd edn. (Basingstoke: Palgrave Macmillan, 2005).

72 There is not space here to enter into a detailed discussion, but in brief, my position is that the voluntarist and Foucauldian conceptions of power are complementary positions, the former focusing on the nature of power exerted at the point of origin and the latter focusing on the dissemination of power through discursive practices. Only for those who take literally Foucault's more radical-sounding statements on the nature of power does it follow that those who exert power and those on whom it is exerted are caught in a seamless web from which there is no escape for either party. As Steven Lukes argues in "Power and the Battle for Hearts and Minds," *Millennium* 33, no. 2 (2005): 477–93, p. 492, that interpretation "strips the subject of power of both freedom and reason." On the interpretation of Foucault's position that I use here, there is no *necessary* incompatibility between the voluntarist and Foucauldian positions. As I have argued in *Molecular Politics* (Chicago: University of Chicago Press, 1994), pp. 13–14, power can be exerted both at the center of a political system as well as through the discursive practices of its legal, military, medical, educational and other institutions.

73 Michel Foucault, *Power/Knowledge: Selected Interviews and Other Writings, 1972–1977*, ed., Colin Gordon (Brighton: Harvester Press, 1980), p. 119.

74 Ibid., p. 131.

75 Hedley Bull, "Strategic Studies and Its Critics," *World Politics* 20, no. 4 (July 1968): 593–605, at p. 599, emphasis added.

76 Jean Elshtain, "On Beautiful Souls, Just Warriors and Feminist Consciousness," *Women's Studies International Forum* 5, nos 3/4 (1982): 341–8, at p. 343; Sjoberg, *Gender, Justice, and the Wars in Iraq*, pp. 96–9.

77 Bull, "Strategic Studies and Its Critics," p. 597.

78 R. J. Lifton and Richard Falk, *Indefensible Weapons: The Political and Psychological Case Against Nuclearism* (New York: Basic Books, 1982).

79 Cohn, "Sex and Death in the Rational World of Defense Intellectuals;" Lifton and Falk, *Indefensible Weapons*, pp. 100–10.

80 Bull, "Strategic Studies and Its Critics," p. 598.
81 Bull, *The Control of the Arms Race*, p. 102.
82 Ibid., pp. 34–5.
83 Cf. Carol Cohn, "Wars, Wimps, and Women," pp. 240–1 on emotion in nuclear strategy.

11 Beyond border security[1]

Feminist approaches to human trafficking

Jennifer K. Lobasz

> While some classify such crime types as "non-traditional" threats to security—
> in many ways they are the most traditional threats to a nation's security, to a
> nation's interest. Slavery has ever been a threat to national unity and national
> interest. As long as there has been slavery, from the Jews enslaved in ancient
> Egypt, to black Africans trafficked to North America, there has been dissent
> and unease within nations (defined here as "an agglomerated people" rather
> than the modern concept of a "State") about the nature of the act. Modern
> human trafficking is no different.[2]

It is not remarkable that Brian Iselin, a regional legal policy advisor for the
United Nations, refers to international human trafficking as a major threat.
What is significant is how trafficking is seen as a threat: what kind of a threat
does it pose and to whom or what? A traditional security approach—one in
line with the mainstream, primarily realist, security scholarship that emerged
in the 1950s—would call for analysis of trafficking as a threat to the state and
particularly to the control of its borders. Traditional security solutions to
human trafficking have focused primarily upon enhanced border security and
swift deportation of trafficked persons, who are considered "illegal immigrants." Like the traditional security scholars who focus primarily on war and
military security, those who focus on crime and borders are concerned first
and foremost with the security—indeed, the survival—of the sovereign state.
Yet the meaning of security has come under greater scrutiny following the end
of the Cold War, with security scholars seeking to broaden conceptions of
security beyond the military realm to incorporate issue areas such as economics, the environment, and health and to deepen approaches to security
through additional levels of analysis.[3] The broadening and deepening of the
concept of security suggest that there might be more than one way to understand
the threat of international human trafficking.[4]

Feminist analyses of human trafficking have eschewed a traditional security
framework, considering instead the security of trafficked persons, recognizing
the manner in which both traffickers and the state itself pose security threats.
Table 11.1 summarizes the traditional security and feminist approaches to

Table 11.1 Traditional and feminist security approaches to international human trafficking

Approach	Security referent	Security threat	Policy focus
Traditional	States	Traffickers, undocumented migrants	Border security, migration controls, international law enforcement cooperation
Feminist	People	Traffickers, border patrol and law enforcement officials, abusive employers and clients	Social services, human rights, safe migration, worker protections, attention to status of prostitution

human trafficking and demonstrates how changing the referent object of security leads to a change in policy focus as well.[5]

Feminists challenge the traditional security approach to international human trafficking on two levels: the ethical and the pragmatic. Feminists argue that as an issue of ethics, human trafficking is first and foremost a violation of human rights.[6] Focusing on trafficking as a security threat to the state neglects the voices of trafficked persons, whose human rights the state is legally obligated to protect. Founded on the premise that scholars of trafficking need to shift their focus from state security to the security of people, feminist research on trafficking began with analyses of the experiences of trafficked persons, emphasizing in particular the plight of women trafficked for sexual exploitation. From a standpoint of efficacy, feminists hold that traditional security approaches compound rather than solve the problem of trafficking. First, repressive border control policies make migration more difficult and dangerous and increase migrants' vulnerability to traffickers. Second, trafficked persons who are deported are themselves prone to re-trafficking. In short, feminists maintain that traditional security approaches to human trafficking are both morally and practically deficient.

Feminist analyses of human trafficking do more than expand the referent of security from states to people. While many feminists highlight the plight of trafficked persons—and this remains an important and worthy endeavor—it is important to note that to simply expand the referent of security is insufficient: care must be taken in regard to how actors are constructed as threatened. This is because prevalent constructions of human trafficking rely upon and reproduce gender and racial stereotypes that (1) discount women's agency; (2) establish a standard for victimization that most trafficked persons cannot meet; and (3) unjustly prioritize the sexual traffic of white women over the traffic of women and men of all races who are trafficked for purposes including, but not exclusive to, the sex trade.

Feminist approaches to human trafficking clearly share a good deal with the alternative security frameworks that have arisen in the past two decades.

In J. Ann Tickner's words, "Feminists' commitment to the emancipatory goal of ending women's subordination is consistent with a broad definition of security that takes the individual, situated in broader social structures, as its starting point."[7] In particular, feminist approaches are largely congruent with the concept of "human security" proposed in the UN Development Program's (UNDP) 1994 Human Development Report.[8] Though the concept itself has been subject to debate and criticism, human security, in general, is characterized by a shift in focus from security of the state to the security of people, changing the referent of security in much the same way that feminists have done with trafficking.[9] This is not to say, however, that a human security approach to trafficking would subsume a feminist approach; feminist analyses of trafficking establish the necessity of gender as a category of analysis in a way that traditional and human security theories do not. As noted, feminists not only establish women as a referent of security and focus on gender-related human rights abuses but also, and perhaps more significantly, study the manner in which gender stereotypes are used to establish and reproduce categories of practices, perpetrators, and victims.

In this chapter, I show that feminists have made two essential contributions to the analysis of international human trafficking: expanding the focus of trafficking analyses to account for the exploitation of trafficked persons and paying attention to how the concept of human trafficking is socially constructed in the first place. I argue that these feminist contributions can serve as a foundation for a reformulated approach to human trafficking for Security Studies. To begin, I briefly present international human trafficking as an issue for global concern, highlighting the ambiguities and debates that characterize contemporary analyses of trafficking. Second, I discuss traditional security approaches to human trafficking, explaining how trafficking is presented as an organized crime threat to the state as well as a threat to state borders. I then provide feminist critiques of traditional security analyses and analyze the feminist debates regarding human trafficking and the status of prostitution. I conclude that, far from being irreconcilable, the two sides of these feminist debates together suggest important directions for the future study of human trafficking, attracting greater attention to trafficked persons while using gender as a category of analysis to reflect on the representation of those persons.

The issues of human trafficking

Analysts and practitioners of International Relations use the term "human trafficking" to refer to a variety of illicit activities, including sexual exploitation, forced labor, debt bondage, slavery and slavery-like practices, serfdom, and forced marriage.[10] Trafficking is practiced in many different ways. Recruiters deploy strategies from kidnappings to deceptive job advertisements for nannies, wait staff, or dancers to "mail-order-bride" services.[11] The hidden nature of the crime, coupled with the reluctance of victims to risk deportation from the state or retribution from their traffickers, and the conceptual confusion surrounding what and who counts as trafficked, make this activity hard to measure.[12] For example, a United Nations Educational, Scientific and Cultural Organization (UNESCO) chart featuring a compilation of various indicators of worldwide human trafficking states that estimates of individuals trafficked each year range from 500,000 to four million.[13] The disparity between estimates is also related to the difficulty in distinguishing—conceptually and in practice—among the trafficked, the smuggled, legal migrants in illicit industries, and refugees.[14] Challenges here reflect both the complexity of the issues and the political agendas of the researchers and funding institutions.[15]

The complexity of the trafficking issue has led to equally complex scholarly and policy responses to the problem. Whereas the 1904 and 1910 International Agreements for the Suppression of the White Slave Traffic, the 1921 and 1933 League of Nations Conventions on the Traffic in Women and Children, and the 1949 UN Convention for the Suppression of the Traffic in Persons and the Exploitation of the Prostitution of Others focused exclusively on forced prostitution, contemporary measures target a greater variety of activities. Moreover, whereas past measures were concerned with the threat to societal virtue, contemporary measures reflect a greater concern for the threat to state security.[16]

Though it disappeared from the international agenda for most of the Cold War, combating human trafficking re-emerged as an international priority in the late 1980s as a number of states, non-governmental organizations (NGOs), human rights activists, and various feminist and religious groups sought to publicize the issue.[17] David Kyle and Rey Koslowski note that law enforcement busts of major trafficking rings, statements by world leaders, international conferences, and popular films all contributed to a rise in awareness regarding the issue.[18] In the late 1990s, US president Bill Clinton established interagency working groups to explore the ramifications of human trafficking and potential strategies for prevention, and Congress subsequently passed the landmark Trafficking Victims Protection Act of 2000 (TVPA) in October 2000. International organizations have likewise begun to address human trafficking, particularly in terms of its relation to transnational organized crime and human rights protection. There are at least 15 international organizations with significant countertrafficking efforts, including the UN, the International Labor Organization (ILO), the International Organization on Migration (IOM), the Organization for Security and Cooperation in Europe (OSCE), the Organization of American States (OAS), the Association of Southeast Asian Nations (ASEAN), and the World Bank.[19]

Increasing government and activist attention to international human trafficking is complemented by increasing scholarly attention to the issue. Trafficking research has largely confounded the theory/policy divide, and even putatively academic research is often funded by or conducted under the auspices of governmental or intergovernmental organizations. According to Frank Laczko, "One of the strengths of trafficking research is its action-oriented approach, with studies often designed to prepare the ground for counter-trafficking interventions."[20] This supposed strength is not without its disadvantages. Others have argued that research on human trafficking is very much shaped by the immediate policy needs and political commitments of researchers and "does not necessarily ensure a deepening of the knowledge base."[21]

A threat to borders and orders

Although international human trafficking does not present a specifically military threat, government officials worldwide argue that trafficking nonetheless gravely endangers the state.[22] In the United States, for example, the Government Accountability Office (GAO) observes that

> the top goal of [Immigration and Customs Enforcement's] trafficking in persons efforts—to disrupt and dismantle criminal organizations involved in trafficking, including intelligence gathering on these organizations—is aligned with [Department of Homeland Security] strategic goals of assessing vulnerabilities and mitigating threats to the homeland.[23]

These threats to national security center largely on transnational organized crime and security of state borders.

In response to the apparently growing menace posed by trafficking, the United Nations passed the Protocol to Prevent, Suppress and Punish Trafficking in Persons, Especially Women and Children, a supplement to the 2000 United Nations Convention Against Transnational Organized Crime.[24] This protocol mandated the criminalization of trafficking, repatriation of victims, strengthened border controls, and more secure travel and identity documents.[25] The Trafficking Protocol also includes measures to protect the human rights of trafficking victims, but Ann Gallagher argues that "while human rights concerns may have provided some impetus (or cover) for collective action, it is the sovereignty/security issues surrounding trafficking and migrant smuggling which are the true driving force behind such efforts."[26]

The specter of organized crime networks and menacing mafiosi looms large in discussions of trafficking. The Center for European Policy studies notes:

> Anti-trafficking policies have put an emphasis on organized and transnational crime and harsher penalties for perpetrators of human trafficking crimes. Transnational organized crime is seen as the dark side of globalization, threatening and damaging democracy and the economic basis of societies, weakening institutions and confidence in the rule of law.[27]

Rather than representing a departure from traditional organized crime, trafficking is said to complement the existing activities of criminal networks.

Separate from human trafficking's relationship to transnational organized crime networks, trafficking is figured as a security threat insofar as trafficked persons are often undocumented migrants.[28] According to the European Commission, "The prevention of and the fight against human trafficking is an essential element of the EU's efforts to improve the checks and surveillance at the external borders and to enhance the fight against illegal immigration."[29] Following the collapse of communism in the Warsaw Pact states and the breakdown of the Soviet Union, EU officials feared an influx of economic migrants from the East and sought to balance relaxation of internal border controls with a strengthening of border controls outside the Schengen area.[30] This context facilitated the EU's securitization of not only trafficking but migration in general, placing "the regulation of migration in an institutional framework that deals with the protection of internal security."[31] Thus, "throughout the 1990s, the United States and Europe expanded the policing of their borders, increased the use of technology to monitor and regulate these borders, and generally militarized and securitized border crossings."[32]

The connection between trafficking and migration poses difficulties for traditional security approaches to border control since differentiating international human trafficking from immigrant smuggling is difficult. In fact, it was not until the adoption of two separate UN protocols to the 2000 Palermo Convention that there was an international legal effort to distinguish between the two phenomena, where trafficking in persons was distinguished by the use of coercion, abduction, fraud, deception, or abuse of power. Yet some argue that human trafficking and migrant smuggling are better thought of as two ends of a continuum.[33] Adam Graycar notes, "It is frequently difficult to establish whether there were elements of deception and/or coercion, and whether these were sufficient to elevate the situation from one of voluntary undocumented migration, to trafficking."[34] Many trafficking victims consent to being smuggled across borders but do not consent to the exploitation that occurs in the host country.[35] Likewise, smuggled migrants often experience exploitation and abuse, sometimes sexual, while in transit.[36] According to a Clinton White House fact sheet on human trafficking and migrant smuggling, "While at their core distinct, these related problems result in massive human tragedy and affect our national security, primarily with respect to crime, health and welfare, and border control."[37]

Feminists and other human rights activists have been, to some degree, complicit in presenting human trafficking as a threat to state security and for understandable reasons. Critical security scholars have long argued that securitization, or the incorporation of a given issue under the umbrella of "security," is a potent, though not unproblematic, strategy for increasing the attention and resources devoted to that issue.[38]

> While service providers, NGOs and women's groups have been concerned primarily with the victimization aspect of trafficking in women, for the problem to get government attention, they had to present it in a sufficiently alarming way … thus, the transmogrification into an organized crime and/or illegal migration issue—issues that the public feels strongly about and expects governments to act on.[39]

The time has come to recognize the drawbacks of this strategy.

A threat to persons

Since the mid-nineteenth century, feminists have lobbied states and international organizations to fight human trafficking while challenging the traditional security approach to trafficking on grounds of both ethics and efficacy. The ethical argument rests on three claims: (1) human trafficking represents a violation of victims' human rights; (2) states are obliged under international law to prevent human rights abuses; and (3) state efforts to address human trafficking thus far are unsatisfactory in protecting human rights and indeed may contribute to the violation of those rights in state treatment of persons who are trafficked.

Rather than seeing trafficked persons as undocumented migrants or otherwise "undesirable" threats to state security, feminists emphasize their status as victims, focusing on the wide array of human rights violations that trafficking often entails. Feminists use narratives from trafficked persons to dramatize abuses and to make their plight more concrete. This draws upon a long-standing tradition of valuing women's voices and of incorporating women's experiences into theory.[40]

The Global Alliance Against Trafficking in Women (GAATW) notes that traffickers routinely violate the human rights enumerated in the Universal Declaration of Human Rights (UDHR). It is both rhetorically and legally significant that human trafficking entails not only aspects that most people would find undesirable or even morally repugnant but abuses that specifically contravene the UDHR. The ability of activists to forcefully connect the plight of trafficked persons to a document that "has been endorsed, regularly and repeatedly, by virtually all states" has been essential in the international effort to move from a border-/state-security approach to a victim-centered approach that demands trafficked individuals be viewed as vulnerable humans rather than dangerous threats.[41] Moreover, the language of human rights demands that state governments be legally obligated to protect individuals within their own territory against human rights abuses even if those individuals are not citizens of that state and even if the government itself is not the group abusing human rights.[42] Feminists can therefore claim moral and legal ground with which to reframe the problem of trafficking.

As pioneers of the human rights approach to trafficking, feminists protest the still too common treatment of trafficked individuals—especially women—as criminals rather than victims.[43] While the traffickers may receive little to no punishment, trafficked individuals may be victimized twice: first by the traffickers and, second, by the host governments. The Trafficking Protocol and the Migrant Smuggling Protocol were specifically written to distinguish between voluntary and coercive migration, but, in practice, the coerced trafficking victims are often treated as voluntary undocumented migrants by border control and other state security apparatuses. Trafficked persons in the Czech Republic, for example, are often treated as migrants "who are in many cases perceived as committing the crime of staying in the Czech Republic illegally and are expelled from the country."[44] Likewise, Peter Landesman explains:

> The operating assumption among American police departments is that women who sell their bodies do so by choice, and undocumented foreign women who sell their bodies are not only prostitutes (that is, voluntary sex workers) but also trespassers on U.S. soil.[45]

Feminist work on human trafficking shows that this characterization is inaccurate and oversimplified. Many women who are trafficked either do not consent to immigrate at all or are misled by traffickers about the nature of the work they will be doing and the extent of their obligation to the traffickers. Still others plan to migrate and to work in the sex industry but experience terrible human rights violations, including—though not limited to—rape, assault, debt bondage, sexual exploitation, and slavery.

Various states and international organizations have responded to feminist criticism by introducing measures for victim protection. The Trafficking Protocol, for example, contains measures to protect the human rights of those trafficked, including five articles outlining legal assistance, medical and psychological services, housing, and training, and the UN now retains a Special Rapporteur on the human rights of trafficking victims.[46] These human rights provisions, however, lack the force of the security measures. Still, in the United States, the TVPA provided for medical care and other social services for trafficking victims, as well as the possibility of T visas for victims who agree to work with federal law enforcement in prosecuting their traffickers.[47] Likewise, the EU's 2004 European Council directive on the short-term residence permit called for trafficking victims to have housing, health care, and legal assistance during a short "reflection period," in which they could decide whether to help authorities, and then additional assistance as well as a short-term residence permit if the victims agreed to assist in prosecuting the traffickers.[48]

Feminists argue, however, that tying victim protection and assistance to cooperation with authorities, as UN, EU, and US policies all do, is flawed from a human rights perspective.[49] The needs of the victims are subordinated to the security needs of the state, which may or may not find any given case worth prosecuting.[50] According to Wendy Chapkis, the T visa, which still allows for victims in the United States to be deported once a criminal case is finished, "is designed not so much as a means to assist the victim as it is a device to assist prosecutors in closing down trafficking networks."[51] In short, even the policies that are meant to protect the human rights of trafficked persons still prioritize the interests of the state.

Feminists argue that treating trafficking victims like criminals is not only wrong, it is counterproductive. Given a population of migrants who wish to pursue a better life elsewhere, traditional approaches that focus on policing borders increase the need for migrants to hire a facilitator (smuggler) and the cost of doing so. Migrants who seek the assistance of professional smugglers for unauthorized border crossing become even more vulnerable to exploitation by traffickers.[52] As Jacqueline Berman characterizes the problem:

> A focus on crime and violated borders (rather than on the conditions under which women migrate or are forced to work) extends barriers to migration and renders it more dangerous for women while not necessarily hindering movement or assisting the actual victims.[53]

Moreover, when those who have been trafficked are deported, they risk being re-trafficked. Commenting on the Trafficking Protocol, Ann Jordan, Director of the International Human Rights Law Group's Initiative Against Trafficking in Persons, argues:

> A law enforcement approach, by itself, may endanger trafficked persons, and it often results in the immediate deportation of potential witnesses or else arrest and imprisonment. An approach that treats victims as criminals or immigrants without rights also is responsible for causing trafficked persons to disappear into the underground or to return home without any support. At its worst, it may also lead to their re-trafficking.[54]

For example, prior to the Turkish government's reform of its countertrafficking program, the government's "practice of 'dumping' victims in neighboring countries made them [the victims] vulnerable to re-trafficking by local recruiters and traffickers."[55] Repatriated trafficked persons may find themselves threatened by the same individuals who originally exploited them. Having returned to the circumstances many had originally sought to leave, formerly trafficked persons may also decide to make another attempt to migrate, running the risk of trafficking once more.[56]

Feminist debates regarding trafficking

While feminists agree on the necessity to protect the human rights of trafficked persons, they disagree on who should be considered a victim of trafficking and what precisely should be done to protect victims' rights. Feminist abolitionists focus primarily on women trafficked for sexual exploitation, advocating the abolition of prostitution and enhanced protections for sex trafficking victims. From this perspective, prostitution is antithetical to women's human rights, and all prostitutes are victims of trafficking. Feminist critics of the abolitionist approach take issue with the notion that prostitution is inherently harmful. They support the decriminalization or legalization of prostitution and argue that current anti-trafficking activities rely upon and contribute to counterproductive if not harmful stereotypes of trafficking victims.

Heated debate among feminists regarding prostitution threatened to derail UN Trafficking Protocol negotiations for nearly a year.[57] As Jo Doezema describes it:

In effect, the lobby was split into two "camps": both framing their approaches to trafficking in feminist terms, in agreement about the size and scope of the problem, and univocal in demanding an international response. Both groups were made up of feminists and human rights activists from the developing world and the developed world.[58]

Abolitionists' critics remain suspicious of the feminist abolitionist alliance with pro-life evangelical Christians, while abolitionists claim that sex workers' rights advocates are in the pay of pimps and traffickers. These debates set up what appears to be an impasse between abolitionist feminists and those who argue for an alternative view of sex work and human trafficking.

The new abolitionists

Like earlier international campaigns against human trafficking and "white slavery" at the turn of the twentieth century, the first contemporary feminists to launch a major campaign against human trafficking focused primarily on the traffic of women for sexual exploitation. Kathleen Barry's 1979 *Female Sexual Slavery* is credited with renewing feminist interest in stopping sex trafficking and launching the modern anti-trafficking movement. For Barry, the fight against trafficking is a fight against all prostitution.[59] Her position thus entails a rejection of any distinction between "forced" prostitution and "voluntary" prostitution, as the latter is a contradiction in terms. Women who believe they are voluntarily engaged in prostitution have fallen prey to false consciousness as a survival strategy. Worse, women engaged in prostitution who are also proponents of prostitution are actively supporting the patriarchal exploitation of other women.

Female sexual slavery not only crosses borders: it incorporates all women living in patriarchal orders so that women, regardless of class, ethnicity, or nationality, have their sexual victimhood in common. Prostitution is simply one aspect of the sexual oppression of women: the "commonality of women's experience in female sexual slavery ... makes it possible to understand that 'victim' can mean also prostitute, battered wife, incestuously assaulted child, veiled woman, purchased bride."[60] The commonality of women's experiences as victims therefore suggests the possibility for a transnational movement based on these experiences to fight female sexual slavery. Yet even as prostitution is a single facet of women's oppression, it is "the model, the most extreme and most crystallized form of all sexual exploitation."[61] Thus, although Barry understands "prostitute women not as a group set apart, which is a misogynist construction, but as women whose sexual exploitation is consonant with that of all women's experience of sexual exploitation," she nonetheless makes prostitution (and, by extension, trafficking in women for sex) the center of her feminist campaign.[62]

Feminists inspired by Barry's work and led by the influential Coalition Against the Traffic in Women (CATW) hold that the criminalization of prostitution is a necessary step toward ending human trafficking.[63] These feminists found unexpected allies among American evangelical Christians, and they are known jointly as prostitution "abolitionists." In the United States, abolitionists successfully lobbied the George W. Bush administration for a federal "gag rule" that requires anti-trafficking groups who receive federal monies to explicitly reject legalized prostitution.[64] Abolitionists have been less successful at the UN level where they were stymied in their attempts to define all prostitution as trafficking within the Trafficking Protocol.

A competing feminist approach

The opposition to abolitionist approaches comes from a set of feminists who are critical of the grouping of prostitution and trafficking and the assumption that attacking prostitution will end trafficking. These critics take issue with both the traditional security approach to trafficking and with abolitionists, arguing that human trafficking represents an instance of the larger problem of abusive treatment of migrants and low-wage laborers, including, but not limited to, prostitutes or "sex workers." From this perspective, it is essential to protect the rights of all trafficked persons, whether victims of forced sex or forced non-sex labor. Exploitation, rather than prostitution, is seen as the problem.

One criticism of the abolitionist approach is that not all trafficked persons are sex workers, and not all human trafficking is a part of the sex industry. Compared to the traffic of women for sexual exploitation, the traffic of women and men for non-sex labor has received short shrift.[65] Numerous transnational organizations aligned against human trafficking specifically resist the "traffic in women," which is understood to take place for the purposes of sexual exploitation, and the notion that sex trafficking victims are perceived as distinct from labor trafficking victims and other immigrants becomes readily apparent upon even cursory reviews of academic literature and governmental and activist websites. Books and articles written putatively about human trafficking restrict their focus to sex trafficking only; news reports and documentaries overwhelmingly focus on titillating reports of "sex slavery" instead of enslaved domestic staff or abused farm workers.[66] Richard Friman and Simon Reich point to media sensationalism of, and public fascination with, incidents of female sexual exploitation.[67] Of his three-year "Smuggled for Sex" series for *Newsday*, DeStefano writes, "Admittedly, we focused on the sex industry because it was a good subject for newspaper treatment."[68]

Yet while women (as well as male and female children) are trafficked and enslaved for sex, men and women are trafficked for other labor as well. One feminist account of this is Christine Chin's work on the human rights violations experienced by trafficked female Filipino and Indonesian domestic workers in Malaysia. Chin highlights the abuse these women suffered and argues that the trafficking they experience is complex and multifaceted. She contends that the Malaysian state supported the (forced) importation and employment of foreign female domestic workers as part of a strategy to curry favor with the middle class and promote ethnic harmony. Chin's work demonstrates that human trafficking extends beyond sex trafficking, as do its gendered implications.[69]

Insofar as prostitution is the issue at hand, feminist critics of abolitionism hold that sex work is not synonymous with human trafficking. While the sex industry is often abusive and exploitative, as are other low-status and low-wage industries, it is not inherently so.[70] Thus, states, scholars, and activists alike must "identify prostitution as work, as an occupation susceptible like the others to exploitative practices."[71] This perspective is espoused primarily by "sex-positive feminists," who see sexual liberation as a key component of women's liberation and by sex workers' rights activists, who have organized sex worker unions and advocacy groups across the world.[72]

Sex worker unions and sex workers' rights activists propose the principle of harm reduction as opposed to abolition. They argue that legalizing prostitution provides resources for sex workers to use, if they so choose, to protest abusive conditions without rejecting the entire industry.[73] Focusing on sex trafficking to the exclusion of other forms of trafficking unfairly stigmatizes women in the sex industry and places them in a disempowered position. As Jo Bindman writes, "The distinction between 'the prostitute' and everyone else helps to perpetuate her exclusion from the ordinary rights which society offers to others, such as rights to freedom from violence at work, to a fair share of what she earns, or to leave her employer."[74]

Sex workers have also worked together with anti-trafficking activists on behalf of women who have been forced into prostitution. For example, sex workers allied with GAATW during the UN Trafficking Protocol negotiations and were instrumental in defining sex trafficking as "forced" prostitution rather than prostitution *per se.*[75] Likewise, the Durbar Mahila Samanwaya Committee (Durbar), an organization of 65,000 sex workers in West Bengal, India, takes an active role in anti-trafficking work, establishing self-regulatory boards (SRBs)

> to prevent entry of minor girls and unwilling adult women into the sex sector, control the exploitative practices in the sector, regulate the rules and practices of the sector and institute social welfare measures for sex workers and their children.[76]

The social construction of trafficked persons

Beyond specific arguments against the prohibition of prostitution, critics of abolitionism make a more general, and perhaps more significant, claim regarding human trafficking: it matters how trafficked persons are socially constructed. I argue that this more critical insight should be recognized as one of feminist theorists' central contributions to the study of human trafficking. Current constructions of human trafficking rely on gender stereo-types that discount women's agency. The conflation of "international human trafficking" with "trafficking of women for sexual exploitation" reflects gen-dered notions of agency that frame men as actors and women as victims—those acted upon.[77] Trafficking discourses rest upon stereotypes of men actively going out into the world to make their way and women passively staying at home unless duped, seduced, or kidnapped by a trafficker.[78] Hence, Melissa Ditmore and Marjan Wijers note that the full title of the UN Traf-ficking Protocol is the Protocol to Prevent, Suppress and Punish Trafficking in Persons, Especially Women and Children; the emphasis on women and children upholds stereotypical perceptions of men as autonomous actors and women as passive victims.[79] Representations of trafficking based upon women's assumed lack of agency conflict with how many trafficked women perceive themselves. Mertus and Bertone explain,

> The narrative of individuals labeled as victims in this process, however, often reflects a far more complicated self-understanding of their own status, one that is not static and devoid of agency. These individuals stress that they were not always victims. At some early state, their involvement was completely willing, albeit tremendously ill-informed.[80]

Bindman argues that analyses of trafficking must recognize that women, like men, make choices and take risks within the international labor market for a wide range of reasons—from the need to financially support themselves and their families to the desire to seek adventure and new experiences. This should not be read as a call to ignore or downplay the sense in which trafficking victims are coerced or misled but rather to begin analysis of human traffick-ing with the recognition that it occurs within a larger context in which labor migration is a reasonable pursuit.[81]

These inherited notions of trafficking betray a reliance on sex-based ste-reotypes of women's capabilities which create unrealistic perceptions of victims as innocent, pure, and sexually exploited. Sex trafficking discourses emphasize elements such as sexual innocence and naïveté, kidnapping, and sexual brutality in order to produce a sympathetic victim who would be politically unpala-table to criminalize. The commonly held picture of the trafficking victim depicts a young, naïve woman who seeks a better life away from her rural home by answering an advertisement to become a waitress or nanny and then ends up a sex slave, repeatedly raped, brutalized, and resold to other mafia pimps.[82] The UN's informational website on human trafficking is indicative of this trope, describing enslaved young women who are beaten, raped, and forced to work up to 18 hours a day, garnering enormous profits for those who sell them.[83]

According to Nora Demleitner, however, the kidnapping of women repre-sents the least likely scenario of human trafficking, as many women willingly leave their homes to join traffickers; it is the subsequent enslavement or coercion that constitutes trafficking.[84] She argues that kidnapped women are used as paradigmatic cases because "these women represent the innocent, the 'true' victim, a victim who did not choose to migrate illegally, let alone prostitute herself."[85] The end result of portraying the referent of security as brutalized young women who are trafficked for sex and lack agency entirely is that a hierarchy of victims is created. Women who have chosen to work as sex workers, but not as sex slaves, do not garner the same kind of sympathy, and men and women trafficked for non-sex labor are easily relabeled "illegal immigrants."[86] For instance, Europol Deputy Director Willy Bruggeman distinguishes between exploited, deceived, and kidnapped sex trafficking victims, arguing that only kidnapped victims "are sex slaves in the truest sense."[87] Such narratives do not assist feminists in forcing the state to incorporate human rights concerns into countertrafficking policies. Moreover, this approach puts sex-trafficked women themselves at a disadvantage if they cannot portray their status as entirely involuntary or that the conditions of their exploitation were merely undesirable instead of horrifically brutal. Bindman elaborates:

> People, including police officers, prosecutors and judges, can easily identify with women who comply to the stereotype of the naïve and innocent victim, unwittingly forced into prostitution. But the moment a woman has worked as a prostitute or wants to continue to do so, or even when she just stands up for herself, compassion turns into indifference or outright hostility. Common opinion holds that once a prostitute, a woman loses all her rights and is no longer entitled to protection against violence, exploitation, abuse, blackmail, and being held prisoner.[88]

Such women fail both the test of innocence and the test of pain: Claudia Aradau explains that "raw physical suffering" is required to distinguish insufficiently "innocent" trafficking victims from illegal immigrants and prostitutes.[89] In other words, the "legal process may tend to declare any woman not fitting this childlike image—and most victims of unscrupulous traffickers will not conform to this model—as unworthy of support and protection."[90] These stereotypes construct an idealized notion of trafficking victims that is applicable to a small subset of trafficked persons, effectively removing all who do not fit this construction from rights protections.

The definition of trafficking victims as naïve and innocent is tied up in a stereotyped assumption of the purity of white women and the impurity of women of color. Historical advocacy against international human trafficking— which was taken to mean the traffic in women for sexual exploitation—arose in the context of concern for the virtue of white women. Tales of white women kidnapped and forced into prostitution made their way from Europe to the United States at the turn of the twentieth century, prompting an international campaign against "white slavery." The white slave trade was thought to center on virginal and naïve young white women who were deceived, kidnapped, or even sold into slavery by parents for the purpose of prostitution. Eileen Scully notes that during this time period, approximately 99 percent of sexual trafficking victims were women of color (including Jews, who were considered non-white). It was the relatively few women of European descent engaged in both voluntary and coerced prostitution, however, whose condition provoked widespread public outrage.[91] Feminists connect the panic regarding white slavery to

> anxieties about changing gender, sex, class, and race relations at the turn of the century. The idea of a "white slave" unconsciously spoke not only to the experience of the white working class laboring under harsh conditions of early industrial capitalism, but also to the racial fears of an increasingly ethnically diverse population.[92]

A number of scholars connect contemporary trafficking discourses to the racially-charged "white slave panic."[93] Some argue that human trafficking only rose to international prominence as an issue once again in the context of increasing numbers of white sex workers. Galma Jahic and James Finckenauer note that the influx of trafficked women from Eastern Europe and the former Soviet Union during the early 1990s contributed to the resurgence of interest in human trafficking, particularly the so-called "Natasha Trade" in white women of Slavic origin.[94]

Furthermore, Doezema finds parallels between the white slavery discourses of the past century and contemporary discourses about trafficked women of all colors. She argues that contemporary emphasis of trafficking victims' lack of agency performs the same function as historic articulations of (white) victims' purity and innocence, reproducing a "colonial gaze" that claims to protect women's virtue but at the expense of recognizing their autonomy, sexual and otherwise.[95]

Conclusion: feminism, security, and human trafficking

Feminist approaches to international human trafficking are essential for security scholars who wish to address the activity as a threat to states and people. Feminists have shown that traditional security approaches to human trafficking are inadequate, not only on moral grounds, but on pragmatic ones as well. Perhaps the most significant issue feminists have raised is the question of who or what is being secured. If the referent object of security is the state, then countertrafficking will focus primarily on border control policies and therefore will consider trafficked persons to be criminals rather than victims. Not only does this further threaten the human rights of trafficking victims, it may also lead to a victim's re-trafficking upon being deported into the same situation. If the referent of security is broadened to include trafficked individuals, then countertrafficking would incorporate social services and human rights protections, which should make victims less vulnerable in the future.

Both abolitionist feminists and their critics are concerned with the security of people (women especially) who are the victims of human trafficking. Abolitionists feminists primarily address prostitution, conflating human trafficking with sex trafficking and assuming that the elimination of prostitution will both end the need for sex trafficking and promote gender equality more generally. Their critics point out that this approach is problematic in its theoretical and policy implications. Theoretically, this approach risks reifying gender stereotypes about women's purity and women's helplessness. Practically, it ignores the many people trafficked for reasons other than sex while also failing to account for sex workers' rights. Still, the abolitionist feminist approach focuses on a number of important elements in human trafficking. These include traffickers' frequently deceptive and abusive recruitment strategies, the terrible human rights abuses trafficked people face at the hands of their traffickers and host governments, and the disproportionate effect that human trafficking has on women.

The critics of the abolitionist approach offer important insights as well. First, they point out that not all persons who are trafficked—and in fact not all women who are trafficked—are trafficked for the purposes of sexual exploitation. The international labor market is a significant motivation for trafficking and a significant destination for trafficked persons. Critics of abolitionism also reject the conflation of trafficking and prostitution because, unlike abolitionists, they see it as possible for women to consent to doing sex work. They argue for an alternative solution to human trafficking that involves legalizing prostitution and establishing legal frameworks to ensure human rights protection for all workers, including sex workers and those in low-wage and low-status jobs.

This impasse seems, at first glance, irreconcilable, and, perhaps as relates to the moral status of prostitution, it is. Yet whatever specific moral and political stance is taken in regard to prostitution, I argue that it is crucial for scholars, activists, and policy-makers not only to protect and empower trafficked persons but to consider the implications of how trafficked persons are produced as subjects. Greater attention to the social construction of trafficked persons, in addition to greater attention to trafficked persons overall, is necessary because of the effects such representations have in perpetuating sexist and racist stereotypes that harm trafficked and otherwise marginalized people. More work must be done on the effects of representing trafficked persons in various ways and on how they might be considered instead in a manner that empowers rather than further exploits them. Tickner has warned that "Notions of security that rely on protection reinforce gender hierarchies that, in turn, diminish women's (and certain men's) real security."[96] The issue for future analyses of human trafficking, explicitly feminist or otherwise, is to discover how we might escape this cycle.

Notes

1 Jennifer K. Lobasz is grateful to Janice Bially Mattern, Bud Duvall, Lene Hansen, Peter Howard, Patrick Jackson, Ron Krebs, Sheryl Lightfoot, John

Picarelli, Aaron Rapport, Will Schlickenmaier, Laura Sjoberg, Lauren Wilcox, and the editors and two anonymous reviewers of *Security Studies* for their helpful comments. An earlier version of this chapter was presented at the 2007 Workshop on Feminist Contributions to Security Studies, the 2008 Annual Meetings of the International Studies Association-Northeast and the International Studies Association, and the Minnesota International Relations Colloquium. The author thanks all who participated in these forums for their constructive criticism.

2 Brian Iselin, "Addressing the Challenge to Security from the Trafficking in Human Beings," paper presented at the OSCE-Thailand Conference on the Human Dimension of Security, Bangkok, 20–21 June 2002.

3 Keith Krause and Michael C. Williams, "Broadening the Agenda of Security Studies: Politics and Methods," *Mershon International Studies Review* 40, no. 2 (1996); Jessica Tuchman Mathews, "Redefining Security," *Foreign Affairs* 68, no. 2 (1989).

4 Subsequent references to "trafficking" should be understood to mean international human trafficking, sometimes called trafficking in persons, rather than drugs, arms, or any other kind of trafficking.

5 This should not be taken to mean that there is only one set of feminist approaches to international human trafficking. The aim of Table 11.1 is to characterize what the feminist approaches share in common and to distinguish them from traditional security frameworks.

6 It should be noted that while this is not a uniquely feminist argument, feminists were the first to widely insist upon protecting the human rights of trafficked persons, especially in regard to women and children trafficked into prostitution. See Kathleen Barry, *Female Sexual Slavery* (New York: New York University Press, 1979).

7 J. Ann Tickner, *Gendering World Politics* (New York: Columbia University Press 2001), p. 48.

8 United Nations Development Program, *Human Development Report* (New York: Oxford University Press, 1994).

9 United Nations Commission on Human Security, *Human Security Now* (New York: United Nations, 2003). See also Special Issue on Human Security, *Security Dialogue* 35, no. 3 (2004). While there is much overlap in the principles of advocacy for human security and against human trafficking, there has yet to be significant overlap within political movements. Key documents establishing the human security framework do include trafficking as a grave threat to, in the words of the UN Commission on Human Security, "people on the move," but the specific language of human security is much less prevalent in the anti-trafficking movement than in the language of human rights. For notable exceptions, see H. Richard Friman and Simon Reich, eds., *Human Trafficking, Human Security, and the Balkans* (Pittsburgh, PA: University of Pittsburgh Press, 2007); Michelle Anne Clark, "Trafficking in Persons: An Issue of Human Security," *Journal of Human Development* 4, no. 2 (2003): 247–63.

10 Ann D. Jordan, *The Annotated Guide to the Complete UN Trafficking Protocol* (Washington, DC: International Human Rights Law Group, 2002), 9–10.

11 Donna M. Hughes, "The 'Natasha' Trade: The Transnational Shadow Market of Trafficking in Women," *Journal of International Affairs* 53, no. 2 (2000): 634.

12 Galma Jahic and James O. Finckenauer, "Representations and Misrepresentations of Human Trafficking," *Trends in Organized Crime* 8, no. 3 (2005): 24–40; Frank Laczko and Marco A. Gramegna, "Developing Better Indicators of Human Trafficking," *Brown Journal of World Affairs* 10, no. 1 (2003): 179–94.

13 United Nations Educational, Scientific and Cultural Organization (UNESCO), "Data Comparison Sheets." Available at: www.unescobkk.org/index.php?id = 1963.

14 Nora Demleitner, "The Law at a Crossroads: The Construction of Migrant Women Trafficked into Prostitution," in *Global Human Smuggling: Comparative*

Perspectives, eds., David Kyle and Rey Koslowski (Baltimore, MD: Johns Hopkins University Press, 2001).

15 Guri Tyldum and Anette Brunovkis, "Describing the Unobserved: Methodological Challenges in Empirical Studies on Human Trafficking," *International Migration* 43, nos 1–2 (2005): 17–34.

16 Tom Obokata, *Trafficking of Human Beings from a Human Rights Perspective* (Leiden: Martinus Nijhoff, 2006); Eileen Scully, "Pre-Cold War Traffic in Sexual Labor and Its Foes: Some Contemporary Lessons," in Kyle and Koslowski, *Global Human Smuggling*; Joel Quirk, "Trafficked into Slavery," *Journal of Human Rights* 6 (2007): 181–207.

17 Frank Laczko, "Introduction," Special Issue on Human Trafficking, *International Migration* 43, nos 1–2 (2005): 5–16; Elzbieta M. Gozdziak and Elizabeth A. Collett, "Research on Human Trafficking in North America: A Review of Literature," Special Issue on Human Trafficking, *International Migration* 43, nos 1–2 (2005): 99–128.

18 Kyle and Koslowski, eds., *Global Human Smuggling*, p. 5.

19 Government Accountability Office (GAO), *Human Trafficking: Better Data, Strategy, and Reporting Needed to Enhance U.S. Antitrafficking Efforts Abroad* (Washington, DC: GPO, 2006), pp. 37–9.

20 Laczko, "Introduction to Special Issue on Human Trafficking."

21 Liz Kelly, "'You Can Find Anything You Want': A Critical Reflection on Research on Trafficking in Persons within and into Europe," *International Migration* 43, nos 1–2 (2005): 236.

22 Joanna Apap, Peter Cullen, and Felicita Medved, "Counteracting Human Trafficking: Protecting the Victims of Trafficking," paper presented at the European Conference on Preventing and Combating Trafficking in Human Beings, Brussels, 18–20 September 200, p. 8; Willy Bruggeman, "Illegal Immigration and Trafficking in Human Beings Seen as a Security Problem for Europe," paper presented at the European Conference on Preventing and Combating Trafficking in Human Beings, Brussels, 18–20 September 2002.

23 GAO, *A Strategic Framework Could Help Enhance the Interagency Collaboration Needed to Effectively Combat Trafficking Crimes* (Washington, DC: GPO, 2007), p. 18. The Department of Homeland Security's interest in combating human trafficking is closely connected to its interest in preventing all unauthorized border crossing of, for example, "terrorists."

24 This convention is known as the "Palermo Convention" after the Italian city in which it was signed.

25 Jordan, *The Annotated Guide to the Complete UN Trafficking Protocol*.

26 Ann Gallagher, "Trafficking, Smuggling and Human Rights: Tricks and Treaties," *Forced Migration Review* 12 (2002): 936.

27 Apap, *et al.*, "Counteracting Human Trafficking," p. 7.

28 See Anna M. Agathangelou, *The Global Political Economy of Sex: Desire, Violence, and Insecurity in Mediterranean Nation States* (New York: Palgrave Macmillan, 2004).

29 Commission of the European Communities, "Fighting Trafficking in Human Beings."

30 George Katrougalos, "The Rights of Foreigners and Immigrants in Europe: Recent Trends," *Web Journal of Current Legal Issues*, available at: webjcli.ncl.ac.uk/articles5/katart5.html; Wyn Rees, "Organised Crime, Security and the European Union," draft paper for the ESRC Workshop, Grenoble, 2000; European Consortium for Political Research, www.essex.ac.uk/ecpr/events/jointsessions/paperarchive/grenoble/ws8/rees.pdf.

31 Jeff Huysmans, "The European Union and the Securitization of Migration," *Journal of Common Market Studies* 38, no. 5 (2000): 756–7.

32 Fiona Adamson, "Crossing Borders: International Migration and National Security," *International Security*, 31, no. 1 (2006): 178.

33 Moisés Naím, *Illicit: How Smugglers, Traffickers, and Copycats Are Hijacking the Global Economy* (New York: Doubleday, 2005), p. 89.

34 Adam Graycar, "Trafficking in Human Beings," paper presented at the International Conference on Migration, Culture & Crime, Israel, 1999, p. 2.

35 Quirk, "Trafficked into Slavery," p. 191.

36 Apap *et al.*, "Counteracting Human Trafficking," pp. 17–18.

37 White House Office of the Press Secretary, news release, "Fact Sheet on Migrant Smuggling and Trafficking," 15 December 2000.

38 See note 2; Karin M. Fierke, *Critical Approaches to International Security* (Cambridge: Polity Press, 2007).

39 Jahic and Finckenauer, "Representations and Misrepresentations of Human Trafficking," p. 28.

40 See, for example, Cherríe Moraga and Gloria Anzaldúa, eds., *This Bridge Called My Back: Writings by Radical Women of Color* (New York: Kitchen Table Women of Color Press, 1983).

41 Jack Donnelly, *Universal Human Rights in Theory and Practice*, 2nd edn. (Ithaca, NY: Cornell University Press, 2002), p. 22. See also Margaret E. Keck and Kathryn Sikkink, *Activists Beyond Borders: Advocacy Networks in International Politics* (Ithaca, NY: Cornell University Press, 1998).

42 GAATW, *Human Rights and Trafficking in Persons.*

43 Janice G. Raymond and Donna M. Hughes, *Sex Trafficking of Women in the United States: International and Domestic Trends* (New York: Coalition Against Trafficking in Women, 2001).

44 Europol, *Legislation on Trafficking in Human Beings and Illegal Immigrant Smuggling*, Europol Public Information. Available at: www.europol.eu.int/publications/Other/Reports%202005/Legislation%20on%20THB%20and%20IIS%20Public.pdf.

45 Peter Landesman, "The Girls Next Door," *The New York Times*, January 25, 2004.

46 United Nations, "Protocol to Prevent, Suppress and Punish Trafficking in Persons."

47 United States Department of Justice, "Department of Justice Issues T Visa to Protect Women, Children and All Victims of Human Trafficking," news release, 24 January 2002.

48 Europol, *Legislation on Trafficking in Human Beings and Illegal Immigrant Smuggling.*

49 Phyllis Coontz and Catherine Griebel, "International Approaches to Human Trafficking: The Call for a Gender-Sensitive Perspective in International Law," *Women's Health Journal* 4 (2004): 47–58.

50 Ibid., p. 57.

51 Wendy Chapkis, "Trafficking, Migration, and the Law: Protecting Innocents, Punishing Immigrants," *Gender & Society* 17, no. 6 (2003): 932.

52 Nandita Sharma, "Anti-Trafficking Rhetoric and the Making of a Global Apartheid," *NWSA Journal* 17, no. 3 (2005): 91; Bruggeman, "Illegal Immigration and Trafficking," p. 3; Quirk, "Trafficked into Slavery," p. 197; Ann D. Jordan, "Trafficking and Globalization," Center for American Progress, available at: www.americanprogress.org/issues/2004/10/b222852.html.

53 Jacqueline Berman, "(Un)Popular strangers and crisis (un)bounded: discourses of sex-trafficking, the European political community and the panicked state of the modern state," *European Journal of International Relations* 9, no. 1 (2003): 37. See also Wendy Chapkis, *Live Sex Acts: Women Performing Erotic Labor* (New York: Routledge, 1997), 94.

54 Jordan, *The Annotated Guide to the Complete UN Trafficking Protocol*, p. 4.

55 United States Department of State, *Victims of Trafficking and Violence Protection Act of 2000: Trafficking in Persons Report*. Available at: www.state.gov/g/tip/rls/tiprpt/2004/.

56 William Finnegan, "The Countertraffickers: Rescuing the Victims of the Global Sex Trade," *The New Yorker*, May 5, 2008.

57 Anthony DeStefano, *The War on Human Trafficking* (Rutgers, NJ: Rutgers Univesity Press, 2007), p. 26.

58 Jo Doezema, "Now You See Her, Now You Don't: Sex Workers at the UN Trafficking Protocol Negotiation," *Social & Legal Studies* 14, no. 1 (2005): 67.

59 Barry, *Female Sexual Slavery.*

60 Ibid., p. 41.

61 Ibid., p. 11.

62 Ibid., p. 9.

63 See Kathleen Barry, Charlotte Bunch, and Shirley Castley, eds., *International Feminism: Networking against Female Sexual Slavery; Report of the Global Feminist Workshop to Organize against Traffic in Women* (Rotterdam: International Women's Tribune Center, 1983); Raymond and Hughes, "Sex Trafficking of Women in the United States"; Sheila Jeffreys, "Trafficking in Women Versus Prostitution: A False Distinction" (paper presented at the Townsville International Women's Conference, Townsville, Australia, 2002); Julie Bindel, "False Distinctions between Pornography, Prostitution, and Trafficking," in *Trafficking and Women's Rights*, ed. Christien L. van der Anker and Jeroen Doomernik (Houndsmills, Basingstroke, Hampshire: Palgrave Macmillan, 2006).

64 DeStefano, *The War on Human Trafficking*, pp. 108–11.

65 Gozdziak and Collett, "Research on Human Trafficking in North America," p. 117.

66 Kelly, "'You Can Find Anything You Want.'"

67 H. Richard Friman and Simon Reich, "Human Trafficking and the Balkans," in *Human Trafficking, Human Security, and the Balkans.*

68 DeStefano, *The War on Human Trafficking*, p. xvii.

69 Christine B. N. Chin, *In Service and Servitude: Foreign Female Domestic Workers and the Malaysian "Modernity" Project* (New York: Columbia University Press, 1998).

70 Shannon Bell notes, "Prostitutes' rights groups do not claim that prostitution is a free choice; they claim that it is as free a choice as other choices make in a capitalist, patriarchal, and racist system." Shannon Bell, *Reading, Writing, and Rewriting the Prostitute Body* (Bloomington, In: Indiana University Press, 1994), p. 111.

71 Jo Bindman, "An International Perspective on Slavery in the Sex Industry," in *Global Sex Workers: Rights, Resistance, and Redefinition*, eds., Kamala Kempadoo and Jo Doezema (New York: Routledge, 1998), p. 67.

72 See Carol Vance, ed., *Pleasure and Danger: Exploring Female Sexuality* (New York: Pandora Press, 1989); Jill Nagle, ed., *Whores and Other Feminists* (New York: Routledge, 1997); Chapkis, *Live Sex Acts.*

73 Priscilla Alexander, "Feminism, Sex Workers, and Human Rights," in *Whores and Other Feminists*, ed., Jill Nagle (New York: Routledge, 1997).

74 Bindman, "An International Perspective on Slavery in the Sex Industry," 65. See also Jo Doezema, "Forced to Choose: Beyond the Voluntary V. Forced Prostitution Dichotomy," in *Global Sex Workers*, p. 42.

75 Alison Murray, "Debt Bondage and Trafficking: Don't Believe the Hype," in *Global Sex Workers*, p. 98.

76 Durbar Mahila Samanwaya Committee, "Anti-Trafficking Website of Durbar – Our Mission," available at: www.antitrafficking-durbar.org/our_mission.html. See also Finnegan, "The Countertraffickers."

77 Laura María Agustín, *Sex at the Margins: Migration, Labor Markets, and the Rescue Industry* (London: Zed Books, 2007).

78 Julia O'Connell Davidson and Bridget Anderson, "The Trouble with 'Trafficking'," in *Trafficking and Women's Rights*, p. 21.

79 Melissa Ditmore and Marjan Wijers, "The Negotiations on the UN Protocol on Trafficking in Persons," *Nemesis* 4 (2003): 82.

80 Julie Mertus and Andrea Bertone, "Combating Trafficking: International Efforts and Their Ramifications," in *Human Trafficking, Human Security, and the Balkans*, p. 51.

81 Ditmore and Wijers, "The Negotiations on the UN Protocol on Trafficking in Persons," pp. 82–3.

82 Berman, "(Un)Popular Strangers and Crises (Un)Bounded"; Jahic and Finckenauer, "Representations and Misrepresentations of Human Trafficking."

83 United Nations Office on Drugs and Crime, "Trafficking in Persons: The New Protocol," (2000). Available at: www.unodc.org/unodc/en/trafficking_protocol_background.html.

84 Demleitner, "The Law at a Crossroads," p. 264. The most common recruitment strategies focus not on kidnapping or abduction but on deceptive job advertisements and promises of employment. See Louise Shelley, "Human Trafficking as a form of Transnational Crime," in *Human Trafficking*, ed., Maggy Lee (Devon: Willan Publishing, 2007), pp. 116–37; Ilse van Liempt, "Trafficking in Human Beings: Conceptual Dilemmas," in *Trafficking and Women's Rights*; Kevin Bales, *Understanding Global Slavery*, pp. 142–3.

85 Demleitner, "The Law at a Crossroads," p. 264.

86 Chapkis, "Trafficking, Migration, and the Law," p. 930; Quirk, "Trafficked into Slavery," pp. 298–9.

87 Bruggeman, "Illegal Immigration and Trafficking," p. 5.

88 Bindman, "An International Perspective on Slavery in the Sex Industry," p. 77.

89 Claudia Aradau, "The Perverse Politics of Four-Letter Words: Risk and Pity in the Securitization of Human Trafficking," *Millennium Journal of International Studies* 33, no. 2 (2004): 262.

90 Demleitner, "The Law at a Crossroads," p. 273. See also Tyldum and Brunovkis, "Describing the Unobserved."

91 Scully, "Pre-Cold War Traffic in Sexual Labor and Its Foes," p. 86.

92 Chapkis, *Live Sex Acts*, p. 42. See also Jo Doezema, "Loose Women or Lost Women? The Re-Emergence of the Myth of 'White Slavery' in Contemporary Discourses of 'Trafficking in Women,'" *Gender Issues* 18, no. 1 (2000): 23–50.

93 See Jacqueline Berman, "The Left, the Right, and the Prostitute: The Making of U.S. Antitrafficking in Persons Policy," *Tulane Journal of International and Comparative Law* no. 14 (2005–6): 278.

94 Jahic and Finckenauer, "Representations and Misrepresentations of Human Trafficking," p. 26. See, for example, Hughes, who writes: "As a result of trafficking, Russian women are in prostitution in over 50 countries. In some parts of the world, such as Israel and Turkey, women from Russia and other republics of the former Soviet Union are so prevalent, that prostitutes are called 'Natashas'." (Hughes, "The 'Natasha' Trade: The Transnational Shadow Market of Trafficking in Women," p. 629) See also Donna M. Hughes, "The 'Natasha' Trade: Transnational Sex Trafficking," *National Institute of Justice Journal*, no. 246 (2001); Victor Malarek, *The Natashas: Inside the New Global Sex Trade* (New York: Arcade Publishing, 2004).

95 Doezema, "Loose Women or Lost Women?" pp. 37–8.

96 Tickner, *Gendering World Politics*, p. 62.

12 When are states hypermasculine?

Jennifer Heeg Maruska

Jon Western's 2005 *Security Studies* article "The War over Iraq" tells a convincing story of President George W. Bush's administration's quest to "sell the war" in Iraq to the American public.[1] Western argues that popular support for the war was largely due to the Bush administration's active propagandizing and marketing campaign. According to Gallup polls, although public support for invading Iraq receded after its early peak in November 2001 (74 percent), it never dipped below 52 percent and stayed solid around 60 percent immediately preceding the invasion in March 2003.[2] If the war in Iraq was *sold* to the American people, however, I am interested in how.

By using gender as a theoretical tool, I will demonstrate how American hegemonic masculinity—or a significant subsection of it—became *hypermasculine* in the days, months, and years following September 11, 2001. This development is key to understanding how the war Iraq was sold to and bought by the American people. The consequences of this hypermasculinity include popular support for the March 2003 invasion of Iraq as well as the re-election of President George W. Bush in 2004. In this chapter, I will elaborate the concepts of hegemonic masculinity and hypermasculinity, based on previous theorizing (largely by R. W. Connell and Charlotte Hooper). I will then apply these principles to the post-9/11 era, suggesting that both the Bush administration (the agent) and American mainstream culture itself (the structure) contributed to the invasion of Iraq. By applying a gender-sensitive lens, and putting hypermasculinity into a historical context, both the decision to invade Iraq and the popular support such an idea received will be made much clearer.

The first section provides a background to the concept of gender, focusing on plurality among masculinities and femininities. In the second and third sections, I will define and elaborate on two concepts introduced in section one: specifically, hegemonic masculinity and hypermasculinity. It will be shown that hegemonic masculinity is dominant in international politics, and occasionally takes hypermasculine forms. In the fourth section, two such cases will be analyzed (the closing of the American frontier in the 1890s, and the beginning of the Cold War in the late 1940s and 1950s). With these cases in mind, the fifth section will discuss how and why US hegemonic masculinity became hypermasculine after the September 11, 2001 terrorist attacks. Finally, in the conclusion, I argue that an understanding that the international system constrains actors, both male and female, to adhere to hegemonic masculinity, raises provocative questions about who can change the system and how it can be changed. In this context, I will also briefly remark on the election of Barack Obama to the United States presidency in 2008.

Gender as constructed, fluid, multiple

Charlotte Hooper writes:

> Gender is neither a thing nor a property of individual character. It is a property of collectivities, institutions, and historical processes. It is also a linking concept, whereby biological difference is engaged with, and social practices are organized in terms of, or in relation to, reproductive divisions.[3]

Understood this way, *sex* has a biological, anatomical meaning, whereas *gender* is socially constructed. Traditionally, attributes such as rational, autonomous, and aggressive have been assigned to men (whereas their counterparts irrational, dependent, and passive have been assigned to women).[4] These essentializing labels can be highly problematic, and are often not rooted in biology (sex), but rather in socially constructed assumptions about what the male and female genders should be. For example, the modern military often challenges recruits (who are still predominantly male) to act like "real" men.[5] This "real" man is actually a caricatured version of manliness, and does not reflect individual beliefs of predispositions. Feminist IR theorist J. Ann Tickner has written, "much of basic training involves overcoming men's reluctance to kill."[6] In an earlier piece (referring to the military of the 1980s and early 1990s), Tickner explains:

> Because military recruiters cannot rely on violent qualities in men, they appeal to manliness and patriotic duty. Judith Stiehm avers that military trainers resort to manipulation of men's anxiety about their sexual identity in order to increase soldiers' willingness to fight. In basic training the term of utmost derision is to be called a girl or a lady. The association between men and violence ... depends not on men's innate aggressiveness, but on the construction of a gendered identity that places heavy pressure on soldiers to prove themselves as men.[7]

So, although individual soldiers may not possess an abundance of violent or aggressive characteristics, they are taught to cultivate (to *construct*) these characteristics in order to conform. The ideal to which these soldiers conform may be defined as *hypermasculine hegemonic masculinity*. The concept of hegemonic masculinity, and its hypermasculine variant, will be made clearer throughout this chapter.

To say that feminist work uses a gendered perspective is to say that it looks not at men but at socially constructed masculinity; it looks not at women but at socially constructed femininity. A gendered perspective recognizes that the story is more complicated: there are more than one type of masculinity and femininity operating at any one time and place. Instead, Hooper identifies variations on the divide formerly understood as "male/female," expanding the range of possibilities to include hegemonic masculinity, subordinate masculinities, and multiple femininities. Hooper builds on the work of Ann Tickner, who argues, "hegemonic masculinity is sustained through its opposition to various subordinated and devalued masculinities, such as homosexuality, and, more important, through its relation to various devalued femininities."[8]

Hegemonic masculinity

R. W. Connell is widely cited as the first to define hegemonic masculinity, and to describe it in opposition to subordinate masculinities.[9] In the 1995 book *Masculinities*, Connell explains that gender relations work within and between males, so that hegemonic masculinity occupies a higher place on the hierarchy than do subordinated masculinities (such as non-white, homosexual, or lower-class masculinities).[10] This Foucauldian network of power relations extends to a variety of femininities as well. As Connell describes:

> Hegemonic masculinity can be defined as the configuration of gender practice which embodies the currently accepted answer to the problem of the legitimacy of patriarchy, which guarantees (or is taken to guarantee) the dominant position of men and the subordination of women.[11]

This is not to imply that hegemonic masculinity is an elite-driven conspiracy meant to oppress women and minorities. Instead, in Hooper's account, "elites are implicated in the dissemination of cultural hegemony through their participation in a lived system of meaningful practices that reproduce and confirm their own identities, rather than through a conscious or deliberate strategy of domination."[12] Elites and non-elites alike are complicit in maintaining hegemonic masculinity every time they act in a way that reifies the institutions of mainstream (hegemonic) culture.

Following Hooper's analysis, "[masculinism/hegemonic masculinity] is endemic at all levels of society as different groups and interests jockey for position in networks of power relations."[13] Connell's move in naming this culture "hegemonic masculinity" came with the identification of gender as a major component, and with the idea that power relations are implicated in and between every group. For Connell, "everyday life is an arena of gender politics, not an escape from it."[14] Where there is patriarchy, there is hegemonic masculinity, and most (if not all) societies, and inter-society relations, have been patriarchal. Therefore, hegemonic masculinity is a concept that helps us to understand power relations at the family, association, state, and interstate levels.

To say that hegemonic masculinity is inescapable is not to say that it is the same unbiversally. However, as Charlotte Hooper points out, without some set of characteristics from which to draw, the concepts of masculinity and femininity can become unrecognizable.[15] I follow in the tradition of Hooper and Harry Brod, who draw on Wittgenstein's concept of "family resemblances," arguing that " just as members of a family may be said to resemble each other without necessarily having any single feature in common, so masculinities may form common patterns without sharing any single universal characteristic."[16] Along these lines, then, hegemonic masculinity may privilege martialism, paternalism, heterosexism, honor, or a variety of intuitive characteristics.[17]

This chapter will establish that in the case of American hegemonic masculinity, hypermasculinity has been a repeated theme, although what counts as hypermasculine varies over time. Insofar as warfare includes violence, it could be postulated that US hegemonic masculinity is hypermasculine at every juncture where the US goes to war. I believe this is an oversimplification. Similarly, what hegemonic masculinity *is*, is time- and place-dependent; it is also multiple, contested, and fluid. It is one type of identity construct, at the top of a hierarchy that includes subordinate masculinities and femininities. The value of the theory of hegemonic masculinity, according to John Tosh,

> does not lie primarily in identifying what the generality of men subscribed to at a given time, or in revealing the gender practices of the ruling elite … [rather, it] has proved its worth because it keeps the power relations always in view, and it reminds us that structures of … dominance operate at several levels, all of which must be identified in their complementary relations.[18]

So, rather than focusing on what exactly constitutes hegemonic masculinity and subordinate masculinities and femininities at any one time an place, the theory of hegemonic masculinity focuses on how these categories are challenged, and how they transform. In lieu of a definition, then,

> hegemonic masculinity is taken to stand for those masculine attributes which are most widely subscribed to—and least questioned—in a given social formation: the "common sense" of gender as subscribed to by all men save those whose masculinity is oppositional or deviant.[19]

Females, along with "oppositional or deviant" males, take up subordinate power relations to hegemonic masculinity. The resultant picture is one not of a male-female divide, but rather one that allows for a proliferation of identities drawn along lines of sex, gender, race, class, and sexual preference. None of this is meant to imply that these racialized, gendered, class-conscious identities are essentialized or fixed. Rather, identity is fluid; it is different from person to person, from year to year. Likewise, the ideals of any given "masculinity" or "femininity" are fluid, so that for example, what constitutes a cultural ideal—hegemonic masculinity—vary through time and space.

This section has demonstrated that hegemonic masculinity and subordinate masculinities and femininities take different forms at different times. The thrust of my argument is that US hegemonic masculinity has become hypermasculine since 9/11.[20] Hypermasculinity is a recurring theme in US hegemonic masculinity; it is not a new phenomenon. The next section will describe this particular variant of masculinity.

Hypermasculinity

Meghana Nayak uses the concept of hypermasculinity in an analysis of post-9/11 American identity formation that relies theoretically on Said's orientalism:[21]

> Hypermasculinity is the sensationalistic endorsement of elements of masculinity, such as rigid gender roles, vengeful and militarized reactions and obsession with order, power and control. Ashis Nandy coined "hypermasculinity" to refer to reactionary masculinity that "arises when agents of hegemonic masculinity feel threatened or undermined, thereby needing to inflate, exaggerate, or otherwise distort their traditional masculinity."[22]

In short, hypergendered behavior is generally understood to be characterized by extreme behavior within gender roles, brought about by a reaction to some internal or external threat. According to the psychology literature, hypermasculinity is not a permanent state, but rather, "most males demonstrate signs of hypermasculinity" at various points in their lives—aggressiveness when angered or provoked, for example.[23] Recent feminist IR theorizing suggests that in states, as in individuals, hypermasculinity is a transient condition; one possible component of a larger identity.

Like the concepts of gender and hegemonic masculinity, hypermasculinity has no fixed meaning. In fact, defining hypermasculinity is a two-fold process: first, we must identify whether we are describing hypermasculinity as a characteristic of the hegemonic masculinity, or a subordinate masculinity. Second, we must determine which gender characteristics this particular masculinity (hegemonic or subordinate) embodies. L. H. M. Ling, a prominent feminist and post-colonial IR theorist, has discussed what she terms *subaltern hypermasculinity*, which she defines as a potential Asian male reaction to feminization by Western imperial powers.[24] So, hypermasculinity takes on a specific, sexualized and muscular meaning for that particular subordinate (or subaltern) masculinity. More pertinent to this chapter, American hegemonic masculinity itself has particular characteristics (possibly based on the old frontier mentality, and now manifested in male sports),[25] and hypermasculinity within that ideal takes on a very different meaning.

New psychological research by Kreiger and Dumka states that "hypergender may represent an independent domain of gender" in humans.[26] Similarly, hypergendered behavior is somehow more reified than other forms of masculinities and femininities in the international realm, because warfare by definition is hypermasculine. So, during periods of war, hegemonic masculinity takes on hypermasculine (violent, reactionary) characteristics. As the next section will show, however, hypermasculinity surfaces in society in times of peace, as well. While a determination of exactly when symptoms of hypermasculinity become hegemonic may be impossible at this stage, I hope to show in the following pages that hypermasculinity is an enduring and recurrent symptom of masculine-dominated society.[27]

The history of hypermasculine hegemonic masculinity in the US

The following section will provide a brief sense of the historical context of hypermasculine hegemonic masculinity in the United States. The idea that hypermasculinity is an element of hegemonic masculinity is not entirely new. However, it has not yet received extensive treatment in the case of post-9/11 US foreign policy; or, where it has, hypermasculine hegemonic masculinity has not been put into historical context. Too often, the term "hypermasculine" is used editorially, to condemn the current administration's policies; however, if we look more closely, we will see that hypermasculinity has been a repeated theme in American hegemonic masculinity.

Some theorists do mention hypermasculinity in the American context. Charlotte Hooper makes reference to hypermasculine hegemonic masculinity in the 1890s and 1950s (also describing hypermasculine subordinate masculinities based on race and class).[28] In a transcribed conversation, reflecting on Carol Cohn's groundbreaking feminist work analyzing the discourse of nuclear strategy in the 1980s, Cynthia Enloe says that Cohn was "surrounded by men and operating as a sort of mole in a hypermasculinized subculture."[29] The questions at hand, then, are: how does US hegemonic masculinity change over time? What explains its various forms? Further, how does hegemonic masculinity interplay with subordinate masculinities and femininities at all levels, leading to a multi-layered US identity at any given time and issue area? Perhaps the answers of these questions are out of the scope of this chapter; the goal at this stage is to pose the questions and hope that the answers will be uncovered upon close analysis in the book of which this chapter is a part. As a start, I will elaborate on the hypermasculine characteristics of hegemonic masculinity that attended the closing of the American frontier in the 1890s, and the start of the Cold War in the late 1940s–early 1950s.[30]

The 1890s

In the year 1890, the United States Census report declared the American frontier officially closed.[31] In 1893, historian Frederick Jackson Turner delivered a paper at an academic conference declaring that the American frontier had been seminal in the creation of a multi-cultural, "composite nationality for the American people," as development stretched westward and was accomplished by various peoples.[32] Frontier life had engendered staunch individualism, leading to the particular character of American freedom, nationalism, and democracy, its influence spreading back to Europe.[33]

After the closing of the frontier, then, the United States began the second period of American history, of a differing character than the one preceding it. As the safety valve of land became unavailable (officially at least), American cities grew and industrialized. A strong movement for American imperialism beyond its now-finite borders took hold, resulting in the Spanish-American War. The closing of the frontier led to restlessness and hopelessness, urbanization and unemployment.[34] The backlash against these constraints was the "crisis of masculinity" and a shift to the hypermasculine in American hegemonic masculinity.[35] This period culminated in World War I.[36] According to theorist Michael Egan:

> At the turn of the last century, the tail-end of the great period of invented tradition, Americanism was steeped in or preoccupied with the rediscovery of American masculinity – displaced by Civil War and the economic depression and uncertainty of the Gilded Age – the closing of the frontier, and a growing appreciation of outdoor recreation. The result was division over the expansionist tendencies of proponents for war against Spain, continued labor resentment, and a reinvigorated surge of white supremacy.[37]

The "crisis in masculinity" that developed in the 1890s was a result of the twin factors of the closing of the frontier and an emerging depression. "Between 1873 and 1896, tens of thousands of bankruptcies suggested that the age of the self-made man had drawn to a sputtering close."[38] When Theodore Roosevelt was elected president, he embodied the principles of self-reliance and virility under pressure by the economic and social pressures of the day:

> On the new "throne" of manliness in America was President Teddy Roosevelt, a self-made "man," Dakota rancher, Rough Rider, big game hunter, outdoorsman par excellence, naturalist, and intellect. Roosevelt was a living embodiment of a new American manhood, one that balanced *civilized* morality and intellectual exploits with a more *primitive* physical muscularity.[39]

Much as we will see in the more-fully developed post-9/11 case, President Theodore Roosevelt was elected because he spoke to the electorate's yearnings. Like President George W. Bush, Roosevelt serves as a marker of American hegemonic masculinity during his presidency. And similarly to Bush, Roosevelt embodied a combination of muscularity and moral certitude, both personally (both are ranchers and Christians) and on the level of foreign policy (with the Spanish-American War and the War on Terror). It is plausible to jointly define these two eras as ones of *hypermasculine hegemonic masculinity*, when American superiority, expressed muscularly abroad, was imbued with a sense of destiny or morality.

Post-World War II

After World War II, the United States emerged as a clear hegemon in the world order. Germany and Japan were occupied by American forces, and all of western Europe was inside the American "sphere of influence." The main threat to American primacy (and all of world peace, as it was framed) was a rising Soviet Union.

By the end of the war, the Truman administration was already becoming leery of Stalin's policies. In fact, many scholars argue that Truman used George Kennan's 1946 Long Telegram—the document that introduced the strategy of containment—as justification for polices that Truman was already leaning toward.[40] The Long Telegram stated that the socialist Soviet government considered itself to be fundamentally at odds with democracies, and the Soviet Union therefore absolutely was not to be trusted. Although Kennan was clear that the Russian people were not to be feared, he painted the Soviet government in strict terms: from this point and throughout the Cold War, the conflict was painted in dichotomous terms: good versus evil. Kennan writes, that people "in Europe at least, are tired and frightened by experiences of past, and are less interested in abstract freedom than in security. They are seeking guidance rather than responsibilities."[41] The United States, according to Kennan, should take this paternalistic role, in the defense of (abstract) freedom. The US is seen as the sole defender of this universal right, which is pitted against the evils of communism. These Manichean ethics are a marker of a hypermasculine hegemonic masculinity, and the Soviet threat provided an opportunity for its expression. By the time NSC-68, which laid out US national security objectives, was circulated in 1950, the Long Telegram (which called for containment) was supplanted by more bellicose policy prescriptions. Writes Efstathios Fakiolas, "By interpreting the Soviet threat almost completely in military terms, NSC-68 left no room for negotiations with the Soviets."[42]

American foreign policy in the 1950s was a signal of a broader hypermasculine movement in American culture. In the Long Telegram, Kennan had an early insight: "there would be far less hysterical anti-Sovietism in our country today if realities of this situation were better understood by our people. There is nothing as dangerous or as terrifying as the unknown."[43] Like the post-9/11 fear of (and at times violent backlash against) Arabs and Muslims in America and worldwide, Americans during the early Cold War met the exotic threat of the Soviet Union with a desire for retribution. Led by Senator Joseph McCarthy in the early and mid-1950s, the United States government (and Hollywood film studios) engaged in a witch-hunt for communist sympathizers within the US.

Hypermasculinity in US foreign policy and popular culture

As we have seen, hypermasculine hegemonic masculinity most often arises from a "crisis of masculinity"—not as a reaction to one isolated event. In the cases under investigation here, hypermasculinity differs widely, but takes the general characteristics of muscular foreign policy, Manichean moral certitude, and opportunity windows. In the period from the 1890s to World War I, hypermasculinity was a reaction to the closing of the American frontier and economic depression. The United States, it was argued, could be a rare civilizing force in the colonial world. World War I provided an opportunity for hypermasculinity to fully realize, to such an extent that "martial" elements of hegemonic masculinity were exhausted.[44] In the 1950s, hypermasculinity arose as a response to the emerging Soviet threat, but it took on paternalistic and moral character as America's role in the world was to defend not only its own borders, but the entire free world in a fight of good (freedom) versus evil (communism).

The next section will demonstrate similar themes in the post-9/11 era.

Hegemonic masculinity in the post-9/11 context

While 9/11 gave the Bush administration an opportunity window for bellicose foreign policy decisions, hypermasculinity was gaining steam well before then. Even as the post-Cold War peace ushered in a more tender, less hypermasculine foreign policy, significant elements in American culture acted as a backlash, including the anti-capitalist/anti-globalization movement and the significant portion of the American military who did not want to be "kinder and gentler." These hypermasculine characters represented a viewpoint that was still not hegemonic in the 1990s, or during the presidential elections of 2000. The terrorist attacks of 9/11 gave hypermasculinity the chance to re-enter mainstream, hegemonic masculinity. But as always, this hegemonic masculinity contains internal and external challenges.

A look at popular song lyrics after 9/11 will help to illuminate what it might mean for American hegemonic masculinity to be hypermasculine. Consider the sentiments that inspired country music superstar Toby Keith to write these words a few days after September 11th: "we'll put a boot in your ass; it's the American way." The song in which these lyrics appear, "Courtesy of the Red, White, and Blue (The Angry American)" peaked at Number One on the country music charts over the July 4th, 2002, holiday weekend.

This song reveals characteristics of a *hypermasculine* hegemonic masculinity. In this post-9/11 American case, hypermasculine hegemonic masculinity exhibits violent and jingoistic qualities, but always for a normatively good cause. "It's the American way," Keith sings, to "put a boot in your ass." The US was "sucker punched from the back" by the terrorists (a cowardly way to fight), and in exchange, Keith announces to the terrorists, Uncle Sam will boldly "put your name at the top of his list" and "[light] up your world like the Fourth of July." American hegemonic masculinity here is more than willing to bring about harsh and violent retribution—perhaps dispropor- tionate to the initial blow—but it does all of this proudly, in the name of *justice*. "Mother Freedom" is valorized, and the cowards who waged the attacks have angered the Statue of Liberty, who is "shaking her fist." It is clear that when the Bush administration repeatedly justifies its policies with reference to protecting American justice, liberty, and freedom, it does not fall on deaf ears. In fact, this hypermasculine strand of American hegemonic masculinity already believes in fighting violently for such ideas if they are perceived to be challenged.

Immediately following September 11, 2001, hypermasculinity took the form of support for invading Iraq (despite substantial objections). In the 2004 election, President Bush's rhetoric of fear and patriotism led him to victory over Senator Kerry. The next sections will analyze how hypermasculine hegemonic masculinity can help to explain both sets of events.

The Iraq War; or, "When Osama became Saddam"[45]

I opened this chapter discussing the "selling" of the Iraq War to the American people, and asking how it was sold, and how much the "sale" affected the outcome of the war. But how much did this "sale" actually affect the policy outcome? Some scholars have intonated that even if there had been no pop- ular support for the war, the Bush administration would have invaded Iraq— or at least, popular support played no large role in the decision-making process.[46] A gendered perspective is interested in discussing this in terms of shifts in the nature of hegemonic masculinity.[47] I argue that *hypermasculine* elements within hegemonic masculinity—on both the elite and mass levels—were present before 9/11, but gained strength and clarity after the terrorist attacks.

According to Andrew Flibbert, on the level of the foreign policy elites (including President Bush, Vice President Cheney, and then-Secretary of Defense Paul Wolfowitz), commonly held beliefs included: "a belief in the necessity and benevolence of American hegemony, a Manichean conception of politics, a conviction that regime type is the principle determinant of foreign policy, and great confidence in the efficacy of military force."[48]

Flibbert argues that these four elite-held beliefs led to the 2003 invasion of Iraq. But the foreign policy did not exist in a vacuum, and the majority of Americans supported going to war with Iraq from September 2001 through the invasion in March 2003. Indeed, the American public's support for the war stemmed from many of the same sentiments as were held by the foreign policy elites. As we saw immediately following September 11, 2001, when anti-Arab and anti-Muslim violence proliferated race and/or religion may have also played a role in the public's willingness to go to war.[49] All of these factors—America's role as benevolent world leader, a belief in good's triumph over evil, faith in democratic institutions, belief in military force, and Western exceptionalism—can collectively describe the particular strain of hegemonic masculinity in America after 9/11. The typical "American" worldview followed these general patterns, although vocal opposition to the invasion of Iraq was also omnipresent.[50] On both the elite and popular levels, the war was favored by a majority. Hegemonic masculinity, therefore, took on hypermasculine characteristics. The war's opponents represented a diminished vision of hegemonic masculinity, one not based on hypermasculinity. Hegemonic masculinity was contested; the hypermasculine variant won out after 9/11. Elements of hypermasculinity (recalling Meghana Nayak's definition) that were particularly salient post-9/11 include rigid gender role, vengeful and militarized reactions, obsession with order, power, and control, and a reactionary bent.[51]

In the wake of the 9/11, there was a sense that "someone must pay" for attacking America.[52] Keith's lyrics are typical of the "vengeful and militarized reactions" that Nayak describes. Justice took retributive meaning, as a result of America feeling "threatened or undermined." It is in this logic that it was possible to see Iraq and Al Qaeda as linked. Someone had to pay for the 9/11 attacks; Iraq seemed to resonate as part of the War on Terror, since the Bush administration promised to "finish what we started" in the 1991 invasion, to remove Saddam Hussein from power once and for all. Whether or not Hussein had actual ties to Al Qaeda was beside the point—under a Manichean conception of politics, there are "bad guys" and "good guys"—as a "bad guy," Hussein had to be taken out. Andrew Flibbert's observation that this "Manichean concept of politics" was pervasive after 9/11 is perhaps a greater clue that hegemonic masculinity became hypermasculine than the invasion of Iraq itself. The next section will demonstrate that hypermasculine hegemonic masculinity extended through the presidential elections of 2004.

The 2004 presidential election

The first sections of this chapter have described how hegemonic masculinity is often contested, and may take hypermasculine forms on different occasions. When describing the role of hegemonic masculinity in politics, electoral campaigns make the perfect case study. During presidential campaigns, the American public decides which candidate's vision for the future they find most convincing, and they vote accordingly. If we understand the 2004 presidential elections as a contest between two differing manifestations of hegemonic masculinity, and put President George W. Bush's re-election into that context, it becomes clear that the form of hegemonic masculinity Bush portrays was more resonant with the general public than that of his contender, Senator John Kerry. Comparing the two also strengthens my argument that American hegemonic masculinity in the wake of 9/11 has taken on *hypermasculine* characteristics.

Political scientist Cheryl Schonhardt-Bailey undertook a computer-assisted content analysis of Bush and Kerry's speeches focusing on national security in the run-up to the 2004 elections.[53] The candidates' differing styles throughout the campaign were quite striking. In general, "the 2004 election pitted emotive appeal [Bush] against logic [Kerry], and in the end, emotive appeal appears to have won."[54] When emotional appeals were made by both candidates, Kerry made attempts to identify with "fellow veterans" and "men and women in uniform," in order to show solidarity with the troops and highlight his war-time experience. Bush, for his part, concentrated his energies on describing the terrorist enemy as a force to be feared, and contrasted terrorists with a valiant United States. Schonhardt-Bailey provides examples of Bush and Kerry's speeches focusing on the "War on Terror." First, read and consider the emotions evoked in Bush's speech: "There's nothing they can do to inti-midate, to make us change our deepest beliefs. They're trying to kill to shake our will; we're too tough, too strong, too resolute, and too determined to have our will shaken by thugs and terrorists."[55] The America portrayed here is most definitely the "good guy" in a Manichean battle to the death against evil. Kerry, instead, focuses on the need to fund the Department of Homeland Security when he describes how to combat terrorism. Kerry says:

> The threats of terrorism and the conflicts of the future can only be met with more engineers, more military police, more psychological warfare personnel and civil affairs teams, more special operations forces and more training for peace keeping missions.[56]

The difference between the two stump speeches is striking. Whereas Kerry presented much more practical, logistical details about how he would manage the threat of terrorism, Bush focused almost entirely on painting a fearful image of the terrorists. In addition to focusing much more than Kerry on "images of fear and courage" throughout the campaign, Bush repeatedly mentioned ideals such as freedom and democracy to a much greater extent.[57] In Schonhardt-Bailey's words, "[Bush] invoked the image of America as defender and proponent of Western, democratic values ... he painted an image of America's pursuit of 'freedom', 'democracy', 'political and economic liberty', 'human dignity', and 'peace' in world affairs."[58] On the other hand, Schonhardt-Bailey sums up Kerry's failed rhetorical strategy by citing Matt Bai, in an article in the *New York Times Magazine*:[59]

> Bai characterized Kerry's "multinational, law-enforcement-like approach" to terrorism as "discordant" with a frightened American electorate, con-cluding that Kerry's "less lofty vision might have seemed more satisfying ... in a world where the twin towers still stood."[60]

Of course, Bush did gain re-election. It is logical that the electorate ultimately voted for the worldview they found most persuasive. But by re-casting these conflicting worldviews as competing visions for American hegemonic mascu-linity, we are able to see much more deeply how the sentiments of the Amer-ican public changed after 9/11, and how Bush was able to capture votes because he won the majority of hearts and minds in the end. This is unsur-prising if we consider that after September 11, 2001, hegemonic masculinity took on *hypermasculine* characteristics. Emotion was privileged over logic; terrorists were to be dealt with by the military, and not the civilian police and justice systems.[61] Again, while it is impossible to define what exactly constitutes hypermasculinity (because it is time- and place-dependent), the general exaggeration of male gender roles appears obvious here.

In the field of media communications, Anna Cornelia Fahey points out that in the run-up to the 2004 elections, John Kerry was painted as "French and feminine" by the Bush administration, implying that Kerry did not possess the necessary masculine characteristics to be president.[62] Fahey cites Trujillo's list of five key characteristics of American hegemonic masculinity: physical force and control, occupational achievement, familial patriarchy, frontiersmanship, and heterosexuality.[63] There are two major problems with this argument. First, Fahey sets up a false masculine/feminine dichotomy that obscures subordinated masculinities, class and race identities, and other more complex processes of identity formation. She writes, "While cultural constructions of masculinity may shift over time, masculinity is consistently defined both by and against the concept of femininity and the feminine 'other.'"[64] This seems to be contradicted in the first line of her article's title: "French and feminine," where racial (French) as well as gendered (feminine) identities are set up as subordinate to hegemonic masculinity.

Second, although Fahey does allow that hegemonic masculinity shifts over time, this relatively static list of characteristics downplays the nonlinearity of the shift. Instead, I argue that hegemonic masculinity is a process of contestation between competing visions of what that hegemonic masculinity should be. Fahey neglects to discuss how the 9/11 terrorist attacks were a watershed event in the hypermasculinization of US hegemonic masculinity.[65] In times of hegemonic hypermasculinity, physical force and control becomes the dominant characteristic, overshadowing all else. Were she to recharacterize the post-9/11 Bush regime as representative of hegemonic *hyper*masculinity, Fahey's argument would be strengthened. As she points out, Kerry was painted not just as feminine (gender), but also as "French" (race). Hegemonic hypermasculinity does not discriminate in its subordination: it considers both race and gender in its superiority.

Not every presidential contest displays such clearly contrasting views of hegemonic masculinity. In 1992, for example, sitting president George H. W. Bush was defeated by then-Governor Bill Clinton. Neither of these candidates portrayed hypermasculine traits; as James Carville famously said about the election, "it's the economy, stupid!" The threat of global annihilation was gone, and the candidates were left to deal with more mundane, domestic matters like the economy and health care. In the post-Cold War era, it seemed, the United States did not need to be cowboy-tough, as it had during the "hottest" periods of the Cold War. In the 2000 presidential debates, which serve as a marker of hegemonic masculinity at the end of the (Bill) Clinton era, then-Vice President Al Gore and then-Governor George W. Bush seemed to agree that the United States should pursue a "humble" foreign policy.[66]

This is not to say that hypermasculinity played no role during the Clinton administration. Nor do I mean to imply that American hegemonic masculinity did not contain elements of hypermasculinity, either. On the contrary: it is evident that a small but strong minority in the 1990s lamented America's turn to what they perceived as "wimpy" or "weak" internationalism. Variations on that theme would eventually pick up enough steam to enter hegemonic masculinity in the aftermath of 9/11.

Conclusion: hypermasculine politics

State behavior (by foreign policy elites and within popular culture) reflects hegemonic masculinity, which is just one type of masculinity that occurs at the top of a hierarchy of power relations. As previously discussed, various forms of masculinities manifest on the international stage, including hegemonic masculinity (of Western elites) and other, subordinated masculinities (such as gay men, men of color, and non-Western men), as well as many forms of subordinate femininity. Hegemonic femininity is perfectly sound as a theoretical concept, but it is present only when "feminine" values dominate the social structure under analysis. But insofar as states are "manly," the field of international politics is dominated by states with differing hegemonic masculinities. American hegemonic masculinity's most recent turn towards hypermasculinity is in stark contrast to Germany's focus on economic primacy. But it does not matter whether Gerhard Schroeder or Angela Merkel is at the helm: like all other states, Germany must behave in a manly way in order to compete against other manly states—and to survive in a feminine anarchy.[67]

The point is well theorized by now that "when women enter politics, particularly in areas of foreign policy, they enter an already constructed masculine world where role expectations are defined in terms of adherence to preferred masculine attributes such as rationality, autonomy, and power."[68] This is adherence to a generalized description of hegemonic masculinity. What I propose as *hyper*masculinity goes further than this, and refers to aggressive and bellicose behavior. It is possible that female heads-of-state may be more likely to adhere to a hypermasculine hegemonic masculinity, in order to minimize their anatomical female-ness. Television pundits make this point: Andrew Sullivan refers to Queens Elizabeth and Victoria, Margaret Thatcher, and now Hillary Clinton as "Warrior Queens."[69] The concepts of hegemonic masculinity, and subordinate masculinities and femininities, give this punditry (based on intuition and a specific reading of history) real theoretical heft.

The field of international politics in the US is dominated almost completely by straight white men—or women who "act like men" (as is frequently said about Hillary Clinton)—or by non-white men and women who conform (by choice or necessity) to the culture of Washington. Even the 2008 election of President Barack Obama, unprecedented as it was, does not fundamentally alter this reality. After all, current First Lady Michelle Obama's senior thesis at Princeton reflected on her experiences as a Black American at an Ivy League university, stating that "the path I have chosen to follow by attending Princeton will likely lead to my further integration and/or assimilation into a White cultural and social structure that will only allow me to remain on the periphery of society; never becoming a full participant."[70] Furthermore, she continues in the next paragraph, "as I enter my final year at Princeton, I find myself striving for many of the same goals as my White classmates." It remains to be seen, but while some may hope that the Obama administration ushers in an era where the particular strand of hegemonic masculinity is less hypermasculine than it was immediately following 9/11, international politics remains as imbued with hegemonic masculinity as ever.

Acceptable behavior in international politics transcends the individual's race or gender; to get to a position of power, all participants (gay, straight, male, female, light or dark-skinned) must conform to the "cult of [hegemonic] masculinity."[71] As Carol Cohn has showed us in the field of nuclear strategy, "learning the language is a *transformative*, not an *additive*, process."[72] Heads of state must be perceived as strong on national security; national security relies on war or the threat of war. This is hegemonic masculinity in the extreme. Hegemonic masculinity *is* international politics, and international politics *is* hegemonic masculinity. In the words of two feminist theorists, "international politics is a process which is *always already gendered* and which is maintained as gender-neutral only in reducing gender to 'women' and their particular concerns."[73] If gender is not widely considered to be useful as a line of inquiry into politics, it is only because politics are dominated so completely by the mindset of hegemonic masculinity. As R. W. Connell wrote:

> Most of the time, defence of the patriarchal order does not require an explicit masculinity politics. Given that heterosexual men socially selected for hegemonic masculinity run the corporations and the state, the routine maintenance of these institutions will normally do the job. This is the core of the collective project of hegemonic masculinity, and the reason why this project most of the time is not visible as a project. Most of the time masculinity need not be thematized at all. What is brought to attention is national security, or corporate profit, or family values, or true religion, or individual freedom, or international competitiveness, or economic efficiency, or the advance of science. Through the everyday working of institutions defended in such terms, the dominance of a particular kind of masculinity is achieved.[74]

Connell's work is foundational, but it is important to note that the understanding of hegemonic masculinity as an elite-driven conspiracy is partial. Instead, hegemonic masculinity can be understood as the "top dog" in a set of power relations that include subordinate masculinities and femininities, and in which we *all* participate, whether or not we want to, by virtue of membership in society at large.

Hegemonic masculinity, therefore, can be understood as the predominant set of beliefs in foreign policy and popular culture. Men (and much more importantly, *masculine* values such as strength and autonomy) have become the norm in the international arena.[75] But in the modern era, only occasionally does hegemonic masculinity become hypermasculine. This chapter has expanded on two main concepts: first, that hypermasculinity has been a dominant feature of hegemonic masculinity in historical periods before 9/11 (including, but not limited to, the closing of the American frontier in the 1890s, and the beginning of the Cold War in the late 1940s and 1950s). The second phenomenon I have hoped to demonstrate is that American foreign policy does not occur in a vacuum: presidential hypermasculinity is often attended by hypermasculinity in mainstream American culture. As examples from popular culture have illuminated, hypermasculinity is ever-present, but it is a major component of hegemonic masculinity only when there are windows of opportunity. September 11, 2001, provided just such a window.

Noted linguistics scholar Deborah Tannen has repeatedly referred to President Bush as hypermasculine. Tannen cites Bush's refusal to identify mistakes he's made, as well as his "stay-the-course, go-it-alone, never-waver profile" as evidence for this hypermasculinity.[76] But Tannen does not pin hypermasculinity on Bush alone. Rather, as Anna Quindlen writes:

> it would be a mistake to overlook how deeply ingrained resistance to admitting mistakes is in the American male. "The public persona of authority is hypermasculine," Tannen says. "The masculine approach in our culture is never to apologize because it indicates weakness."[77]

Were I the journalist, this quote would be rephrased to say, "it would be a mistake to overlook how deeply ingrained resistance to admitting mistakes is in American *hypermasculine hegemonic masculinity.*" Properly understanding the dynamics both of Bush's behavior, and that of the American public, requires an understanding of the internal dynamics of contestation within hegemonic masculinity in the time period between 9/11 and the invasion of Iraq. The hypermasculine won out, in the administration and with the general public—but within the general public, at least, there was dissent from hypermasculinity, coming mainly from those who did not see 9/11 as a valid reason for invading Iraq.

Now that we understand the negative effects of hypermasculinity, what is to be done? It is sometimes assumed that feminist International Relations theorists are interested purely in putting more women in positions of power, or making the world a more "feminine" place. While many scholar-activists are at work at the first task, few would support the second. This particular chapter takes an entirely different route from either of these, and considers instead how the *structure* of international politics is gendered; that is, how states exhibit various masculinities and femininities. As Spike Peterson writes:

Feminist IR, in spite of a dramatic increase in publications and conference visibility, remains foreign to mainstream IR. More specifically, while "woman" as an empirical referent has gained visibility, feminist claims that gender is an analytic category ... remain poorly understood ... Gender is decidedly "not a synonym for women," but a structural, pervasive feature of how we "order" social life. And taking gender seriously involves much more than the important but limited problem of "adding women in."[78]

This chapter has sought in part to demonstrate that the ascension of females to the upper echelons of American government will not have a measurable impact, because both males and females face the constraints of hegemonic masculinity. But the goal of feminist theorists is most certainly *not* a shift towards hegemonic femininity. In the words of Ann Tickner, the goal is not "a more feminized world, whatever that may mean," but one with lessened hierarchies of power based on gender (as well as race, class, and sexuality.)[79] It is unlikely that we will be able to replace war with peace in all cases; rather, the goal is to "challenge violence with politics."[80] When hegemonic masculinity is hypermasculine, there is no place for women *or* men in politics. Caricatured, reactionary, violent ideals (hypermasculinity) take the place of sentiment and reasoning skills possessed by actual people (men and women).

Rather than reacting in a hypermasculine way, heads of state (and public opinion within states) would be better served to respond with diplomacy and multilateralism. While this approach does not eradicate hegemonic masculinity, the goal is twofold: first, to consciously shift hegemonic masculinity away from hypermasculinity, and second, to lessen the power hierarchy that puts hegemonic masculinity on top. Theoretically, the goal would be to eradicate all constraining masculinities and femininities, because (as I have discussed) these gender constructions are based on false essentializing and dichotomizing. On the practical level, although we may never reach a non-gendered reality, we can do our best to minimize the polarizing and bellicose effects of hypermasculinity, and other violent manifestations of gender. Insofar as the core of International Relations scholarship is directed towards understanding the roots of violence, scholarly work that promotes an understanding of hypermasculine hegemonic masculinity is useful to the field at large.

Notes

1 Jon Western, "The War Over Iraq: Selling War to the American Public," *Security Studies* 14, no. 1 (January–March 2005): 106–39.
2 Ibid., p. 119.
3 Charlotte Hooper, *Manly States* (New York: Columbia University Press, 2001), p. 35.
4 See, for example, J. Ann Tickner, *Gender in International Relations: Feminist Perspectives on Achieving Global Security* (New York: Columbia University Press, 1992), pp. 38–9, 103.
5 Hooper, *Manly States*, pp. 81–2.

6 J. Ann Tickner, "Why Women Can't Run the World: International Politics According to Francis Fukuyama," *International Studies Review* 1, no. 3 (Autumn 1999): 3–11, at p. 7.

7 J. Ann Tickner, *Gender in International Relations*, p. 40, citing Judith Hicks Stiehm, *Women and Men's Wars* (Oxford: Pergamon Press, 1983), p. 371.

8 Tickner, *Gender in International Relations*, p. 6.

9 T. Carrigan, R. W. Connell, and J. Lee, "Toward a New Sociology of Masculinity," *Theory and Society* 14, no. 5 (1985): 551–604. R. W. Connell expanded on the concept of hegemonic masculinity in *Gender and Power* (Stanford, CA: Stanford University Press, 1987).

10 R. W. Connell, *Masculinities* (Berkeley, CA: University of California Press, 1995).

11 Ibid., p. 77.

12 Hooper, *Manly States*, pp. 57–8, citing Raymond Williams, *Marxism and Literature* (Oxford: Oxford University Press, 1977), p. 110.

13 Hooper, *Manly States*, p. 57.

14 Connell, *Masculinities*, p. 3.

15 Hooper, *Manly States*, p. 62.

16 Harry Brod, "A Case for Men's Studies," in *Changing Men: New Directions in Research in Men and Masculinities*, ed., Michael S. Kimmel (London: Sage-Focus, 1987), pp. 275–6; cited in Hooper, *Manly States*, p. 62.

17 See, for example, Jean Bethke Elshtain, *Women and War* (Brighton: Harvester Press, 1987) and Hooper, *Manly States*.

18 John Tosh, "Hegemonic Masculinity and Gender History," in *Masculinities in Politics and War: Gendering Modern History*, eds. Stefan Dudink, Karen Hagemann, and John Tosh (Basingstoke: Palgrave Macmillan, 2004), p. 55.

19 Ibid., p. 47. Later in this chapter, it will be made clear that women as well as men are complicit in maintaining the "common sense" of gender.

20 All types of masculinities can take on hypermasculine characteristics; hypermasculinity is not limited to hegemonic masculinity. It is also not limited to the American case. The fact that I am studying American hegemonic masculinity, and its recent turn towards hypermasculinity, is less because it is an "ideal case", or the only case, and more because of my personal interest in contemporary US foreign policy.

21 Meghana Nayak, "Orientalism and 'Saving' U.S. State Identity after 9/11," *International Feminist Journal of Politics* 8, no. 1 (March 2006): 42–61.

22 Ibid., p. 43; citing Anna Agathangelou and L. H. M. Ling, "Power, Borders, Security, Wealth: Lessons of Violence and Desire from September 11," *International Studies Quarterly* 48, no.3, p. 519.

23 Pamela C. Zamel, "Hypervulnerable Youth in a Hypermasculine World: A Critical Analysis of Hypermasculinity in African American Adolescent Males," PhD dissertation, University of Pennsylvania, 2004.

24 L. H. M. Ling, "Hypermasculinity on the Rise, Again: A Response to Fukuyama on Women and World Politics," *International Feminist Journal of Politics* 2, no.2 (Summer 2000): 279.

25 Hooper, *Manly States*, p. 180.

26 Tyson C. Kreiger and Larry E. Dumka, "The Relationships Between Hypergender, Gender, and Psychological Adjustment," *Sex Roles* 54, nos 11–12, abstract.

27 The use of "masculine-dominated" rather than "male-dominated" is conscious, to remind the reader that gender characteristics of strength, valor, and rationalism are not biologically predetermined, but are generally associated with the constructed concept of "manliness," more so than with actual men.

28 Hooper, *Manly States*, pp. 66, 72.

29 Carol Cohn, "A Conversation with Cynthia Enloe: Feminists Look at Masculinity and the Men Who Wage War," *Signs: Journal of Women in Culture and Society*

12, no.4 (2003): 687–718; for hypermasculine warfare in Iraq, see Laura Sjoberg, *Gender, Justice, and the Wars in Iraq: A Feminist Reformulation of Just War Theory* (Lanham, MD: Rowman & Littlefield Publishers, 2006), p. 135.

30 Other cases, such as the Cuban Missile Crisis and the Reagan Administration, are under examination and may be included in the full-length version of this project.

31 Superintendent of the Census, cited by Frederick Jackson Turner, "The Significance of the Frontier in American History," *Report of the American Historical Association* (1893): 199–227.

32 Frederick Jackson Turner, "The Significance of the Frontier in American History."

33 Ibid., p. 227.

34 Michael S. Kimmel, "The Contemporary Crisis in Masculinity in Historical Perspective," in *The Making of Masculinities: The New Men's Studies*, ed., Harry Brod (Winchester: Allen & Unwin, 1987), cited in Hooper, *Manly States*, p. 66.

35 Hooper, *Manly States*, p. 66.

36 Ibid.

37 Michael Egan, "Wrestling Teddy Bears: Wilderness Masculinity as Invented Tradition in the Pacific Northwest," *Gender Forum* 15 (2006): 3.

38 Ibid., p. 9.

39 Ibid., p. 10.

40 According to John Lewis Gaddis, as quoted in Barton D. Gellman, *Contending with Kennan: Toward a Philosophy of American Power* (New York: Praeger, 1984), p. 12.

41 George Kennan, "Long Telegram."

42 Efstathios T. Fakiolas, "Kennan's Long Telegram and NSC-68: A Comparative Analysis," *East European Quarterly* 31, no. 4 (January 1998): 10.

43 Ibid.

44 Hooper, *Manly States*, p. 66, citing Peter Filene, "The Secrets of Men's History," in Brod, *The Making of Masculinities: The New Men's Studies*.

45 Adapted from the title of Scott L. Althaus and Devon M. Largio, "When Osama Became Saddam: Origins and Consequences of the Change in America's Public Enemy #1," *Political Science and Politics* 37, no. 4 (October 2004): 795–9.

46 See, for example, Michael J. Mazarr, "The Iraq War and Agenda Setting," *Foreign Policy Analysis* 3, no. 1 (January 2007): 1–23.

47 What I term the "chicken–egg problem" here is known to some social scientists as the "agent–structure problem" or "agent–structure dialectic". See, for example, Colin Wight, *Agents, Structures and International Relations: Politics as Ontology* (New York: Cambridge University Press, 2006).

48 Andrew Flibbert, "The Road to Baghdad: Ideas and Intellectuals in Explanations of the Iraq War," *Security Studies* 15, no. 2 (April–June 2006): 310–52.

49 Attacks on Muslim Arab-Americans skyrocketed after the 9/11 terrorist attacks. See, for example, Associated Press, "Schools Deal with Anti-Arab Backlash," *CNN.com*, 20 September 2001, accessed online July 20, 2007.

50 To take an example from our field, on September 26, 2002, 33 prominent political scientists took out a full-page ad in the *New York Times*, stating that "War With Iraq Is *Not* In America's National Interest."

51 Nayak, "Orientalism and 'Saving' U.S. State Identity After 9/11," p. 43; citing Anna Agathangelou and L. H. M. Ling, "Power, Borders, Security, Wealth: Lessons of Violence and Desire from September 11," *International Studies Quarterly* 48, no. 3, p. 519.

52 Popular polls taken immediately following 9/11 point to the same sentiments. An *ABC News/Washington Post* poll taken on September 11, 2001, showed that 86 percent "supported military reprisals even if that means war", and a full 80 percent "also support military action against countries that assist or shelter terrorists." Available at: abcnews.go.com/sections/us/DailyNews/wtc_abcpoll010911.html; accessed 20 July 2007.

53 Cheryl Schonhardt-Bailey, "Measuring Ideas More Effectively: An Analysis of Bush and Kerry's National Security Speeches," *Political Science and Politics* 38, no.4 (October 2005): 701–11.

54 Ibid., p. 701.

55 Ibid., p. 706.

56 Ibid.

57 Ibid., p. 707.

58 Ibid., p. 706.

59 Matt Bai, "Kerry's Undeclared War: *John Kerry* Has a Thoughtful, Forward-looking Theory about *Terrorism* and How to Fight It. But Can It Resonate with *Americans* in the Post-9/11 World?" *New York Times Magazine*, 10 October 2004, 38–45, 52, 68, 70, emphasis in original title.

60 Schonhardt-Bailey, "Measuring Ideas More Effectively," pp. 708–9, citing Bai, p. 70.

61 Peter Katzenstein has compared the approach to terrorism of the United States with Germany and Japan, arguing that most liberal democracies including Germany and Japan (but unlike the United States) are more likely to respond to terrorism with police (not military) action, and to utilize their civilian justice systems in order to try and convict suspected terrorists. See Peter Katzenstein, "Same War, Different Views: Germany, Japan, and the War on Terrorism," *Current History* 101, no. 659 (December 2002): 427–36.

62 Anna Cornelia Fahey, "French and Feminine: Hegemonic Masculinity and the Emasculation of John Kerry in the 2004 Presidential Race," *Critical Studies in Media Communication* 24, no. 2 (June 2007): 132–50.

63 Ibid., citing Nick Trujillo, "Hegemonic Masculinity on the Mound: Media Representations of Nolan Ryan and American Sports Culture," *Critical Studies in Media Communication* 8, no. 3 (1991): 290–308.

64 Fahey, p. 133.

65 Ibid.

66 11 October 2000 debate (accessed 26 July 2007, Commission on Presidential Debates, www.debates.org/pages/trans2000b.html); Bush suggested a "humble foreign policy," and Gore agreed that was an appropriate direction.

67 The idea that anarchy is constructed as feminine is discussed in the full-length project, as well as in Tickner, *Gender in International Relations* and Hanna Fenichel Pitkin, *Fortune Is a Woman: Gender and Politics in the Thought of Nicolò Machiavelli* (Chicago: University of Chicago Press, 1999).

68 Ann Tickner, "Feminism Meets International Relations: Some Methodological Issues," in *Feminist Methodologies for International Relations*, eds., Brooke A. Ackerly, Maria Stern, and Jacqui True (New York: Cambridge University Press, 2006), p. 39.

69 Quoted on the *Chris Matthews Show*, in a segment entitled "Lead, Lady, Lead!" originally aired October 8, 2006.

70 Michelle LaVaughn Robinson, "Princeton-Educated Blacks and the Black Community," BA thesis, Princeton University, 1985.

71 V. Spike Peterson, ed., *Gendered States: Feminist (Re)Visions on International Relations Theory* (Boulder, CO: Lynne Rienner, 1992), p. 45.

72 Cohn, "Sex and Death in the Rational World of Defense Intellectuals," *Signs*, 12, no. 4 (1987): 716.

73 Louiza Odysseos and Hakan Seckinelgin, *Gendering the "International"* (New York: Palgrave Macmillan, 2002), p.5.

74 Connell, *Masculinities*, pp. 212–13.

75 Tickner, *Gender in International Relations*, p. 39.

76 Deborah Tannen, "Being President Means Never Having to Say He's Sorry," *New York Times*, October 12, 2004.

77 Anna Quindlen, "Contrition as Leadership," *Newsweek*, January 8, 2007.

78 V. Spike Peterson, "Rereading Public and Private: The Dichotomy that Is Not One", 12. Peterson quotes the title from Terrell Carver, *Gender is Not a Synonym for Women* (Boulder, CO: Lynne Reinner Press, 1996).

79 Tickner, "Why Women Can't Run the World: International Politics According to Francis Fukuyama," p. 11.

80 Elshtain, *Women and War*, p. 257.

13 Peace building through a gender lens and the challenges of implementation in Rwanda and Côte d'Ivoire

Heidi Hudson

United Nations Security Council Resolution 1325 asks that member-states ensure the consideration of gender in peace building processes.[1] This chapter explores what "considering gender" would mean, arguing that, it requires more than acknowledging gender inequality and foregrounding women's needs in peace processes. Considering gender also includes seeing the differential impact of conflict on men and women and the unique knowledge and experiences that both groups bring to the peace table. The benefits of such a strategy reach beyond improved gender relations. Considering gender in peace building also increases the chances of successful planning, implementation, and institutionalization of a post-conflict order. On the other hand, the exclusion of women and/or the failure to consider gender in peace building processes risks not only women's rights, but also the general failure of peace building as an enterprise.

Inspired by Cynthia Enloe's argument that patriarchy "is a principal cause both of the outbreak of violent societal conflicts and of the international community's frequent failures in providing long-term resolutions to those violent conflicts," this chapter contends that considering gender is a key part of an effective peace building process.[2] I argue there is a link between gender inequality and violence, and the prevalence of discrimination against women increases the likelihood that a state will experience internal conflict.[3] If this observation is true, this chapter contends, the success of post-conflict reconstruction can be seen as dependent on the inclusion of women and the pursuit of gender equity.

Building peace is an idea at once broader than and an important framework for the peace making and peace keeping work done by soldiers and diplomats.[4] Perhaps peace keeping can be seen as an effort to contain the violence of a conflict, peace making can be seen as an attempt to change the attitudes of current combatants, and peace building encompasses both while attempting to understand and change the root causes of the conflict.[5] For this task, feminist thinking not only offers an alternative vision of security through the lens of gender, but also presents an inclusive view of global security. Feminist theorizing uses gender as the lens to point out gender inequalities, and then pays attention to the effects of these gendered power relations as they manifest between men and women during and after conflict.[6] This chapter contends that the evidence gathered by studying peace building from a feminist perspective can be used to reconceptualize the peace agenda in more inclusive and responsible ways.

If gender analysis generally is essential to peace building for its specified or bottom-up approach, this chapter argues that a culturally contextual gender analysis is a key tool both for feminist theory of peace building and the practice of implementing a gender perspective in all peace work. In other words, rather than treating women as if they had essential qualities (and therefore applying *a* feminist approach as if it were universal), it is important to look for a contextually situated feminist approach. Using the tools of African feminisms to study African conflicts, this chapter problematizes essentialist approaches to women's roles in conflict and peace, warns against "adding women" without recognizing their agency, emphasizes the need for an organized women's movement, and suggests directions for the implementation of international laws concerning women's empowerment and protection at the local level.

The first section of this chapter explores what it would mean to take a feminist approach to peace building processes. The second section begins applying those insights by suggesting the use of four gender-sensitive "tools" to first analyze women's varied and often invisible roles in conflict and their needs in peace building; second, to establish a post-conflict reconstruction framework that takes account of gender and women's issues; third, to empower women's groups to effectively build the bridge between the current neglect of gender in peace building processes and gender mainstreamed processes which would be more effective and more gender-emancipatory; and finally, to adapt international frameworks for gender equality in culturally sensitive ways. The third section illustrates through case studies of peace building in Rwanda and Côte d'Ivoire that there is an empirical correlation between both *if* and *how* women are included in peace processes and the quality of the peace that is finally achieved. The chapter concludes by suggesting that considering gender fully, through mainstreaming, inclusion, and transformational strategies, peace building processes could be more representative and more effective.

Approaching gender and peace building

Though peace building efforts in Africa have been fundamentally transformed by the implementation of human security approaches over the last two decades, critics (especially feminists) have noted that these changes have not been fundamental enough, since they have allowed the maintenance of a top-down view of security and preserved the illusion that the "human" in "human security" can be gender-neutral.[7] Since gender does influence what is considered a threat or violence, as well as policy-making about security,[8] security needs to be viewed in terms of voice, identity, power and location—and to include the specific concerns of women. Feminists have argued that gender analysis delivers legitimacy and substance to a wider security concept, and offers a bottom-up foundational logic.

At the same time that it is important to reformulate the human security agenda to pay attention to women's needs, it is equally crucial to avoid representing women as a group with the same security needs. This hides differences among women, as well as the power dynamics between women. Specifically, in the international arena, discourses about women's roles in peace building emphasize women's equal representation (liberal feminism) or women's unique (but uniform) characteristics (standpoint feminism).[9] In liberal approaches, women are "added" to the peace building discourse[10] with the assumption that they will behave like *men* when given men's roles, and that the fundamental frameworks of peace building, though they were created by men for men, are unproblematic and will remain intact. Such a feminism contradicts the lived experiences of many women in Africa.[11] Standpoint feminism, in contrast, argues that "men's dominating position in social life results in partial and perverse understandings, whereas women's subjugated position provides the possibility of more complete and less perverse understandings."[12] This is a universalistic approach as well, however, assuming that all men have certain traits (dominance and violence) and all women have certain traits (peacefulness and motherhood).[13] It reifies traditional gender stereotypes. Each of these approaches inadequately distinguishes the differences between masculinities and femininities, and the differences between women.

A more productive approach would recognize that identities are overlapping and women's diverse experiences cannot be understood without reference to context. Such an approach would recognize diversity as an important factor in explaining how and why systems of domination exist and are maintained, while paying attention to the global implications of subordination.[14] In search of such an approach, African women have begun to reassert their own brands of feminism.[15] African feminisms recognize hybrid identities which at once connect with international feminisms' protests against gender subordination and delineate specific ground for African approaches to African women's specific needs and goals.[16] The main difference between these African feminist approaches and the liberal and standpoint approaches described above is that African feminisms not only acknowledge other oppressions, but consider the possibility that "in that context, gender is but one unit of analysis that sometimes has to subject itself to the universal bond between men and women against racism and imperialism."[17] To signify this difference, African feminists prefer to refer to their political project in "womanist" terms.[18] "Womanism" tries to balance the strategic emancipatory project with the tactical dimension of African women's reality, their overlapping identities and the dynamics of empowerment.[19] African feminisms therefore represent a balance between universal normative principles of gender equality and traditional values such as *ubuntu* (the interconnectiveness of each human being, consensus-building and social solidarity).[20]

Using Christine Sylvester's understanding of empathetic cooperation as feminist methodology,[21] African feminisms can be seen as tools for "managing, working with, respecting, and surpassing rigid standpoints, positions, and issues without snuffing out difference."[22] Using a notion of gender equality that embraces cultural difference but does not reinforce cultural subjugation, an African feminist approach takes its cue from the locationality or situatedness embodied in the African Charter on Human and Peoples' Rights, which emphasizes communitarian rather than individualist rights and duties toward family, community, the state and the international community.[23] This approach produces different observations than both the human security framework and its Western feminist critics—observations which, I contend, enrich and empower peace building processes.

Specifically, an African feminist approach focuses on peace building in order to argue for the importance of inclusion of gender *not only* in the formal processes of reconstruction and reintegration *after* the cease-fire has been signed, but also during the pre-settlement phase (e.g. during negotiations), since inclusion or exclusion of marginalised groups here already indicates the potential success or failure of long-term societal reconstruction.

African feminists note that women's important contributions to informal peace building and grassroots activism have been recognized in the policy arena.[24] These successes, however, have not led to the regular inclusion of women in formal processes as peace negotiators and political decision-makers. In fact, statements that praise women's success at the grassroots level often serve to legitimate the non-governmental sphere as the appropriate one for women's activism. There is evidence that this marginalization of women allows the perpetuation of the violent discourses which are key to sustaining conflict, and that women's substantive and representative inclusion can lead to more sustainable peace deals.

This gender critique of current peace building practices underlines two challenges. First, it highlights the problem of how to make the formal peace process benefit from the efforts of women at the informal grassroots level without the latter being subsumed by contestation at the elite level. The symbiotic relationship between these two levels must be recognized. Second, it is crucial to instil the elements of peace building, including security, justice and reconciliation, social and economic well-being, and governance and participation with a feminist perspective that transcends the private–public divide.[25] Feminist analysis contends that gender justice should be the central organizing principle for this new peace building process.[26]

African feminist tools for peace building

Tool 1: Where are the women in conflict and peace building?

The first theme that a feminist approach to peace building suggests is that theorists and practitioners alike re-vision their understanding of women's roles both in conflict and post-conflict processes. Women in wars and conflicts play a variety of roles—as peace protesters, as war supporters, as members of the workforce, as military support, as soldiers, as terrorists, as revolutionaries, and as citizens of belligerent states otherwise uninvolved in the conflict.[27] In fact, myths of women's gender-stereotypical roles in conflict obfuscate women's real contributions while entrenching gender-subordinating ideal-types of womanhood. The (invisible) variety of women's roles is an important piece in the peace building puzzle.

There are two implications of the realization that women play diverse roles in conflict. First, not all women in one conflict zone have the same needs. Combatant women have different needs in peace building than women peace advocates. Similarly, rape victims or mothers may have special (and different) needs. Second, despite the variety of women's roles in wartime, women are still very often described in essentialized terms that frame their capacity as limited to motherhood and their domain as the private sphere. In these discourses, women's aggressive or atypical roles in war are ignored and women's desire to be a part of the peace process signals that they are trouble-makers. These discourses deny women's agency in violence and their importance as peace builders—both of which should not be underestimated in contemporary conflict, especially on the African continent.

Many women suffer disproportionately in conflict and/but many women also gain from conflict. Where women suffer from conflict, it is important that peace building processes take account of that suffering in the construction of a lasting settlement. Where women benefit from conflict, it is equally crucial that peace building processes acknowledge and consolidate those gains. Where both occur (which is in the majority of conflicts in Africa and around the world), peace building processes has the complicated task of paying attention not only to the many and varied roles that women play in war but also to the many and varied impacts of war on women. Attention to these details, however complicated, is essential for planning regarding gender issues in the post-conflict period.

Tool 2: Towards a gender-responsive and integrated post-conflict reconstruction

A second tool is some applicatory suggestions for establishing a post-conflict reconstruction framework that takes account of gender and women's issues. It is necessary to consider these issues carefully because of the complexity of post-conflict reconstruction. Peace building is not just one process of changing from war to peace, but often several processes of transforming inter-group relations, forms of government, and forms of economy. A suggested transition between gender subordination and gender emancipation, while crucial, adds another complicated element.

Gender concerns have been largely absent from peace building processes in Africa thus far, even in the atmosphere of policy reforms based on the shift to human security frameworks. For example, the African Union (AU) Post-Conflict Reconstruction Policy Framework[28] emphasizes that humanitarian and development issues must be at the center of any plan for sustainable peace. Although women are labeled as among the vulnerable groups for whom resources should be mobilized, the Policy Framework does not pursue gender mainstreaming or recognize the gender-specific situations of men and women in war.[29] This Policy Framework has been implemented by a number of African states, which use it to form context-specific action plans. In these action plans, women are omitted, both as members of the political community generally and as persons who have special roles in peace building through their positions in their families and social networks.

Still, peace building *without* gender mainstreaming faces two major threats to its success. First, the reconstruction is often disconnected due to the fact that while women's activists are preoccupied by grassroots human rights violations, gender violence and lack of basic service provision, the warring parties and external actors strike deals without them. Second, differential security needs and particular rights are overlooked during the process and are consequently under-resourced within Security Sector Reform processes. Protection against gender-based violence includes protection not only from the local militia but also from international peacekeepers. Peace agreements written or supervised by Western diplomats often bestow civil and political rights on African women, while failing to pay attention to their priorities, which would often rank social, economic, and cultural rights before those civil and political rights.[30]

These threats to the success of peace building can only be alleviated with a focus on women as agents in political and social life. This is critical because, while many see peace building as a process to return a state to some sort of stable status quo, women are often uninterested in returning to their subordinate positions. Were gender a key and uniting element of peace building, women's organizations would play a key role in moving societies forward, both in reconstruction and in terms of gender equity.

Gender mainstreaming, as defined by the UN, refers to

> a strategy for making women's as well as men's concerns and experiences an integral dimension of the design, implementation, monitoring and evaluation of policies and programmes in all political, economic and societal spheres so that women and men benefit equally and inequality is not perpetuated.[31]

In this understanding, then, the success of mainstreaming depends on achieving gender balance[32] *not just by including equal numbers of women* but through including women's perspectives, encouraging gender awareness, promoting cultural sensitivity, and emphasizing local knowledge.[33] Still, in practice, the concept is often understood as treating men and women the same with the result that so-called gender-neutral goals overshadow women's specific security needs.[34] Further, mainstreaming is still far from universal practice. As such, the responsibility falls on women and women's organizations and movements to demonstrate the importance of gender mainstreaming in post-conflict reconstruction.

Tool 3: Women's groups as a connection between gender and peace building

If the responsibility to promote gender mainstreaming often falls on women's groups, then those groups' strategies, successes, and shortcomings are important factors in the success of peace building processes.

Nadine Puechguirbal observed that, despite the fact that gender mainstreaming has become almost exclusively the responsibility of women's movements, many African women's groups in the 1990s did not have the sort of organization or long-term political strategies that would be required to achieve transformative political goals.[35] In order to inspire the inclusion of women in peace processes, women's groups must engage in organized advocacy. Currently, African women's movements advocate using "a variety of modes of expression such as poems, plays, marches, prayers, physically barricading peace talks with their bodies as human shields, and intercepting delegates in corridors."[36] These approaches demonstrate creativity and attract attention, but women's movements have been unsuccessful in parlaying them into invitations to sit at official peace negotiations.

In order to get those invitations, women need coherent political movements invested in gender mainstreaming and feminist consciousness. Such movements could inform policy initiatives to include women in political institutions, democratize political processes, and reduce conflict-related and domestic violence.

A successful strategy that women's movements have used in Africa is networking to share common experiences and practical training for conflict resolution and trauma counselling. These efforts have contributed towards significantly reducing violence.[37]

Networking has also been used successfully to accomplish dissemination of information. On the continental or regional level, the Federation of African Women Peace Networks (FERFAP) has linked more than 20 women's organizations in over 15 countries.[38] The combined innovation of the new African Union (formed in 2001) and the Pan-African Parliament (formed in 2003) has significantly boosted women's formal participation in political decision-making. The African Union organized a Directorate on Women, Gender and Development with the mission of coordinating its gender-related activities. In 2005, Femmes Africa Solidarité (FAS) established the Pan-African Centre for Gender, Peace and Development.[39] Women's movements armed with data about the gender-specific impacts of armed conflict generally and each African conflict specifically would have a substantially higher chance of impacting state and international policy-making arenas. Women's groups could and should thus try to increase local awareness of the international legislative tools available to increase gender equality.

Tool 4: Culturally sensitive approaches to gender-mainstreamed peace building

Though international legal frameworks on human rights were largely created by men and for men, women's rights, needs, and interests have gradually become a part of the international legal cannon. Though many of the gendered structures of international law remain, international law offers women, "a language recognised by states in which to claim an entitlement to be involved in policy and decision making about peace-building" and creates a framework for assessing policies and practices against stated criteria.[40]

A number of legal tools created in recent decades combine to make up a comprehensive international framework for women's rights which most governments in Africa have adopted. These legal tools include the Convention on the Elimination of All Forms of Discrimination against Women (CEDAW), the United Nations Security Council Resolution 1325, the Protocol to the African Charter on Human and People's Rights on the Rights of Women in Africa, the Heads of State Solemn Declaration on Gender Equality in Africa, and the Southern African Development Community (SADC) Declaration on Gender and Development with its Addendum on Prevention and Eradication of Violence Against Women and Children. It is also encouraging to note that the UN recently established a Peacebuilding Commission, which affirmed the important role of women in peace building.[41]

Although generally regarded as a political watershed for women involved in peace and security work, many of these international legal frameworks remain rhetorical commitments. For example, in Resolution 1325, the United Nations has no mandate to enforce implementation and regular feedback on progress from states. Though Kofi Annan reported in 2004[42] that the Resolution had seen success in terms of global understanding of its purpose, improvement of gender balance in some divisions of the United Nations, and some substantive expansion of other international laws, this progress has not led to a watershed success for gender mainstreaming. Instead, women's exclusion from peace talks remains the norm rather than the exception, women's inclusion (when it happens) tends to be piecemeal and ignore gender analysis. I argue that gender mainstreaming should be seen as about women's representation but not only about women's representation. Inclusionary tools that increase representation from the top-down, like gender quotas, are an important first step but need to be understood as a temporary measure awaiting the implementation of a more transformational strategy, which takes account of women's perspectives, emphasizes gender awareness, promotes cultural sensitivity, and emphasizes local knowledge.[43] As such, top-down measures need to be combined with methods to find and eradicate the structural barriers to women's active participation in formal peace processes. It is here that the African Union and other leaders of the continent should lobby for the inclusion of hybrid gender-sensitive approaches to building peace. This would help international organizations realize that women's presence at the "official peace table" is only part of a larger strategy of gender-sensitivity and of peace building.

The expectation that peace building will be conducted according to international legal standards is in itself insufficient to guarantee women the same protection of their rights as men. For that to happen, the institutionalization of a common international framework should take place through incorporation into national legal systems and being given constitutional priority over customary or religious law. Whether these guidelines are indeed implemented in a culturally sensitive manner or whether lip-service is paid to these commitments and institutions, depends very much on the complex dynamics on the ground.

Rwanda and the paradox of "sameness"

The peace building process in Rwanda has been heralded for its inclusion of women and gender-based perspectives. Rwanda has embarked on a massive peace building effort in the aftermath of the 1994 genocide, where 800,000 people died in one hundred days.[44] The historical rivalry between the elite, minority Tutsi and the peasant Hutu minority dates back to pre-colonial times. The genocide was set off by the assassination of Rwanda's president, Juvénal Habyarimana, on 6 April 1994. Most accounts agree that Habyarimana (a Hutu) was assassinated by extremist Hutu forces who objected to his agreement to share power with the Tutsi Rwandan Patriotic Front (RPF).

After the genocide, the peace building process in Rwanda has been slow and methodical, and continues almost fifteen years later. While reconciliation is practiced by many, healing remains a lengthy process fraught with difficulties in overcoming differences and fostering forgiveness and trust. For Rwanda, the challenge in general is to create "safe spaces" within which to develop an alternative value system as a precursor to sustainable peace. Women—being affected in very particular ways—similarly face very specific challenges to help make this work. In the next section I analyze this task in terms of the four African feminist tools outlined earlier.

Where were the women in the Rwandan genocide?

The fastest and most efficient genocide in history had disproportionate impacts on women. Estimates place the number of rapes during the genocide as between 250,000 and 500,000.[45] Rape does not only inflict humiliation and terror on individual women but also aims to degrade the women's ethnic groups, their men and community as a whole.[46] In addition to these gross bodily violations women suffered loss of livelihood, displacement, separation from family, food insecurity, psychological trauma and loss of traditional social networks.[47] The HIV prevalence rate has dramatically increased from 1 percent before the conflict in 1994 to 11 percent in 1997.[48]

During the genocide, Tutsi women were portrayed in the Hutu Ten Commandments as beautiful and desirable, but "too good" for Hutu men, and therefore needed to be subjugated, i.e. raped.[49] In this sense, rape served as a marker of ethnicity—a deliberate strategy to target women in their role as child bearers to destroy the purity of the ethnic group, by forcing them to give birth to "impure" babies.

Rwandan women not only experienced conflict differently than their male counterparts, but also held different identities as actors in conflict than men. There is evidence that women have not only been victims but also perpetrators of violence during the genocide. African Rights (1995)[50] cites cases of Hutu women encouraging and abetting mass rape and sexual enslavement. For example, Pauline Nyiramasuhuko, former minister of Family and Women's Affairs, is the first woman ever to be charged with rape as a crime against humanity.[51]

The Rwandan peace process has a mixed record on recognizing women's multiple roles in the conflict. On one hand, women's victimization in the conflict is widely recognized. On the other hand, women's participation is downplayed or ignored. Women have been included in the post-conflict reconstruction process in record numbers, but often this inclusion has emphasized the purity and peacefulness of feminine women as something that the Rwandan society desperately needs to call upon. In Rwanda, there was, for instance, no gender-disaggregation of the disarmament process.

Gender-responsive and integrated reconstruction

There were very few women at the official peace talks in Arusha and consequently the agreement made little reference to the gendered impact of conflict or the role of women in peace building.[52] In this way, the peace negotiations represent an absence of gender mainstreaming and an exclusion of women from the peace building process. Still, the transitional government was quick to act on the inclusion of women in governance.

In 1994, Rwanda's transitional government established structures for women's inclusion and implemented progressive gender policies. The government recognized the disproportionately strong impact the war had on women. Rwandan officials openly stated that they considered women's participation in peace building and governance to be crucial for longer-term democratization and sustainable peace.[53]

The Constitution enshrines a commitment to gender equality, and reserves at least 30 percent of posts in decision-making positions for women.[54] Although gender quotas are regarded as a "quick" way of addressing gaps in women's representation, this, combined with innovative decentralized structures of governance did succeed in facilitating broader participation of women in decision-making. In 2003, Rwanda achieved the world's highest representation of women in parliament with women constituting 48.8 percent of parliamentarians[55] and nine out of 28 ministerial posts went to women.[56] Now, Rwanda has the only woman-majority parliament in the history of the world.

Rwanda has also implemented gender mainstreaming in the judicial system. The *Gacaca* system[57] illustrates how traditional forms of peace building can be combined with a progressive approach to gender matters. In Rwanda's case, women are being elected as judges[58] in this system and the system recognizes that since women are the primary witnesses of genocide they play a key role in reconciliation and the building of a post-conflict dispensation.[59]

In many senses, Rwanda's peace building process has become gender-responsive and inclusive of women, even if the peace negotiations that set up the transitional government excluded women. Still, as discussed above, there have been some shortcomings in terms of cultural sensitivity, gender analysis, and valuing local knowledges, which are discussed below. Even given these shortcomings, however, it is important to note the key role of women's movements in achieving gender-responsiveness in post-conflict Rwanda.

Women's movements in post-conflict Rwanda

After the conflict women started participating in Rwandan society as community leaders, heading households, rebuilding homes, caring for orphans and survivors and occupying non-traditional jobs in banking, as cab drivers, and mechanics.[60] By 2000, 57 percent of the adult working population aged 20 to 44 was female, and women produced up to 70 percent of the national agricultural output.[61] By 2003, the number of female-headed households had risen to 35 percent.[62] In the same year, 64 percent of the labour force in basic production was female.[63] However, access to economic resources and rights to education and employment have not increased proportionately. It illustrates that the "gains" made through acquiring new roles in society may at times mask (and clash with) 'untransformed' aspects of women's and girls' social life. For instance, girls as heads of family live in constant fear and insecurity, particularly at night. Hence, gender inequality is perpetuated in the post-war phase.[64]

In the post-genocide period, women have drawn upon their traditional roles as mothers, wives or daughters, community conciliators, and the moral authority which comes with theses roles to call for an end to the conflict.[65] These roles are not only reinforced by stereotypical perceptions that women are better at reconciliation, but also by experiences at community level that women are less corrupt than men.[66] While this observation may come dangerously close to an essentialist interpretation, it is nevertheless in line with the notion of African feminisms. It could become counterproductive if these "informal" roles are the *only* roles women are allowed to play, or if these conciliatory roles become viewed as the "exclusive" responsibility of women.

Women's organizing in the aftermath of the conflict reflects a practical engagement with the notion of empathetic cooperation—building peace across ethnic, religious, national and cultural divides.[67] Many women found a "political" home in civil society organizations as the middle space between the public sector and the private sphere of the family.

Funding incentives provided by the international community helped make the period from 1994 to 2003 the "golden age" of women's civil society organizations. Pro-Femmes/Twese Hamwe ("All Together")—a collective of 32 women's organizations across ethnic lines—was formed in 1994 after the genocide to promote social justice, respect for women's rights and to campaign against impunity for those responsible for the mass killings. Their work associated with their "Action Campaign for Peace" was awarded the UNESCO-Madanjeet Singh Prize for the Promotion of Tolerance and Non-Violence in 1996.[68] Micro-credit programmes for displaced and widowed women were among the first types of assistance during the reconstruction period.[69] In recent years, Rwanda's women have become famous for their handicrafts, such as the peace baskets (*Agaseke*) which are sold on the international market.

Women's everyday existence and their socially constructed roles in the community force them to recognize their interdependence. Such pragmatism allows them to work across ethnic lines more easily than men. Similarly, women's organizations in Rwanda have adopted a strategic approach of cooperation rather than confrontation in relation to government.

Culturally sensitive approaches to gender-mainstreamed peace building

While there have been many successes in the Rwandan peace building process, and many successes in the integration of women and gender concerns in Rwandan society, both processes remain incomplete. Though it has an elected legislature, Rwanda is consistently classified by Polity and other evaluators as a non-democratic state. While relatively free debate is allowed regarding non-security matters, issues classified as involving security are the site of increasing authoritarianism. For instance, political party activity has been banned in the name of suppressing ethnic divisions.[70] Civil society is viewed by the government as serving the ends of the state. Women's movements, and women's opinions, then, are important to the government to the extent that they agree with and further the purposes of the government.

The Rwandan government is also struggling in terms of the fourth tool outlined above, a culturally sensitive approach to reconstruction, where top-down inclusionary measures need to be combined with methods to eradicate structural barriers to women's participation and promote cultural sensitivity. Cultural sensitivity is especially key in a society recovering from genocide. Officially, as a strategy for post-conflict healing, the government has adopted a programme of "co-existence".[71] This refers to efforts to include former genocide victims and perpetrators together in joint projects and programmes, such as health and HIV/AIDS education, vocational school development for both Hutu and Tutsi girls and Hutu and Tutsi women in peace programs.

This strategy has been criticized because it fails to foster a truly "inclusive" political community, not built on erasing or evading differences between people, but rather including all people and groups (regardless of their differences) in the nation-building project. While today it is no longer permissible to refer to another Rwandan in terms of his/her ethnicity, ethnic belonging remains important in the minds of people. Policies of non-identification do not stifle ethnic tension and in fact make it more difficult to identify cases of discrimination. There is a real risk that overemphasis on national unity may also be to the detriment of the feminist cause where class and ethnic differences among women (women are presumed equal and viewed as a homogeneous group) and relations to men in the national gender discourse are not interrogated.[72]

For example, the International Criminal Tribunal of Rwanda has helped to focus international attention on sexual violence as war crimes and crimes against humanity and have also set certain standards of accountability for such crimes. However, it is at the national level where respect for these instruments needs to be inculcated through systems that can effectively combat impunity for gender violence. This poses a major challenge of implementation for Rwanda, as very few perpetrators of sexual violence during the 1994 massacre have been brought to justice.[73] Despite the inclusion of women in governance, many culturally inscribed stereotypical understandings about women and femininity remain in place.

The successes of gender mainstreaming in Rwanda

The inclusion of women and gender concerns in the peace building process in Rwanda has, by most accounts, been a key factor in the maintenance of peace over the last fifteen years and many of the advances Rwanda has made towards democratization and lasting detente. Still, many involved in the Rwandan peace building process have neglected the complexity of women's roles in the conflict and post-conflict era. Also, there are important ways in which the continued viability of the peace in Rwanda relies on what African feminists call a culturally sensitive approach to gender mainstreaming, which takes account not only of adding women to the ranks of government decision-making but also taking account of women's needs in terms of economic, social, and cultural rights. Rwanda is a "positive" case for gender mainstreaming influencing the construction of a successful peace process, but its struggles show that there has yet to be a perfect case, and that Rwanda's continued success in maintaining peace relies heavily on deepening and broadening its inclusion of women, analysis of gender, cultural sensitivity, and valuing of local knowledges.

Côte D'ivoire: "neither peace nor war"

If the Rwandan case is an example of where the inclusion of women has been a net positive for the process of building peace, the Côte d'Ivoire case is an example of the ways that women's exclusion from peace building has played a role in the failure to build a lasting peace. The root cause of the conflict is a complex mix of identity (mainly ethnic, somewhat xenophobic) issues intertwined with economy disparities.

Under the leadership of Félix Houphouet-Boigny, Côte d'Ivoire was stable and prosperous as the largest cocoa producer in the world. Still, ethnic tensions were prevalent even in good times, since Houphouet-Boigny encouraged migration to Côte d'Ivoire to perform menial labor while conditioning citizenship on pure Ivorian descent.[74] These tensions were exacerbated when economic decline coincided with a succession of weak, ethnically divisive and corrupt leaders. The political situation deteriorated into a civil war in 2002, where the government controlled the south, and insurgents called the New Forces controlled the north. Several attempts to make and build peace failed to end the violence.[75] Implementation of the 2007 Ouagadougou Political Agreement (OPA) has had more success, but the road ahead to build peace in Côte d'Ivoire remains long and difficult.

The new transitional Government of Reconciliation was tasked with: "identification" of the population; elections; security sector reform and disarmament, demobilization and reintegration; restoration of State authority; and national reconciliation, peace consolidation, and guaranteeing security to people.[76] It has struggles with voter registration, the disarmament, demobilization, and reintegration process, and continued rebel activity. Once again, these general developments are evaluated in terms of the four tools for implementing a gender-sensitive peace building process.

Women's diverse roles in the conflict

Women in the southern parts of the country had first-hand experience of the wars of liberation against French colonization. Women played ambivalent roles during the rise of ethno-nationalism in the 1990s. The notion of *Ivoirité* was both supported by and caused the suffering of women. Some women leaders, such as the wife of president Gbagbo, were strong proponents of this law. On the other side, when Ivorian-born men lost their citizenship as a result of a change in law, their wives lost their citizenship as well. Similarly, during the civil war of 2002, the divisions between women followed the dividing lines of the conflict. Both sides of the conflict had their own women's political organizations. The most active were *Cadre de concertation permanente des femmes* and the Coordination of Patriotic Women of Côte d'Ivoire (CFPCI), a pro-government group.[77]

In the recent conflict, however, the victimhood of women dominates in reports and accounts of the struggle. As a consequence of the armed conflict since 2002, approximately 700 000 people are internally displaced, 52 percent of whom are women. During the conflict, women and girls fell victim to widespread, and often systematic rape and sexual violence perpetrated by both rebel and government forces and Liberian and Sierra Leonean mercenaries. Sexual violence towards women was used as a tactic of war to terrorize populations suspected of collaborating with the other side. Women close to "foreign" Ivorians were raped to denigrate the latter. Women of the Burki-nabé ethnic group were targeted mainly by rebel groups.[78] Many women were forced into prostitution. The impact of the violence during the war is reflected in the HIV/AIDS prevalence rate which was 6.4 percent for women and 2.9 percent for men in 2005.[79]

The failure on the part of the belligerent parties and international organi-zations to recognize the diverse roles of women in the conflict is a problem for two reasons: First, in practice it means the main parties to the conflict and members of the international community plan "around" rather than "for" women's specific needs. Second, by overlooking the nuances in planning for dif-ferential impacts, men may also be disadvantaged by being treated as a mono-lithic group. An integrated post-conflict reconstruction is therefore also a gender-responsive process which recognizes the interests of both men and women.

Gender-responsive and integrated post-conflict reconstruction

The Constitution prohibits discrimination on the basis of sex. But in the last ten years very little progress has been made to increase the number of women in leadership positions. In 2001, women held six of the 26 ministerial posi-tions in the Cabinet. There were five women justices in the 25-member Supreme Court, and 19 women held seats in the 225-member National Assembly.[80] While the Ivorian People's Front (FPI) has adopted a 30 percent quota for women on electoral lists, this has been slow to translate to real gains on the national level.[81] Further, women included in Ivorian politics are often assigned tasks traditionally associated with femininity, such as social affairs and peace building.[82]

Outside of the political realm, women occupy a subordinate position in society, especially in respect of educational opportunities. The female literacy rate for 2006/2007 was 34 percent.[83] Domestic violence is viewed as a private matter; women suffer unequal access to loans; and there is slow progress in changing attitudes about female genital mutilation (FGM). Informal dis-crimination governs day-to-day practices of hiring and great disparities exist between urban elite and rural women.

These disadvantages for women in Ivorian society impact peace processes. Women's voices are not heard at the peace table. Only one woman was pre-sent at the Linas-Marcoussis Agreement (2003). The agreement did not con-tain any gender-sensitive language, and its negotiation and text assumed that men and women had the same needs and experiences of conflict. The Oua-gadougou Agreement sidelined not only women but all of civil society and the political opposition. Several UN Security Council Resolutions con-demned the violation of women's rights in Côte d'Ivoire and pushed for the removal of obstacles to women's participation in public life,[84] but they failed to inspire real change in the peace building process.

The exclusion of women from the peace-building process has been linked to the failure to establish a stable peace in Côte d'Ivoire. Nicole Doué, vice-president of the Association for the Defence of Women's Rights, sums it up: "This is because of the absence of women in the peace process ... From Lomé to Ouagadougou women have been shut out."[85] The buffer zone which existed during the peacekeeping mission was dismantled as part of the 2007 peace deal. Violent crime, including sexual violence is now rampant, signifying how easy it is to take decisions in the name of "peace" without planning for women's security.

The role of women's movements

In view of these challenges women continue to build peace informally. Behind the scenes when the Linas-Marcoussis Agreement failed and the relationship between the belligerents deteriorated, women lobbied for an end to the war. Through women's intervention the "Flame of Peace" signified the official launch of the disarmament process for the country.[86] During the war, working committees were formed to sustain community action plans. The committees assisted in developing income generating activities, such as flour mills, handicrafts, and agricultural produce. With the help of international donors, more than 500 women in 25 communities across the country have been trained.[87] The Ivorian Movement of Democratic Women (MIFED), founded in 1990, promotes and protects women's rights (by monitoring the effects of conflict) and supports women's increased participation in the democratic process.[88] Other prominent organizations which promote gender equality and justice include the Ivorian Association for the Defense of Women (AIDF).

Women's organizations in Côte d'Ivoire are cognizant of the fact that regional alliances for peace are crucial in the immediate West-African geopolitical context. In 2007, Search for Common Ground used the lessons of women's leadership in Sierra Leone and Liberia to help kick-start women's leadership on peace and in the elections in Côte d'Ivoire. Two regional and one national symposia brought together leaders from across political party, ethnic and religious groups. Women in the west of Côte d'Ivoire, in Guiglo, experienced the war very differently from women in the north, in Bouake. Exclusionary politics between foreigners and locals was perceived as the key obstacle to women's participation in decision-making at the local level. At the national seminar women from the *Forces Nouvelle* were represented for the first time. The seminars helped these women to unite around their common gendered experience of war. The meetings ended with a resolution to increase the number of women in decision-making positions[89] and women's organizations plan to launch a comprehensive national campaign against gender violence, raising awareness, setting up help centers for victims and working to restore the judicial system.[90]

The Côte d'Ivoire case is a study of women's grassroots struggles against all odds. One of the main structural impediments relates to the fact that civil society organizations are not legally recognized as distinct from other associations, such as trade unions. This lack of recognition leads to a lack of resources and an inability to make an impact in society. Without observer status at the major fora they have little access to information and are therefore not in a favourable position to raise the awareness of the population.[91]

Culturally sensitive gender integration

Ayangafac rightly observes that the peace agreement signifies the formation of a state security regime, rather than one that is founded on the basis of human security.[92] The real cause for delays in the implementation of the peace agreement is the lack of trust and the high political stakes of the process. The rebels fear that government will manipulate the electoral and registration processes in view of the president losing support. Ironically, when a peace process which is built on exclusivist terms break down there is no other party involved to come to the rescue.

In this way, the exclusion of women and other minority groups from the Côte d'Ivoire peace process can be seen as directly responsible for a number of its shortcomings. It is problematic that the follow-up committee to the Ouagadougou Accord (the Permanent Consultation Framework and Evaluation and Monitoring) consists of the very same players who are supposed to implement the peace process, the protagonists of the conflict. This makes them both party and judge. Civil society organizations are thus calling for a reconvening of a National Dialogue Forum to make the peace process more inclusive. So-called "secondary and tertiary stakeholders" such as young patriots and women activists should be afforded a place in the peace process.[93]

The incomplete (or false?) peace in Côte d'Ivoire has failed on two counts. First, it failed to include all relevant stakeholders and constituencies of civil society. No stable government of national unity can simply consist of the old players—new formations of excluded voices are bound to form. Without genuine citizen participation, the current peace process is nothing more than a cease fire with little chance of being implemented. Second, the process failed to take account of women and girls' needs during the conflict and in the post-conflict period. A number of reports argued that the scale of rape and sexual violence in Côte d'Ivoire has been largely underestimated; that women are the forgotten victims of the conflict; and that the peace process has failed to curtail the sexual violence, failed to address the need for accountability and has thus contributed to the culture of impunity that currently rules.[94]

The failures of peace building in Côte d'Ivoire

A long road lies ahead to challenge deeply entrenched cultural beliefs about sexual violence and to build credible institutions for the protection of women. Rape is not considered a serious crime in Côte d'Ivoire. Rape is a crime in Côte d'Ivoire and is punishable under the Ivorian Penal Code, yet the penal code definition of rape is not consistent with international law formulations.[95] The war destroyed the courts in the north, and together with structural discrimination by customary law and an inadequate understanding of how to enforce laws on sexual violence it has helped to entrench a climate of lawlessness. Those who rule are guilty of failure to protect, failure to offer redress, and failure to provide services to the victims.

Gender and peace building in Rwanda and Côte d'Ivoire

There are two important points to be taken out of this chapter's feminist reading of peace building practices in Africa, with special reference to Rwanda and Côte d'Ivoire. First, a feminist approach to peace building is invaluable as it helps to transcend the gap between private and public peace processes thereby making women's informal peace building contributions part of "high" politics. Such an approach offers empirical knowledge of women's and men's differential security and peace needs. In addition, empathetic cooperation as a bridge-building, non-confrontational feminist method not only helps to make women's voices heard in the aftermath of conflict, but also has wider application and extends to include all non-dominant and previously silenced perspectives which might be subsumed under the label "human" security. Second, and more specifically, the differential security and peace needs of people, individuals or communities can only be understood intersubjectively within local contexts. In this regard the particular dynamics of the African peace building context were highlighted. These peculiarities pose very specific challenges to the African women's movement in how they engage with national governments; how they use (domesticate) international rights-based frameworks such as Resolution 1325; and how internal and external stakeholders view women's agency in peace and conflict.

In Rwanda, women have effectively bridged the gap between private and public peace building, but now have to learn to work "with" a somewhat more hostile state in order to consolidate their gains. Their presence right at the onset of the peace process has brought dividends in terms of gender justice. While much still needs to be done in terms of prosecutions and the distribution of economic and social rights, among others, this is a far cry from what women experience in Côte d'Ivoire. Here a general amnesty legally exonerated the soldiers and rebels from the atrocities committed during the civil war, effectively legalizing impunity. Women's glaring absence from all peace agreements does not mean that this is the one single factor causing a breakdown in peace, but it does make it so much harder to exercise agency in a context where lawlessness is tolerated. Furthermore, the quest for a common political platform and feminist consciousness among women's organizations of Côte d'Ivoire is still at an embryonic stage. Both cases offered ample evidence of women's and men's differential needs during and after conflict. Women's groups in both countries drew on their sense of interdependence and gave meaning to the concept of empathetic cooperation through their networking, alliance-building and community work. The empirical evidence not only points towards common strategies, but also directs the reader to observe the peculiar dynamics of each local context.

The remaining message of this chapter has been about implementing these ideas in practice. While African feminist approaches have much to offer peace building processes, they must attempt to navigate hostile waters in national, regional, and international politics. It is key for African women's groups to promote gender mainstreaming, and to remind their governments to consider gender at every phase of the peace building process. Not only could this strategy have substantial payoffs in terms of gender rights, it could serve as the missing link to lend coherence to peace building processes. Attention— both from the top down and the bottom up—to gender and women's rights indeed facilitated a more coherent and integrated transition period in Rwanda. Care should however be taken not to view these gender issues as monolithic and existing in a vacuum. Key to a sustainable peace is the ability to engage with overlapping identities, not just gender.

The evidence shows that the representative nature of a gender-mainstreamed peace building process might make it more likely to succeed in getting to the root cause of the serious problems underlying a number of African conflicts. In Rwanda, decentralized governance structures (e.g. women's councils) helped to address many root causes and effects of the genocide at the local level by also staying connected to the national process through the National Women's Council. Women can make various and important contributions to modelling and implementing African peace building processes. The degree to which this potential is realized will depend on the organization of women's movements, and their employment of inclusionary and transformational strategies within a culturally sensitive context of indigenous peace building processes.

Conclusion: the way forward

The two cases in this chapter suggest a general pattern that women's involvement in African peace processes is beneficial to the long-term sustainability of the peace negotiated. They also suggest the utility of four gender-sensitive "tools": analysis of women's varied and often invisible roles in conflict and their needs in peace building; establishment of a post-conflict reconstruction framework that takes account of gender and women's issues; empowerment of women's groups to effectively build the bridge between the current neglect of gender in peace building processes and gender mainstreamed processes which would be more effective and more gender-emancipatory; and adopting international frameworks for gender equality in culturally sensitive ways. Given the evidence in these cases, it appears that considering gender fully, through mainstreaming, inclusion, and transformational strategies could make peace building processes more representative and more effective. Future case study and other empirical research in this area could suggest specific implementation strategies, highlight the importance of cultural sensitivity in women's inclusion in peace processes, provide insight into the causal mechanisms that link culturally sensitive inclusion and sustainable peace, and explore implications of gender mainstreaming outside of the African context.

Notes

1 United Nations Security Council Resolution 1325, 6 October 2000, S/RES/1325/2000.
2 Cynthia Enloe, "What if Patriarchy Is 'the Big Picture'? An Afterword", in *Gender, Conflict and Peacekeeping*, eds., Dyan Mazurana, Angela Raven-Roberts and Jane Parpart (New York: Rowman & Littlefield, 2005), pp. 280–3.
3 Mary Caprioli, "Gendered Conflict," *Journal of Peace Research* 37, no. 1 (January 2000): 51–68.
4 Johann Galtung, *Peace by Peaceful Means: Peace and Conflict, Development and Civilization* (London: Sage Publications, 1996), p. 112.
5 Hugh Miall, Oliver Ramsbotham and Tom Woodhouse, *Contemporary Conflict Resolution: The Prevention, Management and Transformation of Deadly Conflicts* (Cambridge: Polity, 2000).
6 Marianne H. Marchand and Anne Sisson Runyan, *Gender and Global Restructuring: Sightings, Sites and Resistances* (London: Routledge, 2000).
7 See the Introduction to this book.
8 M. Stern and M. Nystrand, *Gender and Armed Conflict* (Stockholm: SIDA, 2006).
9 Louise Vincent, "Current Discourse on the Role of Women in Conflict Prevention and Conflict Transformation: A Critique," *Conflict Trends* no. 3 (2003): 5–10.
10 Referring to the "add women and stir" notion coined by Marysia Zalewski, "Feminist Theory and International Relations", in *From Cold War to Collapse: Theory and World Politics in the 1980s*, eds., M. Bowker and R. Brown (Cambridge: Cambridge University Press, 1993), p. 116.
11 Isabella Bakker, "Identity, Interests and Ideology: The Gendered Terrain of Global Restructuring", in *Globalization, Democratization and Multilateralism*, ed. Steven Gill (New York: United Nations University Press, 1997), pp. 127–39, 135.
12 Sandra Harding, cited in Bakker, "Identity, Interests and Ideology," p. 133.
13 Bakker, "Identity, Interests and Ideology," p. 135.
14 J. Ann Tickner, "Feminist Perspectives on 9/11," *International Studies Perspectives* 3, no. 4 (November 2002): 333–50.
15 It must be noted that feminist criticisms against Western feminism come from many circles: that is, not only from developing world, African or Asian women, but also from Western women who – on the basis of religion, race or class – feel excluded from the lily-white middle-class discourse.
16 Heidi Hudson, "Gender, Peace-building and Post-conflict Reconstruction in Africa: Breaking the Chain between Inequality and Violence", in *Post-conflict Reconstruction and Development: Lessons for Africa*, eds., Dirk Kotzé and Hussein Solomon (Pretoria: Africa Institute of South Africa, 2008), 9–29, 13.
17 Beverly Guy-Sheftall, "African Feminist Discourse: A Review Essay," *Agenda* no. 58 (2003): 31–5, citing Carole Boyce Davies on the unique features of African feminism (p. 32); Hudson, "Gender, Peace-building and Post-conflict Reconstruction," p. 13.
18 Mary M. Kolawole, "Transcending Incongruities: Rethinking Feminism and the Dynamics of Identity in Africa," *Agenda* no. 54 (2002): 92–8. The term "womanism" was coined by Alice Walker in *In Search of Our Mother's Garden: Womanist Prose* (New York: Harcourt Brace Jovanovich, 1983).
19 Amanda Gouws, "Changing Political Opportunity Structures: A Study of the Women's Movement and Activism in South Africa," paper presented at the SAAPS conference, University of the Western Cape, 5–8 September, 2006.
20 Tim Murithi, "African Approaches to Building Peace and Social Solidarity," *African Journal on Conflict Resolution* 6, no. 2 (2006): 9–33.
21 Christine Sylvester, *Feminist International Relations: An Unfinished Journey* (Cambridge: Cambridge University Press, 2002), pp. 242–64.

22 Ibid., p. 244.

23 Article 18 of the African Charter on Human and Peoples' Rights calls on all states to eliminate every form of discrimination against women and to ensure the protection of women's rights as stipulated in international declarations and conventions. Available at: wwwl.umn.edu/humanrts/instree/zlafchar.htm, accessed 5 May 2008.

24 Dyan Mazurana, Angela Raven-Roberts and Jane Parpart with S. Lautze, "Introduction: Gender, Conflict, and Peacekeeping", in *Gender, Conflict and Peacekeeping*, eds., D. Mazurana, A. Raven-Roberts and J. Parpart (New York: Rowman & Littlefield, 2005), pp. 1–26.

25 Jean Elshtain, "Against Androgeny," in *Feminism and Equality*, ed., Jean Elshtain (New York: New York University Press, 1987), p. 142.

26 Noeleen Heyzer, "Women, War and Peace: Mobilising for Peace and Security in the 21st Century," the 2004 Dag Hammarskjöld Lecture, Uppsala, Uppsala University, 22 September.

27 Jill Steans, *Gender and International Relations: An Introduction* (Cambridge: Polity, 1998), p. 115; Laura Sjoberg and Caron Gentry, *Mothers, Monsters, Whores: Women's Violence in Global Politics* (London: Zed Books, 2007), Chapter 6; Meredith Turshen and M. Twagiramariya, *What Women Do in Wartime: Gender and Conflict in Africa* (London: Zed Books, 1988); C. Bop, "Women in Conflicts, Their Gains and Their Losses," in *The Aftermath: Women in Post-Conflict Transformation*, eds., S. Meintjes, A. Pillay and M. Turshen (London: Zed Books, 2001), pp. 19–34.

28 Protocol to the African Charter on Human and People's Rights on the Rights of Women in Africa, July 2003. Adopted by the Conference of Heads of State and Government, Maputo, Mozambique. Available at: www.portal.unesco.org/shs/en/ev.php/.

29 Tim Murithi, "The AU/NEPAD Post-Conflict Reconstruction Policy: An Analysis," *Conflict Trends* no.1 (2006): 16–21, 17–19.

30 For example, the 2003 Liberian Peace Agreement.

31 Kari Karamé, "Gender Mainstreaming in Peace Building Process," in *Gender and Peace-building in Africa*, ed. Kari Karamé (Oslo: NUPI, 2004), pp. 11–26, 12.

32 See Mazurana *et al.*, *Gender, Conflict, and Peacekeeping*, p. 13.

33 June Lennie, "Deconstructing Gendered Power Relations in Participatory Planning: Towards an Empowering Feminist Framework of Participation and Action," *Women's Studies International Forum* 22, no. 1 (January 1999): 97–112.

34 Christine Chinkin and Hilary Charlesworth, "Building Women into Peace: The International Legal Framework," *Third World Quarterly* 27, no. 5 (2006): 937–57, 940.

35 N. Puechguirbal, "Involving Women in Peace Processes: Lessons from Four African Countries (Burundi, DRC, Liberia and Sierra Leone)", *Pambazuka News*, 177 (2004): 47.

36 Hudson, "Gender, Peace-building and Post-conflict Reconstruction," p. 20.

37 Africa Report, 2006, "Beyond Victimhood: Women's Peacebuilding in Sudan, Congo and Uganda," *Africa Report* 112. 28 June. Available at: www.crisisgroup.org/home/index.cfm?id = 4186& 1 = 1, accessed 27 July 2006; for example, in Burundi, in Liberia, and in the Democratic Republic of the Congo. See the longer version of this article (under the same title, in the July 2009 issue of *Security Studies*).

38 Centre for Conflict Resolution and United Nations Development Fund for Women, 2005. *Women and Peacebuilding in Africa,* Seminar Report of Policy Seminar hosted by CCR and UNIFEM, Cape Town, 27–28 October, 29.

39 King, "What Difference Does it Make?" pp. 28–9.

40 Chinkin and Charlesworth, "Building Women into Peace," p. 943.

41 United Nations Security Council Resolution 1645 S/Res/1645/2005.

42 Kofi Annan, "Women Still Excluded From Peace Table Despite Their Pivotal Role." Press Release. New York, 28 October 2004. Available at: www.un.org/Docs/journal/asp/ws.asp?m = S/2004/814.

43 Puechguirbal, "Involving Women in Peace Processes," p. 62.

44 Sadye Logan, "Remembering the Women in Rwanda: When Humans Rely on the Old Concepts of War to Resolve Conflict," *Affilia: Journal of Women and Social Work* 21, no. 2 (Summer 2006): 234–9.

45 Karen Brounéus, "Truth-Telling as Talking Cure? Insecurity and Retraumatization in the Rwandan Gacaca Courts," *Security Dialogue* 39, no. 1 (March 2008): 55–76, 60.

46 Logan, "Remembering the Women," p. 235.

47 Elizabeth Powley, *Strengthening Governance: The Role of Women in Rwanda's Transition* (Washington, DC: Hunt Alternatives, 2003), p. 172.

48 Catherine Onekalit, "The Frightful Actuality: Girls Tools of War in Africa," in *Gender and Peace Building in Africa*, eds., Dina Rodríguez and Edith Natukunda-Togboa (New York: University for Peace, 2005), pp. 99–112, 105.

49 Logan, "Remembering the Women," p. 236.

50 R. Charli Carpenter, "Recognizing Gender-Based Violence Against Civilian Men and Boys in Conflict Situations," paper presented at the International Studies Association (ISA) Annual Meeting, Montreal, 17–20 March 2004, p. 14.

51 Peter Landesman, "A Woman's Work," *New York Times Magazine*, 15 September 2002; Elisabeth Porter, *Peacebuilding: Women in International Perspective* (London: Routledge, 2007), p. 140.

52 Dyan Mazurana, "Women in Armed Opposition Groups in Africa and the Promotion of International Humanitarian Law and Human Rights," report of a workshop organized in Addis Ababa by Geneva Call and the Program for the Study of International Organization(s), 23–26 November 2005, p. 50.

53 Consuelo Remmert, "Rwanda Promotes Women Decision-makers," *UN Chronicle* no. 4 (2003): 25.

54 Porter, *Peacebuilding: Women in International Perspective*, p. 177.

55 Centre for Conflict Resolution and UNIFEM, "Women and Peacebuilding in Africa," p. 21.

56 Jennie E. Burnet, "Gender Balance and the Meanings of Women in Governance in Post-Genocide Rwanda," *African Affairs* 107, no. 428 (2008): 361–86, 370.

57 The Gacaca courts system represents the revival of a traditional tribal system of justice, used to deal with minor family disputes and cattle theft..

58 Thirty percent of Gacaca judges are women. The President of the Supreme Court is also a woman. (United Nations, 2005, *Facts and Figures on Women, Peace and Security*, October. Available at: www.unifem.org/news_events/currents/documents/currents200510_WPS_facts.pdf)

59 Mzvondiwa, "The role of women in the reconstruction," 105.

60 Ibid., p. 102.

61 Kelly Fish, "Cooperation Among Enemies: Mixity of Women in Post-Genocide Civil Society," paper presented at the International Studies Association (ISA) Annual Meeting, Montreal, 17–20 March 2004.

62 Powley, *Strengthening Governance*, p. 13.

63 Myriam Gervais, "Human Security and Reconstruction Efforts in Rwanda: Impact on the Lives of Women," *Development in Practice* 13, no. 5 (2003): 542–51, 544.

64 E. Rehn and E. J. Sirleaf, "*Women, War and Peace: The Independent Experts' Assessment on the Impact of Armed Conflict on Women and Women's Role in Peace Building* (New York: UNIFEM, 2002). p. 2.

65 John Mutamba and Jeanne Izabiliza, in their study for the National Unity and Reconciliation Commission (NURC) in Kigali (*The Role of Women in Reconciliation and Peace Building in Rwanda: Ten Years after Genocide 1994–2004:*

Contributions, Challenges and Way Forward, May 2005), highlight respondents' emphasis on the role of women as life nurturers and givers, mediators between different families and the way in which women are prepared from early childhood to ensure the togetherness of families, serving the general good of the community, p. 24.

66 Powley, *Strengthening Governance*, p. 17.

67 This refers to the concept "mixity" coined by Cynthia Cockburn in *The Space Between Us: Negotiating Gender and National Identities in Conflict* (London: Zed Books, 1998). See also Fish, "Cooperation Among Enemies."

68 UNESCO-Madanjeet Singh Prize for the Promotion of Tolerance and Non-violence. Available at: www.southasiafoundation.org/saf/about_saf/saf_relations/saf_unesco/saf_unesco_7, accessed 28 November 2008.

69 Rehn and Sirleaf, *Women, War, Peace*, pp. 126–7.

70 Elizabeth Sidiropoulos, "Democratisation and Militarisation in Rwanda: Eight Years after the Genocide," *African Security Review* 11, no. 3 (2002): 77–87, 81–3.

71 Porter, *Peacebuilding*, pp. 82–3.

72 See Erin K. Baines, "Le femmes aux mille bras: Building Peace in Rwanda", in *Gender, Conflict, and Peacekeeping*, eds. D. Mazurana, A. Raven-Robers, and J. Parpart (New York: Rowman & Littlefield, 2005), pp. 220–41, 232.

73 Gervais, "Human Security and Reconstruction Efforts," p. 545.

74 Jenny Wong, "Ethnic Animosity: Côte d'Ivoire's Precarious Peace," *Harvard International Review* 27, no. 3 (Fall 2005): 7.

75 Including the 2003 and 2004 Accra agreements, the UN Operation in Côte d'Ivoire (UNOCI), and the 2005 Pretoria agreements. See Megan Bastick, Karin Grimm and Rahel Kunz, *Sexual Violence in Armed Conflict: Global Overview and Implications for the Security Sector* (Geneva: Geneva Centre for the Democratic Control of Armed Forces, 2007), p. 39.

76 United Nations and Government of Côte d'Ivoire, 2008. *Peace Building Fund (PBF) Priority Plan: Support to the Ouagadougou Political Agreement and the Government Crisis Recovery Programs, Republic of Côte d'Ivoire*, 17 July. Available at: www.unpbf.org/docs/Cote_d'Ivoire.

77 "Women in Côte d'Ivoire," Wikipedia.

78 Bastick *et al.*, "Sexual Violence in Armed Conflict," p. 39.

79 UNDP Crisis Prevention and Recovery, *Focus on Women in Côte d'Ivoire*. Available at: www.undp.org/cpr/whats_new/focus_on_cotedivoire.shtml, accessed 2 January 2009.

80 United Methodist Women's Action Network, *Action Alert: Côte d'Ivoire: A Country in Distress, An Opportunity to Act*; June 2003. Available at: www.peace-women.org/resources/Cote_d'Ivoire/action.pdf.

81 Goetz *et al.*, *Progress of the World's Women*, p. 138.

82 *Female Ministers of the République de Côte d'Ivoire/Ivory Coast*. Available at: www.guide2womenleaders.com/Cote_dIvoire.htm, accessed 24 October 2008.

83 Kemi Ogunsanya, "Women Transforming Conflicts in Africa: Descriptive Studies from Burundi, Côte d'Ivoire, Sierra Leone, South Africa and Sudan," *ACCORD Occasional Paper Series* 2, no. 3 (2007): 11.

84 United Nations Security Council. SC/9409. "Security Council Extends Mandate of United National Operation in Côte d'Ivoire until 31 January, allowing Mission to Support November elections," *Resolution 1826 (2008)*. Available at: www.un.org/News/Press/docs/2008/sc9409.doc.htm; Security Council Resolution 1842 (2008).

85 UN Integrated Regional Information Networks. 10 November 2008. *Appeal for Help to Stop Violence Against Women*. Available at: www.allafrica.com/stories/printable/200811101258.html, accessed 28 November 2008.

86 Ogunsanya, "Women Transforming Conflicts," p. 23.

87 Ibid., p. 19.
88 University of Minnesota Human Rights Library. *The Status of Human Rights Organizations in Sub-Saharan Africa. Côte d'Ivoire.* Available at: www1.umn.edu/humanrts/africa/cote.htm, accessed 24 November 2008.
89 Search for Common Ground, November 2007. *CdI Information Letter.* Available at: www.sfcg.org/programmes/cote/programmes_cote.html, accessed 2 January 2009.
90 UN Integrated Regional Information Networks, "Appeal for Help".
91 United States Institute of Peace, August 2006. "Creating a More Inclusive Peace in Côte d'Ivoire," *USAPeace Briefing.* Available at: www.usip.org/pubs/usipeace_briefings/2006/0807_cote_divoire.html, accessed 28 October 2008.
92 Chrysantus Ayangafac, "Peace in Côte d'Ivoire: An Analysis of the Ouagadougou Peace Accord," *Conflict Trends* 2007, no. 3 (2007): 25–31, 26.
93 West Africa Network for Peacebuilding (WANEP), "Ouagadougou Peace Accord: Breakthrough for Peace at last?" *WARN Policy Brief: Côte d'Ivoire Peace Process,* 31 May 2007. Available at: www.reliefweb.int/rw/rwb.nsf/db900SID/EGUA-743M28?OpenDocument, accessed 3 November 2008.
94 Amnesty International, "Targeting Women," in Human Rights Watch, *Trapped between Two Wars: Violence against Civilians in Western Côte d'Ivoire,* Report 15, no. 14(A), August 2003; Human Rights Watch, *My Heart Is Cut: Sexual Violence by Rebels and Pro-Government Forces in Côte d'Ivoire,* Report 19, no. 11 (A), August 2007.
95 See Amnesty International, "Targeting Women," pp. 21, 23, 27–8.

Index

Printed in the USA/Agawam, MA
December 17, 2012

571306.014